The *I Ching* in Tokugawa Thought and Culture

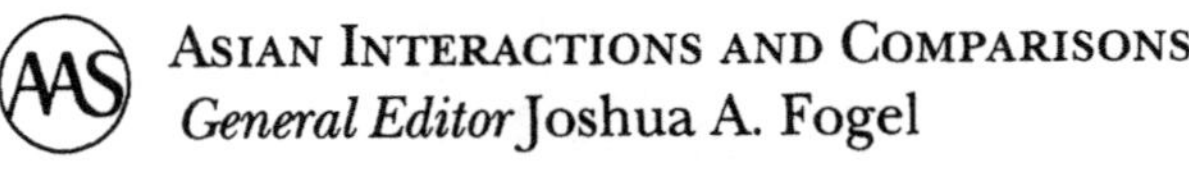

ASIAN INTERACTIONS AND COMPARISONS
General Editor Joshua A. Fogel

*Sovereign Rights and Territorial Space
in Sino-Japanese Relations*
Irredentism and the Diaoyu/Senkaku Islands
Unryu Suganuma

The I Ching *in Tokugawa Thought and Culture*
Wai-ming Ng

ASIAN INTERACTIONS AND COMPARISONS

The *I Ching* in Tokugawa Thought and Culture

Wai-ming Ng

Association for Asian Studies
and
University of Hawai'i Press, Honolulu

ASIAN INTERACTIONS AND COMPARISONS, published jointly by the University of Hawai'i Press and the Association for Asian Studies, seeks to encourage research across regions and cultures within Asia. The series focuses on works (monographs, edited volumes, and translations) that concern the interaction between or among Asian societies, cultures, or countries, or that deal with a comparative analysis of such. Series volumes concentrate on any time period and come from any academic discipline.

00 01 02 03 04 05   5 4 3 2 1

Library of Congress Cataloging-in-Publication Data
Ng, Wai-ming, 1962–
The I ching in Tokugawa thought and culture : Asian interactions and
comparisons / Wai-ming Ng.
p. cm.
Includes bibliographical references and index.
ISBN 0–8248–2215–3 (alk. paper) — ISBN 0–8248–2242–0 (pbk. : alk. paper)
1. I ching. 2. Japan—Civilization—1600–1868. 3. Japan—Civilization—
Chinese influences. I. Title.
PL2464.Z7 N46 2000
299'.51282—dc21   99–046524

Book design by Kenneth Miyamoto
Printed by The Maple-Vail Book Manufacturing Group

For Marius B. Jansen

Contents

Series Editor's Preface

To this day, scholars in the West tend to think of the *I Ching* (Book of Changes) as a strange little book. We know that it was important and that the greatest Confucian minds throughout Chinese and East Asian history revered it, although it was by no means a distinctly Confucian text. Still, unlike the *Analects* of Confucius or the *Mencius* or the *Chuang-tzu*, the *I Ching* seems terribly ethereal. Admittedly, much of this is a response to the aimless way this text has been used by non-specialist Westerners over the past thirty years or so. We have to remind ourselves that, after a hard day at the *yamen*, the most state-craft-oriented, *realpolitik* Chinese thinkers often went home and wrote commentaries on various hexagrams.

Wai-ming Ng's fascinating book on the numerous uses to which the *I Ching* was put in Tokugawa-era Japan reminds us that it was a text claimed by all the major religious and philosophical traditions and that it had a major impact on many areas of public and private life, from the political realm to religion to science to popular culture. We may tend to think of the Tokugawa period as one of quotidian, this-worldly priorities, but that should not dissuade us from recognizing the widespread influence of this text on Japan and the voluminous writings by Japanese on it.

Among his many findings, Professor Ng demonstrates that the *I Ching* in Japan was not only claimed by virtually every school of thought and religious tradition, but was also not rejected as a "Chinese" work by the nativist *(kokugaku)* school. Indeed, the Hirata school sought to transform it into a Shinto text. Japan in the late Tokugawa period even used the *I Ching* as a justification for its adoption of Western weaponry, and thus the text provided a bridge to the West as well.

What can we say about a work that proved to be so flexible, that could be molded by the hands of its adapter into whatever he desired? Some may worry that such a text cannot really have any significant content of its own if it yields to the will of whoever possesses it. This book should disabuse anyone of such an interpretation for Tokugawa Japan.

JOSHUA A. FOGEL
Series Editor

Acknowledgments

The origins of this research can be traced to the second year of my graduate studies in the Department of East Asian Studies at Princeton University. In a seminar on medieval Japanese Zen Buddhism, I read a considerable number of Zen Buddhist writings under the guidance of Professor Martin C. Collcutt. I discovered an extremely interesting intellectual phenomenon—namely, that most Buddhist monks of medieval Japan had painstakingly studied the *I Ching*. I wrote a term paper on the historical significance of *I Ching* scholarship and how Zen monks and other major literate groups of medieval Japan studied and used the text. This paper was the point of departure for the present research.

At the same time, I participated in a seminar on Ch'ing intellectual history. Professor Ying-shih Yü helped me acquire an in-depth understanding of *I Ching* scholarship in China. Without a strong background in Chinese Confucianism, this book would not have been possible.

My specialty is Tokugawa intellectual and cultural history. At the beginning, I did not know how important the *I Ching* was in the Tokugawa period. With the encouragement and advice of Professor Marius B. Jansen, I began to explore this uncharted territory and soon realized that this was a topic of potentially great significance.

I was extremely fortunate to have these three distinguished scholars as my academic advisors to supervise my dissertation research. They kindly read the manuscript at different stages and offered invaluable comments and suggestions. Because of their unfailing help and encouragement, I sometimes feel that this research has been a "team project" rather than my personal academic venture. My gratitude to them defies description.

For my stay in Japan from July 1993 to September 1994, I am especially indebted to Professor Watanabe Hiroshi of the University of Tokyo. I was impressed by his ability in reading texts and by his critical mind. Our stimulating exchange of ideas was an unforgettable part of my stay. More than anyone else, he made me realize the weaknesses and limitations of my scholarship. I would also like to express deep thanks to Professors Kurozumi Makoto, Ogawa Hiroshi, and Tanaka Norichika for their support, and to Ms. Inokuchi Mieko and Mr. Karube Tadashi for proofreading the English translations of Japanese texts in this work.

I am very grateful to the Graduate School of Princeton University for giving me a five-year fellowship, to the Japan Foundation for a generous fourteen-month fellowship to write my dissertation in Japan, and to the East Asian Studies Program at Princeton University for a research grant to study Korean language and history at Ewha Women's University in South Korea.

I would like to thank the following people for their help in various ways: Professors Yue-him Tam, Richard Smith, Samuel Yamashita, Hiraishi Naoaki, Kate Nakai, Ōba Osamu, Wm. Theodore de Bary, Koyasu Nobukuni, John Tucker, Mary Tucker, Robert Kramer, David Howell, Douglas Reynolds, Alan Chan, See Heng Teow, Timothy Tsu, Barry Steben, Sai-shing Yung, Cheuk-yin Lee, Kent Peterson, Jonathan Brown, and Keith Knuuti.

My gratitude also extends to Professor Joshua Fogel, general editor of the series of which this book is a part, for considering this work; to two referees for their recommendations and comments; and to Patricia Crosby, Victoria Scott, Ann Ludeman, Sharon Yamamoto, and the editorial professionals of the University of Hawai'i Press for their skillful editorial work.

Words cannot express my thanks to my wife, Gōda Miho, who gave me love and support so that I could concentrate on completing this work.

Earlier versions of some chapters were published in the *Journal of Asian History, Philosophy East and West, Asian Philosophy, Chinese Science, Journal of Asian Martial Arts, Studies in Central and East Asian Religions,*

East Asian Library Journal, and *Sino-Japanese Studies.* I am grateful to the editors for permission to use the material in this book.

This research is dedicated to Professor Marius B. Jansen as a token of affection and gratitude. Without his tutelage and encouragement, I would have exited academia and Japanese studies a long time ago.

WAI-MING NG
July 1999

A Note on Romanization

The Romanization systems used in this book are as follows: Hepburn for Japanese, Wade-Giles for Chinese, and McCune-Reischauer for Korean. Following the East Asian practice, surnames precede first names. All Japanese, Chinese, and Korean words are italicized, with diacritical marks if necessary, except some words that have come into English, such as Shinto, shogun, and bakufu. English translations of original texts, unless otherwise noted, are my own.

Introduction

This study uses the *I Ching* (*Ekikyō* in Japanese, or *Book of Changes* in English) to investigate the influence of Confucianism and Chinese learning in the Tokugawa period. The text, one of the most influential and popular Chinese classics, is both a book of magic and a book of wisdom. In antiquity, it started as a book of magic that contained sixty-four divinational images, or hexagrams, and their oracles. It was later Confucianized and became one of the Five Confucian Classics. However, the richness of the *I Ching* was not limited to Confucianism but shared its wisdom with different schools of thought and religion. In China, Confucianism, Taoism, the *yin-yang* school, and some schools of Buddhism and folk religion all claimed the text as their own. It is no exaggeration to say that the philosophy and divination of the text became an integral part of Chinese civilization.

In particular, the *I Ching* incorporated two extremely powerful ideas into its system: *yin-yang* and *wu-hsing*. *Yin* and *yang* denote the two primal forces of the universe. They oppose and supplement each other, and their relationship can be represented as the interplay between negative and positive forces, female and male, darkness and brightness. *Yin* and *yang* control the *wu-hsing* (the five basic agents, or stages): wood, fire, earth, metal, and water. Among the five agents, there are two types of relationship: some agents work with each other, whereas some oppose each other. This is called "the theory of promotion and control of the five agents." Corresponding to the five agents, everything in the world can be classified into five, such as five colors, five grains, five organs, and so forth. This is called "the theory of correspondence of the five agents." The doctrine of *yin-*

yang wu-hsing served as the major theoretical framework in philosophy, culture, and science in the Chinese cultural system.

Historically speaking, the concepts of *yin-yang* and *wu-hsing* did not exist in the earliest editions of the *I Ching*, and these terms cannot be found in its main text. Incorporated into the *I Ching* system by the late Chou period (771–221 B.C.E.), they were developed into a sophisticated theoretical framework in the Ch'in (221–206 B.C.E.) and Han (206 B.C.E.–C.E. 200). This research treats the *yin-yang wu-hsing* doctrine as an integral part of the *I Ching* system. In my discussion, therefore, the *I Ching* is not only a Confucian classic but also a powerful metaphysical and symbolic system representing different aspects of Chinese culture.

Traditional Japan was within the orbit of the Chinese cultural sphere, and thus was indebted to the *I Ching* for the development of aspects of its history. Indeed, the *I Ching* penetrated many different areas of Japanese life, including politics, the economy, the military, arts, religion, science, and folklore. This book is the first serious attempt to examine the role of the *I Ching* in Japanese thought and culture. Because secondary references are extremely limited, it relies heavily on primary materials. Using textual analysis of Tokugawa writings as my major research method, I conducted this study within a larger historical context and theoretical framework. Based on a proper and critical reading of the texts, my objective was to formulate narratives and views of historical significance that provide a deeper understanding both of Japanese intellectual and cultural history and of Sino-Japanese cultural relations in early modern and modern Japan.

Each chapter, I believe, represents a bold attempt to address new topics by drawing on many rarely used materials. Part I is a historical narrative of *I Ching* scholarship in Japan. Chapter 1 traces the early adaptation of the text, from its importation to Japan in the sixth century to the end of the medieval period in the sixteenth century. It examines how the *I Ching* became a subject of particular attention among major literate groups in the medieval period, such as Zen Buddhist monks, courtiers, and high-ranking warriors. It focuses on the role of the *I Ching* in medieval Japanese culture and on the continuity of its scholarship from medieval to early modern times. Chapter 2 demonstrates the popularity of the text in the Tokugawa period by analyzing both the numbers of authors and writings on it and the importation, reproduction, and punctuation of Chinese commentaries.

Chapter 3 is an overview of the study and uses of the text in the

Tokugawa period, when *I Ching* scholarship reached its apex and the work itself became one of the most popular and influential Chinese texts among Tokugawa intellectuals. This chapter highlights the *I Ching*'s popularity; the major schools, scholars, and writings that grew up around it; and the characteristics of *I Ching* scholarship. In the Tokugawa period, Confucian scholars replaced Zen Buddhist monks as the main force behind *I Ching* scholarship. Because I discuss Confucian issues in almost every chapter, I have not included a separate chapter on Confucianism.

Parts II and III are the foci of my research. They explore the role of the *I Ching* in the thought and culture of Tokugawa Japan. Part II is an analytical discussion of the text in Tokugawa thought. Chapters 4 and 5 look at the impact of Confucianism on Tokugawa politics and economics through the role of the *I Ching*. Chapter 4 documents its part in the formation of Tokugawa political thought. The abstraction and ambiguity of the *I Ching* meant that its ideas were interpreted in various ways in different political contexts. This chapter shows that whereas early Tokugawa scholars used the text to legitimize the Tokugawa regime, late Tokugawa reformers and loyalists used it to air anti-bakufu ideas. It also surveys how the Japanese altered Chinese political ideals to fit the Tokugawa political system.

Chapter 5 demonstrates the importance of the text in Tokugawa economic thought and analyzes its role in Japan's economic development. The doctrine of *yin-yang wu-hsing* was used as a basic interpretative framework in many agricultural writings. The text was also used by economists and early entrepreneurs to develop their "free-market" economic theories, and provided early entrepreneurs with the wisdom and confidence to engage in modern industry and business.

Chapters 6 and 7 investigate the relationship of Confucianism to religion. Chapter 6 demonstrates how Tokugawa Shinto interacted closely with the *I Ching*. In the early Tokugawa period, a large number of Confucians and Shintoists used the text to uphold the doctrine of the unity of Confucianism and Shinto. Many Shinto doctrines were borrowed from the text, and Shinto was Confucianized in this process. In the late Tokugawa period, however, the Hirata school of national learning *(kokugaku)* attempted to change the *I Ching* from a Confucian classic into a Shinto text.

Chapter 7 looks at the subtle relationship between the *I Ching* and Tokugawa Buddhism. The *I Ching* was an ideological battleground for Buddhists and Confucians. Buddhist monks supported the doctrine of the unity of Buddhism and Confucianism, quoting the text to illustrate that both teachings share the concepts of karmic retribution, transmigration, gods and ghosts, and universal flux. The Confucians, in contrast, interpreted the *I Ching* as denying any affinity with Buddhism.

Part III is an analytical discussion of the role of the *I Ching* in Tokugawa culture. Chapter 8 focuses on the role of the text in the cultural interchange between traditional and Western science. In particular, it highlights the text's role in the adaptation of Western astronomy, calendrical studies, and physics. Japanese scholars of Western learning used the *I Ching* extensively to advocate Western ideas. Some cited it to claim that Western ideas had existed in ancient China, and even maintained that Western ideas had originated in China, while others tried to use the text to transplant Western science and technology into a Confucian metaphysical framework.

Chapter 9 discusses the *I Ching*'s role in traditional medicine and in the adoption of Western medicine. Chinese medicine, which was used extensively by Tokugawa physicians, was based on a number of neo-Confucian doctrines related to the *I Ching*. The text played a less significant role in Western medicine, although some physicians did attempt to use it to fuse Western and Chinese medical ideas.

Chapter 10 explores the importance of the text in traditional military studies and in the importation of Western weaponry. Many military and martial arts schools in the Tokugawa period adopted *yin-yang wu-hsing* as their central philosophy. The *I Ching* was also used by different schools of artillery to explicate and justify the use of Western weaponry.

Finally, Chapter 11 surveys the influence of the *I Ching* on the theory and practice of different forms of Tokugawa art and culture, including the tea ceremony, flower arrangement, popular theater, and music.

The *I Ching*
in Tokugawa Thought
and Culture

PART I # HISTORY

1. The Adaptation of the *I Ching* in the Pre-Tokugawa Period

The *I Ching* has been a book of particular significance and interest for much of Japanese history. Although it was neglected in the ancient period (539–1186), its readership expanded to major literate groups in the medieval period (1186–1603). *I Ching* scholarship reached its apex in the Tokugawa period (1603–1868), when the text became one of the most popular and influential Chinese books. It continued to hold a considerable readership and to be influential into the modern period. This chapter provides a brief overview of *I Ching* studies from the book's importation to Japan in the sixth century to the end of the medieval period.

Reception in the Ancient Period

The history of the *I Ching* in ancient Japan is nebulous and not well documented. We find only a few references to it in the historical period (539–645). The *Nihon shoki* (Chronicles of Japan, 720) traces its importation to the sixth century, although it may have arrived in Japan much earlier.[1] It was quoted in article 3 of the *Code of Seventeen Articles* (*Jūnanajō kempō*, 604) of Shōtoku Taishi (572–612).[2] In 632, a Japanese monk named Min (d. 653) lectured Nakatomi no Kamatari (619–669) and other courtiers on the text after his twenty-five-year sojourn in China.

The study of the *I Ching* was institutionalized during the Nara (712–793) and Heian periods (794–1186). The Bureau of Education (Daigakuryō) treated it as a Confucian text, whereas the Bureau of Divination (Onmyōryō) interpreted it as a book of oracles. The *Yōrō*

Code (718) listed it as an elective subject at the Bureau of Education. All textbooks belonged to the school of textual interpretation *(i-li p'ai)*, which elucidated the philosophy and ethics of the *I Ching* by annotating its main text and the Ten Oldest Commentaries (Ten Wings, or *Shih i*). Cheng Hsüan (127–200) and Wang Pi's (226–249) commentaries were the main references, and some T'ang commentaries were used as supplementary texts. The Bureau of Divination, established in the Heian period, trained its students to study the symbolism and numerology *(hsiang-shu)* of the *I Ching* and their application to divination, astrology, medicine, and court rituals. This knowledge of *yin-yang* was referred to as Onmyōdō (the Way of *Yin-Yang*).

The *I Ching* was never a popular text among educated groups in ancient Japan. Neither government nor private libraries made its commentaries an important part of their collections. According to Japan's oldest catalog of Chinese books, the *Honchō kenzaisho mokuroku* (Bibliography of Chinese Books in My Country, compiled by Fujiwara no Sukeyo [d. 898], later renamed *Nihonkoku kenzaisho mokuroku*), the state library had thirty-one books (177 *kan*, or scrolls) on the *I Ching* in the late ninth century.[3] The famous bibliophile Fujiwara no Michinori (1106–1159) had only nine books (29 *kan*) on the *I Ching* in his personal collection.[4]

There are very few historical records of studies of the text in ancient Japan, and only two people draw our attention. Emperor Uda (867–931) studied it under Zen'en, an officer of the Bureau of Education, in 888. With the help of Zen'en and others, Uda punctuated and annotated some parts of the text using Wang Pi's commentary. Uda's note is considered the earliest commentary in Japan. Fujiwara no Yorinaga (1120–1156), the minister of the left *(sadaijin)*, studied it in 1143 to understand the theory about the change of reign name in the year of *kinoene*.[5] He was conscious of the taboo that prohibited anyone under the age of fifty from studying the text.[6] Fujiwara said:

> The ordinary people say that those who study the *I Ching* will meet misfortune, and that one can only read it having reached the age of fifty. I think this saying is groundless. . . . I am still afraid of this saying, and therefore I had [Abe] Yasuchika perform the *Taizanbukun* worship [a Taoist ritual].[7]

Fujiwara studied the text's philosophy under Fujiwara no Narisuke and divination under Fujiwara no Michinori. His tragic death at the age of thirty-six during the Hōgen Rebellion (1156) reinforced this taboo.

Our understanding of the role of the *I Ching* in ancient Japanese culture is very limited and piecemeal. The text seems to have exerted some impact on historical writings and literature. The *Kojiki* (Records of Ancient Matters, 712) and *Nihon shoki* were influenced by the ideas of *yin-yang* and *wu-hsing*. Yamamoto Yūichi believes that the themes and associations in the *Taketori monogatari* (Tale of the Bamboo Cutter), *Utsubo monogatari* (Tale of the Hollow Tree), *Konjaku monogatari* (Tales of Times Now Past), and *Heike monogatari* (Tale of the Taira House) were inspired by the *I Ching*.[8] Ivan Morris, in his reconstruction of court life in ancient Japan, uses the *Genji monogatari* (Tale of Genji) to describe the influence of *yin-yang wu-hsing* doctrine on Heian politics, medicine, astrology, religion, geography, sexuality, and folklore.[9] Robert Borgen has discussed how the *yin-yang* principle penetrated Heian officialdom.[10] Yoshino Hiroko has investigated the influence of the *I Ching* on court rituals, folklore, and architecture.[11] We know even less about its role in science. The Bureau of Divination applied its principles to calendrical studies, medicine, astrology, and geomancy.[12] Fujiwara no Michinori was famous for applying the principles of the sixty-four hexagrams to mathematics in the *Keishisan* (Mathematics of Numbers, 1157).[13]

Study and Uses in the Medieval Period

For a number of reasons, the *I Ching* gradually became a popular text in medieval times. First, its popularity was promoted by the flow of Chinese neo-Confucian currents into Japan after the thirteenth century. The Sung school had a preference for the *I Ching* and the Four Books (i.e., the *Ta Hsüeh,* or Great Learning; *Chung Yung,* or Doctrine of the Mean; *Lun Yü,* or Analects; and *Meng Tzu,* or Sayings of Mencius). The *I Ching* provided a metaphysical framework on which Sung scholars could construct their neo-Confucian ideas. Many Sung scholars were masters of the text and had produced important commentaries. Famous works—including Chou Tun-i's (1017–1073) *T'ai-chi t'u shuo* (An Explanation of the Diagram of the Supreme Ultimate), Ch'eng I's (1033–1107) *I Chuan* (A Commentary on the *I Ching*), and Chu Hsi's (1130–1200) *Chou-i pen-i* (The Original Meaning of the *I Ching*) and *I-hsüeh ch'i-meng* (Instructions to the Young on the Learning of the *I Ching*)—were imported into medieval Japan and received with great enthusiasm. The new (or Sung) commentaries gradually replaced the old (Han and T'ang) commentaries as the main reference.

Second, Zen Buddhist monks played an important role in promoting the text. In ancient times, the *I Ching* was studied only by a few courtiers and officials of the central court government. In the medieval period, the monks within the five-mountain Zen monastic system *(gozan)* became the dominant intellectual force. A large number of Zen Buddhist monks studied the text, and they punctuated, annotated, and reprinted some important Chinese commentaries.

Third, the *I Ching*'s idea of change fitted the historical atmosphere of medieval Japan. Medieval Japan was a time of chaos and crises. The text equipped medieval Japanese with the wisdom to survive these dramatic changes.[14] As in China, it also provided an ideological support for reform. Thus it is no wonder that some reform-minded medieval Japanese political leaders and warriors studied it with zest.

Fourth, the *I Ching* was well suited to Japan's indigenous beliefs and folklore. The abstraction of the text made its principles applicable to different areas of thought and culture. For instance, early Shintoists employed the ideas of *yin-yang* and *wu-hsing* to conceptualize traditional myths and value systems. The text also penetrated various realms of medieval art and culture, such as *nō* drama, flower arrangement *(ikebana)*, the tea ceremony *(chanoyu)*, and the martial arts.

To understand how and why the *I Ching* was studied and used in medieval Japan, we survey the period's major literate groups: Zen Buddhist monks, members of the imperial family, *hakase* families (specially designated scholarly families), courtiers, teachers and students at the Ashikaga School (Ashikaga gakkō), and high-ranking warriors. Different traditions of *I Ching* studies had close relations and influenced each other.

Zen Buddhist Monks

Zen Buddhist monks were the main force behind *I Ching* studies in medieval Japan. Confucianism was included in the Mahāyāna Buddhist system under the slogan of "the unity of Buddhism and Confucianism" *(Jubutsu itchi)*. Believing that the *I Ching* could help them attain enlightenment, Zen Buddhists monks studied it at the final stage of their training and used it widely to explain Buddhist ideas. However, it seems that some monks studied the *I Ching* and other Chinese texts primarily for cultural, rather than religious, purposes.[15]

With Chinese commentaries reaching monasteries, Buddhist monks began to study the *I Ching* in the early fourteenth century.[16] There were two forerunners of these studies, Kōhō Kennichi (1241–1316) and Issan Ichi'nei (1247–1317). Kōhō employed the text to answer a famous Zen question: "What was our condition before we were born [to our parents]?" He replied: "The origins of the birth of the universe existed before the separation of heaven and earth. The origins of the change in everything existed before the drawing of the first line of the first hexagram *(ch'ien)*."[17] This dialogue was an example of the use of the *I Ching* to explicate Buddhist ideas. Issan, a Chinese monk who spent his last years in Japan, was famous for his mastery of the text. He favored a Han commentary, Yang Hsiung's (53 B.C.E.–18 C.E.) *T'ai-hsüan ching* (Book of the Supremely Profound Principle), an ambitious attempt to replace the *I Ching* with a more complicated symbolic system. Thus we can assume that Issan belonged to the school of symbols and numbers.

The first great master of the *I Ching* in Japan was Kokan Shiren (1278–1346).[18] He was probably the first person in Japan to use both the old and new commentaries of the text. His scholarship benefited from his extensive connections to different traditions of *I Ching* scholarship. At the age of twenty, Kokan studied its philosophy and divination with Minamoto Arifusa, a courtier from the prestigious Minamoto clan. Minamoto pleaded with Kokan: "The *I Ching* is the essence of my family teaching. It has been transmitted for more than thirty generations from the Great Minister Kibi no Makibi [695?–775] to me. The transmission will end if I fail to find an appropriate person to succeed me. I look around but find that no children in my family can be entrusted. Hence I beg you to succeed me."[19]

At the same time, Kokan studied literature with another courtier, Sugawara Arisuke, the *I Ching* instructor to Emperor Hanazono (1297–1348). Ten years later, Kokan met Issan and asked him about the *I Ching*. Issan lent him Yang Hsiung's *T'ai-hsüan ching*. By combining the *T'ai-hsüan ching* with his favorite commentary, Ch'eng I's *I Chuan*, Kokan reached a new understanding. He expressed his gratitude to Issan:

My intelligence is poor and my knowledge is shallow. When I read Ch'eng and Yang's commentaries on the *I Ching*, I did not fully understand. You, Master [Issan], are knowledgeable. I rely on you to solve all my doubts. By combining the ideas of Ch'eng and Yang, thinking deeply and investigating quietly, we can surely find the

explanation. I hope I can be lucky enough to come back one day to
receive your tutelage.[20]

This suggests that Kokan adopted an eclectic approach to studying
both the old and new commentaries and the textual and symbolic
meanings of the text. He trained two outstanding students, Chūgan
Engetsu (1300–1375) and Gidō Shūshin (1326–1389).

Chūgan Engetsu was one of the finest scholars of the text in the
medieval period.[21] He was a champion of the new commentary, and
his explanations were based mainly on Chu Hsi's commentaries. But
he was not a blind follower and corrected some of Chu Hsi's mistakes.
Chūgan also used the text to express his political ideas. In the explanation of the hexagram *ko* (change) in the *Kakukaihen* (A Thesis on
the Hexagram *ko*) and *Jō Kemmu tenshi hyō* (A Memorial to Emperor
Kemmu), he stated that reform was necessary but should avoid being
too radical.[22]

Gidō Shūshin was a popularizer of the text. He remarked, "The *I
Ching* is a book for knowing destiny. It includes everything in heaven,
earth, and man. . . . It cannot be understood without its oral transmission."[23] Hence he put great emphasis on education. To provide
his students with a better edition of the text, he punctuated the standard textbook for the civil service examinations in Yüan China, the
Chou-i chuan-i (The Combination of *I Chuan* and *Chou-i pen-i*), a combination of Chu Hsi and Ch'eng I's commentaries edited by (Yüan)
Tung Kai. Like Chūgan, Gidō stressed the political implications of
the text, and that the ruler must study it in order to equip himself
with the art and philosophy of politics. He discussed the *I Ching* with
the shogunal deputy Uesugi Ujinori (d. 1417) and the shogun Ashikaga Yoshimitsu (1358–1408). He trained a number of brilliant students, including Kiyō Hōshū (1363–1424), Daichin Shūkō, Shinka
Gendai, Seito Myōrin, and Tengan Bokuchū.

Kiyō Hōshū was an ardent reader of Sung commentaries and
favored Chu Hsi's *I-hsüeh ch'i-meng* and Ch'eng I's *I Chuan* in particular. He believed that the *I Ching* was in agreement with Buddhism
and that studying it could help to achieve Buddhist enlightenment.
One day in the spring of 1400, while Kiyō was reading the *I-hsüeh ch'i-
meng*, a fellow Zen monk, Renzan Kenkō, came to ask for his guidance
on the *I Ching*. Renzan said: "I have studied Confucian interpretation
of the *I Ching* in detail. Can I also hear our Buddhist interpretation?"
Kiyō replied:

> Nothing leaves the wonder of the Buddhist law, just as the sixty-four
> hexagrams never leave the trigrams *k'an* (abysmal) and *li* (clinging).
> The Buddha reached his enlightenment for the first time under a
> grapevine. It carries the same meaning as Fu Hsi's drawing the eight
> trigrams. . . . There is a saying of Ch'eng I that [runs,] "I would rather
> read the hexagram *ken* (keeping still) than a set of the *Garland Sūtra*
> *(Avataṃsaka,* or *Kegonkyō)."*[24]

Kiyō's first two comparisons show that the *I Ching* and Buddhism
have similarities in structure and in their stress on enlightenment.
The Ch'eng I proverb implies that the hexagram *ken,* a hexagram of
self-forgiveness and quietness, is in agreement with the spirit of
Nirvāṇa (realization of Buddhahood) expounded in the *Garland
Sūtra.*

Kiyō's teaching of the *I Ching* was succeeded by that of Unshō
Ikkei (1386–1463),[25] who is remembered as a popularizer of Tung
Kai's *Chou-i chuan-i,* a popular text during the *sengoku* (Warring
States period, 1467–1600) and early Tokugawa period.[26] His *I Ching*
scholarship was also indebted to other traditions. He was the elder
brother of the famous *I Ching* court scholar Ichijō Kanera (1402–
1481) and was also closely associated with the Sugawara family, which
lectured to the emperor on the *I Ching.*

Unshō passed his teachings on to Tōgen Zuisen (1403–1489),
who stood at the apex of *I Ching* scholarship in medieval Japan.
Tōgen's mentors were scholars from different backgrounds: *gozan*
monks (Unshō Ikkei, Shōchū Shōzui, Jikuun Tōren [1390–1471],
Tengan Bokuchū, Zuikei Shūhō, and Seito Myōrin), *hakase* families
(Kiyohara Naritada, 1409–1467), courtiers (Ichijō Kanera), and the
Ashikaga School (Hakushū Sōjō).[27] Tōgen developed his own interpretations in the *Hyakunōbusuma* (25 *kan*), the best commentary in
medieval Japan. This influential book was a collection of his teaching notes on the text.

Tōgen annotated Chinese commentaries from all periods.[28] His
scholarship was eclectic; he accepted different schools and approaches, such as textual interpretation, symbols and numbers, and
divination.[29] By combining the old and new commentaries, he developed original interpretations that carried a strong Zen Buddhist tone.
For example, in the explanation of *t'ai-chi* (the Supreme Ultimate)
and the sixty-four hexagrams, he wrote:

> In the state of *t'ai-chi,* there was no difference between big and small,
> high and low, good and evil, and so on. . . . There was no Buddha and

people, no sorrow and Nirvāṇa, no hell and heaven. . . . This is called "the state before the differentiation of the elements in the universe" as well as "the state prior to the birth of father and mother" [in Zen doctrine]. . . . Later, *t'ai-chi* functioned and created the two poles, four symbols, and eight trigrams. Everything is included in the sixty-four hexagrams.[30]

Tōgen's preference for Sung commentaries was clear. He tended to use Sung commentaries to explain the text whenever possible.[31] His favorite commentaries were Chu Hsi's *I-hsüeh ch'i-meng* and Hu I-kuei's *I hsüeh ch'i-meng i-chuan*. The main lineage of *I Ching* scholarship inherited from Kokan ended with Tōgen, who trained no important successors.[32]

In brief, the *I Ching* scholarship of Zen Buddhist monks had the following characteristics. First, it represented the finest scholarship in the medieval period, making major contributions to *I Ching* studies by punctuating and reprinting Chinese commentaries. Some monks even attempted to establish their own explanations. Second, it used both the pre-Sung and Sung commentaries in the beginning and tended to adopt Sung commentaries as the main reference in late medieval times. Third, it was a secret transmission among Zen Buddhist scholars. Its main lineage was kept unbroken for centuries. Fourth, it was eclectic. The approaches of textual interpretation, symbols and numbers, and divination were used. Fifth, it had strong Buddhist overtones in its explanations. The *I Ching* was used to support Zen Buddhist doctrines.

The Imperial Family and Courtiers

The court was another center of *I Ching* studies, where members from the imperial family, *hakase* families, and courtiers learned the text. It became very common, if not obligatory, for the Japanese emperor to study the *I Ching* and the Four Books in the medieval period. In particular, Hanazono, Godaigo (1288–1339), and Sūkōin (1334–1398) were enthusiastic about the text. They supported *I Ching* studies mainly for political reasons—to learn its political philosophy and to claim legitimacy for their policies.

Hanazono rated the *I Ching* as the most important Confucius classic and studied it with great effort. At the age of eighteen, he asked Sugawara Arisuke, the head of the Bureau of Education, to teach him the text, but his request was turned down because of the ancient taboo that prohibited anyone younger than fifty from studying it.[33] He was very disappointed and determined to break this taboo. Having abdicated at the age of twenty-nine, Hanazono began to learn the text. He regarded it as compulsory reading for the emperor because it contained a philosophy of government. He remarked:

> Being in the position of emperor, how can one not know the heavenly will? Therefore Emperor Gouda [r. 1274–1287] and the current emperor [Godaigo] studied the *I Ching*. Although I am not good, I still read books that are worth reading. As I have already become the emperor, isn't it reasonable for me to read the Book of Heavenly Will [the *I Ching*]?[34]

Hanazono stressed the importance of oral transmission and opposed wanton interpretation of the *I Ching* and other Confucian texts. He complained: "[Confucian scholars at court] are all ignorant of the real meaning [of Confucianism]. They develop their own interpretations from their reading of the *I Ching, Lun Yü, Meng Tzu, Ta Hsüeh,* and *Chung Yung.* They advocate their own theories without receiving oral transmissions [of authentic interpretations]. As a result, things like criticisms and attacks arise."[35] Hanazono's major interest was the text's philosophy. He did not believe in apocrypha *(chan-wei),* which insisted that there was a correlation between natural phenomena and human activities, arguing that politics depended on the virtue of the emperor and not on natural phenomena.

Godaigo studied the *I Ching* in his youth and promoted it among his courtiers, so that it became one of the most popular texts at court. Unlike Hanazono, Godaigo was quite superstitious and believed that the text was a book of oracles. He consulted it on almost every major decision in politics. Sometimes he even followed the augury quite irrationally. For example, the *Taiheiki* (Record of the Grand Peace, c. 1372) records that in 1332, Ashikaga Takauji (1305–1358) conquered Kyoto and Nitta Yoshisada (1301–1338) overthrew the Kamakura bakufu (military government). Godaigo and his courtiers disagreed over the timing of returning to the capital, Kyoto. Godaigo wanted to return immediately, but the majority of his courtiers opposed him on the grounds that war-stricken Kyoto was not yet safe. The emperor could not make up his mind and thus consulted the *I Ching.* The result was the hexagram *shih* (army); the augury implied that the emperor should authorize a man of virtue to fight as the general, return to the capital, and award the warriors fairly when the war was over. Following the oracle, he returned to the capital and rewarded the warriors.[36]

The text also seems to have played a certain role in politics during
the Kemmu Restoration. Its idea of change provided ideological support for reform. It was not coincidental that many ardent supporters
of the Restoration, such as Hino Suketomo (1290–1332), Hino Toshi-
moto (d. 1332), and Chūgan Engetsu, were scholars of the text. In
particular, the Hino brothers were Godaigo's close aides and contributed to many important policy decisions. For example, following the
request of Hino Suketomo, who based his arguments on the *I Ching*,
Godaigo changed the era name to Genkyō (1321–1324), a term itself
borrowed from the text.[37] They also held anti-Ashikaga gatherings in
the guise of Confucian seminars.

Sūkōin of the Northern Court studied the *I Ching* under Sugawara Ariatsu and a Zen monk, Kūya. Like Godaigo, he was interested
in the *yin-yang* tradition and used the text as a divination manual. A
monk stated: "[The ex-emperor] is absorbed in the study of the hexagrams [of the *I Ching*] and has a deep understanding of the changes
in time and fate."[38]

Thanks to respectable students like Hanazono, Godaigo, and Sūkōin, the study of the *I Ching* became prevalent among courtiers.
Hakase families produced excellent scholars and became the center
of *I Ching* studies outside the sphere of Buddhism. There were four
major *hakase* families in medieval Japan: The Hino and Sugawara
families were the doctors of letters *(monjō hakase),* and the Kiyohara
and Nakahara were the doctors of classics *(myōkyō hakase).* In particular, the Sugawara and Kiyohara families had a long tradition of *I
Ching* studies.

The Sugawara family specialized in the *I Ching,* and produced important scholars and writings. Their family library had a rich collection of books on the text. Their scholarship was rather conservative;
it aimed to fuse a selected part of the new commentaries with the
old. The Sugawara contributed to the pronunciation, punctuation,
and annotation of the text and had a tremendous impact on all other
schools, including those of the Kiyohara family, the Ashikaga School,
and Zen Buddhism. In particular, prominent *I Ching* scholars such as
Hakushū Sōjō and Tōgen Zuisen were indebted to the Sugawara.
Family members frequently gave lectures on the *I Ching* to the imperial family; many courtiers and Buddhist monks also came to receive
the family's guidance. For example, Sugawara Arisuke taught Emperor Hanazono, and his brother Sugawara Ariatsu taught Emperor
Sūkōin the text in the fourteen century. In the reign of Jōji (1362–

1368), Sugawara Toyonaga went to teach the text in the Kanto area. Many monks from Kamakura came to attend his open lectures. It has been suggested that the teaching of the Sugawara family influenced the Ashikaga School through Toyonaga.[39]

Sugawara Hidenaga (d. 1412), the *I Ching* instructor to Ashikaga Yoshimitsu, was probably the greatest scholar in this lineage. He exchanged opinions on the text with his close friend Gidō Shūshin. Influenced by the rationalism of Chu Hsi and (Sung) Yang Wan-li's commentaries, Sugawara Hidenaga criticized the apocrypha and other superstitions associated with the *I Ching*. Sugawara Ekinaga, in contrast, believed in the apocryphal and *yin-yang* interpretations of the text, and in 1441 submitted an article to Emperor Gohanazono (r. 1428–1464) urging him to alter the era name and government institutions to prepare for the changes that he believed would happen that year.[40] Sugawara Nagaatsu (1502–1549) used Chu Hsi and Ch'eng I's commentaries as the main reference for his lectures. In 1528, he successfully persuaded Emperor Gonara (r. 1526–1557) to change the reign name to Kyōroku, a term from the *I Ching*.

The Kiyohara family began its *I Ching* scholarship in the Heian period. Their conservatism can be seen in their adoption of the Wang Pi's commentary and in their observance of the ancient taboo. At the outset, the Sugawara family outshone them in *I Ching* studies. Kiyohara Naritada was the first to establish Kiyohara family authority vis-à-vis the text; he both introduced Sung commentaries into his family tradition and taught Emperor Hanazono the text and other Confucian classics. His lectures on Chu Hsi's *I-hsüeh ch'i-meng* were published as the *Ekigaku keimō kōgi* (Lectures on the *I-hsüeh ch'i-meng*). His scholarship on the text became so famous that even Tōgen came to study under him. Tōgen borrowed heavily from the *Ekigaku keimō kōgi* in his *Hyakunōbusuma*.

Kiyohara Nobukata (1475–1550), a grandson of Naritada, was one of the greatest *I Ching* scholars of the entire medieval period. He represented the apex of *I Ching* scholarship at court. At first, following family tradition, he began to study the text at the age of fifty and punctuated Wang Pi's *Chou-i chu* the same year. Soon after, he shifted his attention to Sung commentaries and finished two important works: the *Shūeki shō* (A Commentary on the *I Ching*, 4 *kan*) and *Ekigaku keimō tsūshaku shō* (A Commentary on the *I-hsüeh ch'i-meng t'ung-shih*). The *Shūeki shō* included different commentaries from all ages and was one of the most important source books in medieval Japan.

The *Ekigaku keimō tsūshaku shō* was a version of (Sung) Hu Fang-p'ing's *I hsüeh ch'i-meng t'ung-shih* punctuated and annotated in Japan. By combining the old and new commentaries, Kiyohara Nobukata attempted to establish his own explanations. He also developed the other aspect of his family tradition—divination—by writing the *Shūeki zureki ryakketsu* (A Short Note on the Graphic and Calendrical Studies of the *I Ching*), and punctuating the *Eki zeigi* (Divination of the *I Ching*). His students of the *I Ching* included both courtiers and Zen Buddhist monks, such as Sanjōnishi Sanetaka and Ikkin.

While *hakase* families studied the text as a Confucian classic, the two families of the Bureau of Divination, the Abe and the Kamo, used it for divination. The *I Ching* and (Sui) Hsiao Chi's *Wu-hsing ta-i* (Fundamental Principles of *Wu Hsing*, c. 600) were the main texts in the Bureau. The two families applied the *I Ching* to divination, the military, medicine, astrology, and court rituals. The Abe family was famous for its accurate military predications. For example, Hōjō Yoshi-toki (1163–1224) and Hōjō Masako (1157–1225) asked the Abe family for a forecast during the Jōkyū War (1221). They foretold the bakufu's victory, and this helped boost the morale of the bakufu army.[41] Ashikaga Yoshimitsu trusted the head of the Bureau, Abe Ariyo, who had accurately predicted the occurrence of rebellions. He was often beside Yoshimitsu in the army as a military advisor *(gunshi)*.

The *I Ching* was popular reading material among courtiers in medieval Japan. Apart from specially designated families, such as those from the *hakase* and the Bureau of Divination, there were many individual courtiers who studied the text. The most famous of these included Kitabatake Chikafusa (1293–1354), Ichijō Kanera, Yoshida Kanetomo (1435–1511), and the Sanjōnishi brothers.

Kitabatake Chikafusa's *Jimnō shōtōki* (Chronicle of the Legitimate Succession of the Divine Sovereigns, rev. 1343) was indebted to Watarai Ieyuki's (1255–1352) *Ruijū jimgi hongen* (Classified Dictionary on the Origins of Shinto Deities). Watarai used the *I Ching* and *Wu-hsing ta-i* to explain the beginning of the universe. Kitabatake quoted extensively from the *I Ching* and two Chou Tun-i commentaries, the *T'ai-chi t'u shuo* and *I t'ung shu* (A General Explanation of the *I Ching*), to elucidate Shinto.[42] For example, he used the concept of *yin-yang wu-hsing* in the *T'ai-chi t'u shuo* to explain the genealogy of the first seven generations of Japanese deities. Kitabatake discredited the apocrypha of the *I Ching* and argued that politics hinged solely on the virtue of the ruler. Thus he opposed Miyoshi Kiyoyuki's (846–918) idea of changing the era name in the year of *kinoene*.

Ichijō Kanera grew up in an environment that enabled him to learn different traditions of *I Ching* scholarship. His grandfather, Ichijō Tsunemichi, was an advocate of Chu Hsi's commentaries. His grandfather-in-law was Sugawara Hidenaga, the *I Ching* authority at court. His elder brother was the famous monk-scholar Unshō Ikkei. Ichijō Kanera himself was a champion of the Ch'eng and Chu commentaries. In the *Nihon shoki sanso* (A Commentary on the *Nihon shoki*), he used the *I Ching* to expound the doctrine of "the unity of the three teachings" of Shinto, Confucianism, and Buddhism *(sankyō itchi).*

Yoshida Kanetomo was the founder of Yoshida Shinto. The Yoshida family (originally Urabe) had acted as the shamans in the Bureau of Divination since the Heian period. The *I Ching* was the main source of this family tradition. Yoshida Kanetomo also studied with a Zen monk, Ōsen Keisan (1429–1493). Like Kitabatake Chikafusa and Ichijō Kanera, Yoshida attempted to use the text to elucidate Shinto, dwelling on questions such as "What is the meaning of God?" and "What was the situation before the beginning of the universe?"[43] He wrote the *Shūeki zeigi* (Rituals of Divination in the *I Ching*), which became a standard divination manual after it was punctuated by Kiyohara Nobukata. Yoshida also applied the *yin-yang wu-hsing* theory to the military. He was the father of Kiyohara Nobukata, who was later adopted by the Kiyohara family. Kiyohara Nobukata's interest in divination seems to have come from this connection.

Sanjōnishi Saneatsu and his son, Sanetaka, studied the text under Tōgen and Ikkin. In the *Sanetakakōki* (Records of Duke Sanetaka), Ikkin told them that during the transmission of *I Ching* divination methods, they had to obey very strict regulations: They were not allowed to eat any crop threshed by women or to go out for one hundred days, and they were to concentrate on study to the extent that meals and sleep should be sacrificed.[44] Sanjōnishi Sanetaka surpassed his father and became the successor of Tōgen. He studied the text at the age of fifty and later did textual comparisons and punctuated a number of commentaries. He had close relations with *I Ching* scholars at court, including Kiyohara Naritada and Yoshida Kanetomo. He read the *I Ching* and *Eki zeigi* punctuated by Kiyohara Nobukata. Following the advice of Kiyohara Nobukata, Sanjōnishi borrowed the *Shūeki zeigi* from Kanetomo and copied it by hand. He also borrowed the *I-hsüeh ch'i-meng t'ung-shih* from the Kamo family.

In general, the intellectual atmosphere at court was conservative and eclectic. It contained a great variety of students. The philosophical, divination, and practical aspects of the book (such as its use for military, medical, and scientific practices) were all explored. The Sugawara and Kiyohara families in particular achieved a high level of scholarship.

The Ashikaga School

During the latter half of the medieval period, after both the *gozan* and *hakase* traditions had gone into decline, the Ashikaga School established itself as a new center of *I Ching* studies. Its scholarship is characterized by its eclecticism and its emphasis on practical usage. This eclecticism can be seen from two perspectives. First, the Ashikaga School combined different traditions. Inspired by courtiers, sponsored by warriors, and run by Zen monks, it had a tremendous impact on the *I Ching* scholarship of different schools of thought and religion. It was also influenced deeply by the shamanistic practices of Onmyōdō (the Way of *Yin-Yang*) and Shingon Buddhism. Second, the School treated the text both as a book of wisdom and a book of oracles, and adopted both the old and new commentaries. Its emphasis on practical usage was expressed mainly in the form of *gunbai shisō* (military oracles).[45] Its teachers and students served the *sengoku* daimyō (regional military lords of the Warring States period) as military advisors, shamans, physicians, architects, and even weathermen. Neo-Confucian medicine was introduced to Japan through the School. Scholarly discussion of the text was only a sub-current at the School.

The Ashikaga School was famous for its Chinese studies in medieval Japan. The *I Ching* was the most important textbook in its curriculum. Because learning the text was considered a sacred activity, the School had very strict regulations. Its remote location (now Ashikaga City in Tochigi Prefecture) separated it from urban distractions. The transmission of the text was divided into two parts: *seiden* (major transmission) and *betsuden* (minor transmission). The former was the study of its philosophical and ethical meanings, whereas the latter was the process of learning to practice divination.

Seiden relied heavily on Sugawara scholarship. Tōgen explained: "Although there are many Japanese punctuations of the *I Ching*, I think the representative versions are the two punctuations made by the Kō family [Ōe family] and the Sugawara family. Now the Kō family has disappeared, and therefore the Ashikaga School has adopted the Sugawara's punctuation alone."[46] It used the old commentary as its basis and the new commentary as its reference. In particular, Wang

Pi's commentary was the favorite text. The library of the Ashikaga School had an excellent collection of old commentaries on the *I Ching*. Its collection of new commentaries was strengthened by Uesugi Norizane (1410–1466), who brought many Sung and Yüan commentaries from China.[47] It also published and reprinted some books on the text.

Seiden means "primary or fundamental transmission," but *betsuden* emerged as more significant in the actual teachings of the School. The Ashikaga School was a training center for *I Ching* diviners. Its curriculum put more emphasis on divination than philosophy. Using the *I Ching* and *Chou-i ming-ch'i ching* as its major textbooks, it taught fourteen kinds of divinational skills, from the most basic yarrow-stalk oracle techniques to advanced methods such as fate calculation, astrology, and geomancy. Many of these teachings seemed to come from Onmyōdō and Shingon Buddhism. Moreover, the School performed a ritual that was influenced by Onmyōdō: Before using the *I Ching* for divination, scholars of the School read a prayer that invited both Chinese and Japanese deities to come to the School. Here is a standard prayer recited by the ninth rector, Kanshitsu Genkitsu (1548–1612), in 1596:

> In Japan, I—XXX who comes from X province, X prefecture, and X county, on X day of X month—want to use the oracles to solve my doubts. I am wholeheartedly inviting all deities in heaven and earth, Gods of Sun and Moon, Gods of the Five Stars, . . . the Child Holding the Yarrow Stalks, the Child Showing the Oracles, the God of the Six Lines, . . . all deities in Japan, Gods of the Four Directions, hundreds of guardian deities of the mountain, forest, river, and sea, Fu Hsi, King Wen, the Duke of Chou, Confucius, Cheng Hsüan, Wang Pi, Chu Hsi, and the spirit of past masters of the *I Ching*. I hope all of you can come to this place of ritual. This [paper] is the proof of urgency, please come at once, as requested.[48]

The first rector was Kaigen (d. 1469), who was famous for his mastery of the text. He made it the most important subject at the Ashikaga School. Kaigen had close ties to Shingon Buddhism and was more interested in *betsuden* than in *seiden*. He had two great students, Ippaku Genshin and Hakushū Sōjō, who established the School's reputation as the center of *I Ching* studies.

Unlike other Zen monks, Ippaku was initially a scholar of the *I Ching* who later turned to Zen Buddhism because of his understanding of the text. He was highly respected as a great *I Ching* master.

When he traveled to Western Japan, people said that the center of *I Ching* studies also shifted to the West with him. He relied on old commentaries, such as those of Ma Jung, Cheng Hsüan, Wang Pi, and Han K'ang-po, as the basis for his ideas, and selectively used those of Shao Yung, Chang Tsai, Ch'eng I, and Chu Hsi as references. Ippaku was at odds with Kaigen over the direction of the School. He insisted that *seiden* was the core of *I Ching* studies and criticized the misuse of divination:

> The *Chou-i meng-ch'i ching* is descended from ancient times, but we should not use it too often. Nowadays, people are indulging in this learning. They foretell their death by themselves, pointing out that a certain year will have a bad influence on a certain months and days. They frequently become a laughingstock.[49]

Ippaku seemed particularly interested in Chu Hsi's *I-hsüeh ch'i-meng*. His lectures on the books *Shūeki keimō tsūshaku kōgi* (The Oral Explanation of the *Chou-i ch'i-meng t'ung-shih*) and *Shūeki keimō yoku-den kōgi* (The Oral Explanation of the *Chou-i ch'i-meng i-chuan*) mainly adopted the interpretations from two commentaries: (Sung) Hu Fang-p'ing's *I-hsüeh ch'i-meng t'ung-shih* and (Yüan) Hu I-kuei's *Chou-i ch'i-meng i-chuan*. Ippaku's lectures received warm praise from his contemporaries. Even the Kiyohara family included them in their family library (by then known as the Kiyohara bunko). Influenced by (Ming) Hsiung Tsung-li, Ippaku applied the *I Ching* to medicine. His teachings had a great impact on *gozan* monks, and he was succeeded by Gesshū Jukei.

Hakushū entered the Ashikaga School in 1440, at the age of twenty-five. His performance impressed Kaigen so much that he was allowed to study the *I Ching* under Kaigen's own mentor, Kizen, at the age of thirty-one. Hakushū's edition of Kaigen and Kizen's lectures became the *Shūeki yōjiki* (Major Events in My Study of the *I Ching*). Soon there-after, Hakushū became a celebrated master of the *I Ching* himself and traveled extensively to spread his teachings. He had a preference for Sung commentaries, although he did not deny the value of old com-mentaries. In his teaching, he used the *Hsi Tz'u* (The Commentary on the Appended Judgments), one of the Ten Wings, as the textbook for beginners. For advanced students, he used Sung commentaries, particularly Chu Hsi's *I-hsüeh ch'i-meng* and Shao Yung's *Huang-chi ching shih shu* (Supreme Principles Governing the World), as his main references. His greatest contribution was his *Shūeki shō* (A Commentary on the *I Ching*, 3 *kan*), a source book on Chinese scholarship. Its structure and content influenced Tōgen's *Hyakunōbusuma*. Hakushū's students included Tōgen Zuisen, Osen Kensan, and Keijo Shūrin (1440–1578).[50]

Teni, the second rector, adopted the punctuation of the Kiyohara family and absorbed more from the new commentary than Kaigen did. The Ashikaga School reached its peak during the tenure of the seventh rector, Kyūka (d. 1578). The enrollment of regular students rose to three thousand, and the School's *I Ching* seminars attracted large audiences from different parts of Japan. More than a hundred people received the "secret transmission" of the text. One of them was Kishun Ryūki (1511–1574), who taught Bunshi Genshō (1555–1615), the most famous punctuator of the *I Ching* in the early modern period. Kyūka also taught the text to the daimyō of Odawara, Hōjō Ujiyasu (1515–1571) and his son, Hōjō Ujimasa (1538–1590). Kyūka wrote a book on *I Ching* divination entitled *Jūrijōhenketsu* (Divination Based on Changing Lines). His lectures on the *I Ching* became the *Ekikyō kōgi* (Lectures on the *I Ching*).

Kyūka's beloved student, Kanshitsu Genkitsu (also called Sanyō), became the ninth rector of the School. He is remembered more as a diviner than as a teacher or monk. Under his leadership, the image of the school as a training school for military shamans was firmly established. Many of his students were employed by regional warriors as military advisors. He himself had close relations with Takeda Shingen (1521–1573) and Tokugawa Ieyasu (1542–1616). Takeda's strong belief in the *I Ching* may have been influenced by Kanshitsu. Takeda would have no one but graduates of the Ashikaga School as his military advisors.[51] Kanshitsu was famous for his role as a shaman in helping Tokugawa Ieyasu at the Battle of Sekigahara in 1600, and in checking the *feng-shui* (geomancy) of Hagi Castle for Mōri Terumoto (1552–1625). Following the orders of Tokugawa Ieyasu, he was put in charge of the publication of the Fushimi (or Keichō) edition of the *I Ching*.

Characteristics of *I Ching* Studies in the Medieval Period

I Ching scholarship was an eclectic form of learning included in the Mahāyāna Buddhist system, but one that also fused many elements from Onmyōdō and Shinto. Confucianism had been the mainstream school of thought in traditional China, whereas it was only a "maidservant" to other currents of thought in medieval Japan, where Confucians did not exist as an independent intellectual or social group. Rather, there were only "amateur Confucians" (Buddhist monks, courtiers, Shintoists, and the like) who employed the *I Ching* and other Confucian texts to elucidate and enrich their beliefs. *I Ching* scholarship had to wait until the Tokugawa period to establish itself as a part of Confucianism in Japan.

Moreover, new commentaries were adopted and became the main reference in the latter half of the medieval period. The traditional view that Sung learning only became influential in Confucian circles after the efforts of early Tokugawa Confucians is now untenable. Our investigation clearly demonstrates that the development of Confucianism in medieval Japan was, in a sense, the history of new commentaries replacing the old. Zen Buddhist monks began to use the new commentaries as early as the beginning of the fourteenth century. Other traditions of *I Ching* studies also adopted the new commentaries no later than the early fifteenth century. During the latter half of the medieval period, the new commentaries became the main references for all traditions—*gozan* monks, *hakase* families, courtiers, and the Ashikaga School.

Medieval scholarship made the earliest efforts to naturalize the *I Ching* in Japan. Both Japanese-punctuated texts and Japanese commentaries contributed to the naturalization of Confucianism. At first, the purpose of punctuation was probably to popularize Chinese texts for people unable to read classical Chinese. But the reading of Chinese texts through a Japanese form somehow shaped both their content and Japanese readers' perception of the text. Japanese scholars also wrote commentaries and discussed Chinese texts in the context of Japanese history and culture. Buddhist, Shinto, and Onmyōdō elements were added to the Japanese *I Ching* tradition in this process.

Study of the *I Ching* was a rudimentary kind of scholarship that was basically limited to scholars adding Japanese punctuation to, and commenting, on Chinese texts. Medieval scholarship was not mature enough to develop its own interpretations. With the possible exception of Tōgen Zuisen, very few *I Ching* scholars showed levels of originality and intellectual rigor comparable to those of Chinese scholars.

In addition, *I Ching* scholarship was highly pragmatic. Unlike their Chinese and Korean counterparts, the *I Ching* scholars of medieval Japan did not organize sophisticated discussions about metaphysical and scholarly topics, such as *li-ch'i* (principle and material force) and *jen-hsing* (human nature). Instead, they applied the *I Ching* to politics, the military, medicine, calendrical studies, and other practical areas. The Ashikaga School was the best example of practical *I Ching* scholarship.

Divination was an important part of *I Ching* studies, and almost all traditions used it. The *Chou-i meng-ch'i ching* was one of the most widely read and cited commentaries. Divination became extremely popular during the *sengoku* period. *Gunbai shisō* was a peculiar form of *I Ching* divination. The Ashikaga School served as a training school for shamans. Professional *I Ching* diviners *(ekisha)* also appeared in the *sengoku* period; they consulted people on street corners.

Finally, *I Ching* studies spread from aristocrats and elite Buddhist monks to the lower social strata. The *I Ching* was at first an exclusive text used by a very limited number of political and religious elites. The ancient taboo against it being studied by anyone younger than fifty and its oral transmission also prevented it from being popularized. But with the publication of Japanese-punctuated texts, the decline of the nobility, and the better opportunities for a basic education available to the lower classes during the *sengoku* period, the *I Ching* became open to all classes. Its acceptance in the life and folklore of the common people also had an important impact on the popular culture of medieval Japan.[52]

These characteristics help us understand the continuity of *I Ching* scholarship between medieval and Tokugawa times. Some distinctive features, such as its eclecticism, naturalization, and practical usage, continued to characterize Tokugawa scholarship. New developments that occurred in late medieval times—such as the independence of Confucianism, the prominence of new commentaries, and the *I Ching*'s growth in popularity among the populace—grew to maturity in the Tokugawa period.

2. The Popularization of the *I Ching* in the Tokugawa Period

I Ching scholarship reached its apex during the Tokugawa period (1603–1868), becoming one of the most popular and influential Confucian texts among Tokugawa intellectuals.[1] Among Japanese scholars who acknowledge this development is Miyazaki Michio, a scholar of Tokugawa thought, who has remarked: "There was a consensus reached by [Tokugawa] Confucians regarding the *I Ching* as the highest classic."[2] Imai Usaburō, a leading scholar of the *I Ching,* has commented: "Supported by the bakufu's policy toward Confucianism, *I Ching* studies and *I Ching* divination prospered as never before during the Tokugawa period."[3]

Two major factors contributed to the growth of *I Ching* studies in the Tokugawa period. First, medieval Japanese had laid down a solid foundation for Tokugawa scholarship by punctuating, annotating, and reprinting Chinese writings on the text. Second, the rise of neo-Confucianism gave further momentum to *I Ching* studies. Its preference for the *I Ching* became a decisive factor in shaping the intellectual map. Other factors—such as the patronage of the bakufu and the domains, the intellectual influence of Chinese and Korean scholars, a flourishing publishing industry, a relatively high rate of literacy, the emergence of professional *I Ching* diviners, and the practical value and flexibility of the text itself—should also be taken into account.

This chapter demonstrates the popularization of the text in Tokugawa Japan, using publication, reprint, importation, and punctuation as the barometers. The story of this popularization has important implications for an understanding of the naturalization of Confucianism, the influence of Chinese learning, and some characteristics of intellectual history in Tokugawa Japan.

Published Writings

How many books were written on the *I Ching* during the Tokugawa period? An early attempt to count the number of Confucian writings in the Tokugawa period was made by Terada Hiroshi, an ex-official of Satsuma domain in the Meiji period (1868–1912), in the *Nihon keikai* (An Explanation of Confucian Books in Japan).[4] According to Terada, there were 338 books written about the *I Ching* by 116 Tokugawa scholars. His calculations indicate that the *I Ching* was more popular by an overwhelmingly margin than other Confucian classics in the Tokugawa period.

During the Taishō period (1912–1926), Hayashi Taisuke, a former professor of Chinese philosophy at the University of Tokyo, revised these figures in the *Nihon keikai sōmokuroku* (A Complete Index of the *Nihon keikai*, 4 volumes). He raised the number of books and authors to 395 and 212, respectively.[5] Hayashi's prewar statistics are rough and underestimated. My own count suggests much larger figures: I have found the titles of 1,085 texts on the *I Ching* written by 416 authors in the Tokugawa period. Although precise figures for other Confucian classics are not available, the text seems to have far exceeded other Confucian classics in both the number of authors and the amount of writing commenting on the book.

What is the significance of this large figure of 1,085? It indicates three important characteristics of *I Ching* scholarship in the Tokugawa period: popularity, independence, and maturity. Without a high and

Table 1: Terada's Tally of Confucian Writings in the Tokugawa Period

Confucian Classics	*No. of Books*	*No. of Authors*
I Ching	338	116
Shu Ching	124	68
Hsiao Ching	116	81
Ch'un Ch'iu	108	75
Shih Ching	90	60
Li Chi	37	33

Table 2: Hayashi's Tally of Confucian Writings in the Tokugawa Period

Confucian Classics	No. of Books	No. of Authors
I Ching	395	212
Lun Yü	363	261
Ta Hsüeh	246	183
Ch'un Ch'iu	224	164
Hsiao Ching	199	144
Shih Ching	173	131
Meng Tzu	169	126
Chung Yung	168	131
Shu Ching	147	111
Li Chi	144	91

constant academic interest and a faithful readership, it would not have been possible to produce such a large number of works. Before the Tokugawa, Japanese scholars spent their energy on the punctuation and annotation of famous Chinese texts. Pre-Tokugawa scholarship was not independent and mature enough to develop its own interpretations. The number of Japanese writings on the text was small, and very few showed a high level of originality and scholarship. In the Tokugawa period, in contrast, the number of Japanese writings far exceeded the number of imported, reprinted, and punctuated Chinese texts. In addition, Tokugawa writings on the *I Ching* demonstrated a high level of scholarship and originality.

There were many groundbreaking works on the philosophy and divination of the text. For instance, Yamazaki Ansai (1618–1680) reconstructed a lost Chu Hsi commentary in his *Shueki engi* (An Explication of Chu Hsi's Commentaries on the *I Ching*, 1677). Itō Tōgai (1670–1736) separated the main text from the Ten Wings and combined Ch'eng I's *I Chuan* with other commentaries in his *Shūeki keiyoku tsūkai* (A Comprehensive Explanation of the Text and the Ten Wings of the *I Ching*, 1728). Dazai Shundai (1680–1747) attempted to restore Han commentaries through philology and textual criticism in his *Shūeki hansei* (Return to the Correct Interpretation of the *I Ching*, 1746). Nakai Riken (1732–1817) criticized Chu Hsi's commentaries and the Ten Wings in his *Shūeki hōgen* (An Investigation of the Origins of the *I Ching*). Kaihō Gyoson (1798–1866) restored ancient divination methods in his *Shūeki kosenhō* (*I Ching* Divination in Ancient

Times, 1840). Hirata Atsutane (1776–1843) Shintoized the *I Ching* in his *Koeki taishōkyō* (The Great Images in the Ancient *I Ching*). All these works made breakthroughs in East Asian *I Ching* scholarship.

Tokugawa writings on the text can be classified into four categories according to their content and approach: textual interpretation *(i-li)*, symbols and numbers *(hsiang-shu)*, divination, and application.[6] Table 3 demonstrates the popularity of the school of textual interpretation over other schools. More than 60 percent of the writings were works of textual study. This emphasis also characterized Confucian studies and scholarship in general in Tokugawa Japan. Tokugawa intellectuals were less interested in developing sophisticated discussions about abstract, metaphysical, and numerical topics. Like their Ch'ing counterparts, they were fond of textual study, focusing on the ethical, political, and pragmatic aspects of the texts.

Compared with the *I Ching* scholarship in Ch'ing China and late Yi Korea, Tokugawa scholarship was eclectic. Ch'ing and late Yi scholarship represented two extremes. The former preferred textual study, whereas the latter leaned toward symbolic and numerical approaches. In Tokugawa Japan, textual interpretation was the largest but not the dominant school. Other schools also enjoyed considerable support and accounted for about 40 percent of *I Ching* writings. For instance, divination was an important part of *I Ching* studies and was extremely popular during the Tokugawa period. One fifth of the *I Ching* writings were on divination.

The authors of *I Ching* writings can be grouped into three cate-

Table 3: Writings on the *I Ching* in the Tokugawa Period

Categories	*Approaches*	*No. of Books*	*Percentage*	*Ranking*
Textual	explanation	367	33.8	
Interpretation	commentary	172	15.9	1
(659/60.7%)	textual criticism	120	11.0	
Symbols & Numbers	/	146	13.5	3
Divination	/	223	20.5	2
Application	/	57	5.3	4
Total: 4	6	1,085	100.0	1–4

Table 4: Tokugawa Authors Commenting on the *I Ching*

Categories	Schools	No. of Authors	Percentage
Confucianism (354/85.1%)	Chu Hsi school	204	49.0
	ancient learning	42	10.1
	Wang Yang-ming school	13	3.1
	eclectic school	46	11.1
	oracle school	49	11.8
Non-Confucian schools of thought & religion	national learning, western learning, Shinto, Buddhism, etc.	39	9.4
Application	medicine, science, art, military, etc.	23	5.5
Total	7	416	100

gories according to their intellectual orientation: Confucianism, non-Confucian schools of thought and religion, and the application school. Table 4 indicates two important characteristics of *I Ching* scholarship in Tokugawa Japan. First, Confucianism was the dominant force in *I Ching* scholarship. Confucianism refers to both the Han (or old) and the Sung (or neo-Confucian) schools. In particular, the Chu Hsi school of neo-Confucianism was extremely influential, accounting for almost half the authors. However, it would be simplistic to view the popularity of the text as merely a byproduct of the rise of neo-Confucianism. We should not overlook the contributions of old Confucian and even non-Confucian schools. For instance, the school of ancient learning *(kogaku)*, which accounted for about one tenth of the authors, produced the finest and the most original *I Ching* scholarship of the Tokugawa period.

Second, although a majority of authors of works on the text were Confucians, the *I Ching* was not an exclusive text for Tokugawa Confucians and was pursued by scholars from different schools of thought and religion. Buddhists, Shintoists, students of Western learning *(Rangaku)*, scholars of national learning *(kokugaku)*, political leaders, scientists, and artists studied the text's ethics, metaphysics, and divination and accommodated them to their teachings. Their *I Ching* scholarship mixed with many non-Confucian elements, and the text was naturalized in the process, coming to saturate Tokugawa thought and culture.

It became compulsory reading for every Tokugawa intellectual and played an integral role in the development of Tokugawa intellectual life.

These 416 authors of *I Ching* related works included the leading intellectuals of the era. Very few prominent Confucians failed to write on it. Some specialized in the text and produced a large number of works. These prolific writers included Arai Hakuga (1725–1792, oracle school, 39 titles), Asami Keisai (1652–1711, Chu Hsi school, 36 titles), Mase Chūshū (1754–1817, oracle school, 35 titles), Minakawa Kien (1735–1807, eclectic school, 26 titles), and Miyake Shōsai (1662–1724, Chu Hsi school, 26 titles). Regardless of the quality of their works, their enthusiasm and devotion to *I Ching* studies was unparalleled in East Asian history.[7]

Reprinted Books

The popularity of the text was also evident in the reproduction of Chinese works. Tokugawa Japanese reprinted at least sixty-nine Chinese books (166 editions) on the text. These sixty-nine titles were all important works that represented the best Chinese scholarship of all periods. They were imported to Japan no later than the seventeenth century and were reprinted in Japan both as textbooks for official and private academies and as popular books for general readers. Virtually all important Chinese books on the text were reprinted, demonstrating that the persistent influence of Chinese scholarship became the point of departure for Tokugawa intellectuals in their pursuit of a more independent, naturalized, and original scholarship. Most of these books were new commentaries by famous scholars from the Sung to Ch'ing periods. The works listed as "uncertain" were also mostly new commentaries. According to my estimation, almost 80 percent of the reprints were new commentaries. In particular, Sung and Ming works were widely accepted. Very few Chinese texts were reprinted in their original form; most were punctuated, annotated, edited, or collated by Tokugawa intellectuals.

Of these sixty-nine titles, forty were only reprinted once. Of the rest, a number of popular texts were reprinted more than ten times, while a few were reprinted by the bakufu or the domains as official texts. The majority were reprinted by commercial publishers in Edo, Osaka, and Kyoto. Such active reprinting points to the existence of a large and constant demand for excellent *I Ching* texts.

**Table 5: Reprints of Chinese Writings on the *I Ching*
in the Tokugawa Period**

Commentaries	Eras	No. of Titles	No. of Editions	Percentage
Pre-Han	Uncertain	2	12	
Pre-Sung	Han	3	4	
(14/36)	Six Dynasties	2	13	
	Sui	1	1	
	T'ang	6	6	20.3
Post-Song	Sung	16	63	
(47/121)	Yüan	8	13	
	Ming	14	28	
	Ch'ing	9	17	68.1
Uncertain	Uncertain	8	9	11.6
Total	All	69	166	100

The most popular texts were Chu Hsi and Ch'eng I's commentaries. Chu Hsi's *Chou-i pen-i* was reprinted eleven times. There were two outstanding editions. One was Yamazaki Ansai's edition, which first appeared in 1675. It was adopted by the bakufu's Confucian academy, the Shōheikō (School of Prosperity and Peace, established in 1630), as the official edition in 1688, and was also reprinted by a private publisher in 1689. The other was the Hayashi edition. Punctuated by Hayashi Razan (1583–1657), it was rearranged and published by his son, Hayashi Gahō (1618–1680), in 1664, with a second edition appearing in 1674. Chu Hsi's *I-hsüeh ch'i-meng* also had eleven editions, the best of which was punctuated by Yamazaki Ansai in 1677. This later became an official edition and was reprinted many times in Kyoto by the bakufu.

Ch'eng I's *I Chuan* came to Japan during the *sengoku* period through Korea. It was punctuated by Fujiwara Seika (1561–1619) and was reprinted at least five times in the Tokugawa period. First published in 1628 and reprinted in 1684, it was adopted by the Shōheikō as the official textbook during the Genroku period (1688–1703) and was reprinted twice by the bakufu and once by a private publisher.

Some combinations of Chu and Ch'eng's commentaries were also very popular. The most frequently reprinted text was the *Chou-i chuan-i* compiled by Tung Kai in the Yüan period (1271–1368). It was used as the textbook for the civil service examinations in Yüan China. It was reprinted fifteen times (ten times in the seventeenth century, three times in the eighteenth century, and twice in the nineteenth century). There were two popular editions: Bunshi Genshō's (1555–1620), published in 1627 and reprinted in 1648 and 1649, and Matsunaga Sunun's (1618–1680), published in 1664 and reprinted many times in the eighteenth and nineteenth centuries. Hayashi Razan and Yamazaki Ansai also punctuated the text, but their works were not well received and were only printed once or twice.

Other popular combinations of Chu and Ch'eng's commentaries were the *Chou-i chuan-i ta-ch'üan* (An Anthology of *I Chuan* and *Chou-i pen-i*, edited by Hu K'uang) and *I Ching chi-chu* (A Collective Commentary on the *I Ching*, edited by Lai Chih-te). The anthology was a textbook for the civil service examinations in Ming China and was reprinted four times. Two of these reprints were punctuated by Bunshi Genshō; the other two were punctuated by Hayashi Razan and Ukai Shinshi (1615–1664), respectively. The collective commentary was punctuated by Matsunaga Sunun and was reprinted six times.

The popularity of old commentaries declined, and they consisted of only about one fifth of the reprints. The only popular old commentary was Wang Pi's *Chou-i chu*, which had been the one of the most popular *I Ching* writings in Japan since the medieval period. It was reprinted twelve times in the Tokugawa period. The most influential was the Keichō edition, edited by the rector of the Ashikaga School, Kanshitsu, and the Zen monk Seishō under the auspices of Tokugawa Ieyasu. Printed on movable woodblocks in a large quantity, it played an important role in stimulating the *I Ching* boom in the early Tokugawa period.

Moreover, in 1805, Hayashi Jussai (1768–1841), the head of the Shōheikō, reprinted a number of Chinese books that were already lost in China but that were extant in Tokugawa Japan as the *Etsuzon zōsho* (A Collection of Lost Texts in China). This collection included two Sung texts—Kung Yüan's *Chou-i hsin chiang-i* (A New Lecture on the *I Ching*) and Li Chung-cheng's *T'ai-hsüan i-chuan* (*I Ching* commentary by T'ai-hsüan)—that had been lost in China since the Yüan period. The *T'ai-hsüan i-chuan* was reprinted based on the Ashikaga edition copied in 1372. These two lost books, together with the *Etsuzon zōsho*, were brought back to Ch'ing China, marking a memorable event in Sino-Japanese cultural interchange.

In addition to the sixty-nine Chinese books reprinted in Tokugawa Japan, two Korean texts—Yi T'oegye's (1501–1570) *Chuyŏk kyemong chŏnŭi* (A Critical Review of the Commentary Literature on the *I-hsüeh ch'i-meng*, 4 *kan*, published in Korea in 1557, reprinted in Japan in 1657 and 1669), and Ch'oe Dan's *Yŏkhak kyemong poyohae* (A Supplement and Explanation of the *I-hsüeh ch'i-meng*, reprinted in 1669)— were also reprinted in the early Tokugawa period. Both were commentaries on Chu Hsi's interpretations. The *Chuyŏk kyemong chŏnŭi* exerted a considerable influence on Tokugawa scholarship.[8]

Imported Books

Another barometer of the popularity of the *I Ching* was the importation of Chinese writings. According to the data provided by Ōba Osamu, the *I Ching* topped the list of imported Chinese Confucian classics entering through Nagasaki.

Ōba's data are based mainly on the records of Chinese cargo ships, and they thus exclude the importation of books through illegal trade or other channels outside Nagasaki.[9] My own count raises the number of imported *I Ching* writings to 219 titles. Each title might have arrived in multiple copies. Although I can only confirm that 101 titles came through Nagasaki, it is beyond question that most of these imported books were brought to Japan through this channel. Only a small number of books could have come through Korea and the Ryūkyū Kingdom.

Imported items were completely different from those reprinted in Japan. Imported books were usually new in Japan, whereas reprinted books had already existed there for some time. Imported works were usually little known and less influential in both China and Japan,

Table 6: Confucian Books Imported in the Tokugawa Period

Books	No. of Titles	Books	No. of Titles
I Ching	118	*Ta Hsüeh*	8
Ch'un Ch'iu	64	*Hsiao Ching*	5
Shih Ching	44	*Meng Tzu*	5
Shu Ching	36	*Lun Yü*	3
San Li	20	*Chung Yung*	0

Table 7: Books on the *I Ching* Imported in the Tokugawa Period

Commentaries	Eras	No. of Titles	Percentage
Old	Han	3	
(7)	Wei	1	
	T'ang	3	3.2
New	Sung	10	
(120)	Yüan	4	
	Ming	25	
	Ch'ing	81	54.8
Uncertain	Uncertain	92	42.0
Total	All	219	100

while reprinted works were without exception famous and representative. Moreover, imported works were mostly written by Ch'ing scholars, while reprinted works were selected from different periods and included a higher proportion of the Sung and Ming texts. In addition, book importing was largely in the hands of Chinese merchants, who did not see it as a profitable business, whereas reprinting was a big business to Tokugawa publishers, who made their decisions according to market demand. Finally, imported books usually came in quantities of no more than a few copies, responding to the orders of book dealers or book collectors, while reprints were produced in numerous copies and were well planned by Japanese publishers.

In the titles that were imported, the preference for new commentaries over the old is striking. Books listed under "uncertain" in Table 7 were mostly Ch'ing works, and most imported books were Ch'ing editions regardless of when they had been written. In my count, of these 219 books, 204 were Ch'ing editions, 14 were Ming editions, and one was a Yi Korean edition. At least three books were unpublished manuscripts. No book was older than a Ming edition, showing that Chinese books on the *I Ching* were not brought to Tokugawa Japan as rare books.

Works by famous *I Ching* scholars, such as Cheng Hsüan, Wang Pi, Chou Tun-i, Shao Yung (1011–1977), Ch'eng I, and Chu Hsi, were seldom on the list of imports because they had been brought to Japan before the Tokugawa period in considerable quantities and had even been reprinted by Tokugawa publishers. The 219 titles in question here were imported mainly for collections in public and private libraries, rather than for general readers. Most of these imported works remained untouched and noncirculating and thus made little impact on *I Ching* studies in Tokugawa Japan. The few exceptions include Kuo Ching's *Chou-i chü-cheng* (Rectification of the *I Ching*, T'ang work, Ming edition) and Hui Tung's (1697–1758) *Chou-i shu* (A Narrative of the *I Ching*, Ch'ing edition).

Although more than half of imported items were Ch'ing works, they were not taken seriously by Tokugawa scholars, who did not rate Ch'ing scholarship highly. Ch'ing works on the *I Ching* had little impact on Tokugawa scholarship, save for a small group of people like Igai Keisho (1761–1846) who were influenced by the methodology of *k'ao cheng* (the Chinese philological tradition of evidential research).

Japanese-Punctuated Texts

The punctuation of Chinese and *kambun* (composition, by Japanese, of prose in Chinese) works *(kunten)* helped the Japanese read Chinese texts according to Japanese syntax *(kundoku)* by changing the order and pronunciation. The project of punctuating the *I Ching* began in the medieval period with Zen Buddhist monks and courtiers and was largely completed in the seventeenth century by Chu Hsi scholars. Table 8 shows punctuators and their punctuated writings on the text in the Tokugawa period. I have found eighteen punctuators of the text in Tokugawa Japan—sixteen Chu Hsi scholars and two scholars of the eclectic school. Eleven of them lived in the early Tokugawa, five in the mid-Tokugawa, and two in the late Tokugawa. They punctuated twenty-four Chinese commentaries (seven pre-Sung and seventeen post-Sung). These twenty-four works also represented the core readings for *I Ching* studies in Tokugawa Japan.

In the Tokugawa period, Japanese punctuation of the *I Ching* was done almost exclusively by Chu Hsi scholars. In particular, the seventeenth century was the age of Japanese punctuation. Punctuators were usually prominent Confucians because they could boost the sales of the Chinese texts. There were five major punctuators of the *I Ching* in this period: Bunshi Genshō, Fujiwara Seika, Hayashi Razan, Yamazaki Ansai, and Matsunaga Sunun.

Bunshi Genshō, a Rinzai monk, inherited the punctuation methods started by Keian Genju (1427–1508). Bunshi popularized the Sung school by punctuating two of its most popular *I Ching* textbooks, the

**Table 8: Punctuation of Chinese Writings on the *I Ching*
in the Tokugawa Period**

Punctuators	*Years*	*Schools*	*Books Punctuated*
Bunshi Genshō	1555–1620	Chu Hsi	1. *Chou-i chuan-i* (Yüan)
			2. *Chou-i ta-ch'üan* (Ming)
Fujiwara Seika	1561–1619	Chu Hsi	1. *I Chuan* (Sung)
Hayashi Razan	1583–1657	Chu Hsi	1. *Chou-i pen-i* (Sung)
			2. *Chou-i chuan-i* (Yüan)
Ukai Shinshi	1615–1664	Chu Hsi	1. *Chou-i ta-ch'üan* (Ming)
Hayashi Gahō	1618–1680	Chu Hsi	1. *Chou-i pen-i* (Sung)
Yamazaki Ansai	1618–1682	Chu Hsi	1. *Chou-i pen-i* (Sung)
			2. *I-hsüeh ch'i-meng* (Sung)
			3. *I-kua k'ao-wu* (Sung)
			4. *Chou-i chuan-i* (Yüan)
Matsunaga Sunun	1618–1680	Chu Hsi	1. *I-ching chi-chu* (Sung)
			2. *Chou-i chuan-i* (Yüan)
Koide Eian	d. 1684	Chu Hsi	1. *Chou-i chü-chieh* (Yüan)
Nakamura Tekisai	1629–1702	Chu Hsi	1. *Chou I* (pre-Sung)
Murota Yoshikata	early Edo	Chu Hsi	1. *Ch'i-meng i-ch'ien* (Ming)
Miyagi Ryūtetsu	early Edo	Chu Hsi	1. *I-ching chih-chieh* (Ming)
Inoue Kindai	1704–1761	eclectic	1. *Chou-i chu* (Wei & Chin)
Gotō Shizan	1720–1782	Chu Hsi	1. *Chou I* (pre-Sung)
Kimura Sonken	1735–1779	Chu Hsi	1. *I ken tsao tu* (Han)
Kazuyama Kikō	mid Edo	Chu Hsi	1. *Chou I* (pre-Sung)
Ichikawa Kan	mid Edo	Chu Hsi	1. *I-san-yen* (Yüan)
Satō Issai	1772–1859	eclectic	1. *Chou I* (pre-Sung)
Tōjō Hōan	late Edo	Chu Hsi	1. *Chou I* (pre-Sung)
	early Edo 11	Chu Hsi 16	pre-Sung commentaries 7
Total: 18	mid Edo 5		
	late Edo 2	eclectic 2	post-Sung commentaries 17

Chou-i chuan-i and *Chou-i chuan-i ta-ch'üan*. (An Anthology of *I Chuan* and *Chou-i pen-i*). With assistance from a Ming scholar, Huang Yu-hsien (1538–?), Bunshi spent seven years finishing his punctuation of a Korean edition of the *Chou-i chuan-i*. Bunshi's edition was promoted and published by his student Tomari Jochiku (1570–1655) in 1627. Bunshi did not finish punctuating the *Chou-i chuan-i ta-ch'üan;* two unfinished chapters were later punctuated by his student Seien, also in 1627.[10]

Fujiwara Seika punctuated the *I Chuan* and *Chou-i chuan-i* with the help of a Korean Chu Hsi scholar, Kang Han (1567–1618). The former text was adopted by the Shōheikō as the textbook during the Genroku period.[11] Hayashi Razan punctuated the *Chou-i pen-i, Chou-i chuan-i,* and *Chou-i chuan-i ta-ch'üan.* Hayashi Razan's punctuated *Chou-i pen-i* was improved and published by his son Hayashi Gahō in 1664, and later became an official edition.[12] Yamazaki Ansai punctuated Chu Hsi's three books: the *Chou-i pen-i* (in 1675), *I-hsüeh ch'i-meng* (in 1677), and *I-kua k'ao-wu.* The first two became official editions in the eighteenth century. Matsunaga Sun'un punctuated the *I-ching chi-chu* (A Collective Commentary on the *I Ching*) and *Chou-i chuan-i.* These two editions were published in 1664 and were reprinted many times thereafter.

Thanks to these five punctuators, all of Chu Hsi and Ch'eng I's commentaries were punctuated and published by the early Tokugawa period. Most of these punctuated books were reprinted multiple times by both official and private publishers throughout the Tokugawa period. They were adopted by the bakufu, the domains, and most private academies as their textbooks.[13]

To conclude, quantitative analysis of the publication, reprinting, importation, and punctuation of the *I Ching* in Tokugawa Japan demonstrates the process, means, and degree of the popularization of the text as well as some characteristics of its scholarship, thus deepening our understanding of the complexity of, and problems in, the adaptation of Confucianism in Tokugawa Japan. For instance, it reveals that the *I Ching* boom came mainly from the "inner logic" of intellectual developments, the pragmatic value of the text, and the efforts of scholars from different intellectual schools. Hence the role of the bakufu in promoting *I Ching* scholarship and Confucianism should not be overemphasized. Moreover, Tokugawa Confucianism was highly eclectic and should not be generalized as consisting primarily of either the Chu Hsi school or neo-Confucianism. The school of ancient learning and some non-Confucian schools also played a significant role in the development of *I Ching* studies. This research also helps us understand the nature of Tokugawa Confucianism. As seen from *I Ching* studies, Tokugawa Confucianism was popular, influential, plebeian, eclectic, accommodating, textual, and pragmatic.

3. Study and Uses of the *I Ching* in the Tokugawa Period

I Ching **Scholarship in the Early Tokugawa Period**

During the early Tokugawa period (the seventeenth and early eighteenth centuries), Confucian scholars replaced Zen monks as the main force behind *I Ching* studies. Although recent research indicates that Confucianism was not the official learning or orthodoxy of early Tokugawa Japan, its vitality and influence were undeniably strong in the intellectual world.[1] The three schools of Confucianism —the Chu Hsi school, Wang Yang-ming school, and the school of ancient learning—produced the majority of scholars and writings during this golden period of *I Ching* studies.

The Chu Hsi school was the largest school of *I Ching* studies. During the first half of the Tokugawa period, many scholars of the highest caliber emerged from it and began to develop their own interpretations and commentaries. In general, however, their explanatory works on Sung commentaries were more safe than stimulating because they tried to be faithful to Chu Hsi's commentaries.

Fujiwara Seika (1561–1619) favored Ch'eng I's (1033–1107) *I Chuan* and Chu Hsi's (1130–1200) *Chou-i pen-i*. His understanding of Sung texts was influenced by Yüan and Ming scholarship. For example, following the Yüan-Ming practice, he combined these two books in his readings. He held that the essence of the Chu Hsi school could only be attained through a secret transmission of the *I Ching*. Besides textual analysis, he was also interested in divination and accepted only the yarrow-stalk divination method as orthodox.[2]

Hayashi Razan (1583–1657) studied under the guidance of a disciple of Kiyohara Hidekata in his youth. He recalled that he had not read important Sung commentaries, such as the *I-hsüeh ch'i-meng, T'ai-chi t'u shuo*, and *Huang-chi ching-shih shu*, until he turned to Fujiwara Seika for guidance.[3] According to a record kept in the library of the Hayashi family, before giving Hayashi a copy of the *Ekigaku zukai* (An Illustrative Explanation of the *I Ching*), which explained various *I Ching* charts and diagrams, Fujiwara had Hayashi make a pledge that he would not transmit this teaching to anyone except one of Hayashi's own sons.[4] Like Fujiwara, Hayashi relied heavily on the *Chou-i chuan-i* and *Chou-i chuan-i ta-ch'üan*, and he developed some interesting political and religious views from his reading of the *I Ching*.

Hayashi Gahō's (1618–1680) interpretations of the *I Ching* surpassed his father's. Unlike Fujiwara Seika and Hayashi Razan, he opposed the common practice of combining the Chu Hsi and Ch'eng I commentaries. He wrote: "The *Chou-i ta-ch'üan* appeared and combined Ch'eng I's *I Chuan* and Chu Hsi's *Chou-i pen-i*. Although the teaching of Chu Hsi is in agreement with that of Ch'eng I, his ideas on the *I Ching* are different. Although the *Chou-i pen-i* is very popular, it mixes with elements from Ch'eng I's *I Chuan*. As a result, the meaning of the ancient *I Ching* is not understood."[5] He pointed out that the *I Chuan* offered fine textual interpretation, whereas the *Chou-i pen-i* was better in its analysis of symbols and numbers. He studied them separately and wrote a number of books. His representative works were the *Shūeki hongi shikō* (My Investigation of the *Chou-i pen-i*, 1662, 13 *kan*) and *Shūeki kunten idō* (Similarities and Differences in the Punctuation of the *I Ching*, 1677).

Yamazaki Ansai (1618–1682) was a great scholar of the *I Ching*, believing it to be the greatest book from China.[6] He made great efforts to restore the true teachings of Chu Hsi and to distinguish Chu Hsi's scholarship from the distorted ideas that had been the byproduct of the textbooks used for the civil service examinations. He was critical of all post-Sung commentaries and opposed the fusion of the Chu Hsi and Ch'eng I commentaries.[7] He was proud to have reconstructed a lost Chu Hsi commentary on the *I Ching, Shueki engi* (An Explication of Chu Hsi's Commentaries on the *I Ching*, 1677, 3 *kan*). This book was later adopted by the Tokugawa authorities as the official text in the eighteenth century.

Yamazaki put great emphasis on the *I Ching* in education and made the Ansai school the most important and productive force in *I Ching* studies within the Chu Hsi school. In his four-stage curriculum, the

Chou-i pen-i and *I Chuan* were the readings for the final stage in a student's development.[8] The *I Ching* occupied a central position in the school. Most of Yamazaki's disciples, including Satō Naokata (1639–1719), Asami Keisai (1652–1711), and Miyake Shōsai (1662–1741), specialized in the text.[9] Disagreement over interpretation of the text later brought internal strife to the school.[10]

Kaibara Ekken (1630–1714) studied under Yamazaki Ansai and Matsunaga Sekigo (1592–1657) in his early years. When he read the hexagram *i* (increase), he changed his name to Ekken. He borrowed from the *I Ching* to formulate his cosmological, ethical, and medical ideas. His famous questioning of Chu Hsi's dualistic metaphysics was inspired by his reading of the text. He argued that since the *I Ching* never distinguished between *li* (principle) and *ch'i* (material force), Chu Hsi was incorrect in emphasizing the priority of principle over material force. He suggested that everyone should read the *I Ching* because it was capable of unifying the way of heaven and the way of man. He stated: "The way of heaven and earth is the root and source of the human way. . . . Therefore, after first learning the way of daily human relations, we should learn the way of heaven and earth. Is not this way why the sage studied the *Book of Changes*?"[11] He wrote the *Eki-gaku teiyō* (An Outline of *I Ching* Scholarship, 1665) as a textbook for his students. One of his students, Nakamura Tekisai, surpassed Kaibara in the quality of his *I Ching* scholarship. Nakamura punctuated the text and wrote several books to interpret Sung commentaries.

Muro Kyūsō (1658–1734) wrote a number of books on the *I Ching*, the most notable being the *Shūeki shinso* (A New Commentary on the *I Ching*, 10 *kan*), in which he gave his own commentary. Other works included his lectures on Sung commentaries. Muro borrowed heavily from the text to develop his ethical and religious ideas and was also famous for his divination skills. Even the famous "rational" thinker Arai Hakuseki (1657–1725) asked Muro to use the *I Ching* for advice on the marriage of his daughter.[12]

The Wang Yang-ming school was a small school of *I Ching* studies, though its characteristics can be seen in its *I Ching* scholarship. Compared with Chu Hsi scholars, Wang Yang-ming scholars were more eclectic and usually included both the old and new commentaries in their writings and lectures.

Nakae Tōju (1608–1648) studied the Chu Hsi commentaries in his early years,[13] becoming absorbed in the *I Ching* later in life. His scholarship had two major characteristics. First, the *I Ching* became the point of departure for his Confucian training. He noted: "Because the *I Ching* includes the essence of the Thirteen Confucian Classics, we should study it thoroughly. However, the wonder and subtlety of the *I Ching* make it difficult for ordinary people to understand. If they read the *Hsiao Ching, Ta Hsüeh* and *Chung Yung* wholeheartedly, they will come to grasp the outline [of the *I Ching*] easily."[14] The *I Ching* provided Nakae with a framework for interpreting other classics. Although he was a specialist in the *Hsiao Ching,* he told his students that if they had to choose one Confucian classic to study, it should be the *I Ching.* Indeed, his famous scholarship on the *Hsiao Ching* was related to his reading of the *I Ching.* In the *Kōkyō keimō* (An Introduction to the *Book of Filial Piety*), Nakae used the *I Ching* to interpret the *Hsiao Ching.* He adopted the same approach to explicate the *Chung Yung* in the *Chūyōkai* (An Explanation of the *Doctrine of the Mean*).

Second, Nakae practiced a very peculiar ritual of the *I Ching.* He made a statue of Ekishin, the God of the *I Ching,* and worshipped it every day—and every time he used the *I Ching* for divination. He identified Ekishin with Taiitsushin, a Taoist deity. This kind of practice was not uncommon in medieval times but became rare in the Tokugawa period. Nakae lamented that the influence of Sung school's rationalism meant that people no longer worshipped the God of the *I Ching.* He wrote: "I worship the statue of the spirit frequently. I believe that all Confucians should worship the statue of the God of the *I Ching.* However, Sung Confucians discredited talismans and symbols, and thus had no sources of authority. No wonder that, when in doubt, they became indecisive and could not make decisions for a long time."[15]

Kumazawa Banzan (1619–1691) was the greatest *I Ching* scholar in the Wang Yang-ming school. He claimed that the *I Ching* was the most important Confucian classic and wrote several books on it to establish his sophisticated political, historical, ethical, and religious views.[16] His *Ekikyō shōkai* (A Modest Interpretation of the *I Ching,* 7 *kan*) was particularly important for its originality. His *I Ching* scholarship had several characteristics. For one thing, he used Japanese history and political reality to explain its principles. By doing this, he rationalized Tokugawa political and social systems and simultaneously criticized the problems facing the bakufu and local administration. Kumazawa also stressed the text's practical nature, stating that "If you understand morality, knowledge, politics, art, and everything [through the *I Ching*], there will be nothing difficult at all."[17] He also favored the *Hsi Tz'u* (Commentary on the Appended Judgments) the most philosophical part of the Ten Wings, and popularized the *I Ching* by annotating a part of the main text, the Ten Wings, and the chart and diagram in Japanese.

The school of ancient learning of the early Tokugawa period produced the finest and most original *I Ching* scholarship of the entire era.[18] *Kogaku* (ancient learning) scholars had several distinguishable features in *I Ching* studies. First, they discredited the Sung commentary and tried to restore the original meaning of the *I Ching*. Second, they believed the text itself to be the only reliable source of knowledge and discarded other approaches, such as divination, symbolism, and numerology.[19] Third, they were equipped with a spirit of doubt and dared to challenge many established ideas. Their views and methodologies were somewhat similar to those of Ch'ing *k'ao-cheng* scholars, as both employed sophisticated philological, phonetic, and historical methods to restore the original meaning of the text.

Itō Jinsai's (1627–1707) scholarship on the *I Ching* was pioneering and insightful. Although the *I Ching* was not his major academic concern, his monistic philosophy was influenced by it, and he was at first close to the Sung school. Having read Chou Tun-i's (1017–1073) *T'ai-chi t'u shuo,* he wrote the *Taikyokuron* (Discourse on *T'ai-chi*) at the age of twenty-seven. In his middle years, he began to question Sung scholarship, criticized Chu Hsi and other Sung scholars for treating the *I Ching* as a divination manual, and held that the *I Ching* was a book of wisdom that had nothing to do with divination.[20] Hence he appreciated Ch'eng I's effort to explicate its philosophy. Itō attempted to restore the ancient meaning of the *I Ching* in his trilogy of the *Tai-shōkai* (An Explanation of the Commentary on the Great Images), *Ekikyō kogi* (The Ancient Meaning of the *I Ching*), and *Shūeki kenkon kogi* (The Ancient Meaning of the Hexagrams *Ch'ien* and *K'un*). The intellectual significance of these works hinged not on their quality but on the new direction they gave to *I Ching* studies—namely, reconstruction of the original *I Ching* through two of the Ten Wings, the *Ta Hsiang* (Commentary on the Great Images) and *T'uan Chuan* (Commentary on the Decision).

Itō came to an astonishing conclusion: that the *I Ching* was a book of divination in the times of King Wen and the Duke of Chou, and that it became a Confucian text only after the time of Confucius and his disciples.[21] He used the *Lun Yü* and *Meng Tzu* as the criteria for judging the creditability of the *I Ching* and other classics. Because these two books never mention divination, he concluded that three of the Ten Wings that do advocate divination—the *Hsi Tz'u, Tsa Kua* (Miscellaneous Notes on the Hexagrams), and *Shuo Kua* (Discussions of the Trigrams)—were not written by Confucius or his students.

Itō Tōgai (1670–1736) was one of the greatest *I Ching* scholars of the Tokugawa period. He was the successor to his father's *I Ching* scholarship, but he went beyond Itō Jinsai in both depth and breadth. Like his father, Itō Tōgai did not believe in divination and was determined to find the original meaning of the *I Ching*. He was a devoted scholar of the *I Ching* and wrote a large number of books on it. The *Shūeki keiyoku tsūkai* (A Comprehensive Explanation of the Text and the Ten Wings of the *I Ching*, 1728, 18 *kan*) has been praised by Hoshino Hisashi (1837–1917) as the most important writing on the *I Ching* in the Tokugawa period.[22] Separating the main text from the Ten Wings and combining Ch'eng I's *I Chuan* with other commentaries, Itō Tōgai gave his own explanation of the whole book—a feat that his father Itō Jinsai had not accomplished.

In another important work, the *Tokueki shiki* (Records on My Reading of the *I Ching*, 1703), Itō Tōgai gave a number of reasons proving that the Ten Wings were not the works of Confucius. His major arguments were that (1) the Ten Wings advocate divination, which conflicts with the teachings of the *Lun Yü* and *Meng Tzu;* (2) Mencius and Tzu Ssu never mentioned that Confucius had written the Ten Wings; (3) the *Shuo Kua* and *Tsa Kua* are very confusing and were not written in Confucius's style; (4) the *Hsi Tz'u* discusses the spirit, a subject that Confucius did not address; (5) the *Hsi Tz'u* is imbued with Taoist ideas; and (6) the four moral principles in the *Wen Yen*—*ching* (reverence), *i* (righteousness), *chih* (endurance), and *fang* (etiquette)—are too strict and narrow.[23]

Dazai Shundai (1680–1747), a disciple of the *kogaku* thinker Ogyū Sorai (1666–1728), wrote highly original interpretations of the *I Ching*. His *Shūeki hansei* (Return to the Correct Interpretation of the *I Ching*, 1746, 12 *kan*) was an ambitious attempt to restore Han commentaries and is regarded as one of the best writings on the text in the Tokugawa period. His attempt to reconstruct Han commentaries through philology and textual criticism paralleled the *k'ao-cheng* scholarship of mid-Ch'ing China. Significantly, Dazai's book was finished about two decades earlier than Hui Tung's (1697–1758), and a century earlier than Chang Hui-yen (1761–1802) and Chiao Hsün's (1763–1820) famous works, which had similar objectives and approaches.[24] Influenced by Ogyū Sorai's politicization of Confucianism, Dazai stressed the political implications of the *I Ching* in his *Ekidōron* (Discourse on the Way of the *I Ching*). He remarked that the *I Ching* is a book of political wisdom for the ruler's benefit in governing the nation; whereas other Confucian classics were intended for people living in peaceful times, the *I Ching* is meant to save the nation in times of confusion.

The methods and ideas of *kogaku* scholars had a tremendous impact on *I Ching* scholarship in the latter half of the Tokugawa period. The Hirata school of national learning *(kokugaku)*, the eclectic school *(setchūgakuha)*, and the oracle school (see below) were all indebted to the school of ancient learning.[25]

While the three Confucian schools acted as the dominant force in *I Ching* studies, Buddhism and Shinto played a respectable role during the first half of the Tokugawa period. Both attempted to accommodate the text to their doctrines.

Zen Buddhism, the dominant force in *I Ching* studies during medieval times, still exerted a considerable influence in the early decades of the Tokugawa period. The center of *I Ching* scholarship for the Rinzai sect was the Ashikaga School. Divination on the basis of the *I Ching* had been secretly transmitted by the School since the fifteenth century, and this tradition was continued by early Tokugawa rectors. They made yearly predications *(nenzei)* on New Year's Eve for the shogun and wrote books on divination. Even outside the Ashikaga School, many Rinzai Buddhist monks studied the *I Ching*. For example, in the preface to the Fushimi edition of the *I Ching*, Saishō Shōtai (1533–1607) expressed his wish that the text become a bridge between Buddhism and Confucianism, and asked his fellow monks to study it. Takuan Sōhō (1573–1645) used it to explicate Buddhist ideas such as karmic retribution. The Sōtō sect pursued *I Ching* scholarship along other lines. A large number of Sōtō Zen monks used the text to explain the doctrine of the five ranks *(goi setsu)*, a central philosophy of Sōtō Zen Buddhism in both China and Japan.

The founders and followers of New Ise Shinto, Yoshida Shinto, and Suika Shinto believed in the unity of Shinto and Confucianism and employed the *I Ching* to enrich their Shinto ideas. For instance, Watarai Nobuyoshi (1615–1690), the founder of New Ise Shinto, suggested that both Shinto and the Way of the *I Ching* were founded on the principles of loyalty and honesty. Kikkawa Koretari (1616–1694), the champion of Yoshida Shinto, identified a Shinto deity, Kuni-no-tokotachi-no-mikoto, as *t'ai-chi* (the Supreme Ultimate), and Izanagi and Izanami as the gods of *yin* and *yang*. Yamazaki Ansai, the founder of Suika Shinto, referred to the *I Ching* as "China's *kamiyo no maki*" (the scroll of the Age of the Gods) and to the *Nihon shoki* as "Japan's *I Ching*," and used them to advocate the unity of Shinto and Confucianism.

I Ching Studies in the Mid-Tokugawa Period

During the mid-Tokugawa period (from the mid-eighteenth century to the early nineteenth century), *I Ching* scholarship underwent dramatic changes. Although the Chu Hsi school, Wang Yang-ming school, and school of ancient learning managed to produce a large number of *I Ching* scholars and works, their scholarship became redundant and few writings from this time match the high level of previous books on the text. The intellectual forces that stole the limelight during the latter half of the Tokugawa period were the eclectic school, the school of national learning, and the oracle school.

The eclectic school was the main force behind *I Ching* studies in the latter half of the Tokugawa period. Despite their anti-Sorai stance, scholars of this school were close to *kogaku* scholarship of the *I Ching*. They did some important philological and historical studies to restore the ancient meaning of the text and also rejected ideas and practices deemed irrational, such as *yin-yang wu-hsing* and divination. The school was based in three big cities: Osaka, Edo, and Kyoto.

The headquarters of the eclectic school in Osaka was the famous merchant academy, Kaitokudō.[26] A founder of the academy, Goi Ranshū (1696–1762), wrote several books to explicate Chu Hsi and Ch'eng I's commentaries on the *I Ching*. His students, the brothers Nakai Riken (1732–1817) and Nakai Chikuzan (1730–1804), became more critical of Sung commentaries and developed their own interpretations by using both the old and new commentaries.

Nakai Riken was a creative interpreter and a skillful historian of the *I Ching*. His masterpiece, the *Shūeki hōgen* (An Investigation of the Origins of the *I Ching*, 6 *kan*), was one of the best commentaries in the Tokugawa period. He was highly skeptical of established interpretations. In the *Shūeki hōgen*, he criticized Chu Hsi's commentaries for being too abstract and for losing the original meaning of the *I Ching*. He also attacked the Ch'eng I and Shao Yung commentaries.

Next, Naki Riken challenged prevailing ideas about the formation and content of the Ten Wings, questioning the common belief that the Ten Wings had been written or edited by Confucius and pointing out that the *Ta Hsiang* had been composed long before the time of Confucius, whereas the other texts of the Ten Wings had been written toward the end of the Eastern Chou period. He liked the content and writing of the *Ta Hsiang, Hsi Tz'u* and *T'uan Chuan* but criticized the rest, stating that "If [any part of] the *T'uan Chuan, Ta Hsiang,* and *Hsi Tz'u* grasps the meaning of the *I Ching,* we can use it to explicate the main text. If [any part of these texts] misses the meaning of the main text, we can throw it away. . . Confucians since the Han period have esteemed the Ten Wings highly. They all taught the Ten Wings first and used them to interpret the main text. Hence the mistakes in the Ten Wings frequently misled scholars."[27]

Finally, Nakai Riken believed that the original *I Ching* had had nothing to do with the *yin-yang wu-hsing* doctrine, charts and diagrams, or divination, and that the extant *I Ching* was a corrupted version of the original. Criticizing Sung commentaries for adding non-Confucian elements to the *I Ching,* he tried to restore the text's original meaning in his *Ekichōdai ryaku* (An Outline of the Main Ideas of the *I Ching,* 3 *kan*) and *Ekikyō kikigaki* (A Record of Sayings about the *I Ching,* 2 *kan*).

Nakai Chikuzan wrote two interpretative works, the *Ekidan* (My Judgment on the *I Ching,* 5 *kan*) and *Ekisetsu* (Discourse on the *I Ching*). Like his younger brother, Nakai Chikuzan was critical of Sung scholarship. In particular, he attacked Chou Tun-i's *T'ai-chi t'u shuo* for using the *yin-yang wu-hsing* framework to interpret the *I Ching.* However, he avoided criticizing Chu Hsi's commentaries directly. Although Nakai Chikuzan did not enjoy a reputation in *I Ching* scholarship equal to that of Nakai Riken, he taught some brilliant students, including Yamagata Bantō (1748–1821) and Satō Issai.

The founder of the eclectic school in Edo was Inoue Kinga (1732–1784), who chose selectively from the Han and Sung commentaries to develop his *Ekigaku setchū* (A Synthesis of *I Ching* Scholarship, 1761). He did a philological study of the book in his *Shūeki ikō* (A Study of the Terminology in the *I Ching,* 12 *kan*) and *Ekigaku bengi* (A Debate on Questions in *I Ching* Studies, 1767). Inoue was a great *I Ching* educator and trained a large number of *I Ching* scholars.[28]

Ōta Kinjō (1765–1825) was the most famous *I Ching* scholar in this lineage. His works were primarily historical and philological studies of the main text and the Ten Wings. Among many talented students whom Ōta trained, Kaihō Gyoson (1798–1866) was particularly important for his efforts to restore a clear picture of the ancient divination methods in his *Shūeki kosenhō* (Divination of the *I Ching* in Ancient Times, 1840, 4 *kan*).[29] Among Kaihō's other philological surveys, the most noteworthy was the *Shūeki Kanchūkō* (An Investigation of Han Commentaries on the *I Ching*, 21 *kan*), which was a critical review of fragmentary Han commentaries. He also coauthored a book with Ōta to reconstruct the ancient meaning through an examination of the *Ta Hsiang: Shūeki shōgi yoroku* (An Appendix to the Meaning of the *Ta Hsiang* of the *I Ching*, 5 *kan*).

Satō Issai was one of the finest *I Ching* scholars of the entire Tokugawa period. This Edo-based scholar traveled frequently and was indebted to different intellectual traditions. He studied under Hayashi Jussai (1768–1841) in Edo, Nakai Chikuzan in Osaka, and Minakawa Kien (1735–1807) in Kyoto. The combination of these three *I Ching* traditions contributed to his eclecticism. He wrote one of the most important and original commentaries of the Tokugawa period, the *Shūeki rangai sho* (A Commentary on the *I Ching*, 10 *kan*). He also made the best Japanese punctuation of the text in the late Tokugawa period, the "Issai punctuation" *(Issai ten)*. He coined a metaphor that compared the *I Ching* to the root of a tree and Western knowledge to the branch. This idea influenced his student Sakuma Shōzan (1811–1864), who produced the famous phrase, "Eastern ethics and Western techniques."

The founder of the eclectic school in Kyoto was Minakawa Kien, a famous and prolific *I Ching* scholar. In his major work, the *Meichū* (A Categorization of Terms), he used the *I Ching* as a framework to define and categorize the moral terms of Confucianism. Using a methodology that incorporated philology and phonetics (he called it *kaibutsugaku*, or "knowledge of investigation"), Minakawa wrote many important books on the text. His *Shūeki shakukai* (An Explanation of the *I Ching*, 16 *kan*) was one of the best commentaries in the Tokugawa period, while his *Ekigaku kaitei* (A Study Guide to the *I Ching*, 3 *kan*) was written as a textbook and used widely by Tokugawa intellectuals.[30]

In brief, the eclectic school was similar to *kogaku* in its *I Ching* scholarship. Few scholars of the eclectic school researched Sung commentaries; instead, they used philology, phonetics, and textual criticism in studying the main text, and the Ten Wings (especially the *Ta Hsiang*) to restore the ancient meaning of the *I Ching*.

The school of national learning held some interesting opinions of the *I Ching* in the late Tokugawa period. Most early *kokugaku* scholars were indifferent to the text and even critical of it. Motoori Norinaga (1730–1801) commented that the *I Ching* was a deception intended to fool people. Although some early Shinto and *kokugaku* scholars admitted that the *I Ching* had theoretical and divinational value, a real shift in attitude did not come until the rise of the Hirata school.

Hirata Atsutane (1776–1843) insisted that the *I Ching* was not an alien work of literature but the handiwork of a Japanese deity. He wrote the *San'eki yuraiki* (The Origins of the Three Early Versions of the *I Ching*, 1835) and the *Taikō koekiden* (The Original *I Ching* in Antiquity, 1836, 4 *kan*) to trace the alleged Shinto or Japanese origins of the ancient *I Ching*. Hirata believed that Fu Hsi, the putative creator of the *I Ching*, was a Shinto deity who had gone to China to cultivate the Chinese. He blamed King Wen, the Duke of Chou, and Confucius for distorting and Confucianizing the *I Ching*, and held that the only way to restore the ancient *I Ching* was to study the *Ta Hsiang* and *T'uan Chuan*, which he believed were fragmentary commentaries on the lost ancient *I Ching*. The *Koeki taishō kyō* (The Great Images in the Ancient *I Ching*) and *Tan'ekiron* (Discourse on the *T'uan Chuan*) were his ambitious attempts along these lines. He tried to restore the original *I Ching* by rearranging the order of the hexagrams and changing the number of yarrow stalks.[31]

To make his scholarship seem legitimate, Hirata attributed his ideas to Motoori. Hirata's ideas were further developed by his students Ikuta Yorozu (1801–1837) and Ōkuni Takamasa (1791–1871). The *I Ching* scholarship of the Hirata school reveals how national learning and cultural borrowing could coexist when everything foreign was shown to have a Japanese origin.

There was also a group of professional *I Ching* diviners that I call "the oracle school." According to Ogawa Kendō's *Chiritsukadan* (Discussions on Trifling Things), there were more than a thousand *I Ching* diviners *(ekisha)* in the city of Edo alone, and at least one *I Ching* diviner for every village. Ogawa divided these men into three categories: Ordinary diviners who had small stalls on the street corners were called *tachimi;* famous diviners who had their own offices or academies were *sayauchi;* and dispatch diviners were *shikiri.* Scholars of the oracle school belonged to the category of *sayauchi.* They either owned or worked in private academies where the *I Ching* and other Confucian classics were taught. They were prolific writers on the *I Ching,* and their writings were mostly about divination. Their concern was not limited to personal fortune but included medicine, the military, business, agriculture, and meteorology, among other fields. Through their writings, they expanded the practical uses for the *I Ching*. In terms of intellectual lineage, most of them belonged to the Chu Hsi school, but their scholarship on the text was eclectic. They traced the text's ancient meaning and lectured on Sung commentaries together.

Arai Hakuga (1725–1792) was the most famous *ekisha* of the Tokugawa period. He was trained as a Chu Hsi scholar in his early years. Realizing that he could never surpass Ogyū Sorai's Confucian scholarship, Arai concentrated on the *I Ching* and eventually established his own academy of *I Ching* studies in Kyoto. His inferiority complex had an impact on his scholarship. He boasted that his books outsold those of Hattori Nankaku (1683–1759, a disciple of Sorai) and that they stood up to academic scrutiny better than those of Sorai himself. He liked to mix old and new commentaries in his writings. He wrote at least thirty-nine books on the *I Ching;* his important works included the *Koekidan* (My Judgment on the Ancient *I Ching*, 1776, 10 *kan*), *Ekigaku ruihen* (A Collection of *I Ching* Scholarship, 1766, 23 *kan*), and *Ekigaku shōsen* (A Modest Interpretation of the *I Ching*, 1754), in which he popularized divination by suggesting a simplified method. He was confident enough to compare his *Koekidan* to the *Chou-i che-chung* (A Synthesis of *I Ching* Studies), and himself to Shao Yung.[32] The Arai Hakuga school produced some famous diviners in late Tokugawa times, including Mase Chūshū (1754–1817) and Matsui Rashū (1751–1822).

Mase Chūshū enjoyed the same reputation as his teacher Arai Hakuga. His activities were centered in Osaka, where he taught a large number of people. He wrote at least thirty-five books on the *I Ching* and coauthored the *Shūeki shakuko* (An Explanation of the Ancient Meaning of the *I Ching*, 1811–1813, 25 *kan*) with Matsui Rashū. This work was an ambitious attempt to restore the divination practices and original text of the ancient *I Ching*. For instance, Mase argued that the original divination technique used forty-eight yarrow stalks instead of the forty-nine mentioned in the *Chou I*.[33] He also tried to correct mistakes in the main text and Ten Wings that he believed had occurred over the ages.

The oracle school was very popular and influential in Osaka and Kyoto in the late Tokugawa period. Although it has been overlooked by modern scholars because of its emphasis on divination, scholars from this school made important contributions to the theory of divination and helped further the tradition of Shao Yung.

I Ching Studies in the Late Tokugawa Period

The last decades of the Tokugawa period were a time of decline in *I Ching* scholarship. People seem to have lost interest in scholarly pursuits vis-à-vis the text, such as verifying its authenticity or offering criticism of it. As a result, few fine scholars or works appeared. This decline in scholarship did not mean that the *I Ching* became less popular, however, for its readership widened to include the lower stratum of society. The text's practical nature was highlighted by different schools of thought and religion in the late Tokugawa period. People used it to find clues to solve political, economic, and cultural problems. This application of the *I Ching* has important implications for understanding the role of Confucianism in the modernization of Japan.

There were two major approaches to solving the political crises of late Tokugawa Japan: reform and restoration. The Mito school was famous for its ideas of *sonnō* (reverence for the emperor) and reform.[34] The *I Ching* and other Confucian texts became tools of authorization and legitimation in its hands. For instance, Aizawa Seishisai (1781–1863) quoted the *I Ching* extensively in his *Shinron* (New Thesis, 1825, 2 *kan*) to explain some characteristics of Japan's *kokutai* (national polity). He also urged the daimyō of Mito domain to implement reforms according to the political principles of the *I Ching*. In his *Tokueki nissatsu* (Notes on My Daily Reading of the *I Ching*, 1862, 7 *kan*), Aizawa compared the social hierarchy to the six lines in a hexagram, noting that, from bottom to top, society consisted of commoner, samurai, officer, daimyō, emperor, and "nobody." Aizawa himself was by no means anti-bakufu in his views, but his political thought did not legitimate the shogun and thus was vulnerable to being interpreted in an anti-bakufu light.

In addition to Mito scholars, people from other parts of Japan also expressed their ideas on reform. The *I Ching* was cited extensively to advocate reform and the necessity of change. Sakuma Shōzan urged Hitotsubashi Nobuyoshi (1837–1913) to carry out reforms by using an oracle in his explanation.

When the chorus of reform was ignored, some reformers adopted an anti-bakufu stance. Confucianism provided them with the logic to advocate a restoration. Many *shishi* (loyalist) thinkers quoted the hexagram *fu* (return, or restoration) to express their wish for a restoration of imperial power. For example, Kusumoto Tanzan (1828–1883) emphasized the goodness of *yang* returning to its original position to carry out the rule of benevolence. Ogasawara Keisai (1828–1863), in his punctuation of the *I Ching*, added many criticisms of the bakufu and urged the emperor to rule by himself according to the spirit of the hexagram *fu*. Other *shishi*, such as Yoshida Shōin (1830–1859) and Takasugi Shinsaku (1837–1867), also drew on the text to express their anti-bakufu opinions.

Scholarship on economic problems focused on two major issues: improving the old sector (agriculture) and establishing the new sector (modern industry and business). There was a movement for agricultural improvement in late Tokugawa times. Hayakawa Hachirō (1739–1809), a bakufu retainer, used the *I Ching* to suggest ways to improve productivity in his *Kyūsei jōkyō* (Teachings for Many Generations, 1799, 7 *kan*). He encouraged farmers to study the text's philosophy and divination. Many scholars outside the bakufu also concerned themselves with agriculture. Some students of Hirata Atsutane addressed this issue by using the *I Ching* as their basic framework. Two famous examples are Ko'nishi Atsuyoshi's (1767–1837) *Nōgyō yowa* (Discursive Talks on Agriculture, 1828, 2 *kan*) and Tamura Yoshishige's (1790–1877) *Nōgyō jitoku* (Self-Actualization in Agriculture, 1856, 2 *kan*).

One of the most prominent leaders of the rural improvement movement was Ōhara Yūgaku (1797–1858), a charismatic rural reformer whose authority rested on his ability to predict the weather using the *I Ching*. He had studied the divination methods of the Arai Hakuga school in Kyoto before traveling to various rural areas to implement agricultural reforms. He became a famous *I Ching* diviner and formed his own intellectual school, the *seigaku* (school of nature). Ōhara taught people in villages the theory of the text and its ethical implications, believing that it could enhance their material and spiritual lives. Using the theory of *yin-yang*, he made every two households into a mutual cooperative unit. He also used divination and geomancy to decide the locations of houses, paddy fields, and irrigation canals.

The philosophy of change and the divination methods in the *I Ching* gave early entrepreneurs wisdom and confidence. The most striking example was Takashima Donshō (1832–1914), a self-made businessman whose interests extended from the electricity and railway industries to agriculture and the iron and steel industries. In his autobiography, *Takashima Kauemon jijoden* (The Autobiography of Takashima Kauemon), he attributed his own success to the principles he found in the *I Ching*. The philosophy of the text also inspired some officials and intellectuals to advocate a "free-market economy." For instance, in his *Sanka zui* (Illustrative Glossary of Monetary Policy in the Three Countries, 42 *kan*), Kusama Naokata (1753–1831), a famous Kyoto merchant who had served the bakufu and several domains as an economic advisor, held that an economy should follow the natural principle of *yin-yang* and require no human intervention.

The problem of integrating Western ideas into the Chinese-Japanese cultural heritage was a common concern of nineteenth-century Japanese. Some attempted to transplant Western ideas into a neo-Confucian metaphysical framework using the *I Ching*, whereas others cited the text itself, claiming that Western ideas had existed in ancient China. In astronomy and physics, Shizuki Tadao (1760–1806), Yamagata Bantō (1748–1821), and Yoshio Nankō (1787–1843) used it to advocate Newtonian physics and Copernican heliocentrism. Hashimoto Sōkichi (1761–1836) and Kasamine Tachū used the images of the *I Ching* to demonstrate the theory of electricity. In medicine, Ikeda Tōzō, a *Rangaku* (Western learning) physician, used its principles to explicate Western medical ideas in his *Igaku engen* (The Origins of Medicine). Many Tokugawa artillerists used the *I Ching* to explain Western artillery. In the *Shūhatsu zusetsu* (A Graphic Illustration of the Movable Gun Carriage, 1778), Sakamoto Tenzan (1745–1803) used its images to illustrate his movable carriage. In the *Hōka* (The Hexagram of a Cannon, 1852), Sakuma Shōzan attributed his knowledge of explosives and cannons to principles he found in the *I Ching*.

Characteristics of *I Ching* Scholarship in the Tokugawa Period

I Ching scholarship boomed during the Tokugawa period. The number of scholars and writings was not only unprecedented in Japan but outnumbered the Korean output and even rivaled that of the Chinese. The popularity of the *I Ching* can also be seen using other barometers, such as the importation and reproduction of Chinese commentaries, the intellectual attitude of Tokugawa intellectuals, and the text's influence on Tokugawa politics, economics, thought, and culture.

I Ching scholarship was pursued by Tokugawa intellectuals from different schools of thought and religion. Confucians, Buddhists, Shintoists, *kokugaku* scholars, Mito scholars, students of Western learning, artists, merchant and peasant scholars, political leaders, and other intellectuals studied and accommodated the *I Ching* to their teachings.

I Ching scholarship was eclectic. It maintained a delicate balance between different approaches: philosophical and divinational, practical and academic, Han and Sung, Chinese and Japanese. Each group of scholars pursued *I Ching* studies in its own way and mixed in many non-Confucian elements. Ch'ing scholars were text oriented and exceedingly critical of divination and of symbols and numbers, whereas Yi scholars preferred using symbolic and numerical approaches. In Tokugawa Japan, all three approaches enjoyed considerable support, although textual analysis seems to have been more influential than the others.

I Ching scholarship went through Japanization. The making of Japanese-punctuated editions and Japanese commentaries demonstrated scholars' high degree of independence. The *I Ching* was also used by some Tokugawa intellectuals to advocate the unity of Confucianism and Shinto. Late *kokugaku* scholars even attempted to give it Japanese origins. It also played a considerable role in the development of many "indigenous" cultural practices, like the tea ceremony, flower arrangement, popular drama, and the martial arts.

I Ching studies also demonstrated a high quality of scholarship. There were many brilliant scholars and groundbreaking writings on its philosophy and divination. In particular, *kogaku* and the eclectic school were famous for their efforts to reconstruct its ancient meaning through sophisticated research methods.

I Ching scholars had a strong preference for Sung commentaries —evidence of the dominance of the Sung school in the Tokugawa intellectual world. Chu Hsi and Ch'eng I's commentaries were overwhelming in their influence. The bakufu, the domains, and most private academies adopted the Sung commentaries as their main references.[35]

I Ching scholarship underwent three dramatic changes but did not show a clear direction or continuity.[36] The early period was the heyday of the Chu Hsi school and produced the greatest number of scholars and writings. In mid-Tokugawa times, the eclectic school, *kokugaku,* and the oracle school emerged and stole the limelight. During the *bakumatsu* (last decades of the Tokugawa) period, different schools put emphasis on practical aspects of the text. *I Ching* scholarship demonstrates both the vitality and the discontinuity of Tokugawa intellectual developments.

Finally, *I Ching* scholarship put emphasis on the practical aspects of the text. In general, *I Ching* scholarship was textual and historical in Ch'ing China, philosophical in Yi Korea, and eclectic and practical in Tokugawa Japan. The *I Ching* penetrated different areas of the culture and lives of Tokugawa Japanese. It had a strong impact on medicine, politics, martial arts, sciences, performing arts, literature, agriculture, commerce, religion, and folklore. In particular, during the last decades of the Tokugawa period, people drew wisdom from the *I Ching* to find solutions to political, economic, and cultural crises.

Part II THOUGHT

4. The *I Ching* and Political Thought

The *I Ching* had strong political implications. As a book of wisdom it became an integral element of political thought, while as a divination manual it played a significant role in policy making, ceremonies, and in the formation of institutions. This chapter focuses on the role of the *I Ching* in Tokugawa political thought.[1] The text was, in a sense, a book of political philosophy. It functioned as a source of political guidance, a reform manual, and a tool for political legitimization. Its political ideas, such as the unity of heaven and man, change and reform, revolution, modesty, frugality, and simple administration, became important elements of political thought in Japan and all of East Asia.[2] In the past, the Japanese emperor and his ministers were obliged to study the text to learn the art and philosophy of politics. They cited it frequently in their political discussions and writings. The abstraction and ambiguity of its philosophy left it open to interpretation and meant that its ideas could function in different ways in different political contexts.

In China the *I Ching,* together with *Ch'un Ch'iu* and *Meng Tzu,* exerted a tremendous impact on politics, and there seems to have been an even closer connection between the *I Ching* and politics in Japan. While the emperor-centered ideology of the *Ch'un Ch'iu,* and the ideas of revolution and the way of the king *(ōdō)* of the *Meng Tzu,* were less suited to the Tokugawa political system, the flexibility of the *I Ching* made it an influential Chinese classic in Tokugawa politics.

Political ideology in the Tokugawa period has been the subject of academic attention in Western scholarship for many years.[3] Most scholars regard the *bakuhan* system (coexistence of a shogunate and

hundreds of daimyō domains)—which defined bakufu-court relations, the four-class social hierarchy, economic and cultural growth,
and diplomatic affairs—as the core political structure of the Tokugawa period. The rise and decline of the *bakuhan* system stimulated
intense debates over political ideology during the Tokugawa period.

Examining how Tokugawa intellectuals interpreted the *I Ching* to
support their political ideas, this chapter describes the changes in
Tokugawa political thought. The first section documents political
interpretations of the *I Ching* by Tokugawa intellectuals to see how
they accommodated Chinese political ideals to the Tokugawa political
system. The second section researches the role of the text in early
Tokugawa politics, focusing on how it was employed to legitimize the
Edo shogunate and the *bakuhan* system. The third section discusses
the *I Ching* and late Tokugawa politics, highlighting its role in supporting reformist and anti-bakufu ideas.

The *I Ching* and Political Ideals

The *I Ching* enriched the political thought of many Tokugawa intellectuals, although their interpretations of the text should be understood
as an attempt to accommodate Chinese political ideals to the Japanese
political system. They employed several devices to achieve this goal.
First, they completely transplanted ideas that did not conflict with
the Tokugawa setting, such as the politics of benevolence and the idea
of "simple administration." Second, they edited ideas, deleting unwanted elements, such as ideas of change and revolution in the
hexagram *ko*. Third, they distorted ideas, using the framework or terminology of an idea but changing its content, an example being the
tendō (heavenly way) theory in Tokugawa Japan, which did not imply
ekisei kakumei (change of imperial house following dynastic revolution). Fourth, they downplayed sensitive concepts, such as the *sonnō*
(reverence for the emperor) ideology. Fifth, they extended or elaborated on some ideas, such as loyalty and filial piety, which became
bushidō (the way of the samurai) and family-state ideology. Sixth, they
associated Chinese political ideas with Shinto, an example being
ikan (simple administration).

Here we examine the adaptation of Confucian political thought
in Tokugawa Japan by looking at the role of the *I Ching* in the discussion of six major political issues.

The Nature of the Hexagram *Ko* (Change)

The hexagram *ko* (change) contains two important concepts: reform and revolution.[4] The idea of reform was powerful in both China and Japan. It encountered no ideological resistance in Japan and was used frequently to support various reform programs in the bakufu. For example, before the submission of his financial reform plan, Arai Hakuseki said:

> It appears in the *Chou I* that when things are at their worst, a solution appears. The situation at the present time is not as bad as that, for though the treasury is bare, His Highness [the shogun] possesses the wealth of the empire. There is bound to be a solution. Let him not distress himself about these matters. Tell him I will think of a plan.[5]

And Ogyū Sorai (1666–1728) asserted that the new replacing the old was a natural law, applicable to politics:

> It is a general law of nature that old things gradually disappear and new things come into being. All things in heaven and earth are like this. We might like to keep old things forever, but this is beyond our power. Timber rots; grain varies in yield from year to year. So, too, with men: the old pass away and the young come in. In this they follow the law of nature, by which things from below rise gradually to the top and, on reaching the top, decline and disappear. This is an invariable rule, with which even the law of [the *Book of*] *Changes* accords.[6]

In China, starting with the Emperors T'ang and Wu, the concept of revolution was used frequently to justify dynastic changes. However, revolution was a sensitive topic in Japanese history. The myth of unbroken imperial lineage opposed this notion. The *tendō* philosophy in Japan did not imply a Chinese-style political revolution. In general, Japanese people believed that those who received the heavenly mandate were authorized to govern the nation but not to replace the imperial family through dynastic changes. In Japan, the theory of *ekisei kakumei,* or revolution to replace the throne, was unpopular.

Tokugawa intellectuals used three major devices to accommodate the hexagram *ko* to the Edo establishment. The first was reinterpretation. The hexagram *ko* implies both revolution and change. Most Tokugawa Confucians stressed the second definition and downplayed the first. Famous examples of scholars who interpreted the idea this way include Yamazaki Ansai (1618–1682), Yamaga Sokō (1622–1685), Itō Jinsai (1629–1709), Asami Keisai (1652–1711), and Wakabayashi

Kyōsai (1697–1732).[7] As Itō Jinsai explained the hexagram, "If the sages lived in today's world, they would have to act according to today's customs and apply today's laws. Therefore, [the *I Ching* says,] 'The superior man changes like a panther; the inferior man molts in the face.' The nation naturally will be well governed."[8]

The second method was to deny the veracity of the *Chou I*. For instance, Ban Nobutomo (1773–1846) and Hirata Atsutane (1776–1843) blamed King Wen for altering the *I Ching* in order to justify the revolution that overthrew the Shang dynasty. The *Chou I*, Hirata argued, had been further distorted by the Duke of Chou and by Confucius and his students, giving Chinese traitors an ideological means to justify their political ambitions.

The third method was distortion. Hayashi Razan (1583–1657) and Itō Jinsai twisted the meaning of *ko-ming* (revolution), employing this term to support the old idea that the Tokugawa family had received the heavenly mandate and to downplay the idea of revolution in the Chinese sense.[9]

The Political Ideal of *Ikan* (Simple Administration)

Ikan literally means "easy and simple," and it was a very powerful political idea accepted by many Tokugawa intellectuals. The *I Ching* suggests that political policy must be simple to understand and easy to carry out. The *Hsi Tz'u* (Commentary on the Appended Judgments) reads:

> The Creative is known through the easy; the Receptive can do things through the simple. What is easy is easy to know; what is simple is easy to follow. He who is easy to know attains fealty. He who is easy to follow attains works. . . . By means of the easy and the simple, we grasp the laws of the whole world. . . . The people use it day by day and are not aware of it. . . . Because of the good in the easy and the simple, it corresponds with the supreme power.[10]

Famous advocates of this idea in the Tokugawa period included Takuan Sōhō (1573–1645), Hayashi Razan, Kumazawa Banzan (1619–1691), Kaibara Ekken (1630–1714), Nishikawa Joken (1648–1724), Tokiwa Tanhoku (1685–1744), and Jiun Sonja (1718–1804). Takuan explained:

> The sage-king sits and lives in the palace with ease. Four classes and hundreds of professions live in the world with ease. When they do their own jobs diligently, the nation will be peaceful and stable. This

virtue of the sage-king is called the ultimate virtue. The goodness of simple administration *(ikan)* can match the ultimate virtue of the sages.[11]

Compared to the Ch'ing Chinese and Yi Korean central governments, the bakufu administration was small in scale and relatively efficient. It did not face serious problems of overstaffing, corruption, or trivial administrative and legal codes, and thus was frequently praised by Tokugawa intellectuals as fulfilling the ideal of *ikan.*

This idea of *ikan* also helped scholars fuse Confucianism and Shinto. Some Confucians, such as Hayashi Razan, Kaibara Ekken, and Kumazawa Banzan, pointed out that both Shinto and Confucianism stressed this idea of simplicity. A scholar of national learning, Izumi Makuni (1765–1805), asserted that Japan was superior to other nations because *ikan* had been a political principle in Japan since the Age of the Gods:

> When the ruler follows a great principle created by the majestic gods of our nation without using other trivial ways and teachings, the nation will be well governed and people will be safe and comfortable. Until the end of heaven and earth, and the extinction of the light that shines from the sun and moon, it will always remain unchanged and give prosperity to the nation. The *Chou I* says: "Be simple *(ikan)* and you get the truth of everything," "The goodness of simplicity *(ikan)* is the utmost virtue," and "The people enjoy their daily lives unconsciously." Isn't this the virtue? Isn't this the Way?[12]

The Relationship Between Ruler and Subject

In medieval Japan, loyalty to the ruler was conditional and reserved. Disobedience, betrayal, assassination, and usurpation were common. The rise of neo-Confucianism provided a new political ethic that made loyalty unconditional and unlimited. The *I Ching* played an important role in this transformation. Tokugawa intellectuals used its ideas of *yin-yang* and *ch'ien-k'un* (the first two hexagrams) to justify and promote this new political ethic.

The view that the natural principle of *yin-yang* could be applied to political morality and human relationships had strong appeal. For example, Hayashi Razan, in his *Chitentai kaigi* (An Explanation of the Hexagram Earth-Heaven *T'ai*), stated that the loyalty of subject (or retainer) to ruler was a natural law:

> The Way of the ruler and the father is the Way of Heaven, and the way of the subject and the son is the way of the earth. . . . The nobility of

the ruler and the father and the baseness of the subject and the son can be compared with the fact that the places of heaven and earth are fixed and cannot be disordered. But the hearts of those above reach those below, and the feelings of those below extend to those above. The way of ruler and subject, and of father and son, are mutually upheld; the righteousness that governs the relationship between the high and the low, and the noble and the base, are closely related, and the principles of *yin* and *yang,* in the house and in the outside world, are harmonious.[13]

Tokugawa Confucians sowed the seeds of family-state *(kazoku kokka)* ideology, which combined loyalty and filial piety into one. The idea of loyalty was well explicated by Matsunaga Sekigo (1592–1657), who argued that the relationship between ruler and subject was one of the four constant relationships mentioned in the *I Ching,* and that loyalty to the ruler was a natural principle that every subject must obey. He remarked:

The *I Ching* also reads: "At the beginning, we had heaven and earth, then husband and wife followed. Father and son came after husband and wife. Ruler and subject came after father and son." Who can live without these relationships? If you apply filial piety to your parents to serve your ruler, it becomes loyalty. Using the method of settling family affairs to govern the nation will bring peace and stability.[14]

Matsunaga's interpretation of the hexagram *ch'ien* in relation to the ruler-subject relationship was orthodox. He explained: "*Yang* is the ruler and *yin* is the subject. The ruler is like heaven above, and the subject is like earth below. This is the principle of heaven and earth. The hexagram *ch'ien* of the *I Ching* also holds that nine in the fifth place is the supreme position of the ruler, while nine in the second place is the humble position of the subject."[15] This kind of neo-Confucian ethical interpretation of the *yin-yang, ch'ien-k'un* dualism became a part of the political mentality prevalent among Tokugawa officials and intellectuals.

If Hayashi and Matsunaga's ideas of the ruler-subject relationship sound strict, Satō Issai's can be considered absolutist. Satō lectured to the twelfth shogun, Tokugawa Ieyoshi (1793–1853), on the *I Ching* and advocated unconditional loyalty to the ruler: "Heaven is respectable, and earth is despicable. This is the way to establish the relationship between *ch'ien* and *k'un.* The relationship between ruler and subject is decided by heaven. Each performs its own functions. The subject should repay his indebtedness to the ruler regardless of how the ruler treats him."[16]

The Relationship Between Ruler and People

Compared to the ruler-subject relationship, that between the ruler and the people was less coercive and unilateral. Confucianism regarded the people as the basic unit of politics and advised the ruler to show benevolence *(jen)* toward them. Benevolence meant pursuing the interests of the people as one's ultimate political goal. Yamaga Sokō cited the *Hsi Tz'u:* "It is the great treasure of the holy sage to stand in the right place. How does one safeguard this place? The answer is through benevolence."[17]

Perhaps no one was more articulate in discussing this issue than Kumazawa Banzan. He held that if the ruler did not treat his people with benevolence, his regime was bound to fall. He used the hexagram *po* (splitting apart) to explicate his idea of *minpon,* or people-oriented politics:

> The process of splitting apart starts from the bottom. It takes no time to finish this process. . . . A nation shows its decline in its people. When the people live in poverty, the nation begins to split apart. The *I Ching* reads: "The mountain rests on the earth: The image of Splitting Apart. Thus those [who rule] can ensure their position only by giving generously to those below." This is the way to stop [the nation from] splitting apart. The ruler adheres to the people like the mountain rests on the earth. . . . When a nation is in decline, gentlemen retreat and evil men progress. When evil men come forward, the world will become arrogant and extravagant. Therefore, when the world is wasteful, the people will fall into ruin.[18]

Kumazawa believed that the ruler should consult the people before making decisions:

> The hexagram *k'uei* (opposition) . . . symbolizes the lack of communication between the high and the low. When there is no interchange between the high and the low, the heart of the people will lose respect for the ruler. When this happens, it is a sign that there is no leadership; it is the root of great turmoil. If the ruler makes every decision himself, and hates listening to public opinions or good advice, this scenario will occur. . . . When the ruler puts everything in his hand, punishment will be increased. That is not the way of heaven.[19]

Although it was not democracy in the modern sense—consultation did not mean the sharing of power, and the ruler made final decisions—the idea of the benevolence of the ruler toward the people had a liberalizing influence on Tokugawa political ideology.

Similarly, Yamagata Dai'ni (1725–1767) used hexagrams to define benevolent rule. According to Yamagata, the change from hexagram *t'ai* ▤ (peace) to hexagram *sun* ▤ (decrease) meant that if the ruler pursued his own interests at his people's expense, the peace of the realm would disappear. In contrast, the change from hexagram *p'i* ▤ (stagnation) to hexagram *i* ▤ (increase) indicated that when the ruler sacrificed his own interests for the sake of his people, the stagnation in the realm would disappear.[20]

The Qualities of a Ruler

Tokugawa intellectuals generally agreed on the following qualities of the sage-ruler. First, he should not use excessive force. For instance, in the explanation of the top line of the hexagram *ch'ien,* "Arrogant dragon will have cause to repent," Kumazawa Banzan wrote: "Since ancient times, there has never been any authority with excessive power that did not lose its position. People always say that something in a position that is too high is bound to fall."[21]

Second, the ruler should employ gentlemen *(chün-tzu)* to assist him. To acquire help from gentlemen, the ruler should give them respect and power. Kumazawa stated:

> The six lines of [the hexagram *ch'ien* of] the *I Ching* put the ruler on the fifth line [from below]. The nine in the sixth place [the top line] should be given to gentlemen. The nine at the top of the hexagram *ku* (decay) says: "He does not serve kings and princes, and sets himself higher goals." The six in the fourth place of the hexagram *kuan* (contemplation) reads: "Contemplation of the light of the kingdom. It forces one to exert influence as the guest of a king." In ancient times, when there were gentlemen, the ruler treated them as guests. Thus gentlemen came to the court to serve the ruler. This is the meaning of [the word] "guest."[22]

Third, the ruler should be modest. Yamaga Sokō cited the hexagram *ch'ien* (modesty) to argue that modesty was a crucial political virtue. It reads: "[Modesty] is the way of heaven; it sheds its influence downward and creates light and radiance."[23]

Fourth, a ruler should be determined, courageous, and cautious. Yamagata Shūnan (1687–1752) reminded the shogun that he should not be satisfied with "the Tokugawa Peace" (i.e., the early half of the Tokugawa, when Japan experienced political stability and cultural and economic growth); rather, he should always rule the nation with caution and courage, just like a man crossing a river—a metaphor used in the hexagram *t'ai* (peace). Shūnan explained: "In the six in the second place of the hexagram *t'ai* of the *I Ching*, politics is compared to crossing a river. During peaceful times, if the ruler indulges in pleasure and becomes lazy, the nation will gradually decay. It is like a house that collapses because no one fixes a decaying pillar."[24]

Fifth, the ruler should be impartial in handing out rewards and punishments. Many Tokugawa intellectuals criticized the Edo administration for its harsh punishments and its reluctance to grant rewards. Shūnan said: "Rewards and punishments are like *yin* and *yang*. If you have punishments, then you should have rewards. . . . It is easy to punish too harshly, and to reward too little."[25]

The Relation Between the *I Ching* and Politics

There was a consensus among most Tokugawa Confucians that *ekidō* (the way of the *I Ching*) and *seidō* (politics) were inseparable, and that political leaders were supposed to be familiar with the text. Dazai Shundai (1680–1747) gave the most provocative arguments. Viewing the *I Ching* as a political manual that was needed for times of degeneration, he pointed out that in times of peace, people could study literature, history, or other Confucian classics, but that in times of turmoil, the *I Ching* was the only book that could save the nation. He praised his master, Ogyū Sorai, for rediscovering the political implications of the text:

> When the early kings created the rituals and music to govern the nation, they must have based their principles on this [the *I Ching*]. If we go against the way of the *I Ching*, not even a little thing can be carried out, not to mention national politics. The reason the *I Ching* belongs to the Six Arts is that it is the tool for governing the nation. Since the Han and Wei periods, Confucians have not understood this idea, and have treated it as a way for periods of normalcy. Hence the *I Ching* was not understood. We students of the *I Ching* must know that my teacher [Sorai] discovered this [relationship between the *I Ching* and politics], and obviously surpassed the people of the past.[26]

In his *Keizairoku* (A Record on Political Economy), Dazai wrote a whole chapter entitled "Ekidō" to explain the relationship between the *I Ching* and politics. He suggested that every political ruler should know the three political dimensions of the text: time, numbers, and *yin-yang*. Time means following the changes of time that occur in politics. Numbers help people know what is inevitable in history. *Yin-yang* reveals the rise and fall of gentlemen and evil men. Dazai guaranteed that rulers who know these three principles would make no major mistakes in politics.[27]

From these six issues, we can conclude that the political ideals gleaned by Tokugawa intellectuals from the *I Ching* were generally not very different from the ideals associated with the text in China. In a word, both emphasized the politics of benevolence, which had three basic characteristics. First, the ruler should pursue the way of the sage-kings, who possessed the virtues of modesty, constraint, determination, courage, fairness, and caution. Second, a good government must use talented people to create a simple administration and carry out reforms. Third, the people are the origin and purpose of politics.

However, there were some significant adaptations made to accommodate the political ideas of the *I Ching* to the Tokugawa political system. First, the notion of revolution was not accepted. Second, Shinto was linked with *ikan,* the ideal of the *I Ching.* Third, certain aspects of Confucianism were developed into *bushidō* and family-state ideology. In the second half of this chapter, we investigate how Tokugawa rulers and intellectuals accommodated Chinese political thought to Tokugawa politics through the *I Ching* from a historical perspective, focusing on the issue of legitimization.

The *I Ching* and Early Tokugawa Politics

Japan had a long tradition of using the *I Ching* in politics. In the ancient past, the imperial family had studied its political principles to rule, and also carry out political reforms. The decline of central authority during the late medieval period brought warrior families into positions of prominence. A new political philosophy, the idea of *tendō* (the heavenly way), was used by some military leaders to justify their authority in the scramble for power, and to legitimize the new power that replaced the imperial court.[28] The content of the *tendō* philosophy, as well as its terminology, borrowed heavily from the *I Ching.* *Tendō* was described as "the principle of heaven," a principle that was higher than any secular power (including the imperial court). Warrior leaders claimed that they had received the heavenly mandate *(tenmei)* to govern their domains *(tenka)* in accordance with *tendō.* Thus their authority was granted by heaven, not the imperial court. If they acted against *tendō,* they would receive heavenly punishment *(tenbatsu).*

Following the establishment of the *bakuhan* system in the early Tokugawa period, the *I Ching* took on a new role in politics. The Tokugawa shogunate in Edo, rather than the imperial court in Kyoto or the regional warriors, became the major "consumer" of political ideology. One of the Tokugawa bakufu's main political concerns in the first decades was its legitimacy. Literate groups such as Confucians, Buddhists, and Shinto priests competed to legitimize the new regime. The Edo bakufu did not direct or manipulate this intellectual activity but passively used these intellectual forces that it had at its disposal.

Did the early Edo shoguns use the *I Ching* for their own political purposes? This is not an easy question to answer. The early Edo bakufu did not have a unified intellectual policy, and seems to have used whatever was felt to be appropriate from the Three Teachings (Confucianism, Buddhism, and Shinto). Read and used as a Confucian text in different political contexts, the *I Ching* played a considerable role in educating the shogun and the people, and in defining bakufu-daimyō relations and the image of the shogun in diplomacy.

Tokugawa Ieyasu recognized the philosophical and divinational value of the *I Ching*. He had two Zen monks, Kanshitsu Genkitsu and Saishō Shōtai, who were masters of the text, act as his advisors, and put them in charge of the publication of the Fushimi (or Keichō) edition of the *I Ching*. Ieyasu's motivation was to use the concept of *yin-yang* to cultivate a new political ethic of loyalty and obedience. This project helped promote the popularity of the text in the early Tokugawa period; it was used to politically educate the shogun, daimyō, and the people.

The *I Ching* played a subtle role in Ieyasu's policies. For instance, the *Buke shohatto* (Laws Governing the Military Households, 1615), the standard behavioral code for the daimyō and samurai, contained the following clause on marriage between daimyō families:

> Marriage follows the principle of harmony between *yin* and *yang*, and must not be entered into lightly. In the *Book of Changes*, under the thirty-eighth hexagram [*k'uei*], it says, "Marriage should not be contracted out of enmity [against another]. Marriages intended to effect an alliance with enemies [of the state] will turn out badly."[29]

This clause prohibited the old practice of using strategic marriages among daimyō to reconcile and ally families; thus it balanced each family's power and prevented the formation of cliques in the *bakuhan* system. Hereafter, marriages between warrior families had to be approved by the bakufu, becoming a tool with which the bakufu could regulate its relationship with daimyō from different backgrounds.

Tokugawa Iemitsu (1604–1651), the third shogun, perfected the *bakuhan* system. He reshaped and enhanced the image of the shogun by cultivating the Ieyasu cult and *taikun* (great ruler) diplomacy. The *I Ching* was not directly related to the Ieyasu cult, but it provided the inspiration for *taikun* diplomacy. The term *"taikun"* was borrowed from the *I Ching* and referred to a great ruler who did not have an imperial lineage or vassal status; using it in diplomatic correspondence increased the prestige of the bakufu and emphasized the independence of Japan. Iemitsu chose *taikun* to replace "king of Japan" *(Nihon kokuō)* and other titles that were either associated with the emperor or that put Japan into a subordinate position within the Chinese world order.[30]

The most enthusiastic sponsor of *I Ching* scholarship was the fifth shogun, Tokugawa Tsunayoshi (1646–1709). From April 4, 1693 to November 21, 1700, a period of seven years and ten months, he held 240 *I Ching* seminars. The average number of seminars was 2.6 per month, but in some months the seminar was held more than six times. Tsunayoshi was the chairman of the seminar, and he made a large number of courtiers, monks, officers, daimyō, and Confucians (including Ogyū Sorai) join.[31] A minister described this unprecedented "*I Ching* boom" in East Asian political history as follows:

> The shogun [Tsunayoshi] sometimes lectured on the *Chou-i pen-i*. That day, he talked about the first half of the *Chou I* in the seminar. Hereafter, the seminar was held six times a month and took eight years to finish. [The audiences were] not only from his close retainers, but also included daimyō, high-ranking samurai, local administrative officers, executive officers and officials, Buddhist monks, and Shinto priests under his administration. Anyone interested was welcome to attend.[32]

Tsunayoshi ordered the reprinting of the *Chou-i pen-i* (The Original Meaning of the *I Ching*, by Chu Hsi) and *I Chuan* (A Commentary on the *I Ching*, by Ch'eng I) to spread the orthodox interpretation of the *I Ching*, using them as standard textbooks for the *I Ching* seminar and the Shōheikō (School of Prosperity and Peace, founded in 1630).[33] His enthusiasm for *I Ching* scholarship was motivated by political rather than intellectual interest. According to a Japanese historian, Tsunayoshi wanted to use *I Ching* studies to achieve two political goals: to show that he was a contemporary sage-king who embodied virtue, talent, and scholarship, and to obtain the ability to predict and take precautions against natural disasters.[34]

During Tsunayoshi's office, the Onmyōdō was developed into a nationwide institution. Its origins can be traced to the Onmyōryō (Bureau of Divination) founded in the early Heian period. Following the decline of central authority in the medieval period, it had ceased to function. In 1683, Emperor Reigen (r. 1663–1683), with the blessing of Tsunayoshi, reestablished the system and renamed it Onmyōdō.[35] The bakufu later enhanced its control over this system and used it for different political purposes.[36]

Tsunayoshi's successor, Ienobu (1633–1712), was also a respectable student of the *I Ching*. He first studied the text under Arai Hakuseki in 1695. When he became the sixth shogun, Ienobu asked Arai to give him "daily lectures" on the *I Ching*.[37]

Having examined the Edo shoguns—the main "consumers" of *I Ching* political philosophy—we now look at the intellectuals who were its "producers." When Confucianism became independent of the sphere of Buddhism in early Edo times, they sought political patronage from the bakufu. Although their training was closely related to politics, Tokugawa Confucians enjoyed neither privileges nor authority in the political arena.[38] Hence they exerted their political influence by advocating pro-bakufu ideas and by performing advisory and secretarial work for the bakufu and daimyō. They used Confucian classics, the *I Ching* in particular, to provide ideological support for the bakufu.

In general, early Tokugawa Confucians tried to illustrate several political ideas using the *I Ching*. These included the notions (1) that a hierarchical political and social order could be deduced from nature;[39] (2) that the *bakuhan* system was equivalent to feudalism in ancient China (and that since feudalism was a device of the sages, the *bakuhan* system was the creation of the contemporary sage Ieyasu); (3) that the shogun was the legitimate ruler of Japan; (4) that the imperial family and courtiers *(kuge)* should not hold political power because they had lost the heavenly mandate to the warrior families *(buke);* and (5) that the shogun should not take over the throne.

Confucians from different schools used the *I Ching* to legitimize the Tokugawa shogunate. Asayama Soshin (1589–1664), for example, was famous for his *I Ching* scholarship. Explaining the political implications of the most widely quoted hexagram, *ch'ien* (creativity), in his

Kiyomizu monogatari (Tale of Kiyomizu, 1638), Asayama used the *tendō* philosophy to legitimize the Edo shogunate and discuss the political role of the shogun. He wrote:

> On the six unbroken lines, the lord's place is indicated by the second stroke from the top, the fifth from the bottom: ☰. Why not the first stroke on the very top, as some would argue? If the ruler of the realm and the nation thinks that he is the top in everything, that in terms of status, rank, honor, fame there is no one above him, he should be told that this clearly is contrary to *tendō,* that he will do evil things. The place at the top has the negative commentary in the *I Ching* of a "Dragon at the top will have cause to repent." The dragon at the top is a dragon that has climbed to heaven. Such a dragon has no higher place to go and therefore has to come down. If one goes too high, one will have cause to repent.[40]

It was commonly thought in Tokugawa Japan that the shogun was the political ruler in both name and substance. Unless the title *"tennō"* was used or mentioned specifically, "the ruler" in Tokugawa literature referred to the shogun. "The ruler of the realm and the nation" and "the lord" in this quotation also referred to the shogun, who ruled over the people of the four classes (represented by the bottom four strokes). The emperor had no place in this political hierarchy, and thus was not supposed to play an active role in politics. The hexagram *ch'ien* was thus used to rationalize the bakufu-court relationship in the Edo period and the emperor's role in performing ceremonial and symbolic functions.[41] Asayama was convinced that the shogun, on the fifth line, should be satisfied with this position; any ambitions to assume the highest position (i.e., the throne) would only cause misfortune.

Kumazawa Banzan established some insightful political views based on the *I Ching*. Like Asayama, he rationalized the Tokugawa social hierarchy in his explanation of the six lines in the hexagram *ch'ien*.[42] Kumazawa remarked:

> In today's Japan, the emperor is on the top line. Although he is very high, he has no people. Although he is respectable, he holds no real position. In the position of nine-five is the shogun. In nine-four are the three dukes and hereditary great ministers. Although they are only next to the shogun *(taikun),* they are in the position of darkness and thus should not hold power. If they acquire power, the nation will suffer and their families will also meet misfortune. They enjoy prestigious positions and good pay, and watch politics from a distance. In nine-three is the nobility. . . . As the lords of their domains, they are

the masters of their lands. Although they are small, they have officers and administrations. Because they are also rulers, the shogun should treat them as guests. The nine-two, . . . although in a low position, is more powerful than the nine-four. This is the position of the administrative officer. The nine-one is the position of the people. Samurai also belong to this rank, because soldiers should be based on farmer-soldiers. Although the samurai are in the lowest position, their aspirations should be high, and their talents can be good or bad. Since they are numerous, there must be virtuous people among them. They are in a position to know the changes of human emotions and the course of events.[43]

Here Kumazawa adopted a new social-class categorization system that was more congenial to Japan. In China, Confucians usually classified people into four classes: scholar-officials, peasants, artisans, and merchants. Inspired by the *I Ching,* Kumazawa divided the social hierarchy into six groups: the emperor, the shogun (or *taikun*), courtiers, daimyō, officers, and the people (which included peasants, artisans, merchants, and samurai).[44] This categorization fitted the *bakuhan* system well. This social hierarchy, however, did not imply the necessity of a proportional distribution of power. Only the shogun, daimyō, officers, and samurai were supposed to be active in politics. The imperial house was deprived of real political influence.[45]

Arai Hakuseki used the periodization of Japanese history to legitimize the Tokugawa shogunate. According to the hexagram *ch'ien,* the ruler was in the position of nine in the fifth place. Arai, in his *Tokushi yoron* (Some Opinions after Reading the History of Our Country, 1712), became convinced that the Edo shogunate was in the legitimate position of nine in the fifth place. He wrote: "In our country, the government of the realm after nine epochal changes fell to *buke* rule; in the age of *buke* rule, there were five further epochal changes leading to the rule of the present house. . . . Lord Ieyasu brought the realm to submit through the agency of his martial virtue."[46] Arai's concept of historical change seems to have been influenced by the theories of change expounded in the *I Ching.*[47] In his historical narrative of medieval Japan, he seldom mentioned the court because he believed that the imperial house had lost the heavenly mandate to the military houses.[48]

Dazai Shundai was an ardent supporter of the Edo bakufu and saw the court in Kyoto simply as a decoration. He praised the *bakuhan* system for being the political system that best combined noble intentions with practical measures, and compared it to the feudal structure established by the sage-kings in ancient China. He found support for feudalism in the *I Ching:*

> In antiquity, the sage-kings of the Three Dynasties did not consider the nation their own. They established domains of different sizes, and ennobled the people as lords. . . . The *I Ching* reads: "Just like the water on the surface of the land, the former kings used this principle to establish thousands of domains, and were on intimate terms with the nobles." Therefore, feudalism was a device of the sages.[49]

Dazai portrayed Ieyasu, the founder of the Edo *bakuhan* system, as a contemporary sage-king, and joined the chorus of the Ieyasu cult.

These examples show that the *I Ching* was used extensively both by the bakufu and by intellectuals to legitimize the new political system and ideology in Tokugawa Japan.[50]

The *I Ching* and Late Tokugawa Politics

When the bakufu was in its heyday, people produced pro-bakufu ideas whether or not they were invited to do so. When the bakufu was in trouble, however, people began to attack it. The *I Ching* was used in both situations because its principles did not have any internal or necessary links to either pro-bakufu or anti-bakufu ideas. Used to legitimize the bakufu in early times, the *I Ching* assumed the opposite role in the *bakumatsu* period (the last decades of the Tokugawa), becoming an ideological tool of reformers and of those who espoused anti-bakufu and *sonnō* ideas. Here we examine the writings of late Tokugawa intellectuals from different backgrounds to understand the role of the *I Ching* in late Tokugawa political thought.

Andō Shōeki (1703–1762) made the first frontal assault on the ideas underlying the *bakuhan* system.[51] The framework of his anti-feudal thought was built on criticizing the *I Ching*. He blamed Fu Hsi, Shen Nung, and other Confucian sages for stopping the practice of "direct cultivation" and creating the evil emperor system, and regarded the principle of *yin-yang wu-hsing* as the origin of social unfairness and class exploitation. He wrote:

> Using cleverness founded on self-interest, they ascribe to [the agent of] fire a princely character. . . . They wished to place themselves above the people as the possessors of princely character, and to live and eat in comfort without cultivating the soil. In order to be respected by the people, they equated the fire of the sun with the symbol of the prince and the fire on earth with the symbol of the ministers. Heaven is

equated with the principle of *yang* and is held in high respect, while the earth is equated with *yin* and is held to be base. In this way they distinguish between the high and the low and, proclaiming this to be the law, they claim to possess princely characters and place themselves above others.[52]

Kaihō Seiryō (1755–1817), like Andō, was a critic of the basic premises of feudalism, and believed that the natural law of hierarchy should be replaced with the logic of commercial exchange. Having traveled across the nation to different domains to advocate reforms to the samurai class, Kaihō's main concern was with solving the problem of the uneven distribution of wealth in a commercial economy. He blamed the *bakuhan* system for creating corruption in domains; the daimyō, he believed, had lost the qualities of their ancestors and now gained their positions by inheritance rather than ability. He stated:

> The old saying is: "The parents take pains [in working]. Their sons enjoy [their fruit]. Their grandsons beg for food." This is in accord with the principle in the *I Ching*. . . . Nowadays, the daimyō are in the position of the sons. [They forget that] their ancestors lost their blood, faced danger to acquire success and fame, and fought with their spades to obtain merit and repute.[53]

He also used the hexagram *t'ai* to describe the ideal political attitude of the ruler, and pinpointed the problems of the day: Leaders were idle and absentminded, the social order was in chaos, and malpractice among bureaucrats was prevalent.[54]

Voices for reform became much louder in the nineteenth century. People from various backgrounds urged the bakufu and the domains to carry out timely reforms. Hirose Tansō (1782–1856) wrote the *Ugen* (Outdated Opinions, 1840) to advocate political reforms. He criticized the warrior families for being arrogant and extravagant, and chastised the bakufu for setting a bad example. He used the hexagram *p'i* (standstill, or stagnation) to express his criticism:

> In the hexagrams of the *I Ching*, *k'un* at the top and *ch'ien* at the bottom is the hexagram *p'i*. The air *(ch'i)* in the earth does not rise; the air in the sky does not fall. The distance between above and below makes no communication possible. Therefore, applying this idea of the blockage of communication [to politics], it shows that the sovereign and the subject are not in harmony. This is a symbol of a nation without proper rule. Today, the ruling style of the warrior families makes this mistake. We have to be frugal and refrain from wasting now. We have this opinion in different domains, [but they do not

know that] the origin of extravagance is arrogance. If the rulers do not change their arrogant attitude, no matter how hard they save, the situation will be like adding water to the wood which I mentioned before, and it will bring no good in the end.[55]

He praised the ideal of *ikan* and suggested abolition of the alternate attendance system that required daimyō to reside in Edo in alternate years. According to Hirose, in addition to frugality, the key to successful politics was the use of *jinzai* (talent), and to cultivate *jinzai*, a sound educational system was needed. He quoted the hexagram *ta ch'u* (the taming power of the great) to illustrate the importance of primary education for children.

Date Chihiro (1802–1877), a retainer of Kii domain, criticized the bakufu for wasting resources and for usurping lands from the people to construct and maintain their mansions and mausoleums. He believed that a good government should make the well-being of the people its top priority and not waste the people's resources. He said: "[The hexagram *i* (increase) of] the *I Ching* tells us that [the best politics means] a decrease in what is above and an increase in what is below. [The hexagram *chieh* (limitation) reads]: If the ruler applies this principle to the creation of institutions, property will not be encroached upon and people will not be harmed."[56]

The Mito school was very much concerned with the political crisis in the late Tokugawa period. Drawing on the *I Ching* and other Confucian texts, Mito scholars advocated the ideas of *sonnō* and reform. Here are two examples.

Aizawa Seishisai (1781–1863) quoted the *I Ching* extensively in his *Shinron* (New Thesis, 1825) to define Japan's *kokutai* (national polity). In the *I Ching* he found symbolism showing the relationship between ruler and subjects. He used the images of the hexagram *kuan* (contemplation) to explain three ideas. First, there was an intimate relationship between ancestor worship and political order. He remarked: "*Kuan* shows its subject washing his hands, but not [yet] presenting his offering with sincerity. This is an appearance of dignity."[57] Here the object of loyalty and respect was the emperor, not the shogun. Second, it was necessary to have good communications between above and below: "*Kuan* shows that those above observe those below, and that those below observe those above. The high and the low communicate and observe each other."[58] This was intended to urge the bakufu to create a more open political environment. Third, Aizawa argued that Shinto was in agreement with Confucianism and that the center of Shinto worship was the imperial family.

Aizawa also used other political and ethical principles from the *I Ching* to address problems such as the management of property and valuables, the judgment of right and wrong, the consolidation of the nation, the pursuit of both righteousness and profit at the same time, and the use of men of talent and virtue.[59] In the conclusion of the *Shinron,* he urged the daimyō of Mito to carry out timely reforms: "The *Book of Changes* says, 'The Way does not implement itself; that requires the man of talent and virtue.' To solve difficulties as these arise and to devise methods of dealing with changed situations—these tasks await the appearance of the Great Hero."[60]

There was no place for the shogun in Aizawa's political thought. In his comparison of the six lines with the social system, he portrayed the social order as consisting of commoners, samurai, officers, daimyō, the emperor, and "nobody."[61] Most Mito thinkers were by no means anti-bakufu, but their writings created an anti-bakufu logic that was later developed by *shishi* (late Edo loyalist) thinkers.

Like many Tokugawa intellectuals, Aizawa used the *I Ching* to assert that Japan was a divine nation: "Our Divine Realm lies to the east, in the direction of the sun. The *Book of Changes* says, 'Emperors emerge from the East.' The East corresponds to wood and is appropriate for cultivating grains."[62] In response to the intrusion from the West, he commented: "The way of heaven is to respect *yang* and despise *yin.* The earth is in the center of the universe. The East is the beginning [head] and is in the position of *yang.* The West is the end [tail] and is in the position of *yin.* Compared to China, the Land of the Gods [Japan] faces closer to *yang* and is in a respectable location."[63] Hence the concepts of the *I Ching* became an inspiration for modern nationalism and pan-Asianism.

Fujita Tōko (1806–1855) submitted his reform proposal to Mito domain in 1830. He described the hexagram *t'ai* and asked the new daimyō of Mito domain to choose talented men, to keep close contact with the people, and to maintain their well-being. He argued:

The *I Ching* uses the hexagram earth-heaven, *t'ai,* to refer to a world with the Way, and the hexagram heaven-earth, *p'i,* to a world without the Way. Heaven is up above and earth is down below, and therefore we might think that the world with the Way should be represented by heaven-earth. However, why did [the sages] arrange the hexagram as earth-heaven [and not heaven-earth]? The reason is that although heaven is high, it provides the light of the sun and moon, and the moisture of rain and dew to the ground. Although earth is humble, it provides cloud and fog, and makes the grass and tree grow. The air [on the ground] always rises. The air *(ch'i)* of heaven and earth meet and mix, and give birth to everything. If heaven climbs up and earth falls down, nothing can survive even a day.[64]

Sakuma Shōzan (1811–1864) advocated reforms in his explanation of an augury. In 1864, Hitotsubashi Nobuyoshi (1837–1913) asked Sakuma to analyze the current situation in Japan by using the oracles. The result was the hexagram *ku* (decay). Sakuma explained that the image of this hexagram was like a bowl containing worms, and that it served as a metaphor of warning for the nation. He explained: "If one uses vessels and bowls for a long time, they will give rise to worms; if the body indulges in too much banqueting, it will become ill; if a realm is idle or inactive, it will produce abuses. All of this must be decay."[65] He knew that tradition and ancestral law were no longer sufficient to solve the problems of present-day Japan, and thus urged Hitotsubashi to implement reforms according to the principles of the *I Ching*. He stated:

> If there exists disturbance and decay, it is a principle that order must be restored. From antiquity it has been a natural principle for political tranquillity to follow prevalent disorder, and for disorder to follow the creation of tranquillity. [The *I Ching* reads:] "If one investigates, one will achieve change; when one changes, he will pass over to prosperity.". . . If one observes profound difficulties and is overcome by fear, he will not advance; if one stops short in idleness and inaction, he will end in decay and disorder.[66]

Reformism had the potential to become an anti-bakufu ideology. When the chorus for reform was ignored by the bakufu, more and more reformers assumed an anti-bakufu stance. This happened during the last two decades of the Tokugawa period. When we examine the writings of late Tokugawa intellectuals, we gain the impression that it was Confucianism, not other intellectual forces, that provided the major framework, logic, and spirit for the Meiji Restoration.

In the writings of late Tokugawa loyalists, there were many discussions of the meaning of the hexagram *fu* (return, or restoration). This hexagram suggests that it is the time for *yang* to return. Its reads: "Return. Success. Going out and coming in without error"; "Return has success. The firm returns. Movement and action through devotion. . . . In the hexagram of *fu*, one sees the minds of heaven and earth"; "Noblehearted return. No remorse"; "Missing the return. Misfortune."[67] This hexagram seems to have provided some loyalists with the logic for advocating a restoration, and with the belief that restoration was historically inevitable. We investigate several loyalists who were inspired by this hexagram.

Kusumoto Tanzan (1828–1883) discussed this hexagram with his teacher and friend Ōhashi Totsuan (1816–1862) in a letter. He wrote:

> Recently, when I was carefully reading the hexagram *fu,* I realized something about the first (or bottom) line where *yang* comes back. The 364 lines of the *Chou I* begin with this line, and it also has the word *"jen"* (benevolence). I deeply believe that there is something important here. Undoubtedly, it shows that the principle of love is sympathy. One *yang* comes out from the area of all *yin* in the first line. It moves slightly but vigorously. This is the purest, the best, and the most interesting thing. The root of every goodness is inside it.[68]

These lines emphasize the goodness of *yang* returning to the original position to carry out the rule of benevolence. If Kusumoto's idea was perhaps too abstract, then his friend Ogasawara Keisai was more explicit and provocative in using this hexagram to discuss late Tokugawa politics. Ogasawara wrote:

> To explain to the commoners the *I Ching,* I added *katakana* [to my book,] in which I have severely criticized the shortcomings of the bakufu and condemned the evils of overlords. Sometimes my assertions might be too radical, but if I am prosecuted for doing this, I am willing to accept it. . . . As for the rulers, if they want to save the nation from collapsing, or want to govern the nation to stop disorder, they are not without the means. Heaven regards life as a virtue, and does not want [to see the nation in] chaos. If the emperor shakes himself up, and seeks sound government by declaring policies to implement benevolence, then his will shall match the universe. If his will fits the heavenly will, then heavenly decisions can be changed. Therefore, [the hexagram *fu*] reads: "Return from a short distance. No need for remorse." Nowadays, if people discuss politics by only stressing historical trends, and overlook [the power of] will, they are not qualified to lecture on the *I Ching.*[69]

He was optimistic that things could be fixed if the emperor came to power and carried out the way of benevolence.

The most famous loyalist, Yoshida Shōin (1830–1859), also drew on the *I Ching* to express his anti-bakufu opinions. According to Shimohodo Yūkichi, Yoshida's *shishi* morality was inspired by his reading of the text.[70] The hexagram *k'an* (the abysmal) became the motto of his life, cited numerous times by Yoshida. It reads: "If you are sincere, you have success in your heart, and whatever you do succeeds."[71] Influenced by its romantic elements, Yoshida saw success as something that exists within our hearts and that cannot be judged by results alone. A few months before his execution, he wrote a poem to express his *sonnō* idea by quoting the hexagram *chien* (obstruction). The text gave him strength to face death. The hexagram reads: "The king's servant is beset by obstruction upon obstruction, but it is not his own fault."[72] Yoshida's poem contained this line: "Royal subjects die for the nation. Although they are beset by obstruction upon obstruction, they only devote themselves to the cause [of the nation]."[73]

Studying the *I Ching* in prison was a common practice in China and Japan. Yoshida spent his last days reading the text in prison. He composed this poem:

> With nothing to do in prison,
> I contemplate the principles of the *I Ching*
> to understand the philosophy of change.
> Through the hole of this broken hut,
> sometimes I look up and watch the clouds floating.[74]

He placed two books—the *Chou-i chuan-i* (Combination of Chu Hsi and Ch'eng I's Commentaries on the *I Ching*, edited by Tung Kai) and *I-hsüeh ch'i-meng* (Instructions to the Young on the *I Ching*, by Chu Hsi) —beside his pillow in the cell.

Yoshida's political ideas were shaped by the *I Ching* to a considerable extent. For instance, he advocated *ikan* as a political ideal and suggested abolishing the trivial forms of etiquette that alienated subjects from the ruler. For the same reason, he criticized the alternate attendance system. He was also very critical of the domestic and foreign policies of the bakufu. In 1851, he used the hexagram *po* (splitting apart) to analyze the crises in Japan. He said: "The mean plans of the aliens contribute to strange events in Japan. The situation is like the splitting of the leg of a bed [as described in the *I Ching*]. Ordinary officials and old-fashioned Confucians are not qualified to discuss this. People who pursue the way of military affairs must not be indifferent. We should worry about this situation."[75]

In 1858, Yoshida cited a passage from the *Hsi Tz'u* to criticize the bakufu for being too dictatorial and refusing to listen to advice from the court and daimyō. Finally, he called for the destruction of the bakufu. Again he quoted from the *I Ching* to show that the anti-bakufu movement would be successful, both because loyalists were imbued with the power of loyalty *(gi)* and because the timing *(toki)* was right.[76]

The harmony of the *shishi* spirit and the *I Ching* was echoed by

Yoshida's top student, Takasugi Shinsaku (1837–1867). In 1864, Takasugi thought he was going to be executed and composed the following poem to demonstrate his will while he was in jail:

> I have so many grievances that I want to cut my breast out [to show them].
> I have learned how to distinguish evils and dangers from the
> *I Ching.*
> From ancient times to the present, gentlemen have died for loyalty.
> Unfortunately, they have not been recognized by the people.[77]

Concluding Remarks

This chapter has discussed three old topics of Tokugawa history—the legitimization of the bakufu, the naturalization of Confucianism, and the intellectual origins of the Meiji Restoration—from a new perspective, namely, the textual analysis of Tokugawa writings about the *I Ching* and politics.

The *I Ching* played an important role in the history of political thought in Tokugawa Japan. The principles of the text did not contain any necessary links to either pro-bakufu or anti-bakufu ideas, so people were able to interpret the book differently to serve their own political purposes. Early Tokugawa intellectuals used the text to support the legitimation of the Tokugawa bakufu. They pointed out that the *bakuhan* system and its power distribution and social hierarchy were in agreement with the principles of the *I Ching*. The early shoguns also promoted *I Ching* studies to cultivate a new political ethic and to enhance their authority, whereas late Tokugawa intellectuals employed the text to advocate a restoration of power to the imperial house. The text's philosophy and logic contributed to reformist, anti-bakufu, and loyalist ideologies, indicating that Confucianism provided the intellectual underpinning for the Meiji Restoration.

In addition, throughout the Tokugawa period, Chinese political ideas were adapted to suit the Japanese setting. Tokugawa Confucians naturalized Confucianism in their explanations of the *I Ching*, developing several devices to achieve this goal, such as transplantation, editing, distortion, downplaying, and extension. The Japanese interpretation of the text provided the Tokugawa Japanese with political doctrines and also with a system of ethics. Elements from both these arenas seem to have survived even into the modern period.

5. The *I Ching* and Economic Thought

Economics was perhaps the weak part of Tokugawa *keizai* (economic) thought.[1] Few if any Tokugawa economic scholars matched the caliber of Adam Smith (1723–1790) or Karl Marx (1818–1883). In the area of theory, most Tokugawa intellectuals simply applied the *yin-yang* principle to agriculture and business. They were primarily concerned with practical and basic economic issues, such as agricultural productivity and the accumulation of wealth. The main sources of Tokugawa economic thought were Chinese; native and Western learning played a less significant role.[2]

As an integral part of Chinese learning, the *I Ching* played a significant part in the formation of Tokugawa economic thought. This chapter investigates the role of the *I Ching* in the discussion of agriculture and business through a textual analysis of Tokugawa writings. It focuses on economic matters, so political, social, and ethical issues of agriculture and business are not highlighted. Because the Tokugawa economy was basically agricultural, this chapter is more detailed in its analysis of agriculture than of business.

The *I Ching* in Tokugawa Agriculture

The *I Ching*, agriculture, calendrical studies, geomancy, astronomy, and divination were woven together in traditional China. The *yin-yang wu-hsing* theory in the *I Ching* system influenced agricultural practices and ideas. The theory is omnipresent in Chinese agricultural writings, whether or not it serves as the central philosophy. Because the Japanese did not produce their own agricultural writings until the Tokugawa period, little is known about agricultural thought in ancient and medieval Japan. Chinese agricultural literature came to Japan in the Heian period, and the *yin-yang wu-hsing* theory seems to have penetrated medieval agriculture.[3] Influenced by Chinese scholarship, Tokugawa agricultural writings used the *yin-yang wu-hsing* principle extensively. Iinuma Jirō, a historian of Japanese agriculture, notes that the application of the *yin-yang wu-hsing* doctrine was a characteristic of agricultural studies in Tokugawa Japan.[4] This section investigates the role of the doctrine in the discussion of agriculture through an analysis of Tokugawa writings, focusing on the impact of topography, soil, climate, labor, and technology on agricultural productivity.

The seventeenth century saw a boom in Japanese agricultural studies. For the first time, the Japanese produced their own agricultural works and attempted to discuss agriculture within the context of Tokugawa Japan. Two agricultural classics were created in early Tokugawa Japan: the *Hyakushō denki* (Records of the Peasant, 1682, 15 *kan*) and *Nōgyō zensho* (An Anthology of Agriculture, 1697, 10 *kan*). Both employed *yin-yang wu-hsing* as the theoretical framework for comprehensive and insightful discussions.

The *Hyakushō denki* (author unknown), praised by a modern Japanese historian as the best agricultural book in pre-Meiji Japan, is a very useful guide to every detail of the lives of the peasantry.[5] It stresses Confucian morality and metaphysics and uses the *yin-yang wu-hsing* doctrine extensively in its explanations. The *Hyakushō denki* set the precedent for Tokugawa agricultural works of applying the principles of the *I Ching* to show Japan's geographical superiority over other nations. It bases its arguments on the *yin-yang wu-hsing* theory—and on inaccurate geographical and astronomical information—and also appeals to readers' patriotic sentiments. It argues that because of the rotation of the sun and the moon, the Northwest part of the globe is *yin*, which is too cold for agriculture, whereas the Southeast is *yang*, which is ideal for agriculture because it has plenty of sunlight and a mild temperature. Japan, the book claims, is the only nation located at the center of the Southeast, and thus it enjoys the best agricultural environment in the world:

> In regard to this world, the Northwest is a huge land. Since it receives less from the sun and the moon, it is extremely cold and very difficult for things to grow and ripen [there]. The Southeast is a narrow "treasure land" that receives plenty from the sun and the moon. It is full of

the *yang* force, and thus everything can grow and ripen. Among nations of the Southeast, only Japan has its entire territory inside the East and the Eastern Ocean. Hence its growing and ripening environment exceeds [those of] all foreign nations.[6]

In addition, the *Hyakushō denki* employs the *wu-hsing* principle of promotion and control to explain why the insularity of Japan makes it a *yang* nation rich in natural resources:

> Japan has much water. Since water promotes wood, an abundance of water causes plants to thrive. Since wood promotes fire, thriving plants produce the rich supply of the *yang* force. Since fire promotes earth, the strong *yang* force produces a large quantity of soil. The soil is thick and plentiful, and therefore our nation is rich in gold [because earth promotes metal].[7]

The book is characterized by its preference for *yang* over *yin*. Determining the *yin-yang* nature of a land is one of its central themes, because choosing a *yang* land is the first key to success. Associating *yang* with the Southeast and the flatlands, and *yin* with the Northwest and the mountains, the author—probably a rural scholar from Eastern Honshū—believed that the Kantō plain and the Tōkai region were the most fertile lands in Japan.[8] But how does one determine the fertility of soil? The author applied the *wu-hsing* theory, which identified the five agents (earth, metal, fire, wood, and water) with the five colors (yellow, white, red, green, and black) to analyze soil quality. Soils with these five colors were considered to be high in quality, and their order of fertility was the same as that of the five colors.[9]

The *Hyakushō denki* uses the *yin-yang wu-hsing* interpretative framework but sometimes modifies it to accommodate the peculiarities of Japan. According to the Chinese tradition, the annual circular movement of *yin-yang* in the Chinese lunar calendar means that the winter solstice comes in December. This is represented by a hexagram with five *yin* lines at the top and one *yang* line at the bottom ䷗. *Yang* increases by one line each month, until a state of full *yang* is reached in May ䷀. From June on, one *yin* is added to the bottom monthly, so that a state of full *yin* is reached in November ䷁. Cultivation and harvest of different crops must accord with the *yin-yang* nature of each crop. Realizing the climatic difference between China and Japan, the author modified the whole cycle by pushing it forward one month. This means that the winter solstice arrives in November, and so on.[10] The author regarded spring and summer as the best seasons in which to farm because *yang* is ascendant; his ignorance of autumn and winter crops is an obvious shortcoming of the book.[11]

The *Nōgyō zensho* was a classic of Japanese science as well as agriculture. It is commonly viewed as the finest, most comprehensive, and most influential agricultural book in pre-modern Japan. Its author, Miyazaki Yasusada (1623–1697), was a *rōnin* (masterless warrior) turned peasant from Fukuoka domain. Relying heavily on Hsu Kuang-ch'i's (1562–1633) *Nung-ch'eng ch'üan-shu* (An Anthology of Agricultural Policies, 1639) and other Chinese texts, Miyazaki used the *yin-yang* theory frequently throughout his book. He was also influenced by Kaibara Ekken's (1630–1714) scholarship on botany, which used the *yin-yang wu-hsing* doctrine to categorize and analyze different plants in Japan. Kaibara Ekken wrote the preface for, and his brother Rakuken edited, Miyazaki's *Nōgyō zensho*.

There are two distinguishable theoretical differences between the *Hyakushō denki* and the *Nōgyō zensho*. First, the former prefers *yang* to *yin*, whereas the latter pursues the harmony of *yin* and *yang*. This difference also illustrates the two major approaches, or schools, of the *yin-yang* theory. Second, the former uses the concepts of *yin-yang* and *wu-hsing* extensively, while the latter seldom mentions the idea of *wu-hsing*. These differences in basic assumptions lead to some interesting contrasts. For instance, although both books claim Japan's geographical superiority over other nations, the *Hyakushō denki* points out that Japan is a land of *yang* because it is located in the Southeast, whereas the *Nōgyō zensho* states that Japan enjoys the harmony of *yin* and *yang* because it lies between the Northern and Southern hemispheres:

> The land of Japan lies between the North and the South of the world. It enjoys the right combination of the forces of *yin* and *yang* and a mild temperature. It suffers basically no natural disasters from either heaven or earth. It has wide plains and fields suitable for the cultivation of rice and wheat.[12]

Miyazaki believed that *yin* and *yang* circulate endlessly in the universe, and that one should seek to achieve a balance of the two in agriculture. Thus he denied the basic premise of the *Hyakushō denki* and remarked: "The coordination of the rise and fall of *yin-yang* will promote budding. We should not lose the balance [between *yin* and *yang*]. Solely relying on one aspect is contrary to the heart of heaven."[13] Like the *Hyakushō denki*, Miyazaki identified the Southeast with *yang* and the Northwest with *yin*. However, he did not regard the land of *yin* as agriculturally less valuable and pointed out that some plants, such as tea, are more fit for *yin* land. In terms of humidity, he treated dry land as *yang* and wet land as *yin*. Since excessive *yin* and excessive *yang* are equally unwanted in agriculture, he suggested using wet night soil for dry land and dry night soil for wet land to achieve the harmony of *yin* and *yang*.[14] For the same reason, he suggested directing water (which is *yin*) into land where the *yang* level is too high.[15]

The use of the *yin-yang* theory in these two agricultural classics represents a continuation of the East Asian cultural tradition, and should be understood as an attempt to apply rational explanation to agricultural issues in pre-modern times. Neither the *Hyakushō denki* nor the *Nōgyō zensho* advocates superstitious practices and ideas, such as divination, geomancy, or Onmyōdō rituals.

Most other early Tokugawa agricultural texts were also influenced by the *yin-yang wu-hsing* theory. A notable work that appeared soon after the two classics was the *Kōka shunjū* (Cultivation and Harvest in Spring and Autumn, 1709, 7 *kan*). The author, Tsuchiya Matasaburō (1642–1719), a regional official of Kaga domain, extensively cited Chinese texts and the *Nōgyō zensho* in his discussions of agriculture in Western Honshū. Accepting the traditional Chinese view that the *I Ching*, astronomy, and calendrical studies were derived from the same principle, Tsuchiya urged the peasants to understand and apply them in farming. He wrote:

> The *I Ching* is the natural principle. Calendrical studies is an astronomical skill, whereas the theory of the five agents and the six climatic factors is an application of astronomy. Hence the *I Ching*, calendrical studies, and the theory of the five agents and the six climatic factors are said to share a common origin. Officials have to study them. If capable farmers contemplate the relationship between these subjects, they will surely reach the same conclusion that I have.[16]

In brief, early Tokugawa scholars successfully established Japan's agricultural studies. Although they were heavily influenced by Chinese scholarship, they attempted to accommodate Chinese theories to the Japanese setting. Their ideas demonstrate a high level of sophistication and a national consciousness. In particular, the *Hyakushō denki* and *Nōgyō zensho* exerted a far-reaching impact on Tokugawa agriculture.

The excellence of these early texts made late Tokugawa times almost an anti-climactic period in agricultural studies. Despite the emergence of a large number of writings in late Tokugawa times, very few could match the scholarship of their predecessors. Many of these were interpretations, condensations, or interpolations of earlier Tokugawa and Chinese scholarship. In general, the *yin-yang wu-hsing* theory maintained its influence in late-Tokugawa agricultural studies.[17]

There was a spontaneous popular movement to improve agriculture in late Tokugawa times. Leaders of this movement came from various backgrounds and included bakufu retainers, regional officials, peasants, *kokugaku* scholars, and *rōnin*. They left many records of their ideas and activities. We examine some of their writings to see how they used the *I Ching* to advocate agricultural and rural reforms.

Under the auspices of the bakufu, Hayakawa Hachirō, a bakufu retainer, suggested ways to improve productivity in his *Kyūsei jōkyō* (Teaching for Many Generations, 1700, 7 *kan*). This book, which was similar in nature and style to the *Liu yü yen-i* (*Rokuyu engi*, Amplification of the Six Maxims), was comprised of six maxims and their interpretations.[18] It was written in simple language so that regional officials could read it aloud to the peasants throughout the year. Its agricultural ideas seem to have come mainly from earlier texts, such as the *Hyakushō denki* and *Nōgyō zensho*. The first chapter, entitled "Kannōsō" (Encouraging Agriculture), discusses methods of cultivating different crops and uses the principles of the *I Ching* to enhance the authority and interest of its arguments. Identifying the principles of the *I Ching* with the natural law that could determine and explain everything in agriculture, the book encourages the peasants to study the text's philosophy and divination and to employ these to agriculture:

> Now, when we study the principles [of the *I Ching*], [we know that] wheat is *yang* and rice is *yin*. Understanding this essence of agriculture to grow these two plants, and following ancient methods and the change in hexagrams and lines of the *I Ching*, are good [for the farmers]. However, farmers do not know these things and only associate the *I Ching* with divination. They should understand the *yin-yang* theory of change because undoubtedly the way of agriculture is also subject to the same principle. As mentioned, I want to teach the farmers that when they grow and harvest wheat and rice, they can understand important things in agriculture through the hexagrams [of the *I Ching*] and the lines [of the hexagrams].[19]

This chapter even holds that the principles of the *I Ching* could also be applied to industry and commerce.

The "Kannōsō" focuses on two major crops in Japan: wheat and rice. Identifying wheat as a *yang* crop and rice as a *yin* crop, it explains their complementary growing seasons in detail. It points out that the growing season of wheat is from October to April, following the increase of *yang* from zero to six, as represented by hexagrams of the *I Ching*:

> In this month [October], we sow the seeds of wheat on the ground where *yang* begins to grow. November brings the winter solstice, represented by the hexagram *fu* ䷗ (return). While a single *yang* begins to rise from the earth, wheat buds. December is the hexagram *lin* ䷒ (approach), which has two *yang* lines. January is the hexagram *t'ai* ䷊ (peace), which has three *yang* lines. February is the hexagram *ta chuang* ䷡ (power of the Great), which has four *yang* lines. March is the hexagram *kuai* ䷪ (breakthrough), which has five *yang* lines. Accordingly, wheat grows as *yang* increases gradually. April is the hexagram *ch'ien* ䷀ (creation), when *yang* reaches its peak. *Yang ch'i* makes the wheat ripe and the land dry.[20]

Likewise, the growth of rice follows the rise of *yin* from May to October. One plants rice sprouts in May, when there is only one *yin* line. It grows steadily after June and becomes ripe in October, when *yin* peaks. The book also discusses the impact of *yin-yang wu-hsing* on the colors of wheat and rice. This *yin-yang* interpretation of the growth of wheat and rice was largely borrowed from some Chinese and early Tokugawa texts. Thanks to the *Kyūsei jōkyō* and other agricultural writings, the agricultural application of the *yin-yang wu-hsing* theory gained wider currency among Confucian scholars in nineteenth-century Japan.[21]

This semi-official work was used widely in Central and Eastern Honshū, and spread *yin-yang* agricultural thought to the peasantry. Its brevity allowed peasants and local officials to make copies. Tokuyama Keimō (1761–?) even included the whole first scroll of the *Kyūsei jōkyō* in his *Nōgyō shison yōiku kusa* (A Manuscript for My Offspring on Agriculture, 1826).[22] A commentary on the *Kyūsei jōkyō*, entitled the *Jōkyō danwa* (A Discussion on the *Kyūsei jōkyō*, author unknown), appeared in 1834 and was well received.

Ishida Harunori (1757–1826), a local official from Central Japan, wrote an important book, the *Hyakushō kashokunomoto* (The Essence of Agriculture for Peasants, 1819), that was an attempt to fuse traditional agricultural wisdom with *I Ching* philosophy and Shinto. Ishida used the theories of *yin-yang wu-hsing* and the hexagrams to articulate his agricultural views. First, he used the *wu-hsing* theory to support his idea of agrarianism. Identifying agriculture with the agent of earth, which was located in the middle and which supported the other four agents, he emphasized that agriculture played a central role in the economy.

Second, Ishida applied the *wu-hsing* theory to analyze the soil in Japan. Citing a passage from the *Nihon shoki* to prove that Japanese soil was fertile and that Japan had five kinds of top-quality soil, he used the idea of *wu-hsing* to illustrate the distribution and ranking of the soil in Japan: one found yellow soil in the center of Japan, white soil in the West, red soil in the South, green soil in the East, and black soil in the North.[23] It is not difficult to understand why he claimed that his homeland, Central Honshū, had the best soil.

Third, Ishida believed that people could understand the natural principle through the *I Ching*. He even pointed out that both the *I Ching* and the ancient Chinese land system, the well-field system, shared the same principle because they were both created by the sages in accordance with the natural principle.[24]

Unlike Hayakawa and Ishida, most agricultural scholars had neither positions nor direct links to the bakufu and regional administrations. Thus we also investigate some peasant-scholars and their application of the *yin-yang wu-hsing* doctrine to agriculture.

The Hirata school of *kokugaku* not only claimed that the *I Ching* was a Shinto text but also applied it in agriculture. It produced two major agricultural scholars: Ko'nishi Atsuyoshi (1767–1834) and Tamura Yoshishige (1790–1877). Hirata Atsutane praised them, calling them the two agricultural experts from two sides of Japan who were imbued with the spirit of Japanese deities.[25] Regardless of their nativist affiliation, these two scholars seem to have been influenced more by *yin-yang* theory than by Shinto ideas in the formation of their agricultural thought.

Ko'nishi Atsuyoshi, a farmer from the Osaka area, wrote the famous *Nōgyō yowa* (Discursive Talks on Agriculture, 1828, 2 *kan*), which was read by Hirata Atsutane and collated by his son Atsumasa; Kanetane, Atsutane's adopted son, wrote an afterword. Nor was it an accident that a famous *I Ching* scholar, Inoue Roshū, wrote the preface. This popular book was first published in 1828, and was followed by a number of modified and condensed versions.[26] Ko'nishi was invited by a number of daimyō to visit and spread his teaching. The eleventh shogun, Ienari (1772–1841), even sent him a letter of appreciation.

The *Nogyō yowa* was a description of Ko'nishi's agricultural philosophy based on his own farming experiences. His theoretical narrative developed *yin-yang wu-hsing* thought into a sophisticated and original interpretative framework. In it, he attributed his success in experimental cultivation to the principle of *yin-yang wu-hsing:* "Following the principle of *yin-yang,* I experimented with its application and acquired fruitful results. Now I write them down roughly to teach my offspring."[27]

The point of the book was to show how the forces of *yin* and *yang* penetrate every aspect of agriculture. By knowing the *yin-yang* nature of a crop, one could fix conditions and choose methods and seasons appropriate for cultivating it. *Yin* plants grow better during *yin* seasons, while *yang* plants grow better during *yang* seasons. Ko'nishi even believed that both *yin* and *yang* exist in a plant, even if the plant primarily represents one force, suggesting that the stem, trunk, and leaves are *yin* and the root *yang.* According to his analysis, *yang* parts grow better in spring and summer, while *yin* parts grow better in autumn and winter.

Ko'nishi observed that the forces of *yin* and *yang* in the universe are in a state of circular flux. To understand and predict this change was a crucial aspect of being successful in agriculture. On a large scale, he saw a bumper-crop–lean-year cycle following changes in the balance of *yin* and *yang* in the universe: "*Yin* and *yang* in the universe rise and fall and come and go. They never stop for a moment. Their principle is to change in a thousand times and refuse to settle in one place. The cycle of bumper year and lean year is like this."[28]

Table 9: Ko'nishi's *Yin-Yang* Classification System

Nature/ Item	Attributes	Climate	Agents	Agriculture
Yang	up, right, surface, male, birds and animals, odd, open, light	spring, summer, warm, hot, dry	fire, wood	wood, leaf, bud
Yin	down, left, inner, female, insects and fishes, even, close, heavy	autumn, winter, cool, cold, humid	water, metal	grass, root, seed

Although the large cycle is difficult to see, the small scale is easier to ascertain. Ko'nishi held that there is a daily rise and fall of *yin* and *yang*; odd-numbered days are *yang*, and even-numbered days are *yin*. Choosing a proper day to cultivate difficult crops and do the right job is extremely important. For instance, sowing on a *yin* day would bring poor results:

> We must choose the right day to do sowing. *Yang* days, such as the first, third, and fifth, are good for sowing. During *yin* days, such as the second, fourth, and sixth, we should avoid sowing. Sometimes sowing on *yin* days will bring bitter taste, but sowing on *yang* days will bring good taste.[29]

Ko'nishi also used the *yin-yang wu-hsing* theory to explain the growing conditions of the four seasons and the reasons, in general, that plants and crops grow faster in spring and summer than in autumn and winter. First, he said, the function of *yang* is to help growth, whereas the function of *yin* is to help shape. Since spring and summer are *yang*, crops grow faster. Second, he argued that the four seasons belong to different agents in *wu-hsing* and thus have different functions: spring (wood, growing), summer (fire, fruiting), autumn (metal, rooting), and winter (water, storing).

Tamura Yoshishige, a farmer from the Northern Kantō area, was the author of the *Nōgyō jitoku* (Self-Actualization in Agriculture, 1856, 2 *kan*). Hirata Atsutane edited the writing style of this book, gave it its title, wrote the preface, and had his son Atsumasa collate it. The book contains many original ideas and useful suggestions. Its content and ideas are somewhat similar to those of the *Nōgyō yowa*. Like many agricultural scholars, Tamura believed that agriculture is subject to the natural law of *yin-yang wu-hsing*. His personal success during the famine years of 1833 and 1836 convinced him that he should write down his understanding of the natural principle. He recalled: "I have liked agriculture since my youth. I have worked hard without any distractions and have planted different types of crops, grasses, and trees. I understand the principles of the universe, *yin-yang wu-hsing*, and nature in farming."[30]

One of the secrets of Tamura's success was his ability to distinguish the *yin-yang* nature of the land. He divided paddy fields into two major groups: *yang* fields and *yin* fields. Dry fields and hot fields are *yang* fields, which are good for early crops, whereas wet fields and cold fields are *yin* fields, which are good for late crops.[31]

Tamura concluded that a bumper year and a lean year usually come one after another, following the rise and fall of *yin-yang* in the universe; that the worst situation is an excessive supply of *yin*, which guarantees a lean year; and that a serious famine year will occur every thirty to fifty years. He remarked: "The general pattern of good and bad years is one good year, and one bad year. It is subject to the principle of *yin-yang*. If *yin* is overwhelming, a bumper year is unlikely."[32]

To predict their agricultural prospects, Tamura asked the peasants to keep yearly climatic records, paying special attention to the previous year and the early months of the current year. For instance, he pointed out that large snows in the previous year will bring a bumper year because snow is *yin*, which can protect the *yang ch'i* of the soil from being lost during the winter. When summer comes, *yang ch'i* becomes very active and abundant in the soil. The summer heat then releases that *yang ch'i*, which promotes farming, and the melting snow brings moisture to the soil.[33] If the sky is covered with light clouds when the cherry blossoms bloom, the current year will also be a bumper year because this indicates the release of *yang ch'i* from the soil, which warms and nourishes the soil and humidifies the air.[34] To understand the variation of *yin* and *yang* in nature, Tamura also urged peasants to observe the growth and habits of animals, birds, and plants.

Keeping and utilizing *yang ch'i* is a major topic of the book. Winter is the time to store *yang ch'i* in the earth. Tamura explained: "The winter solstice is a time of great *yin*, when *yang ch'i* enters and warms the earth. Animals, insects, fish, grass, and trees all absorb *yang ch'i* into their bodies, which are surrounded by *yin ch'i*. They are nourished by the inner warmth, and therefore are strong and healthy."[35] Summer is the time when *yang ch'i* is released from the earth. When *yang ch'i* (represented by fire) brings warmth to the soil and meets *yin ch'i* (represented by water) in the air, the ideal growing condition is created: "In the winter, *yang ch'i* enters the earth. In the summer, *yang ch'i* rises to the surface. Fire is great *yang;* water is great *yin*. Their mixing gives birth to everything. Nothing can grow against this principle."[36]

Not all rural reformers wrote down their agricultural philosophy and blueprints for reform. Many were activists who visited villages and helped peasants improve their productivity and livelihood. We can understand the role of the *I Ching* in the thought and action of these activists through records of their lives and work. Ōhara Yūgaku (1797–1858) is a good example. Ōhara was a charismatic rural reformer who frequently claimed authority from the divination of the *I Ching*. Having studied the divination of the Arai (Hakuga) school in Kyoto, he traveled around rural areas implementing agricultural reforms. Believing that it could enhance their material and spiritual lives, Ōhara taught village people the ideas of the *I Ching* and their ethical and economic implications. Based on the ideas of *yin-yang* and *wu-hsing,* he employed his knowledge of geomancy and divination to designate every two households in a village as a mutual cooperative unit and to determine the location of houses, paddy fields, and irrigation facilities.[37]

To summarize, late-Tokugawa agricultural scholars were concerned with practical issues and thus produced few works of originality and scholarship. The *yin-yang wu-hsing* doctrine became a theoretical tool that they used to suggest ways to improve Japanese agricultural practices and increase productivity. This doctrine was an integral part of Tokugawa agricultural thought, and its influence was very strong during the entire period. Many agricultural scholars developed their ideas within the *yin-yang wu-hsing* framework, even though these ideas varied. Both the philosophy of the *I Ching* and the use of its hexagrams in divination played a considerable role in Tokugawa agriculture. In particular, the philosophy of the *I Ching* was associated with the natural principle and became a very powerful concept.

Some Tokugawa scholars were faithful to Chinese concepts, while others attempted to modify those concepts to accommodate Japan's agricultural conditions. However, most scholars generally agreed that the *yin-yang wu-hsing* doctrine was a universal principle applicable to both China and Japan. In the rich Tokugawa agricultural tradition, this doctrine was not a part of speculative, abstract discussions but was a basic interpretative framework that was used to explain the details of agricultural practices and to suggest ways of increasing productivity. Unlike medicine, astronomy, and military science, agriculture was almost immune to Western influence during the Tokugawa period, so this Tokugawa agricultural heritage survived into modern times.[38]

The *I Ching* in Tokugawa Industry and Commerce

The role of the *I Ching* in the development of Tokugawa business practices is a nebulous one. Despite the emergence of an undercurrent of commercialism, the prevalent attitude among Confucians remained disapproving. It was unthinkable that an orthodox Confucian might write a book on methods of increasing the profitability of a business venture. Hence most business-related writings in this period were confined to the topics of political economy, commercial ethics, and personal or familial matters, with relatively few discussions of business management and economic theory. I nevertheless attempt to demonstrate the role of the *I Ching* in Tokugawa commerce and industry vis-à-vis two of its facets—divination and theory.

Using divination in business was very popular among Tokugawa merchants. There are many records that attest to the fact that merchants made investments by following the oracles of the *I Ching*, and *I Ching* diviners who specialized in business affairs had appeared by the mid-Tokugawa period. The most sensational was Daikokuya Yoshiji, who became a financial consultant to Kyoto merchants. His name and divination records were frequently found in Tokugawa *zuihitsu* ("loose," or miscellaneous, prose) writings. However, the most interesting story about business divination is about the beginning of Daimaru. According to a late Tokugawa record, the founder of the enterprise, Daimaru Shōemon, stole money on the street and began his business by investing it in accord with advice from an *I Ching* diviner.[39]

When business oracles became very popular, some people began to worry and urged merchants to stop this practice. Their advice is evidence of the prevalence of *I Ching* divination in Tokugawa business. For instance, Nishikawa Joken condemned the use of *I Ching* divination in business as a departure from the heavenly principle in his *Chōnin bukuro* (Secrets for Merchants, 1719),[40] while Shōji Kōki (1787–1857), a merchant-scholar, pointed out that the secrets of business success lay in proper judgment and determination, not in oracles:

> Some people use *I Ching* divination to make business moves. The sages did not create the *I Ching* for pursuing personal desires by fortune-telling. Since business is a lifetime career, one should know how to make profits and do the right thing when in doubt. For merchants, making decisive judgments is the most important quality.[41]

But such warnings were largely ignored. Commercial divination manuals mushroomed starting in the mid-Tokugawa period. Some even became best-sellers and were reprinted many times. Nagasaki Nobukuni, for example, used the ideas of *wu-hsing* and the eight trigrams to predict monthly business situations in his *Nichiyō shōhakka* (The Daily Use of the Eight Trigrams for Business, 1761).

Specialization was another barometer of divination's popularity. A famous *I Ching* diviner, Inoue Kakushū, wrote the *Bokuzei kashoku kō* (Divination of Price Fluctuations, 1845), which uses the images of the sixty-four hexagrams to predict the price fluctuations in the rice market. In it he explains, for example, that the hexagram *ch'ien* means that the rice price is at the ceiling and will soon fall because six *yang* cannot last long and *yin* is bound to come.[42]

In the development of modern industry and commerce, both the philosophy of change and divination seem to have given early entrepreneurs wisdom and confidence. Takashima Donshō (1832–1914), "the sage of *I Ching* divination," was perhaps the most striking example of this. The son of an Edo timber merchant, he was sent to jail for breaking the bakufu's business regulations. Having found a way of doing business from reading the *I Ching* in jail, Takashima accumulated a fortune by cooperating with foreigners in the construction industry and timber trade after his release. He gave financial backing to the anti-bakufu troops and maintained intimate personal ties with *ishin* (Meiji Restoration) leaders like Ōkubo Toshimichi (1830–1878), Kido Takayoshi (1833–1877), and Itō Hirobumi (1841–1909). After the Restoration, he invested in modern industries such as electrical supplies, railways, farms, and iron and steel works.

As a semi-official businessman and a skillful diviner, Takashima also exerted considerable influence on Meiji politics. In his autobiography, *Takashima Kauemon jijoden* (The Autobiography of Takashima Kauemon), he attributed his success in industry and commerce to the principles he found in the *I Ching*. He particularly liked using the divination methods of the Arai (Hakuga) school to make business decisions.

The philosophy of the *I Ching* also played a role in the thought and practice of Tokugawa industry and commerce. Some people actually applied the *yin-yang wu-hsing* doctrine to their specialized field of industry. For example, Kurosawa Motoshige used it to discuss mining in his *Kōsan shihō yōroku* (Records of Ultimate Treasures in Mining, 1691). He described how to distinguish the *yin* and *yang* of a mountain, and held that only *yin* mountains had mining resources.[43] Kurosawa divided the quality of metal into five types according to *wu-hsing*: gold (yellow), silver (white), bronze (red), lead (green), and iron (black).

Kanazawa Kenkō, a famous ship builder, used the *I Ching* and its commentaries extensively in his *Wakan senyōshū* (The Use of Ships in Japan and China, 1761) to explain the theory of ship building. In his explanation of the hexagram *huan* (dispersion), he quoted and paraphrased the *Hsi Tz'u* to demonstrate that ship building was the work of the sages:

> The Yellow Emperor scooped out tree trunks to make boats and hardened wood in the fire to make oars. The advantage of boats and oars lies in providing communication to places that were once isolated. Boats can reach distant places and thus benefit the whole world. I think the sages created the boat from their understanding of the hexagram *huan*.[44]

Asserting that ship building was subject to the principle of *yin-yang wu-hsing*, Kanazawa used the hexagram *chung fu* ䷼ (inner truth) to explain the proportion of materials used in ship building. The main text of this hexagram reiterated the advantage of building ships to cross rivers. By looking into the image of the hexagram, Kanazawa concluded that the ratio between metal and wood in a ship should be seven to nine; wood should be used for the upper half, and metal for the lower half:

> According to the regulations of ship building, a ship is subject to the law of 7–9. This idea comes from the image of the hexagram *chung fu*, which consists of *t'ui* ☱ on the bottom, *sun* ☴ on the top. Why do we get the ratio 7–9 from the trigrams *t'ui* and *sun*? *Sun* belongs to the agent of wood, which is identified with the number nine; *t'ui* belongs to the agent of metal, which is identified with the number seven.[45]

The philosophy of the *I Ching* also helped Tokugawa intellectuals formulate their economic views. In particular, its *yin-yang* theory was identified with the natural law that inspired some "free market economy" ideas.[46] Many early Tokugawa Confucians pointed out that stagnation of wealth is contradictory to the natural principle of *yin-yang*, two dynamic forces that circulate throughout the universe. For instance, Kaibara Ekken said: "When *yin* and *yang* get together, their mixing and dispelling cause frost, snow, rain and dew. Their stagnation and non-moving cause violent air and poisonous fog. The same principle is applicable to human activities."[47] Perhaps Nishikawa Joken was more articulate in linking the natural principle with economics. He wrote:

> There is a principle that when my treasure is reduced, the treasure of others increases; when I increase my treasure, the treasure of others is

reduced. Likewise, the two forces of the universe, *yin* and *yang*, are in motion and do not stop in any place under normal conditions. If *yin* and *yang* stay in a certain place for a long time, it is caused by the imbalance of *yin* and *yang*. This will certainly lead to a natural disaster. The gold and silver in this world are the same. They should circulate around thousands of commoners in the world, and must not stop in any place for long.[48]

This last sentence seems to subtly imply that the bakufu should not accumulate wealth but allow merchants to play a part in circulating it. This idea of the circulation of wealth matches the spirit of the free market economy, which regards the flow of capital as an impetus to economic growth.

Hatanaka Tachū (1734–1797) applied the *I Ching* to economic ethics. In his *Kashokuron* (Treatise on Capital Investment), he strove to prove that business was also a way of the sages, and thus should not be discriminated against. He cited many passages from the *I Ching* to show that even this sacred book talks about business, and that the sages regarded financial administration as the top priority in their political agenda. Blaming Meng Tzu for sowing the seeds of prejudice against business by differentiating between interest *(li)* and righteousness *(i)*, Hatanaka used the *I Ching* and Confucius's commentary to stress that interest is not a bad thing in itself:

> Meng Tzu was unreasonable to regard interest as all evil. The *ch'ien* hexagram of the *I Ching* created by the sages has [the four cardinal virtues of] "sublime" *(yüan)*, "success" *(heng)*, "furthering" *(li)*, and "perseverance" *(ch'eng)*. In the commentary of Confucius, interest *(li)* is in harmony with righteousness.[49]

How did one keep one's wealth, then? Hatanaka underscored the importance of two virtues for the merchants: kindness and frugality. He cited the hexagram *i* (increase) to demonstrate that if a merchant has a kind heart, things will go smoothly and there will be no need to consult an oracle. It reads: "If in truth you have a kind heart. Ask not. Supreme good fortune." On frugality he said: "After all, the foundation of the entrepreneur is frugality. [The hexagram *pi* (grace) of] the *I Ching* reads: I decorate my garden on the hill. The roll of silk I use is meager and small. It looks stingy, but will bring good fortune in the end."[50]

Ninomiya Sontoku (1787–1856) addressed similar issues in economic ethics. He believed that there is a cycle of riches and poverty, and that the only way for the rich to maintain their wealth is to stop pursuing excess wealth and help the poor:

> The riches and poverty of a man are like *yin* and *yang* in the universe. The extreme of *yin* gives birth to *yang*, whereas the extreme of *yang* gives birth to *yin*. Extreme poverty gives birth to riches, whereas extreme riches gives birth to poverty. The everlasting circulation of *yin* and *yang* and riches and poverty is the heavenly way. Strengthening oneself to keep one's wealth is the human way. . . . Having no extreme wealth and helping others are in accordance with the heavenly mandate and human aspirations. Is there any other way to keep wealth?[51]

The ideas of change and of the circulation of *yin* and *yang* inspired merchants to look at the balance of supply and demand. Tsutsumi Masatoshi, a Kyoto Confucian, wrote the *Shōdō kyūhen kokujikai* (An Explanation of the Way of Business in Japanese in Nine Chapters, 1816, 9 *kan*). The central philosophy of the book is that the idea of change in the *I Ching* should be applied to business. Tsutsumi observed that the changes in demand and supply are similar to the changes of *yin* and *yang* in the universe; if a merchant understands patterns of change and accumulates products that are bound to be in great demand, he will make a profitable investment:

> If you do not know the changes in time, you will not understand the principle of hoarding. Hoarding means accumulating a large quantity of a certain product. The principle of hoarding is extremely interesting. If you understand it, you will also realize the essence of the way of the *I Ching* and the wonder of creation.[52]

Tokugawa merchants disliked excessive interference from the bakufu and domains in their economic activities. Indeed, many of them espoused the idea of laissez faire. The natural principle of *yin-yang* became a very convenient and powerful ideological weapon for them. A good example is Kusama Naokata (1753–1831) and his famous work, *Sanka zui* (An Illustrative Glossary of the Monetary Policy in the Three Countries, 42 *kan*). Kusama was a successful merchant in Kyoto who had served as an economic advisor to the bakufu, helping several domains reconstruct their finances and economy. He held that an economy should follow the natural principle of *yin-yang*, and that it required no unnecessary human intervention. In particular, he opposed government intervention in the rice market. As the sages followed nature and the current of time, so a successful merchant should observe and follow the natural principle. He said:

The hexagram *i* of the *I Ching* reads: "The way to increase is to follow the change of time." The way to benefit the world endlessly hinges upon the natural principle. The sages benefited the world by following the principle in a changing current of time, acting in accordance with the universe, and keeping the same pace with time.[53]

The *I Ching* was, however, more significant in Tokugawa writings on agriculture than in those on commerce and industry, where it was not quoted in as much detail or as frequently. Thus discursive discussions on business in this section reflect the subtle and nebulous relationship between the *I Ching* and business in Tokugawa Japan.

Concluding Remarks

The philosophy and divination of the *I Ching* played a considerable role in Tokugawa economic thought. Its *yin-yang* idea, associated with Confucian natural law, was generally accepted by Tokugawa Confucians. The *I Ching* had closer ties with agriculture than business. *Yin-yang wu-hsing* was a very powerful concept in Tokugawa agriculture, used as a basic interpretative framework to advocate the superiority of Japan's agriculture and to suggest ways to increase productivity in many agricultural writings. In business, the natural principle of *yin-yang* was used to discuss some economic issues, such as the positive role of business in national economy, the circulation of wealth, the balance of supply and demand, and the role of the government in economic activities. It was also applied to explain and justify different fields of industry.

The *I Ching* also played a part in Japan's modernization. Economic modernization was concerned with two major themes during the nineteenth century: improving the old sector (agriculture) and beginning the new sector (modern industry and business). The philosophy and divination of the *I Ching* gave some agricultural reformers and early entrepreneurs wisdom and confidence to make their economic activities a success in the early stage of capitalism and industrialization.[54]

The influence of the *I Ching* on Japan's economic thought began to decline after the Meiji period, but never vanished. Even now, not a few Japanese businessmen associate their business philosophy with the *I Ching*. Many businessmen and farmers still believe in divination, geomancy (usually called *kasō*, or "house-reading," in Japan), and the like. The *I Ching* thus maintains a role in the economic life of modern Japanese.

6. The *I Ching* and Shinto

It might seem strange to put a Chinese classic and a Japanese religion together, but in fact the *I Ching* played an important role at
different stages of Shinto's development.[1] It is no exaggeration to say
that the *I Ching* was one of the most important books influencing
Shinto. Our investigation focuses on two main themes: the role of
the text in the discussion of Confucian-Shinto relations, and the
project of transforming the text from a Confucian classic into a Shinto
text. We first examine how early Tokugawa Confucians, as well as
Shintoists, used the *I Ching* to elucidate the doctrine of the unity of
Confucianism and Shinto, and to develop their Shinto ideas. Next,
we outline the changes in Confucian-Shinto relations during the mid-
Tokugawa period through the voices of some Confucian scholars.
Finally, we see how scholars of Unden Shinto, *kokuugaku* (the school
of national learning), and the Mito school turned the *I Ching* from a
Confucian classic into a Shinto or Japanese text in late Tokugawa
times.

The Confucianization of Shinto in Early Tokugawa Times

Although animistic beliefs and shrines existed in ancient times, Shinto
in the ancient and medieval periods did not contain a set of clear
doctrines.[2] "*Shintō*" (or *shen-tao*), a term from the *I Ching*, was uncommon in ancient Japanese vocabulary. It appeared for the first time in
Japan in the eighth century, when it was used in the *Nihon shoki*
(Chronicles of Japan, 720) a mere three times. The meaning of
the term "*shintō*" was never settled on during the medieval period.[3]

Medieval Shinto developed within the Mahāyāna Buddhist system. Using the doctrine of *honji suijaku* (or the idea that Buddha manifested in the form of Shinto deities in ancient Japan), Zen Buddhist monks attempted to include Shinto within the world of Buddhist teaching. Shinto was also affiliated with Confucianism, Onmyōdō, and folk beliefs, and did not generally come to be perceived separately, as an indigenous or national religion, until the late Tokugawa and early Meiji periods.

As neo-Confucianism gradually became a powerful intellectual force in the early Tokugawa era, it had a tremendous impact on Shinto. The two teachings formed an anti-Buddhist alliance in the seventeenth century. Some Confucians sought to include Shinto within Confucianism, while Shintoists wanted to use neo-Confucian metaphysics to enrich their own teachings.[4] In both cases, the *I Ching* was the main text used to progress toward these goals.

Prominent Confucian scholars used the text to promote the unity of Confucianism and Shinto. Most early Tokugawa Confucians, despite their different schools and their disagreements over a number of issues, shared similar ideas about the relationship between Confucianism and Shinto—namely, (1) that Confucianism represented a universal principle and could be used to explicate Shinto, (2) that Confucianism and Shinto were in agreement on political ideology, ethics, and metaphysics, and (3) that Shinto had originated in China and was also a way of the sages, rather than being either subordinate to Buddhism or an exclusive way for Japan. Accordingly, major Shinto currents in Tokugawa Japan were viewed as wrong because they encompassed shamanistic practices. In brief, early Tokugawa Confucians attempted to incorporate Shinto by emphasizing the universality of Confucianism and the similarity of Confucianism and Shinto.

Hayashi Razan (1583–1657) was among the earliest Tokugawa scholars to advocate the unity of Confucianism and Shinto based on the *I Ching*. He was a Confucian first and a Shintoist second, attempting to incorporate Shinto into Confucianism, not vice versa. His view of Shinto can be summarized in two sentences: "Shinto in my country is in agreement with the way of the *Chou I*," and "Shinto is within Confucianism."[5]

Hayashi's major work on Shinto was the *Shintō denju* (The Transmission of Shinto, 1648), in which he introduced the history of Shinto and the main ideas of different Shinto schools. He concluded that any Buddhist efforts to explain Shinto would be in vain, and that Shinto could be understood only through the reading of Confucian classics and Japanese historical writings. In particular, he believed that the *I Ching* and *Nihon shoki* were the keys to unlocking the mystery of Shinto. Hayashi used the theory of *yin-yang wu-hsing* to explain the Age of the Gods. For instance, he identified the Shinto deity Kuni-no-tokotachi-no-mikoto with *t'ai-chi* (the Supreme Ultimate), and asserted that Izanagi and Izanami represented *yin* and *yang* and *ch'ien* and *k'un*, respectively. He also compared the five major Shinto deities to *wu-hsing*.[6]

Attributing the origins of his Shinto ideas to the *I Ching* and *Nihon shoki,* Hayashi stated that while these two books belonged to different ages and countries, they shared the same view on the formation of the universe: "The *Nihon shoki* states that the combination of the God of *Yang* and the Goddess of *Yin,* and their marriage, gave birth to everything. . . . In the *Chou I,* it is expressed in [the form of] *ch'ien* and *k'un*."[7]

In the same book, Hayashi also mentioned two other interesting ideas. First, by putting the doctrine of *honji suijaku* into a Confucian context, he maintained that many Shinto deities were in fact from China, and therefore that Shinto was included in Confucianism.[8] Second, he pointed out that both Shinto and the *I Ching* favored the number eight because it reflected the mystery of the numerology of the universe.[9] In the *Shintō hiden setchū zokukai* (A Synthesis and Simple Explanation of the *Secret Transmission of Shinto,* 1676), he used the hexagram *kuan* (contemplation) to link Confucianism and Shinto together:

> The hexagram *kuan* of the *I Ching* reads: "The sages, in accordance with the spirit-like *(shintō)* way, laid down their instructions, and all under heaven yield submission to them." Isn't this the way of the kings? Isn't this the way of the sages?[10]

Thus Hayashi treated Shinto as a way of the Chinese sages, and believed that Shinto and Confucianism shared the same natural principle.

Yamazaki Ansai (1618–1682) was the founder of Suika Shinto as well as a Chu Hsi scholar. Like Hayashi Razan, he used the *I Ching* and *Nihon shoki* to explain the Age of the Gods and to formulate his Shinto views. Yamazaki regarded the *I Ching* as the most important Chinese book, and referred to it as "China's *kamiyo no maki,*" or scroll of the Age of the Gods. Likewise, he saw the *Nihon shoki* as "Japan's *I Ching*." Using the theory of *yin-yang wu-hsing,* he developed a description of the Age of the Gods that was similar to Hayashi's: "Izanagi was the God of *Yang,* and Izanami was the God of *Yin.* These two gods supported the wonderful forces of *wu-hsing.*"[11] He also wrote: "The first generation of the gods were the Gods of Heaven and Earth. From the second to the sixth generations lived the Gods of Water, Fire, Wood, Metal, and Earth. The seventh generations were the Gods of *Yin* and *Yang.*"[12]

Yamazaki asserted that Confucianism and Shinto possessed the same principle, and that their ultimate purpose was to cultivate a moral character and a proper relationship between the emperor and his subjects:[13]

> In Japan, at the time of the opening of the country, Izanagi and Izanami followed the divination teachings of the Heavenly Gods, obeyed *yin* and *yang,* and thus correctly established the beginnings of ethical teachings. In the universe there is only One Principle, [although] either Gods or sages come forth depending on whether it concerns the country where the sun rises [Japan] or the country where the sun sets [China]. The [two] ways [of Shinto and Confucianism] are, however, naturally and mysteriously the same.[14]

Although Confucianism and Shinto shared the same origin, Yamazaki did not think that they should fuse into a single entity because Japan and China had different national characters. Hence he made few attempts to blend the two.[15] In his later years, he even proclaimed that Shinto was superior to all other teachings. This extreme stance distinguished him from Hayashi Razan and other early Tokugawa Confucian scholars who held Shinto beliefs.

Kumazawa Banzan (1619–1691) elaborated the idea of "the divine way of heaven and earth" *(tenchi no shintō),* which was very similar to Watarai Nobuyoshi's "natural principle" *(shizen no ri).* He stated: "We do not have two principles. The way of the sages in China is also the divine way of heaven and earth. Shinto in my country is also the divine way of heaven and earth. The *I Ching* is also the divine way of heaven and earth."[16] What he meant by "the Shinto of heaven and earth" was the way of benevolence and righteousness. Based on this idea, Kumazawa developed a cultural perspective that treated both the *I Ching* and the Three Regalia as symbols of the divine way of heaven and earth:

> The sages understood the deep and subtle principle of the gods, which
> is hard to manifest since it has neither form nor color. No words and
> essays can fully explicate it. Therefore, [the Chinese] made the hexa-
> grams and came to understand this principle by looking into these
> symbols. . . . The Three Regalia of the Age of the Gods show us the
> subtle and unspeakable virtues in visible form. They are symbols.[17]

He added:

> In the ancient past, we did not have a writing system. In China, the
> works of the sages before Yao and Shun, the indoctrination of virtues,
> and the establishment of institutions were expressed only in the lines
> of *yin* and *yang* in the *I Ching* because there were no books to transmit
> them. Also, in Japan we had the Three Regalia as symbols, and they
> functioned like the lines of the *I Ching*.[18]

Kumazawa concluded from his comparison of these symbols that
"the Three Regalia and the three lines [of a trigram] of the *I Ching* are
alike."[19] The most striking similarity between the *I Ching* and Shinto,
he believed, was that they both favored the number eight, which reflected the universality of the divine way of heaven and earth:

> The Chinese sage Fu Hsi was the first to draw the lines of *ch'ien* and
> *k'un*, which were later developed into the six lines, the eight trigrams,
> and [eight times eight to produce] the sixty-four hexagrams. Similarly,
> we [Japanese] used the number eight in words, such as the *Yatano* [Mir-
> ror] and the *Yasaka* [Jade], because the divine way of heaven and earth
> is one, and it is naturally the same wonderful principle shared by both
> Japan and China.[20]

In addition to his work on symbols, Kumazawa produced a textual
analysis of the *I Ching* and quoted two passages from it to prove the
Chinese origins of Shinto. The first is from the famous hexagram
kuan. The second passage reads: "Manifesting the virtue of the spirit-
like way *(shintō)*, one can consult with the gods and receive their
blessing."[21]

Yamaga Sokō (1622–1685), like Kumazawa, disapproved of Shinto
in its current form but did not reject Shinto itself. Like many Confucian contemporaries, he believed that Shinto was one of the ways of
the sages, which could be practiced in any nation and which had
validity that was not necessarily limited to Japan. Yamaga maintained
that both Shinto in ancient Japan and the way of the Chinese sages
represented the proper way to govern and had nothing to do with
shamanism and magic. One of his disciples recalled Yamaga's view of
the relationship between Confucianism and Shinto:

One question was: "Our country is a divine nation, so why don't we use Shinto to govern?" My master [Yamaga Sokō] replied: "Every nation in the world is a divine nation, and why do you confine it to our country?" The *T'uan Chuan* of the *I Ching* comments on the hexagram *kuan*. It reads: "When we contemplate the spirit-like way *(shintō)* of heaven, we see how the four seasons proceed without error. The sages, in accordance with the spirit-like way *(shintō)*, laid down their instructions, and all under heaven yield submission to them." That is the Shinto of the sages. The way of the sages is to use Shinto to rule the nation. However, nowadays the school of magicians and diviners advocates Shinto because they work in Shinto shrines. What do they know about the Shinto of the sages?[22]

Ogyū Sorai (1666–1728) also advocated the way of the sages. According to Ogyū, both Shinto and the way of the *I Ching* were included in the way of the sages. He quoted the hexagram *kuan* to elucidate the political implications of the way of the sages: "The sages, in accordance with the spirit-like way *(shintō)*, laid down their instructions and acted according to the will of heaven. It is not limited to divination and magic, and should include ritual, music, administration, and punishment. This is the way of benevolence."[23] Ogyū criticized Itō Jinsai for denying the existence of Shinto: "Why did Master Jinsai say that Confucius did not talk about gods and ghosts? Ancient people worshipped the sages because the latter acted according to the way of heaven. Therefore, [the *I Ching*] says: 'The sages, in accordance with the spirit-like way *(shintō)*, laid down their instructions.' "[24]

Ogyū's examination of the ancient history of Japan reinforced his belief that Shinto and the way of the sages were in agreement. He argued: "Worshipping heaven and ancestors, laying down instructions based on the way of the gods *(shintō)*, and making decisions about administration, punishment, and reward in [ancestral] temples and shrines have been practices since the Early Three Dynasties. This is the way of my nation, which is equivalent to the ancient way of the Hsia and Shang."[25] Of course, Ogyū did not believe every story that the Shintoists told. For example, he dismissed the authenticity of the supposed written characters of the Age of the Gods, maintaining that the hexagrams of the *I Ching* were the real origin of Chinese and Japanese characters.[26]

Early Tokugawa Shintoists also studied the *I Ching* and adopted elements from Chinese learning, using the text extensively to interpret and enrich Shinto. While stressing the similarity of Shinto and Confucianism, they did not entertain the idea that Shinto was also a way of the sages imported from China. This differentiates them from Confucians who held Shinto views. We focus on the leaders of two major Shinto schools, New Ise Shinto and Yoshida Shinto.

New Ise Shinto is characterized by its strong association with the *I Ching*.[27] Its founder, Watarai Nobuyoshi (1615–1690), exerted considerable influence on early Tokugawa Confucians and Shintoists. His major work was the *Yōfukki* (Records of the Return of Yang, 1650), a text whose title was borrowed from the hexagram *fu*. He used the *I Ching* and *Nihon shoki* to explain every detail of the Age of the Gods (Izanagi and Izanami, for instance, were represented by the hexagrams *ch'ien* and *k'un*). Watarai believed that these two books were equally important because they shared a similar idea of the way of heaven, earth, and man:

> In our country, many of the ancient stories that have been transmitted agree with the *I Ching*. The authors of Shinto books sometimes borrowed terms and ideas from the *I Ching*. Japan's holy relics are in agreement with the Book of the Sages [the *I Ching*] from China. One might wonder how this could be. The natural way of heaven and earth does not vary with nations. That is the way Shinto should be.[28]

What was the way of heaven, earth, and man? According to Watarai, it was the way of loyalty and honesty to which Shinto and the way of the *I Ching* belonged. He remarked: "Some people say the way of the *I Ching* is flawless. I think the reason for its infallibility is that it is the same as Shinto in our country; both are the way of loyalty and honesty."[29] Here Watarai suggested the interesting duality of *ri* and *dō* (principle and expression), teaching that the way of loyalty and honesty was the natural principle *(ri)*, but that each nation had its own expression *(dō)* of that principle. This explained why Japan had Shinto, China had Confucianism, and India had Buddhism.

Watarai's conclusion was that people should abide by the expression to which their nations belonged, and therefore that Japanese should be faithful to Shinto. He had never forgotten his identity as a Shinto priest, and thus held that Shinto was not subordinate to the way of the *I Ching*. He argued:

> Because both Shinto and the way of the *I Ching* follow nature, their teachings are in accordance with the truth. In particular, the *Nihon shoki* obviously borrowed many words from the *I Ching*. However, Shinto does not derive from the *I Ching*. If people read foreign books

and begin to suspect that Japanese Shinto might have come from the *I Ching*, they merely have the bodies of Japanese and do not realize their indebtedness to the nation. They have the heart of the alien.[30]

In his reading of the *Nihon shoki* and *Gobusho* (Five Shinto Classics, c. thirteenth century), Watarai was convinced that Shinto had existed before the importation of Confucianism, and that it was therefore not a way of the sages imported from China. This was the most significant difference between Shintoists and Confucians in their understanding of the relationship between Confucianism and Shinto.

Kikkawa (Yoshikawa) Koretari (1616–1694), the champion of Yoshida Shinto, enjoyed a reputation equal to that of Watarai Nobuyoshi in early Tokugawa times. Believing that the Age of the Gods had been imbued with the principle of the *I Ching,* he used the theories of *t'ai-chi* and *yin-yang wu-hsing* to construct his theological and ontological views. He identified Kuni-no-tokotachi-no-mikoto, the first Shinto deity who appeared after the beginning of the universe, as *t'ai-chi,* and Izanagi and Izanami as the gods of *yin* and *yang.* The story of Izanagi and Izanami meeting on a floating bridge he interpreted as a metaphor for the harmony of *yin* and *yang.* Kikkawa adopted the theory that metal, water, wood, fire, and earth are the five primal agents in the universe. In the *Tsuchikan no den* (Treatise on the Agents of Earth and Metal), he added that earth and metal were the essences of everything from which the other three agents were created, and that they represented the most important virtues of all—loyalty and righteousness.

Kikkawa also contributed to the discussion of Shinto-Confucian relations by popularizing the explanation of a Shinto prayer. According to tradition, the legendary emperor Sui'nin (29 B.C.E.– 70 C.E.) had composed a prayer that consisted of the words *"to-o-kami-emi-tame, kan-ken-shin-son-ri-kon-sui-ken."* People believed that this prayer had mystic power and recited it from generation to generation, even though no one seemed to understand its meaning. Looking at the phonetic similarities, Kikkawa claimed that the first sentence represented the five agents and that the second sentence stood for the eight hexagrams; on this basis, he concluded that Shinto was in agreement with the way of the *I Ching.*[31] He also explained the extensive use of the number eight in Shinto, such as in the Three Regalia and the architecture of the Shinto shrine, in terms of the combination of the three powers and the five agents—two key ideas of the *I Ching.*[32]

Although Kikkawa's ideas were similar to those of Hayashi Razan and some early Tokugawa Confucians, he put stronger emphasis on Shinto exorcism, prayer, and the virtue of *makoto* (sincerity).

The Separation of Confucianism and Shinto in Mid-Tokugawa Times

Of course, not all Confucians and Shintoists in early Tokugawa times agreed with the doctrine of the unity of Confucianism and Shinto. By the late seventeenth and early eighteenth centuries, we witness growing disagreement over this assumption.[33] It is not easy to explain why Confucians and Shintoists began to separate Shinto from Confucianism by the mid-Tokugawa period. I think this phenomenon was a byproduct of two intellectual movements: the pursuit of purity and the original teaching in Confucianism, and the emergence of an influential nativist current. Strikingly, however, those who opposed the doctrine of the unity of Confucianism and Shinto used the same source material from the *I Ching* as those who advocated it. To demonstrate the characteristics of this brief transitional period of approximately a half century in mid-Tokugawa times, we look at the thought of two representative Confucians, Muro Kyūsō (1658–1734) and Dazai Shundai (1680–1747).

Muro Kyūsō denied that there was any relationship between Confucianism and Shinto, attacking Suika Shinto in particular. According to Muro, people in his times believed in the unity of Confucianism and Shinto because they misread the hexagram *kuan*. He asserted that the term *"shen-tao" (shintō)* in the *I Ching* meant simply "the wonderful way" *(shen-miao chih tao)*, not "the way of the gods" *(shen-tao):*

> "The sages gave instructions according to *shen-tao.*" We call the way of the sages *"shen-tao"* because of its wonder. We can also call it the way of benevolence. Shinto is not the only way. I have tried to understand the theory of today's Shinto, which regards the way of our country as superior to the way of the sages. I find it hard to understand.[34]

According to Muro, the first and most basic difference between Confucianism and Shinto was that the former put emphasis on ethical principles whereas the latter stressed mystery:

> Is the so-called Shinto of the present day the same as the way of the sages or different? Its [Shinto's] books have many subtle words and few explicit [moral] lessons. The more they talk about gods and ether, the fewer ethical lessons they present. . . . The *I Ching* says: "Even if the dif-

ference [at the beginning] is only an insignificant unit of measure, [later] their difference will be as wide as a thousand miles."[35]

The second difference was that Confucianism was universal whereas Shinto was national. In a letter to a friend, Muro criticized Shinto for its exclusiveness and insisted that the Way should belong to the world and not be a private thing of Japan.[36] The third difference was that Confucianism was political while Shinto was religious. He regarded the way of the sages as a way to govern through politics and education, and quoted the following sentence from Ch'eng I to explain this idea: "Rulers before the Early Three Kings laid down their instructions in accordance with the wonderful way. It goes without saying that their purpose was to educate the people. We saw the success of the Way in Yao's times."[37] The fourth difference was that Confucianism was historical and Shinto ahistorical. Muro pointed out that Japan had a short history of slightly more than two thousand years, and that the Age of the Gods was thus only a myth.[38]

Dazai Shundai was also a critic of Shinto. Defining the way of the gods *(shintō)* as a way of the sages, which meant a respect for supernatural beings, Dazai recognized its practical value but denied its authenticity. He asserted that the sages themselves did not believe in Shinto but used it as a means to educate the foolish and superstitious people of primitive times. He explained the hexagram *kuan* in this way:

> Nowadays, people think Shinto is the way of our nation, and regard it as one of the ways along with Confucianism, Buddhism, and Taoism. That is a big mistake. Shinto at first belonged to the way of the sages. The *Chou I* reads: "When we contemplate the spirit-like way *(shintō)* of heaven, we see how the four seasons proceed without error. The sages, in accordance with the spirit-like way *(shintō)*, laid down their instructions, and all under heaven yield submission to them." . . . The [early] rulers knew the truth. The ordinary people were very foolish and had doubts about everything. If gods and ghosts were not used as a means to teach them, the heart of the people would not settle. The sages knew that in order to teach the people, they had to claim [authority] from the gods and spirits to produce order. That is the meaning of the Shinto of the sages, and of the phrase "the sages laid down their instructions in accordance with the spirit-like way *(shintō)*."[39]

According to Dazai, Tokugawa Shinto was completely different from the Shinto of the sages. Japanese Shinto was a kind of shamanism, and historically short. Dazai did not believe that Shinto had ever existed in ancient Japan.[40] He remarked:

> Today's version of Shinto did not exist in pre-medieval times. We can-
> not find any records in ancient historical writings and Japanese litera-
> ture. Hence you should know that in the time of Shōtoku Taishi [574–
> 622] we did not have Shinto yet. . . . The term *"shintō"* was from the
> *Chou I;* it was one of the meanings of the way of the sages. Today,
> people take the way of divination as Shinto. . . . That is a big mistake,
> a ridiculous and unreasonable thing.[41]

Dazai pointed out that medieval Shinto had been built on the
Shingon Buddhist framework, and that Yoshida Kanetomo (1435–
1511), the founder of Yoshida Shinto, had added Buddhist and Confucian elements into Japanese shamanistic practices, which later became the mainstream Shinto school in the early Tokugawa period.
Hence Tokugawa Shinto was an inappropriate combination of Confucianism and Buddhism.

The Shintoization of the *I Ching* in Late Tokugawa Times

Although the relationship between the *I Ching* and Shinto underwent
tremendous changes, the two maintained a very close relationship
throughout the Tokugawa period. In the first half of the Tokugawa
period, Shinto moved closer to Confucianism and away from Buddhism. Many Confucians and Shintoists used the *I Ching* to advocate
both the doctrine of the unity of Confucianism and Shinto and some
Shinto ideas.

During the second half of the Tokugawa period, Shinto distanced
itself from Confucianism and established its status as an indigenous
religion.[42] The relationship between the two teachings became subtle.
Shintoists tended to denounce Confucianism openly but were still influenced by it, consciously or unconsciously. The *I Ching* was no
longer used to uphold the doctrine of the unity of the two teachings.
Although it was still influential in Shinto, it was used with less and
less reference to Confucianism and China.[43] Thus if the Confucianization of Shinto through the *I Ching* was a major theme in early
Tokugawa Confucian-Shinto relations, the late Tokugawa period is
characterized by the Shintoization of the text. Schools that were
strongly nationalist—the *kokugaku* in particular—tried to turn the *I
Ching* from a Confucian classic into a Shinto text. In this section we
investigate the Shintoization of the *I Ching* begun by Unden Shinto,
kokugaku, and the Mito school.

Unden Shinto was founded by Jiun Sonja (1718–1804), a Shingon priest who sought to strengthen the fusion of Shinto with some Buddhist and Confucian ideas.[44] Comparing the similarities between the *I Ching* and Shinto writings on such topics as the heavenly mandate, divination, numerology, gods and spirits, and politics, he suggested that the creation of the *I Ching* might have been influenced by Shinto. According to Chinese tradition, Fu Hsi created the eight trigrams based on the *Ho T'u* (Yellow River Diagram). Jiun speculated that the *Ho T'u* had been inspired by a Shinto mirror: "The images of the *Ho T'u* were manifested through the Okitsu Mirror [one of the ten Shinto treasures, a round bronze mirror kept in the *gekū* (Outer Shrine) of the Ise Shrine]. Fu Hsi used the *Ho T'u* as the basis for drawing the eight trigrams."[45]

Jiun even speculated that the text of the *I Ching* had been derived from Shinto divination in the Age of the Gods. He said:

> Every word and sentence in the *I Ching* is interesting and significant. The two parts of the main text and its Ten Wings are perfect in politics and ethics. [The authors of the *I Ching*] copied our ancient divination of Takama-ga-hara [the plain of the high heaven where Izanagi and Izanami lived] and formulated its text and style. The whole book is completely borrowed from us.[46]

Jiun's discussions on the Shinto origins of the *I Ching* were only piecemeal. He did not address important questions such as how Fu Hsi and other Chinese sages had been influenced by Shinto. A full-fledged theory of the Shinto origins of the *I Ching* did not appear until the emergence of the Hirata school a few decades later.

Early *kokugaku* scholars condemned the *I Ching*, but late *kokugaku* scholars, particularly those of the Hirata school, Shintoized or Japanized the text so that they could use its metaphysical ideas to enrich their thought.[47] This becomes one of the most interesting intellectual themes in late Tokugawa times.

Motoori Norinaga (1730–1801), like earlier *kokugaku* scholars, was indifferent to and even looked down upon the *I Ching*, calling it "a white elephant" *(muyō no chōbutsu)* created by the Chinese sages to deceive people:[48] "Confucians believe that they have grasped the meaning of the universe through the creation of the *I Ching* and its very profound words. But all that is only a deception to win people over and be masters over them."[49] Hence Motoori attacked people who used the idea of *yin-yang wu-hsing* to explain the Age of the Gods.[50] He preferred the *Kojiki* (Records of Ancient Matters, 712) to the *Nihon shoki* because the latter was influenced by the *I Ching* and used the theory of *yin-yang wu-hsing* to discuss the Age of the Gods. Motoori distinguished Japanese Shinto from Chinese "Shinto" *(shen-tao),* holding that the main difference was that Chinese "Shinto" was strange and abstract whereas Japanese Shinto was historical and existent. He wrote:

> However, a book of China [the *I Ching*] reads: "The sages established Shinto." Some people thus believe that our country borrowed the name "Shinto" from this book. These people do not have a mind to understand things. Our understanding of gods has been different from the Chinese from the beginning. In China, they compare gods to the *yin* and *yang* of the universe and the unpredictable spirit. Their discussion is only empty theory without substance. Deities in our country were the ancestors of the current imperial emperor and are not empty theories like the Chinese [notion of gods].[51]

When Motoori wrote this passage, the chief object of his attack was Dazai Shundai. In it, Motoori made three points—that Japanese Shinto was unrelated to the *I Ching,* that Shinto existed in ancient Japan, and that Shinto had strong political implications. In brief, he regarded Shinto as an indigenous religion of ancient origin and condemned both the Buddhist Shinto of the past and the Confucian Shinto of his own times.

Izumi Maku'ni (1765–1805), a student of Motoori, was a maverick in *kokugaku* circles. His knowledge of the Chinese classics was exceptional, and his relationship with other *kokugaku* scholars poor. He wanted to fuse Shinto, the *I Ching,* and the *Chung Yung* (Doctrine of the Mean). In his major work, the *Meidōsho* (Book to Explain the Way, published in 1830), Izumi used the *I Ching* and *Chung Yung* to explicate Shinto. However, his stance was different from that of early Tokugawa Confucians. Being a *kokugaku* scholar, he considered Shinto an independent entity, not a component of Confucianism, and defined it as the natural way of heaven and earth and as an ideal ideology that was in agreement with the teachings in the *I Ching* and *Chung Yung.*[52] Although Shinto was universal, Izumi argued, Japan was the only nation that had been in accordance with it ever since the Age of the Gods:

> The *Chou I, Chung Yung,* and other books have many right words and are well written. However, the so-called way of honesty has from the beginning been merely empty words on paper from the foreign land [China], and thus the Chinese did not gain profit from it at all. In our imperial kingdom, although we did not have the name of the Way or

the books to teach, the thing itself [the Way] has been carried out correctly from the Age of the Gods, and it has filled the nation for ten thousand generations. Its benefits can be seen even now.[53]

Izumi further asserted that *ikan* (simple administration), the political ideal of the *I Ching,* had also been practiced in the Age of the Gods.

Hirata Atsutane (1776–1843) changed the direction of the whole discussion. His early views on the *I Ching* followed those of Motoori closely, and he adopted a similar perspective on the different kinds of Shinto in China and Japan. The main difference between Shinto in these two nations, Hirata pointed out, was that the Shinto of the *I Ching* did not have a real god whereas Japanese Shinto was the way of the gods.[54] Hirata divided Shinto into two categories: the Shinto in Japan, which was real Shinto, and the Shinto of the *Chou I* and other schools of Shinto that interacted with Confucianism and Buddhism, which were vulgar Shinto. He wanted to clear all non-Japanese elements from Shinto, and thus disagreed with those who used the *yin-yang wu-hsing* theory to explain Shinto.

In his later years, Hirata became very interested in the *I Ching* and established his own views on the text. His most original and significant idea about the relationship between Confucianism and Shinto was his distinction between the *Chou I* and *I Ching.* Hirata came up with the idea that the *I Ching* was not an alien work of literature but the handiwork of a Japanese deity, and he wrote the *Saneki yuraiki* (Origins of the Early Three Versions of the *I Ching,* 1835) and *Taikō koekiden* (The *I Ching* of the Ancient Past, 1836) to trace the alleged Shinto origins of the ancient *I Ching.*[55] Turning the *honji suijaku* theory upside down, he argued that all sage-kings and deities in ancient China were from Japan. For example, Fu Hsi was actually a Shinto deity named Ōmono-nushi-no-kami, who was supposedly the creator of the trigrams, *I Ching* charts, oracle bones, and Chinese characters.[56] Hirata asserted: "Later, our god, Ōmono-nushi-no-kami, also called Taikō-fukki-shi, granted [the Chinese] the *Ho T'u* and *Lo Shu* (Writings from the River Lo), and created the wonderful trigrams. . . . Based on the images of oracle bones, he invented Chinese characters."[57] Forced to explain why a Japanese deity went to China, he stated: "[Fu Hsi] was actually a god of our holy land, Ōmono-nushi-no-kami, who went to exploit that land [China] and cultivate the foolish people. In order to teach them the way of human relations, he went [to China] for a short period and acquired this Chinese name."[58]

The *I Ching* was thus, according to Hirata, originally the work of a Japanese deity.[59] Hirata alleged that the text had been modified by Shen Nung and Huang Ti, both of whom he claimed were Japanese deities, and held that the modified *I Ching* later became the *Lien Shan* and *Kui Ts'ang*. According to Hirata, these two early forms of the *I Ching* had also been transmitted orally and adopted by the Hsia and Shang dynasties, respectively. Hirata blamed King Wen, the putative editor of the *Chou I,* for changing the order of the hexagrams and the number of the yarrow stalks to justify the revolution that overthrew the Shang regime. The *Chou I,* he argued, had been further distorted by the Duke of Chou and by Confucius and his students, and had later become a Chinese and Confucian text. Hirata asserted that the only way to reconstruct the ancient *I Ching* was to study the *Ta Hsiang.* In the *Koeki taishō kyō* (*Ta Hsiang* Commentary of the Ancient *I Ching*), he argued that the *Ta Hsiang* was a commentary on the lost *Lien Shan* and thus preserved many elements of the original *I Ching.* Hirata rearranged the order of the hexagrams and reduced the number of yarrow stalks from forty-nine to forty-five, believing that he had restored the ancient *I Ching.*[60]

Hirata trained many students. According to Furukawa Tetsushi, a Japanese historian of Tokugawa thought and religion, the Hirata school is characterized by its active participation in *I Ching* studies.[61]

Ikuta Yorozu (1801–1837), a faithful disciple of Hirata, believed everything his teacher told him about the ancient *I Ching.* Ikuta agreed that the text was the work of a Japanese deity, whom he called Ōkuni-nushi-no-kami, who had felt pity for the Chinese when he saw their stupidity. As a result, this deity had gone to China and written the *I Ching* to enlighten them. Ikuta wrote:

> Alas! When the realms of humans and gods began to separate, our god, Ōkuni-nushi-no-kami, also called the Holy Fu Hsi by the Chinese, went across the ocean to China and taught the foolish people about morality. The *I Ching* was made as a tool for this purpose. This happened four thousand eight hundred and eighty some years ago.[62]

Following Hirata, Ikuta asserted that the ancient *I Ching* had been maliciously corrupted by the Duke of Chou and then by Confucius. The only way to restore the ancient *I Ching,* he felt, was to study the *Ta Hsiang.* He wrote the *Koeki taishōkyō den* (A Commentary on the *Koeki taishōkyō*), a commentary on Hirata's book, but added many original ideas of his own. Ikuta realized that he and some *kokugaku* scholars were making a breakthrough in *I Ching* studies:

People in this world who talk about the *I Ching* all refer to King Wen, the Duke of Chou, and Confucius. Diviners and the like only read the books of several people, such as Hirasawa [Tsunenori], Baba [Nobutake], Arai [Hakuga], and Mase [Chūshū]. Only two or three of us want to learn the ancient *I Ching*. How wonderful our projects are![63]

Ōkuni Takamasa (1791–1871), also a student of Hirata, provided a new explanation for the Japanese origins of the *I Ching*. At first, he adopted the view that the Chinese sage-kings were from Japan, although he changed their names. For instance, Fu Hsi was no longer Ōkuni-nushi-no-kami but Yashima Shinomi-no-kami. Later, having read some Chinese books, Ōkuni adopted the interesting view that Shinto deities had not become Chinese sages but had merely gone to China and acted as the advisors of Chinese sages.[64] His most striking idea was that, in the Age of the Gods, Japan had possessed its own written system, which he termed *"jindai moji"* and believed was the mother of all languages, including Chinese, Sanskrit, and Dutch.

It goes without saying that Ōkuni believed that the hexagrams of the *I Ching*, allegedly the primitive form for all Chinese characters, were derived from these Japanese characters from the Age of the Gods. Table 10 shows his transformation from *jindai moji* to hexagrams and thence to Chinese characters.[65] Ōkuni saw the Japanese language

Table 10: Transformation from *Jindai Moji* to Chinese Characters According to Ōkuni

Jindai moji	Hexagrams	Chinese Characters		
				天
				地
				水
				火

as the most beautiful language in the world because its five basic vowels (a, i, u, e, o) matched the *wu-hsing* (in the order of wood, fire, earth, metal, and water). He claimed that the *wu-hsing* theory existed in ancient Japanese books, that it had been recovered by Motoori and Hirata, and that the Confucian interpretation of *wu-hsing* was false and empty.[66]

This kind of reasoning, although seemingly ridiculous, should be understood as an attempt to put the school of national learning into a global context and to justify Japanese borrowing from other cultures.[67] From Hirata to Ōkuni, we see an expanding intellectual force that sought to include other elements in its system. Such thinking also demonstrates the changing attitude toward China and the West in late Tokugawa times.

Aizawa Seishisai (1781–1863) of the Mito school attacked Motoori and Hirata's ideas in his defense of the *I Ching*. Paraphrasing a passage from the *Naobi no mitama* (The Spirit of the Deity Naobi), he maintained that the *shen-tao* (Shinto) mentioned in the *I Ching* was not an empty theory but had once been put into practice by the sages.[68] Aizawa used the *I Ching* frequently in his discussions on the Age of the Gods, international relations, politics, and morality. His most significant idea was, perhaps, to put the *I Ching* into the context of Japanese politics and history.[69] In his explanation of the hexagram *kuan*, Aizawa used the Japanese deities and imperial ancestors to replace the sages of ancient China. He remarked: "In the past, the imperial ancestors [the Sun Goddess and Shinto deities], in accordance with the way of the gods, laid down their instructions. Hence loyalty and filial piety became known and human relationships were settled."[70]

Aizawa defined Shinto as a natural way of revering heaven and worshipping deities. He again used the hexagram *kuan* to show that Shinto was the teaching created by Japanese deities based on natural human feelings:

> In our heavenly dynasty, leaders [of the ancient times] worshipped the gods of heaven and earth and were respected by the people. Therefore, [the *I Ching* reads]: "The sages, in accordance with Shinto, laid down their instructions, and all under heaven yield submission to them." The *I Ching* is implicitly in agreement with the Shinto of our heavenly dynasty.[71]

Here the *I Ching* was used without any reference to China. The project of Japanizing the text thus went through two stages: it began with Hirata Atsutane and his students, who claimed that the book had Japanese origins, and ended with Aizawa Seishisai, who put it into a Japanese context.

Concluding Remarks

For much of the Tokugawa period, Shinto had no independent status; rather, it was subordinate to Buddhism institutionally and to Confucianism intellectually.[72] Early Tokugawa Shinto was heavily indebted to the *I Ching* for the formation of its ideas. Many Confucians strove to accommodate Shinto to their neo-Confucian syntheses. History then took a reverse course in late Tokugawa times. Thanks largely to the Hirata school, Shinto became conceptualized and politicized, so that the idea that Shinto was Japan's indigenous religion gained wide currency in the nineteenth century. The Hirata school absorbed elements from Chinese and Dutch learning; including the *I Ching* with Shinto was only a part of this expanding discourse.

This chapter has developed two themes. First, the *I Ching* played a crucial role in the discussion of the relationship between Confucianism and Shinto. In the early Tokugawa period, when the relationship was harmonious, both Confucians and Shintoists used the *I Ching* to uphold the doctrine of the unity of Confucianism and Shinto. When the school of national learning became a powerful intellectual force and the arch-rival of Confucianism in the latter half of the Tokugawa period, both *kokugaku* scholars and some Confucians denied any affinity between Confucianism and Shinto. *Kokugaku* Shintoists rebuked Confucianism in public, but many of them were still influenced by it. They used the *I Ching* for its metaphysical and divinational value.

Second, early Tokugawa Confucians endeavored to sinicize or Confucianize Shinto by pinpointing its Chinese origins. The Hirata school turned this argument upside down, initiating the project of Japanizing the *I Ching* by claiming its Japanese origin. This project was completed by Aizawa Seishisai of the Mito school, who used the form of the text but emptied it of its Chinese content. The history of the transformation of the *I Ching* from a Confucian classic into a Shinto or Japanese text demonstrates the emergence of a nativist movement and the subtlety of the relationship between Confucianism and Shinto.

7. The *I Ching* and Buddhism

Scholars commonly believe that, compared to Confucianism and Taoism, Buddhism was less influenced by the *I Ching*,[1] probably because Buddhism's sophisticated metaphysical framework made extensive ideological borrowing unnecessary. Although the relationship between the *I Ching* and Buddhism was subtle, and at times even nebulous, their intellectual exchange is historically significant and deserves close examination.[2] Their relationship in Japan is particularly interesting because there was more interaction between the two there than in China and Korea.

For many centuries in pre-modern Japan, *I Ching* scholarship and its related *yin-yang* tradition, shamanistic practices, and even Confucianism developed within the Mahāyāna Buddhist system. By the sixteenth century, when Buddhism began to lose its intellectual hegemony, a new relationship had developed between it and the *I Ching*. This process and its significance are explained here by examining how Tokugawa Buddhists and Confucians discussed the relationship between Buddhism and Confucianism through the medium of the *I Ching*.

The Making of a New Relationship between the *I Ching* and Buddhism

I Ching scholarship was a component of the Mahāyāna Buddhist system in medieval Japan. The *I Ching* served as a maidservant to Zen Buddhism. Zen Buddhist monks used it and other Confucian texts to explicate their Buddhist beliefs. Many of them advocated the doc-

114

trine of the unity of Buddhism and Confucianism, which regarded the two teachings as "two aspects of one truth" because both Zen Buddhism and neo-Confucianism agreed on many ideas, such as the possibility of self-cultivation.

The intellectual influence of Buddhism had weakened by the end of the sixteenth century, and the relationship between the *I Ching* and Buddhism changed. Compared to their medieval counterparts, Buddhist monks of the Tokugawa period played a less important role in Japanese intellectual and cultural life. Their *I Ching* scholarship produced very few important works or original ideas. In the first half of the Tokugawa period, from the seventeenth century to the mid-eighteenth century, Confucianism worked to separate itself from and even to confront Buddhism by incorporating *I Ching* studies and other teachings into its system of ideas, thus challenging the doctrine of *Jubutsu itchi* (the unity of Buddhism and Confucianism). Confucians rather than Zen monks became the major force in *I Ching* scholarship, a process that took several decades to complete. But during the first few decades of the Tokugawa period, the Confucians maintained their Buddhist ties and Zen monks played a significant role, though no longer as leaders, in *I Ching* studies and in the intellectual world in general.

Under these new conditions, the *I Ching* became the "battleground" for Confucians and Buddhists. This process and the significance of this relationship are the topic of this chapter, which examines how Buddhists and Confucians discussed their mutual relationship by utilizing the *I Ching*.

The *I Ching* in Buddhist-Confucian Relations

Before we examine the arguments of both sides, a fundamental question must be answered—namely, why it was the *I Ching*, rather than some other text that became so widely used in defining the relationship between Buddhism and Confucianism. That the *I Ching* was the most important text to tie Confucianism and Buddhism together in Japan is obvious, because both sides referred to it frequently when discussing their mutual relationship. Moreover, the *I Ching* was commonly used throughout East Asia when Buddhists—but also some Confucians—sought to expound on the basic unity of the two traditions.

From medieval times in Japan, Zen monks often quoted the following passages from the *I Ching* to show that Confucianism also espoused Buddhist doctrines such as the karmic retribution of good and evil, transmigration of three lives, gods and ghosts, and universal flux. The most frequently quoted passage comes from the *Wen Yen* (Commentary on the Words of the Text) on the hexagram *k'un* (the receptive):

> A house that heaps good upon good is sure to have an abundance of blessings. A house that heaps evil upon evil is sure to have an abundance of ills. Where a servant murders his master, where a son murders his father, the causes do not lie between the morning and evening of one day. It took a long time for things to go so far. It came about because things that should have been stopped were not stopped soon enough. In the *Book of Changes* it is said: "When there is hoarfrost underfoot, solid ice is not far off." This shows how far things go when they are allowed to run on.[3]

This excerpt reveals a primitive view of the causal relationship and was the most-quoted passage used by Buddhist monks and Confucians to demonstrate the commonality of the two teachings in both China and Japan.[4] In effect, many used it support the Buddhist view of karmic retribution.

The second most-quoted passage is from the first chapter of the *Hsi Tz'u* (Commentary on the Appended Judgments):

> Going back to the beginnings of things and pursuing them to the end, we come to know the lessons of birth and of death. The union of seed and power produces all things; the escape of the soul brings about change. Through this we come to know the conditions of gods and ghosts.[5]

This ambiguous statement led to arguments about whether or not the change in life form after death implied transmigration. It was cited by some Buddhists who argued that Confucianism also believed in the existence of spirits and an afterlife.

The third most frequently quoted passage is from the second chapter of the *Hsi Tz'u:*

> If good does not accumulate, it is not enough to make a name for a man. If evil does not accumulate, it is not strong enough to destroy a man. Therefore the inferior man thinks to himself, "Goodness in small things has no value," and so neglects it. He thinks, "Small sins do no harm," and so does not give them up. Thus his sins accumulate until they can no longer be covered up and his guilt becomes so great that it can no longer be wiped out.[6]

Suggesting retribution in one's present life, this reasonable moral judgment provides another support for the concept of karmic retribution.

In addition, many Buddhists pointed out that both Buddhism and the *I Ching* contain the idea of universal flux, or *mujō* (evanescence, or impermanence) in Buddhist terminology, a pessimistic idea and one said to be the source of human sorrow. The *I Ching* expounds the idea of *heneki,* or circular change, which has a slightly more optimistic tone because it suggests that things are bound to turn good no matter how bad a current situation may be.[7] For instance, after the bad hexagram *p'i* (stagnation) comes a good hexagram, *t'ai* (peace). The hexagram *p'i* says: "The standstill comes to an end. First standstill, then good fortune." This is central to the logic and philosophy of the *I Ching* and is reiterated throughout the text.

These passages were discussed and interpreted in different ways in Tokugawa Japan. Many Buddhists used them to link Confucianism with Buddhism, whereas some Confucians denied any such affinity. The *I Ching* therefore played a central role in both the defense of and the attack on the doctrine of *Jubutsu itchi.*

The *I Ching* in the Criticism of Tokugawa Buddhism

Many early Tokugawa Confucians discarded the doctrine of *Jubutsu itchi* and the Buddhist interpretation of the *I Ching.* They emphasized the Confucian and Shinto aspects of the *I Ching* and used it as a major textual source for incorporating Shinto into the Confucian system. This changing perspective on Buddhist-Confucian relations is seen in a poem composed by Nakae Tōju (1608–1648) during his 1639 visit to a temple on Takejōjima, a small island in Lake Biwa:

> A mountain [hexagram *ken*] came out from the water [hexagram
>   *k'an*]
> by changing the first line to *yang,*
> The God of the Hexagrams was indeed Daimyōjin,
> Buddhist monks mistook him for the Bodhisattva Sarasvatī
>   (Benzaiten),
> The revolution of the universe will bring back the truth one day.[8]

Nakae found that many people worshipped the Shinto deity Daimyōjin, who was enshrined in the temple on the island. According to the Shingon understanding of *honji suijaku*—the idea that buddhas and bodhisattvas manifested as Shinto deities in ancient Japan—the

Great Sun Buddha (Mahāvairocana, or Dai'nichi Nyorai) appeared at Mount Miwa in Yamato in the form of Daimyōjin.[9] Nakae's poem suggests that Daimyōjin is actually the God of the Hexagrams, not a manifestation of the Great Sun Buddha. As such, the poem serves as a metaphor of the ideological power struggle that took place in this period between Buddhism and Confucianism over the right to incorporate Shinto into their respective systems of belief.

Most Tokugawa Confucians were highly critical of Buddhism. They frequently attacked two aspects of the religion—what they saw as (1) its irrational ideas about the law of karma, heaven and hell, and transmigration, and (2) its anti-social and apolitical character. Often the points of criticism were developed from their readings and discussions of the controversial hexagram *k'un*.

Arai Hakuseki (1657–1725) refuted Buddhist interpretations of the *I Ching* in his *Kishinron* (Discourse on Gods and Ghosts), arguing that the text's view of cause and effect differs from the Buddhist view and lacks the correct understanding of the *san shih* (three generations, or three lives). In Arai's opinion, the *I Ching* discusses good and evil retribution in the present life only, in terms of individuals and families:

> The common saying of the people in this world is "A house that heaps good upon good is sure to have an abundance of blessings. A house that heaps evil upon evil is sure to have an abundance of ills." However, we have seen many cases where good people did not get this blessing, and bad people did. Hence Buddhism advocates the theory of transmigration in three lifetimes in order to explain this phenomenon. [According to this theory,] good people have misfortunes because they are repaying the bad karma of previous lives. If they have repaid all their sins, they will definitely receive blessings in their afterlife. Bad people receive blessings in this life because they did good deeds in a previous life. Once the reward has ended, they are bound to have misfortunes in their afterlife. [I think that] this theory grasps the truth of trivial things but ignores the truth of very important things. . . . In the *I Ching*, you can also find the idea of the accumulation of good and evil. In a family, the grandfather at the top and the offspring at the bottom, the person himself in the middle and his uncles and cousins on both sides are together called this name [i.e., three generations, or *san shih*]. Despite the name *"san shih,"* it only concerns the present life of an individual. Although the sages said that it [i.e., retribution] would pass through the upper, middle, and lower levels and down through thousands of generations, it only involves one family.[10]

Here Arai reinterpreted the hexagram *k'un* to make it strictly Confucian and rational. *San shih* in his definition refers simply to three generations within a family, not to the three lives of a person. Although Arai disagreed with the Buddhist doctrines of karmic retribution and transmigration in three lives, his critique was relatively mild and accommodating.[11]

Okada Hakuku (1691–1767), a Chu Hsi scholar, also compared the understanding of causality in Confucianism and Buddhism, pointing out three main differences. First, Buddhism maintains the idea of retribution of good and evil over three lifetimes (the previous life, this life, and the afterlife) of the same person, whereas the *I Ching* talks about retribution within three generations (parents, the person him- or herself, and his or her descendants). Second, in Buddhism cause and effect is a personal matter that has essentially nothing to do with the family, whereas the Confucian understanding of causality is relevant only in relation to the ancestral lineage (in other words, both a person's own conduct and that of the members of his family affect each person within this structure). Third, Buddhist retribution is essentially ahistorical and based on belief, whereas the Confucian understanding of causality is historical and rational. Okada wrote:

> The *I Ching* reads: "A house that heaps good upon good is sure to have
> an abundance of blessings. A house that heaps evil upon evil is sure to
> have an abundance of ills." This is the teaching of the sages. Buddhist
> causality only concerns itself with one person. For instance, a person
> who does good deeds [will be blessed], even though his parents may
> have done bad things. He is therefore not influenced by the good and
> evil [behavior] of his parents. What the sages wrote in the *I Ching* about
> "a house that heaps good upon good" are words [meant] to encourage
> one's descendants. If a good man has no blessings in the course of his
> life, then his descendants will definitely have them. If a bad man re-
> ceives no misfortune during his life, his descendants will surely have
> it. This has proved true in our historical records. This is the difference
> between Confucianism and Buddhism.[12]

Yamagata Bantō (1748–1821) went one step farther than Arai and Okada in his critique of a Buddhist causality. In his *Yume no shiro* (In Place of Dreams), he categorically rejected the Buddhist idea of retribution as well as the existence of gods and ghosts. Yamagata believed that man himself, not some transcendental heaven, contributes to the cause and effect of good and evil. To this end, he provided the following rational and persuasive explanation of the hexagram *k'un:*

If a man always does many good deeds and never does anything bad, he will be praised by everyone. When he has urgent problems, ten thousand people will come to his assistance. A man who does bad things all the time and does nothing good will be disliked by everyone. When he has urgent problems, ten thousand people will rise and attack him. They will be glad to see his demise. . . . The retribution of good and evil has nothing to do with heaven but depends on man. In a sense, heaven means [the power of] being loved or hated by ten thousand people. That is the meaning of the saying of the *I Ching* to the effect that "A house that heaps good upon good is sure to have an abundance of blessings. A house that heaps evil upon evil is sure to have an abundance of ills." However, there are people who are hated by ten thousand people and enjoy longevity and blessings, whereas some are loved by ten thousand people but meet an untimely and unfortunate death. Yen Tzu and Tao Chih were such examples. How could this happen? It only happens once in a million people. It is an exception, not the rule.[13]

These three examples show that the Tokugawa Confucians used the *I Ching* primarily to attack what they saw as the irrationality of Buddhist doctrines on retribution. However, they employed other texts, such as the *Ta Hsüeh* and *Hsiao Ching,* to criticize Buddhist anti-social and apolitical ideas.

In addition, many Tokugawa Confucians, in particular *kogaku* scholars, blamed the Sung commentaries on the *I Ching* for adding Buddhist ideas to the Confucian meaning. Itō Jinsai (1627–1707) provided a historical and philological analysis of Ch'eng I's misreading of the text. He traced the origins of *t'i-yung* (essence and function) dualism to a commentary on the *Garland Sūtra* by the T'ang dynasty Hua-yen (Kegon) Buddhist monk Ch'ing-liang, and demonstrated how Ch'eng I had misread the *I Ching* by promoting Buddhist ideas of "emptiness" *(hsü,* or *kyo)* and "quietude" *(chi,* or *jaku).* Itō wrote:

In the T'ang, the monk master Ch'ing-liang's commentary on the *Garland Sūtra* reads: "Substance *(t'i)* and function *(yung)* are of the same origin, and they are precise and perfect." Ch'eng I borrowed these two phrases and put them in the preface of his *I Chuan.* . . . The words *"hsü"* (emptiness) and *"chi"* (quietude) come from Buddhism and Taoism, and cannot be found in our books of the sages. However, the *Ta Hsiang* of the hexagram *hsien* (wooing) reads: "A gentleman receives people with modesty *(hsü)."* The *Hsi Tz'u* reads: "The Changes have no consciousness, no activity; they are quiescent *(chi)* and do not move. But if they are stimulated, they penetrate all situations under heaven." Hence we see the words *"hsü"* and *"chi."* However, *hsü* in the hexagram *hsien* means doing without intentions, and *chi* in the *Hsi Tz'u*

Chuan refers to the goodness of the yarrow stalks. They are not meant to explain the substance *(t'i)* of the principle *(li)*. Actually, Ch'eng I only used the word *"chi"* to discuss mind. Beginners do not know the essence of the *I Ching*, and think that the real meaning of the sages is like that. How wrong they are![14]

Hara Sōkei (1718–1767), a student of Itō Tōgai, stressed that the *I Ching* itself was unrelated to Buddhism; that the idea of *wu-chi* (ultimate non-being) in Chou Tun-i's *T'ai-chi t'u-shuo* had been borrowed from a T'ang period Hua-yen monk, Tao Shun (558–640); and that the dualism of *t'i-yung* in K'ung Ying-ta (574–648) and Ch'eng I's commentaries on the *I Ching* had been influenced by Ch'ing-liang.[15] Ōta Kinjō (1765–1825) expressed a similar opinion, adding that Chu Hsi's explanation of the *I Ching* had also been influenced by Buddhism, and that Ch'eng I and Chu Hsi had misread the *Hsi Tz'u* to advocate the Buddhist ideas of *tao-ch'i* (metaphysics-physics) and *li-ch'i* (principle and material force). In the *Gimonroku* (Records of My Doubts, 1831), he wrote:

> Ch'eng I and Chu Hsi adopted the theories of *tao-ch'i* and *li-ch'i*. These terms were borrowed from the idea of *shih-li* (phenomena and principle) of the Tendai sect and the *Garland Sūtra*. Ch'eng and Chu both used the *Hsi Tz'u Chuan* as the textual support for these ideas. Having examined the *Hsi Tz'u*, I cannot find any of the ideas suggested by Ch'eng and Chu. All their arguments are [based on] false evidence.[16]

Ōta gave three examples to illustrate the mistakes in how Ch'eng and Chu interpreted the *Hsi Tz'u*.[17]

Hirose Yokusō (1816–1863) also pointed out the Buddhist influences in Ch'eng I's scholarship on the *I Ching*, writing, for instance:

> In the *I Chuan*, Ch'eng I said: "Stop where you cannot see, and you will have no desires to disturb your heart. Stopping will bring you comfort." This is like Mahākāśyapa [one of the ten disciples of the Buddha] confining himself to a snowy mountain, and Bodhidharma [Daruma] facing the wall.[18]

This distinction between original Confucianism and Sung learning became a powerful device—and one that was skillfully developed by scholars of both *kogaku* (the school of ancient learning) and the eclectic school in their insistence on the separation of Buddhism and Confucianism.

In nineteenth-century Japan, more and more Confucians came to discuss the relationship between Confucianism and Buddhism from a new perspective. Unlike the Buddhists and Confucians of the seventeenth and eighteenth centuries, who admitted and acknowledged the Buddhist influence of Sung interpretations of the *I Ching*, these late-Tokugawa Confucians emphasized just the opposite—namely, Buddhism's indebtedness to the *I Ching* in the formation of its doctrines. One of them, the Chu Hsi scholar Okada Kōtei (1791–1838), made a textual comparison of the *I Ching* and a number of Buddhist texts. He found that the latter had borrowed heavily from the former, and wrote:

> Buddhists have included many words and ideas from our sages to enrich their own theories. As a result [of this], good seeds bring poor crops. There are many [sentences in the Buddhist texts] similar to the teachings of Confucius and Mencius. The *I Ching* reads: "The Changes have no consciousness, no action; they are quiescent and do not move. But if they are stimulated, they penetrate all situations under heaven" *(Hsi Tz'u)*. The Buddhist sūtra reads: "It has no thinking, no activity; it is quiet and does not move. It penetrates every corner of the world" *(Garland Sūtra)*. The *I Ching* reads: "The same voice brings the same echo. The same aspirations meet" *(Wen Yen)*. The Buddha said: "Purity brings a pure echo; the impure and the impurities meet" *(Agongyō* or *Āgama Sūtra)*. . . . Why do scholars only recognize that the ideas of the Sung Confucians resemble Buddhism?[19]

Another Confucian scholar, Isobe Tadakata, also claimed that "Buddhist ideas were indeed borrowed from a superficial reading of the *I Ching*."[20] With his knowledge of the text, he claimed to have easily grasped the purport of the writings of Zen Buddhism. This reverse development reflects the change in the balance of power between Confucianism and Buddhism at that time.

Use of the *I Ching* to Defend Tokugawa Buddhism

During the first few decades of the Tokugawa period, Buddhist monks remained influential in *I Ching* scholarship. Many Zen monks were invited to lecture on the text. For example, Daifukuan taught Hino Sukekatsu, a courtier, during the Kan'ei era (1624–1628), and Zenshu Kanshō (1548–1636), the tenth rector of the Ashikaga School, enjoyed the patronage of the bakufu, the court, and various daimyō. Every new year, Zenshu was asked to use the *I Ching* to predict how upcoming events would unfold.[21]

The Ashikaga School was still very prestigious in *I Ching* studies during early Tokugawa times but gradually ceased to be at their center as it had been during the medieval period. In the period under its ninth rector, Kanshitsu Genkitsu (1548–1636), up to its the sixteenth, Gekkō Genchō, the School continued to produce important ideas and commentaries on the text.[22] Kanshitsu became famous for opening a branch school in Kyoto, and he acted as an *I Ching* diviner both to Tokugawa Ieyasu at the Battle of Sekigahara in 1600 and to Mōri Terumoto (1534–1625), a daimyō from Southern Honshu, for whom he checked the geomancy of Hagi Castle. The rectors were all *I Ching* specialists and familiar with the practice of divination. Under their leadership, the Ashikaga School published or reprinted many books on the *I Ching* on its own printing press.[23]

In terms of intellectual vitality, however, Buddhism was in decline. Many Confucians, including Hayashi Razan (1583–1659), Yamazaki Ansai (1618–1682), and Ogyū Sorai (1666–1728), adopted an ardent anti-Buddhist stance and exerted increasing pressure on Buddhism, which retreated to a position of defense. In response to the strong Confucian challenge, Zen monks in particular made many attempts to reinvigorate Buddhist beliefs during this period. One of their major strategies was to propagate the doctrine of *Jubutsu itchi*. In early Tokugawa Japan, dozens of Buddhist monks, the majority of whom belonged to the Zen tradition, wrote extensively to promote their doctrines. Their writings reflect the differing attitudes that Buddhists and Confucians had toward each other during this time. In general, the Buddhist side was more reconciliatory toward Confucianism and other non-Buddhist doctrines than the Confucian side was toward Buddhism. Moreover, a number of important Buddhist leaders defended their religion from Confucian attacks through their explanations of the *I Ching*.

In 1605, Tokugawa Ieyasu ordered Saishō Shōtai (1533–1607), the abbot of Shōkokuji in Kyoto, and Kanshitsu Genkitsu, the rector of the Ashikaga School, to take charge of the publication of the Fushimi (Keichō) edition of the *I Ching*. Saishō hoped that the *I Ching* would become a bridge that would join Buddhists and Confucians. In the preface, he advocated the unity of the two teachings by writing:

> Confucian scholars from past to present reject the Buddhist scriptures, while Buddhist scholars [on their part] rebuke the Confucian classics. Ordinary people in this world are unable to distinguish the truth. If Śākyamuni Buddha had been born in China, he would have set forth his teaching the same way the Duke of Chou and Confucius did. If the Duke of Chou and Confucius had been born in the Western Heaven [India], they would have presented their teachings in the same manner

as Śākyamuni Buddha. In the beginning, Confucianism and Buddhism did not represent two different ways. [Hence] they can be compared to two wings of a bird, or to the two wheels of a vehicle.[24]

From this it is clear that Saishō believed that the Way set forth in the *I Ching* was in agreement with the path of Buddhism, so that publication of the *I Ching* promoted the true understanding of Buddhism. In his diary, he wrote:

> On the order from our Lord, the Shogun Minamoto [Tokugawa] Ieyasu, we have published the *Chou I* to spread the Way of the sages for [the next] ten thousand years. We have corrected the mistakes and added Lu Te-ming's [556–627] views on sound and meaning to the commentary by Wang Pi to perfect the text. There is an old saying to the effect that "When the Buddha held up a flower on the top of Mount Grdhrakuta, Mahākāsyāpa smiled faintly." [This nonverbal transmission was like] Fu Hsi drawing the first stroke of the trigrams. Bodhidharma [Daruma] facing the wall at the Shao Lin Temple and King Wen's doubling the lines of the trigrams during [the time of] his imprisonment were similar experiences. Because of this, Zen monks must study the way of the *I Ching* thoroughly.[25]

Saishō's edition of the *I Ching* became one of the most popular to be printed during the Tokugawa period; as such, it was probably the single most important Buddhist contribution to *I Ching* scholarship undertaken in Tokugawa Japan.

Takuan Sōhō (1573–1645), the abbot of Daitokuji, was the most famous Rinzai monk of the early Tokugawa period. He strove vigorously to revive Zen Buddhism and enjoyed the patronage of Tokugawa Iemitsu (1604–1651). Takuan used the *I Ching* and other Confucian texts to explain Buddhist concepts and ideas. In his explanation of the karmic retribution of good and evil in the course of three lives, Takuan quoted the *Wen Yen* on the hexagram *k'un*.[26] His ideas on metaphysics, politics, medicine, martial arts, and divination were all influenced to a considerable extent by his reading of the *I Ching*. For instance, he sounded like a Confucian when he used the theory of *yin-yang wu-hsing* to support the doctrine of *Jubutsu itchi* in his *Jitsurigaku no shōkei* (A Shortcut to Practical Philosophy).

Other Zen monks of the Tokugawa era did not hesitate to insist on the superiority of Buddhism over Confucianism. Suzuki Shōsan (1579–1655), a samurai turned Zen monk, agreed with the commonality of the two traditions because they both taught one to praise good and chastise evil. However, he insisted that Buddhism represented a higher teaching because it helped people escape karmic transmigration. While he respected the philosophy of the *I Ching*, Suzuki despised its system of divination, which had been commonly practiced by Buddhist monks ever since medieval times. The use of divination was particularly prevalent among the followers of Zen, Shingon, and Shūgendō (a minor Buddhist school that stressed the importance of esotericism and hermitage). Suzuki's *Kaijō monogatari* (Stories Told on the Sea) includes an interesting story about a father who asked Suzuki to use the *I Ching* to decide whether his son would be a monk or a physician, to which Suzuki replied, "I study the way of Buddha and of the patriarchs, I know nothing of the way of *yin* and *yang.*"[27]

Unshō (1613–1693) was a famous Shingon monk who received the patronage of the bakufu and court. His knowledge of Confucianism was outstanding in Buddhist circles. He used the *honji suijaku* doctrine to explain the origins of Confucianism. According to Unshō, all ancient Chinese sages were manifestations of the buddhas and bodhisattvas. He cited the *Nirvāna Sūtra (Nehangyō)* and other sūtras to prove that Fu Hsi was indeed a bodhisattva.[28]

During the Tokugawa period, Sōtō Zen monks also advocated a doctrine similar to, and in fact influenced by, the philosophy of the *I Ching*—namely, the doctrine of the five ranks *(goisetsu)*. This doctrine, which was central to the traditional teachings of Chinese Ts'ao-tung Ch'an and of Sōtō Zen in Japan, had originated in China with Tung-shan (807–869) and his primary disciple, Ts'ao-shan (840–901). The doctrine of the five ranks is metaphysical as well as dialectic, and illustrates the five-fold relationship between the absolute *(shō)* and the relative *(hen)*. According to this doctrine, the absolute is a true emptiness that serves as the foundation of heaven, earth, and man, while the relative are phenomena, or the condition in which the absolute manifests in concrete form.

According to this system of thought, the absolute and the relative are interdependent, while the five ranks are the different stages in the relationship between the two, and thus illustrate the various possibilities of the universe. The five ranks are: (1) the absolute within the relative—from the absolute to the relative; (2) the relative within the absolute—from the relative to the absolute; (3) the absolute by itself—the absolute prior to any externalization; (4) the relative by itself; and (5) the absolute and the relative together in the state of undifferentiated oneness, which is the highest of the five ranks.[29] Sōtō monks usually used the first five lines of a given hexagram to explain the five ranks. In this way the dialectic system could be used to interpret everything in the world, such as the relationship between the emperor and his subjects, the different stages of development in life, and so on.[30]

Taihaku Kokusui (d. 1700) used the doctrine of the five ranks in his *Sōtō gokokuben* (Sōtō Zen in Defense of the Nation, 1676) to advocate the unity of the three teachings of Buddhism, Shinto, and Confucianism. He openly admitted that Zen Buddhism was indebted to the *I Ching* in the formation of many of its ideas and rituals, and suggested that Tung Shan had used the numerology of the *Hsi Tz'u* in his creation of the doctrine of the five ranks:

> The *Hsi Tz'u* reads: "The number for heaven is five; the number for earth is five." They both contain the principles of the five ranks and are in harmony. Hence the even numbers in the *Ho T'u* and the odd numbers in the *Lo Shu* all take the number five as their basis. The image of [the character] "five" starts with the character "two," which represents heaven and earth, and it becomes five when we add to it [the character] "man" to form the three powers [i.e., heaven, earth, and man]. If heaven and earth have it [the number five], is there any reason that man does not have it? It was for this reason that Tung Shan created the doctrine of the five ranks.[31]

Taihaku also thought that Shōsetu had created the *gozan* (five-mountain) institution in Kyoto based on his understanding of the *I Ching* scholarship of the Chinese monk Ma-i.

Taihaku compared the *I Ching* with Po-ch'eng's *Hyakujō seiki* (Buddhist Monastic Code) as follows:

> The *I Ching* is a book about feelings and [their] regulations. This is where the rites and the music of this world are rooted. The *Hyakujō seiki* is the field of blessing for [those dwelling within] the three boundaries [of a monastery]. The rites and music used in our temple originated there.[32]

Taihaku cited the *I Ching* and other Confucian classics to prove that many Buddhist ideas could also be found in Confucianism. For instance, he believed that the idea of precepts *(kai)* was identical in the three teachings:

> The fulfillment of Buddhism, the achievement of thousands of virtues, and the illumination of thousand of kinds of wisdom are all brought by the virtue of the precepts *(kai-toku)*. This is being emphasized in the three teachings [Shinto, Confucianism, and Buddhism]. The *I Ching* set forth the Confucian prohibition [as follows]: "Using the precepts

(sai-kai) to prohibit [excess human desire], the sages manifested the virtues of the deities." . . . The *Commentary on the Image* of the hexagram *chi chi* (after completion) reads: "Obey the prohibition all day long."[33]

Taihaku's book was widely read and had a considerable impact on the bakufu's policy on religion.

The reviver of Rinzai Zen, Hakuin Ekaku (1685–1768), is remembered as the greatest Zen master of the Tokugawa period. He reminded his followers that although Buddhism and Confucianism look similar on many points, Buddhism actually represents a higher teaching because it deals with the essential problem of life and death. Confucian teachings, in contrast, are "nothing but inessential things" used for "nothing more than giving help in a dream to a dream."[34] Hakuin held that Hayashi Razan's anti-Buddhist ideas were the result of his jealousy over the success of Buddhism and did not reflect the true differences between Confucianism and Buddhism. He argued with Confucians of his day who believed that the driving forces of life, *yin* and *yang,* would die out once life was over:

> Nowadays, when people hear stories [of heaven and hell] such as this, they frequently take them as empty theories and deluded talk, and they will clap their hands and roar with laughter, saying: "For man, with the good functioning of *yin* and *yang,* death is like the extinguishing of a lamp. What heaven can there be? How can there be a hell?" This is the heresy that everything ends with death, and it is a frighteningly evil view. There is no idiocy that exceeds this.[35]

By criticizing those who in his opinion misread the *I Ching* in order to attack Buddhism, Hakuin used the theories found in the text to explicate his Buddhist and philosophical views. He was also a champion of the doctrine of the five ranks. It is said that when his master, Shōju Etan, taught him this difficult doctrine, Hakuin understood immediately because of his prior study of the *I Ching*.[36] When he talked about metaphysics, he sounded like a Confucian paraphrasing the *I Ching:* "When the Way was divided, we had two poles. The fusion of *yin* and *yang* gave birth to human beings and other things. . . . Everything came from two. When the two poles separated, heaven and earth appeared, just like *yin* and *yang.* The four images, the eight trigrams, and the sixty-four hexagrams then came one after the other."[37]

Hakuin became famous for his *I Ching* scholarship and evidently believed that the text could prove a useful reference to Buddhist scholars. Later, he passed these teachings on to his leading disciples, Teishū and Tōrei Enji (1721–1792). The account of the first meeting between Hakuin and Teishū is particularly interesting. Teishū was said to be a highly learned person who understood all Buddhist and non-Buddhist scriptures except the *I Ching*. While on the way to Edo to find a Confucian under whom to study, he met Hakuin, who told him: "If you do not understand your own nature first, you cannot understand the principles of the *I Ching*. Why don't you stay here? You will then come to understand yourself. When you discover your own nature one day, I will lecture on the *I Ching* for you."[38] Following this, Teishū is said to have studied under Hakuin for more than ten years.

The *I Ching* and Anti-Buddhist Sentiment in the Late Tokugawa

The decline of Buddhism was a slow process. During the early Tokugawa period, it remained an important intellectual force in *I Ching* studies. Many talented monks attempted to revive and defend Buddhism, but its influence on the intellectual world of Japan declined further during the second half of the Tokugawa era. By the mid-eighteenth century, Buddhism was in a miserable state of intellectual and moral bankruptcy, although the Ōbaku Zen sect (established in the early Tokugawa to reform decaying Buddhism in Japan) made significant cultural contributions and Buddhist temples in general enjoyed material prosperity.

Not only Confucianism but new forces, such as *kokugaku* and the Mito school, were hostile to Buddhism. Buddhism itself was simply incapable of producing monks with the intellectual caliber needed to deal with the situation. The Buddhists were unable to defend themselves against ferocious attacks from a number of critics, such as Tominaga Nakamoto (1715–1746), Hattori Tenyū, and Hirata Atsutane (1730–1801).[39] Not only did Buddhists lose the ideological battle with Confucians over the issue of *Jubutsu itchi* in early Tokugawa times, but by late Tokugawa times they had to defend their own ideas against severe attacks from other schools of thought as well.[40]

The decline of Buddhism can also be seen in the greatly diminished role of Buddhist monks in *I Ching* studies, where no more important works or ideas were produced. There were also no more records of monks lecturing on the text at court or to the bakufu or daimyō. The Buddhist center for *I Ching* studies, the Ashikaga School, was in decline as well.[41] We therefore examine how Buddhists fought and eventually lost their ideological battle to the anti-Buddhist camp in late Tokugawa Japan by highlighting the role that the *I Ching* played in this process.

In 1728, a bold but futile attempt was made to revive Buddhism when Japanese monks reprinted the *Chou-i Ch'an-chieh* (Ch'an Buddhist Interpretation of the *I Ching*, 1641) by the late-Ming Zen monk Chih-hsü Ou-i (1599–1655).[42] This work represented the finest scholarship on the *I Ching* ever written by a Buddhist monk, and had considerable impact in China. By using Buddhist terms and ideas to interpret the *I Ching*, the *Chou-i Ch'an-chieh* created an original synthesis of neo-Confucianism and Buddhism. For example, in his explanation of the hexagram *ch'ien* (creation), Chih-hsü wrote:

> Creation is production, . . . for if production is directed toward the ten sins of the higher order, then man will fall into hell; if toward the ten sins of the middle order, then man is reborn as an animal; if toward the ten sins of the lower order, then man is reborn as a *preta* (hungry ghost). If production is directed toward the ten good deeds of the lower order, then man will be reborn as a *preta;* if toward the ten good deeds of the middle order, then a man in his future remains a man. . . . If his production is directed toward the ten good deeds of the highest order and he can be useful for himself and for others, then he will be called a *bodhisattva*.[43]

The printing of this book was only a modest success, and it never enjoyed a wide circulation outside of Buddhist circles in Tokugawa Japan.[44] Nevertheless, it was attacked by many Buddhist critics for distorting the original ideas of the *I Ching*.

Chūmoku Gikai (d. 1767), a Jōdo Shin (New Pure Land) monk, used the *I Ching* to uphold Buddhist beliefs. For example, on the prohibition against killing, he wrote:

> The *Chou I* reads: "The neighbor in the East who slaughters an ox does not attain as much real blessing as the neighbor in the West who presents a small offering." Hence we realize that the important thing in offering lies with sincerity, not slaughter. The text also reads: "The greatest virtue in the universe is staying alive." Killing living things to offer them to the ancestors goes against benevolence and heaven.[45]

Inkei Chidatsu (1704–1769) provided a last-ditch counterattack on the Confucian position. He wrote the *Jubutsu gōron* (Discourse on Confucianism and Buddhism) in response to attacks on Buddhism by the famous Confucians Yamazaki Ansai and Kumazawa Banzan (1619–1681). Yamazaki Ansai considered Buddhist ethics immoral because Buddhists ignored their worldly responsibilities. Inkei replied to this accusation by using the ideas of metaphysics *(hsing-erh-shang)* on the one hand and physics *(hsing-erh-hsia)* on the other, as well as the *tao-ch'i* dualism set forth in the *I Ching*. The *Hsi Tz'u* reads: "What is above form is called *tao;* what is within form is called *ch'i*." Inkei argued that Buddhism and Confucianism represent two aspects of one truth—*tao* and *ch'i*, respectively. In his understanding, Confucians pursue worldly wisdom and ethics whereas Buddhists seek the transcendental way to ultimate salvation. Hence Buddhists practice a higher form of ethics.[46]

Kumazawa Banzan attacked Buddhist ideas of transmigration and of ghosts suffering in the hells, and believed that both the body and soul would disappear after death. Inkei strongly defended the Buddhist position, claiming that references to ghosts occur 177 times in the Confucian classics and that both the Duke of Chou and Confucius believed in the existence of such beings. On transmigration, he found support for his views in the *Hsi Tz'u*, where it is said: "The union of seed and power produces all things; the escape of the soul brings about change."[47]

Inkei also argued that the metaphysics of Buddhism are superior to those of Confucianism because, with the exception of the *I Ching*, Confucian texts are rather weak in their discussion of metaphysics compared to Buddhist sūtras:

> Although Confucianism talks about heaven and earth, and *yin-yang*, its teachings are unclear. In the process of transmission, their teachings have become corrupted and have, accordingly, resulted in many heterodoxies. The Confucians are only able to express their secret teachings through the *I Ching*. It is unlike our Buddhist teachings, from which we understand three-thousand-fold world systems as seen through heavenly eyes.[48]

Furthermore, he attributed the use of metaphysical wisdom as found in the *I Ching* to the neo-Confucian scholars of the Sung period, who had used Buddhist doctrines to enrich it.[49]

Jiun Sonja (1708–1804) believed that Buddhism is basically in agreement with Confucianism and Shinto. In his explanation of the hexagram *t'ai*, he pointed out that the political ideals contained in the *I Ching* share the same spirit as Buddhism.[50] In discussing the Ten

Precepts of Buddhism, he quoted extensively from the *I Ching*, and clearly believed that the spirit behind the Ten Precepts could be found therein:

> When Confucius read the hexagrams of *sun* (decrease) and *i* (increase) of the *I Ching*, he sighed. Tzu Kung asked Confucius why he sighed, and Confucius answered: "Increase means in itself decrease. By seeking one's own increase, one will only cause decrease. Therefore, I sighed." . . . From the hexagram *i*, we know that we have to pursue goodness and rectify our mistakes. . . . Obviously, the *I Ching* also contains the spirit of the entire Ten Precepts of Buddhism.[51]

Jiun praised the Chinese sages for discovering the universal principles of *t'ai chi, yin-yang,* the four images, and the eight trigrams, but pointed out that the four-element theory in Buddhism was superior to the theories found in the *wu-hsing* system of thought. He also argued that the original teachings of the *I Ching* and Confucius did not contain the idea of the *wu-hsing,* and criticized certain Shinto writings for borrowing this theory.[52]

By the nineteenth century, there were no more substantial Buddhist responses to the Confucian attacks. The Buddhists had lost the ideological battle for the harmonization of the two creeds and were relegated to a minor supporting role in the intellectual milieu of late Tokugawa Japan.

An interesting story by a famous playwright, Takizawa Bakin (1767–1848), tells of a Buddhist monk who bought the *I Ching* and read it in his temple. While reading it, he could not help clapping his hands and laughing out loud because he found the text ridiculous. Suddenly he felt very sick. A Confucian told him that the book he had bought belonged to a late Confucian who had spent his life studying it; the bad attitude of the monk had angered his spirit. The monk now studied the text seriously, and his illness went away.[53] In a sense this story may serve as a metaphor for the victory of Confucianism over Buddhism in the intellectual history of the Tokugawa era.

Concluding Remarks

Although Buddhism declined gradually, it would be wrong to regard it as having been intellectually moribund. As we have seen, Buddhist monks remained influential in *I Ching* scholarship in Tokugawa Japan. They used the text for several purposes: as a means of promoting the doctrine of the unity of Buddhism and Confucianism, for its divinational quality, and for the development of the doctrine of the five ranks as taught within the Sōtō tradition.

Buddhism produced important *I Ching* scholars and works on the text during the early Tokugawa period. To some extent, the decline of Tokugawa Buddhism can be seen in the greatly diminished role of *I Ching* studies during the late Tokugawa period.

Here I have examined the relationship between Buddhism and Confucianism from the perspective of Tokugawa interpretations of the *I Ching,* and have shown how the text provided an ideological bridge between the two traditions. When Buddhists or Confucians addressed their mutual relationship, the *I Ching* was often their point of departure. In Tokugawa Japan, both Buddhists and Confucians interpreted the *I Ching* to serve their respective purposes; the text also provided them with fuel in an ideological battle that the Confucians wanted to win and that the Buddhists did not want to lose. Buddhists eventually lost the dispute over the doctrine of *Jubutsu itchi* and were forced to cede part of their ideological territory to their Confucians rivals during the early Tokugawa period. From this time on, *I Ching* scholarship and Shinto gradually became connected to the Confucian ideological sphere of interest. By the late Tokugawa, Buddhism had further weakened and was forced to defend its own systems of belief against strong and persistent attacks from a united front of anti-Buddhist ideologies.

Finally, it should be mentioned that *I Ching* studies never existed as an independent tradition in Japan. In the medieval period such studies belonged exclusively to the sphere of Buddhism, but in early Tokugawa times the Confucians wrested them away from the Buddhists, and during the late Tokugawa period *kokugaku* and the Mito school tried to claim *I Ching* studies as their own. From this we see how different intellectual factions within the intellectual milieu of the period used the *I Ching* in their sectarian infighting over what can be best described as "ideological territory."

Part III CULTURE

8. The *I Ching* and Natural Science

The *I Ching* and the Chinese scientific system were inseparable in East Asia. In particular, the text's *yin-yang wu-hsing* theory became a major theoretical framework for explaining physical phenomena and constructing metaphysical ideas.[1] The *I Ching* played a crucial role in formulating theories in Chinese astronomy, calendrical studies, mathematics, geography, architecture, botany, and other fields.[2] Inasmuch as traditional Japan was within the Chinese cultural orbit and its scientific ideas were largely borrowed from China, the *I Ching* was an integral part of pre-modern Japanese science. From the Heian (794–1186) to Tokugawa (1603–1868) periods, astronomy and calendrical studies were subordinate to the Bureau of Divination (Onmyōryō, later renamed Onmyōdō [Office of *Yin-Yang*] in the Tokugawa period) in the central court government.[3] In the intellectual world, following the spread of neo-Confucianism during the Tokugawa period, the *I Ching* exerted a tremendous impact on the thought of scholars who had studied science mainly through Chinese texts.

However, it is not our objective here to examine the role of the *I Ching* in traditional or Chinese science. Rather, our concern is the role of the text in the adaptation of modern or Western science in the Tokugawa period.[4] Historians of Japan usually regard Confucianism and Western science as competitors in the Tokugawa period. They believe that Confucianism was a conservative shield used to resist Western science, and that Western science caused the decline of Confucianism. This chapter challenges this simplistic view by reexamining how the *I Ching* was handled by Tokugawa scholars.[5]

Western science was introduced to Japan in the sixteenth century, and was naturalized and incorporated into Tokugawa culture over time, becoming a part of the neo-Confucian synthesis. It did not challenge the hegemony of the Chinese mode of scientific thought until the last years of the Tokugawa period. Tokugawa Confucianism, as seen from the *I Ching*, transformed, survived, and even played a significant role in the process of the naturalization or Confucianization of Western science. Two major intellectual and cultural themes in Tokugawa history—the role of Confucianism in modernization and the naturalization of Western learning—are different sides of the same coin. We look at this issue by focusing on the role of the *I Ching* in the adaptation of Western astronomy, physics, and related disciplines.

The Introduction of Western Science in Early Tokugawa Times

Although Western military technology and some applied sciences aroused tremendous enthusiasm during the sixteenth century, it was not until the seventeenth century that Japanese writers began to incorporate Western ideas into their own scientific works.[6] Even then, instead of introducing their readers to the new ideas that were products of the scientific revolution of seventeenth-century Europe, Japanese scholars of the early Tokugawa period limited themselves to the theories expounded in texts that had been brought by missionaries during the previous century.[7] They particularly emphasized the Aristotelian theory of the four elements and the Ptolemaic global theory. The former views earth, water, fire, and air as the four basic terrestrial elements; the latter holds that the earth is a sphere located at the center of the universe, with the sun, moon, and stars revolving around it.[8] Though already outdated in the West, these ideas were new and stimulating to seventeenth-century Japanese thinkers.

Early popularizers of Western science remained faithful students of Chinese science. In their translation and interpolation of Western texts, they tried to accommodate certain Western elements to the Chinese-Japanese cultural heritage, but attacked those Western scientific ideas that they found incompatible with *yin-yang wu-hsing* and other concepts central to traditional Chinese thought.

Ironically, the project of translating Western scientific texts was motivated by the Tokugawa bakufu, which strove to purge the country of unwanted Western influences. Under orders of the bakufu, Sawano Chūan (1580–1652), a Portuguese apostate priest who had become a naturalized Japanese, translated a Western astronomy book into Japanese romanization with the title *Kenkon bensetsu* (A Critical Commentary on Cosmography, 1650). This work explains astronomy and physics in terms of the Aristotelian theory of the four elements. The similarities and differences between the Western theory of the four elements and the Chinese theory of the five agents drew the attention of early popularizers like Sawano. He pointed out that while these two theories were alike and compatible, the Chinese theory was superior and more comprehensive. Realizing that Aristotelian theory did not clearly define the relationships among the elements, Sawano tried to make up for this deficiency by applying the principle of control and promotion of the five agents. This approach had a far-reaching impact on early Tokugawa writers on Western science.

In 1656, under the auspices of the bakufu, the book was translated into Japanese and annotated by Mukai Genshō (1609–1677), a Confucian physician from Nagasaki. Upholding the theory of *yin-yang wu-hsing* as the cornerstone of knowledge, Mukai attacked the theory of the four elements—the subject of the first half of the book—for lacking a metaphysical basis and a definition of the relationships among the elements. "Giving up the ideas of *li-ch'i* (principle and material force), *yin-yang* and *wu-hsing* to pursue other things," Mukai argued, "is not practical learning. They [Westerners] do not know the right way."[9] "Since Westerners do not comprehend the significance of *li-ch'i* and *yin-yang,* their theory of material phenomena is vulgar and unrefined."[10] Unlike Sawano, he did not apply the *wu-hsing* theory to explain the four-element theory, and pointed out Sawano's mistake in linking wood in *wu-hsing* to air in the four-element theory.

Mukai was critical of Western ideas. His remarks on climatology and geography were very much in line with orthodox Confucian explanations. For instance, instead of using the Western notion of density to explain the difference in temperature between the earth's surface and its depths, he resorted to an explanation based on variations in *yin-yang wu-hsing:*

In the summer, *yin ch'i* (the force of *yin*) enters the earth and *yang ch'i* (the force of *yang*) comes out from the earth. Therefore the surface is hot, and the earth and well water are cool. In the winter, *yang ch'i* enters the earth and *yin ch'i* comes out from the earth. Therefore the surface is cold, and the earth and well water are warm. The water [temperature] in the sea and the rivers follows the same principle. Those who are familiar with the ideas of the *I Ching* will understand this principle. Scholars of the Southern barbarians know nothing about the ideas of the *I Ching,* and are ignorant of the theory of *ch'ien* and *k'un* [the first two hexagrams of the *I Ching*].[11]

Mukai also used the *yin-yang* principle and the hexagrams to explain earthquakes, lighting, and thunder. He rephrased a passage by Chu Hsi from the twenty-ninth scroll of the *Hsing-li ta-ch'üan* (An Anthology of Nature and Principle, 1405, edited by Hu K'uang) as follows:

In the spring, *yang ch'i* comes out from the earth and gives birth to everything. Hence earthquakes occur frequently in the spring. In the summer, *yang ch'i* rises to the sky. When it is blocked by *yin ch'i* in mid-air, it breaks through it. *Yang ch'i* attacks *yin ch'i* with anger. This explains why thunder and lighting are frequent in the summer. . . . Hence the *I Ching* has the trigram ☳ [*chen*], from which we can understand the fundamental principles of thunder and earthquakes.[12]

The latter half of Mukai's book on astronomy made a major contribution by introducing Japanese scholars to the Ptolemaic system.[13] Although critical of the Aristotelian system, Mukai was ambivalent about Ptolemaic global theory. He acknowledged that the global theory was contradicted by the traditional interpretation based on the *yin-yang* principle. According to *yin-yang* cosmology, heaven is *yang,* and earth is *yin;* and the attributes of *yang* are round and moving, whereas those of *yin* are square and quiescent. Thus the earth should be square. However, Mukai seemed implicitly to favor the Ptolemaic global theory, and even cited the *I Ching* and other Chinese classics to "prove" that this theory had existed in ancient China. In short, Confucian scholars like Mukai were able to accept the Ptolemaic system because it was largely compatible with *yin-yang* cosmology; while the two systems differed on relatively minor questions, such as the shape of the earth, they were in agreement on more fundamental matters, such as the geocentric structure of the universe.

Kobayashi Kentei (or Yoshinobu, 1601–1684), a Nagasaki astronomer, explained global theory and solar eclipses, among other things, in his *Nigi ryakusetsu* (A Brief Explanation of Heaven and Earth, 1667), also based on a Western book. Like Sawano, Koyabashi employed Chinese ideas, such as *yin-yang,* the control and promotion of the five agents, and the six climatic factors, to accommodate the theory of the four elements to the Chinese mode of scientific thought.[14]

European scholarship on astronomy, geography, and mathematics was popularized by Nishikawa Joken (1648–1724), a prolific writer also from Nagasaki. Like many other early Japanese students of Western science, Nishikawa, who had studied Western science by reading Chinese translations of Western texts, believed that the four-element system basically accorded with the more sophisticated *wu-hsing* system. For instance, he pointed out that both theories view water and earth as the most important agents. In his major work on astronomy, the *Tenmon giron* (Discussions of the Principles of Astronomy, 1712), Nishikawa took the notions of *yin-yang wu-hsing* and *wu-yün liu-ch'i* (the five agents and the six climatic factors) as his major theoretical framework, while incorporating some Western ideas. Like Sawano and Kobayashi, Nishikawa compared *wu-yün liu-ch'i* and the Western theory of the four elements and four qualities:

> The Chinese theory has five agents *(yün)*—earth, metal, water, wood, and fire—and six qualities *(ch'i)*—cold, hot, dry, wet, windy, and fiery. The Westerners are said to have four elements—earth, water, air, and fire—and four qualities—dry, wet, hot, and cold. Since we know nothing further of the Western theory, we cannot judge its truth, but it seems to be of the same sort as the Chinese theory. It may be that the Chinese theory is more detailed than the Western.[15]

According to Nishikawa, the *I Ching*, astronomy, and calendrical studies form a trinity: the *I Ching* constitutes the principle *(ri)*, astronomy the form *(tai)*, and calendrical studies the application *(yō)*. "Astronomy is the form of the *I Ching* and calendrical studies; the *I Ching* is the principle of astronomy; and calendrical studies is the application of astronomy," Nishikawa contended, suggesting a common origin for these three teachings in Fu Hsi.[16] By so doing, he assured a respectable place for astronomy and calendrical studies in the neo-Confucian hierarchy,[17] for he linked these teachings to the ultimate Confucian ideal of the unity of heaven and man:

> The origins of astronomy can be found in the *I Ching*. Using the principle of astronomy, calendrical studies, and the *I Ching* to understand thoroughly the meaning of the unity of heaven and man is difficult. Nevertheless, we should study the *I Ching* little by little and fuse it with the principles of astronomy and calendrical studies. Then we can investigate the similarities in all things.[18]

Nishikawa's rich knowledge of world geography and his understanding of the *I Ching* reflected a nationalist sentiment. While introducing various nations of the world to the Japanese for the first time, Nishikawa did not forget to proclaim the superiority of Japan.[19] In his *Nihon suidokō* (An Investigation of Japan's Geography, 1720), he pointed out that on the world map brought by the missionaries, Japan is located in the Northeast. According to the preference for *yang* over *yin* expressed in the *I Ching*, this is the best position (the hexagram *ken*) because it represents "the end of *yin* and the beginning of *yang*." Hence Nishikawa was convinced that Japan was imbued with the spirit of *yang*, which made the country rich in resources and its people kind and brave. This geomancy also justified Japan's name, "Nihon," which literally means "the origin of the sun," because *yang* is associated with the sun.

Another popularizer of Western astronomy was Baba Nobutake, a Kyoto physician who wrote several primers on astronomy. Like Nishikawa and many of his contemporaries, Baba studied Western science through Chinese translations. His most important work, the *Tenmon shogaku shō* (An Introduction to Astronomy, 1706), went a step farther than previous studies in adapting Western views. For instance, instead of the theory of *yin-yang*, Baba employed the idea of magnetics to explain that the tides on earth are caused by the moon. Baba's book was influenced by a Chinese work on astronomy, the *T'ien-ching huo-wen* (Queries on the Classics of Heaven, c. 1675, by Yu I), which is a synthesis of Western and Chinese ideas. Yu I's work uses the *wu-hsing* theory along with the four-element theory, and advocates the Tychonian views of sun and earth as the two centers of the universe. In his own scholarship Baba, who was also a famous *I Ching* specialist, often combined Chinese and Western approaches. For instance, he drew a diagram of the annual variation of *yin-yang* that identified each of the twelve months with a different hexagram and used it to illustrate seasonal changes. On this basis he explained, for example, why May (identified with the hexagram *kou* ䷫) is the rainy season: "In May, a single *yin* comes up from the bottom and *yang* descends. Therefore, the rain falls."[20]

Among these early writers on Western science, we see a huge gap between the ideas they introduced and the ideas they believed in. There had been no structural change in intellectual perception during this period: Scholars' thinking remained dominated by Chinese scientific thought, and none yet saw Western science as an alternative. In accordance with their belief in *yin-yang wu-hsing* and neo-Confucian doctrines, they accommodated Western ideas that they felt were compatible with the Confucian system and rejected all others.

We should be aware that Western science was no more than a weak undercurrent in the stream of Tokugawa thought; the majority of early Tokugawa astronomers and calendrical scholars seem to have been minimally influenced by it. Most Confucian scholars continued to favor traditional scientific approaches and seldom mentioned Western ideas. For instance, in calendrical studies, Shibukawa Harumi (1639–1715), the founder of Japan's own calendar, adopted *yin-yang wu-hsing* as the major principle in his *Tenmon keitō* (Systems of Astronomy, 1698). He made no clear distinction between astronomy and astrology and, in particular, associated changes in natural phenomena with politics and the military. In astronomy, Ida Tsunenori wrote an important book, the *Tenmon zukai* (An Illustrative Explanation of Astronomy, 1689), using the idea of *yin-yang wu-hsing*. Ida accepted the traditional notion of Fu Hsi as the father of astronomy, geography, and the *I Ching,* which he maintained that Fu Hsi had created according to his understanding of heaven and earth. "Fu Hsi," Ida wrote, "investigating astronomy and geography, following the *Ho T'u* (Yellow River Diagram), advocated the theory of *yin-yang* and created the *I Ching* to understand changes."[21]

Western impact was even weaker in mathematics, biology, and botany. For example, Kaibara Ekken (1630–1714) discussed biology and botany solely in terms of *yin* and *yang*. In his *Yamato honsō* (Botany of Japan, 1709), he classified different animals and plants and identified their gender as either *yin* or *yang*. This methodology made some of his ideas seem arbitrary and mechanical. Kaibara's explanation of the main differences between human beings and other creatures is interesting but curious: "Humankind belongs to *yang;* animals, insects, and fishes belong to *yin*. The number of *yang* is limited to nine; the number of *yin* is limited to ten. Hence humankind have no tails, whereas other living creatures have tails."[22]

The Adaptation of Western Science in Late Tokugawa Times

The worldview of Japanese intellectuals gradually changed during the latter half of the Tokugawa period, as the authority of Chinese culture began to be challenged by both indigenous and foreign currents of thought.[23] *Rangaku* (Western learning), a strong undercurrent since the late eighteenth century, became increasingly influential. *Rangaku* scholars, unlike popularizers of the earlier period, were accepting of, and even enthusiastic about, Western science. They not only believed in what they introduced but really admitted the superiority of the West in science and technology. They could directly use Dutch materials, and so relied less on Chinese translations. The result was that they could investigate Western theories without having to look through a Chinese filter. At the same time, throughout Tokugawa Japan the influence of Chinese scientific thought gradually declined. *Yin-yang wu-hsing*, once the central principle of early Tokugawa scientific writings, was no longer used to judge the acceptability of Western ideas.[24]

Some scholars discarded the *yin-yang wu-hsing* approach entirely, while others attempted to modify it in such a way that it became useful merely to illustrate Western ideas. In general, however, Confucianism remained respected and influential in *Rangaku* circles. In other words, the rise of Western learning did not challenge the hegemony of the Chinese cultural system, at least until the last years of the Tokugawa period. The majority of scholars of Western learning were conciliatory toward traditional views and attempted to integrate Western science into the traditional cultural system. The *I Ching* played a new role in this period: It became a tool whereby many late-Tokugawa scholars justified their arguments for the acceptance of Western science.

On the question of the *I Ching* and its *yin-yang wu-hsing* theory, *Rangaku* scholars were divided into two camps. The first camp, a small but strong minority, was critical of *yin-yang wu-hsing* and other traditional scientific views. For instance, Maeno Ryōtaku (1723–1803), a pioneer of Western medicine and physics, criticized Nagasaki scholars of the early Tokugawa period for applying the *wu-hsing* principle to interpret the theory of the four elements. He attacked *yin-yang wu-hsing* as an empty and arbitrary theory, rejecting its use in astronomy and medicine. This iconoclast even dared to challenge some physical views of the *I Ching*, commenting, for example, on the hexagram *ch'ien:*

> The [hexagram *ch'ien* of the] *I Ching* reads: "Fire turns to what is dry; water flows to what is wet." Indeed, water also penetrates into the dry. If dry soil accumulates on the surface for a long time, water will rise from beneath and turn it to wet soil.[25]

Another iconoclast was Motoki Yoshi'naga (Ryōei, 1735–1794), a Nagasaki official translator and the first Japanese to introduce Copernican heliocentrism.[26] In his major work, the *Seijutsu hongen taiyō kyūri ryōkai shinsei tenchi nikyū yōhōki* (Use of the Newly Made Celestial and Terrestrial Globes in Understanding the Origins of Astronomy and the Sun, 1791), Motoki described the heliocentric solar system and also compared Western astronomy with Chinese astronomy:

> Japanese and Chinese scholars use the *yin-yang wu-hsing* theory to elucidate astronomy and geography. The Dutch do not use the theory of *yin-yang wu-hsing* in their discussions of astronomy and geography. They do not even have the term *yin-yang*. For the rest, [Dutch ideas] are similar to those of the Japanese and Chinese.[27]

Because of his official status, Motoki could not openly attack the theory of *yin-yang wu-hsing*. However, he implied that *Rangaku* had nothing to do with it, and he himself did not use it in his writings.

The second camp consisted of scholars who sought to accommodate Western science to the traditional cultural system.[28] In astronomy and physics, they used the *I Ching* to justify their advocacy of Newtonian physics, Copernican heliocentrism, and other recently imported Western ideas.

Shizuki Tadao (1760–1806), a student of Motoki, introduced Newtonian physics to Japan.[29] His main intellectual concern was to accommodate Western science to the neo-Confucian system. Like many seventeenth-century Western authors who found support of Copernican heliocentrism in the Bible, Shizuki used the *I Ching* to demonstrate that many Western scientific ideas had existed in ancient China and were thus compatible with Confucianism.[30] In his work on the origins of the solar system, the *Konton bunhan zusetsu* (An Illustrative Explanation on the Beginning of the Universe, 1802), Shizuki used the *I Ching* and other Chinese classics to explain Western physics and chemistry. For instance, he showed why the different densities and compositions of things were the result of physical and chemical reactions:

> When water evaporates, salt remains. When fire burns, ashes remain. The Chinese classic [the *Huai-Nan Tze*] writes: "Light and pure stuff rose and became heaven; heavy and impure stuff descended and formed the earth." In addition, the *I Ching* reads: "The sages established the way of heaven and called it darkness and brightness. They established the way of earth and called it firmness and softness." Although these quotations refer to physical forces and substances, they are also applicable to [the explanation of] heaven and earth.[31]

Having introduced the laws of Newton in his *Rekishō shinsho* (New Book on Calendrical Phenomena, 1798–1802, published after the Meiji), Shizuki reminded his readers that they could find the same physical principles in the *I Ching*:

The expansion of force always implies the contraction of material. The contraction of material always implies the expansion of force. Because of expansion and contraction, change is everlasting. Since force is monistic, everything is one. We dare not discuss the underlying principle concerning the cause of movement. If you want to understand the subtle principles of movement and density, you should study the *I Ching*.[32]

Shizuki even went so far as to try to reconcile the traditional theory of *ch'i* and Newtonian mechanics:

The space of the universe contains only one substance, *ch'i*, but it can also be either empty or full. Thus in one there is two, and in two, one. If there were only the one, there could be no difference between the rarefied and the condensed. The heavens are light and rarefied. The earth is heavy and condensed. Is there not, then, a difference between the rarefied and the condensed? By the existence of these two contrary principles, the phenomena are caused in endless succession. Because of the oneness of the substance, the universe is monistic. The cause of these principles is beyond my comprehension, but the best way to comprehend the subtlety of these principles is to study the teachings of the *I Ching*.[33]

Shizuki endeavored to unravel Copernican heliocentrism. At the beginning, he was caught in a dilemma because the theory conflicted with the orthodox Confucian idea of geocentricity that regards heaven as moving *yang*, and earth as unmoving *yin*. He recalled this struggle:

Heaven is *yang* and earth is *yin*. Movement is the attribute of *yang* and non-movement is the attribute of *yin*. If the earth moves, it goes against the attributes of *yin-yang*. However, when I examine the idea of the Westerners over and over, it is hard to say that Western theory is not solid in its view of the mathematical principles of movement.[34]

How could this dilemma be overcome? Shizuki did not discard the basic framework of *yin-yang* dualism but added a footnote: *yin-yang* in the *I Ching* is a relative concept. When it refers to force, heaven is *yang* and earth is *yin*. When it refers to material, heaven is *yin* and earth is *yang*. Therefore, *yin-yang* theory did not necessarily conflict with heliocentricity. He even quoted the hexagram *shih ho* (biting through) to demonstrate that the Chinese had long known of heliocentricity:

I have the following idea: The main objective of the *I Ching* is to praise the wonder and function of heaven and earth. When it discusses the force of heaven and earth, or heaven-as-force and earth-as-material, heaven is *yang* and earth is *yin*. However, when it refers to the material of heaven and earth, it undoubtedly treats heaven as soft and light *yin*, and earth as tough and solid *yang*. It is like the hexagram *shih ho* in the *I Ching*. It reads: "There is something between the corners of the mouth." Mouth and the thing are the earth; the space inside the mouth is heaven. *Yang* lines [unbroken lines of the hexagram] represent the mouth and the thing, whereas *yin* lines [broken lines] represent the space [inside the mouth]. Hence, from this explanation, we come to know clearly that the material of heaven is *yin* and the material of the earth moves around heaven.[35]

Shizuki was convinced that Westerners were knowledgeable about physics *(gi)* but not about principle or metaphysics *(ri)*. He could not accept the Western notion of God, in either its Christian or Aristotelian form, as the principle underlying physical phenomena. His ultimate intellectual concern was to replace Western theological metaphysics with a neo-Confucian metaphysics for Western science.[36] Regarding *yin-yang wu-hsing* as the supreme metaphysical principle, he regretted that "Western countries know nothing about *yin-yang wu-hsing*."[37] Shizuki strove to fuse Western physical ideas with the neo-Confucian metaphysical principle of *yin-yang wu-hsing*. In the *Kyūryokuhōron* (Treatise on the Law of Attraction, 1784), he used the *yin-yang wu-hsing* theory extensively to interpret the astronomy and physics of a Newtonian scholar, John Keill (1671–1721). For instance, Shizuki applied *yin-yang* to explain attraction, gravitation, action and reaction, and employed *wu-hsing* to illustrate the theory of particles.[38]

Shizuki's idea of *yin-yang* relativity was widely accepted by students of Western science, and overall, his scholarship powerfully shaped the direction of astronomy and physics in the late Tokugawa period.

Yamagata Bantō (1748–1821), a popularizer of Copernican theory, borrowed heavily from the scientific views of Shizuki's *Rekishō shinsho* in writing his major work, the *Yume no shiro*. (In Place of Dreams, 1802–1820). Yamagata adopted, for instance, Shizuki's idea of the relativity of *yin-yang* to accommodate heliocentricity to traditional *yin-yang* ontology.[39] Unlike Shizuki, however, he was critical of *wu-hsing* theory and rejected its application to medicine and astronomy. Thus, while he believed in the superiority of Western science, he also accepted the superiority of Eastern ethics. According to Yamagata, the Confucian classics, despite their excellence in moral teaching, were deficient when it came to science. For example, he pointed out that the notions of a round heaven and a square earth in the *I Ching* were clearly incorrect in light of Western theories.[40]

Yoshio Nankō (1787–1843), an official translator of Nagoya domain, was also deeply influenced by Shizuki. He restated many of Shizuki's ideas in his *Chidō wakumon* (Inquiry into the Movement of the Earth, 1823). Like many other *Rangaku* scholars, Yoshio asserted China's superiority in metaphysics but admitted the West's excellence in physics. Thus he defended the *I Ching* from the criticism that its scientific views were erroneous. First, he regarded the *I Ching* as the essence of Chinese culture, and as a tool that enabled the people to understand gods and spirits and the wonder of creation. Hence Yoshio did not think humankind in a position to judge this sacred book:

> The ability of the Chinese was to create the ideas of *t'ai-chi* (the Supreme Ultimate) and the two poles, and to investigate the images and numbers. They made the *I Ching*, which enables us to communicate with gods and spirits. Master Shizuki Tadao understands the core of heliocentricity through Tycho Brahe and Nicolaus Copernicus, and the Newtonian system through Isaac Newton and John Keill. In the *Rekishō shinsho*, he writes: "If you do not study the *I Ching*, you will not understand the wonder of creation." How can shallow scholars comment on the *I Ching* lightly?[41]

Second, Yoshio borrowed the notion of *yin-yang* relativity from Shizuki. According to the principle of the *I Ching*, heaven is mobile *yang* and earth is unmoving *yin*. Yoshio added that movement is a relative concept and depends on one's point of reference. When one talks about the principle of the *I Ching* with the earth as one's point of reference, heaven is moving; when one observes the earth from heaven, the earth is moving. "Now we see that mountains, rivers, grasses, trees are motionless *yin*," Yoshio argued, "and the sun, the moon, and stars are moving *yang*. If we talk about the principle of the *I Ching* from the moon's perspective, the moon is a motionless *yin*, whereas the earth is a moving *yang*."[42] Thanks to the theory of *yin-yang* relativity, scholars of Western learning were able to defend Confucianism and promote Western science at the same time.

The *I Ching* also played a role in the introduction of applied physics. In the nineteenth century, some Japanese used the *yin-yang* theory to explain the principles of electricity. Hashimoto Sōkichi (1763–1836), a forerunner of the study of electricity in Japan, absorbed the principles of electricity by reading Dutch texts and proved his understanding by conducting experiments and making simple electrical devices. His book, the *Oranda shisei erekiteru kyūrigen* (An Investigation of the Origins of Electric Devices Invented by the Dutch, 1811) introduced the study of electricity and described the ways it was used in Holland. Hashimoto held that the principles of electricity could be found in the images of the *I Ching* because both those images and electricity were subject to the same natural principle of the universe. In the preface, he wrote:

> The principles of electricity reveal the fact that everything, from big things like heaven and earth to small things like corn dust, is subject to the same principle. Natural phenomena like wind, rain, thunder, lighting, earthquakes, and shooting stars can be created and experimented on by us. We are now able to know the movement of a mini-universe that represents heaven and earth. This knowledge should also be used to promote moral teaching. I use the activity of the *I Ching* to illustrate the principles of the rise and fall of *yin* and *yang*. . . . If you investigate the principles [of electricity] by looking at the activity of the *I Ching* through its images from this book, you will feel like a man who has been awakened from a billion-year sleep by the first rays of sunlight shining through the window.[43]

Hashimoto was thus conciliatory: there was no insurmountable barrier between science and ethics; Western science and Confucianism could enrich each other. Therefore he employed the ideas of *t'ai-chi, yin-yang* and the hexagrams to explain the principles of electricity throughout his book.

Another *Rangaku* scholar, Kasamine Tachū, wrote the *Erikiteru zensho* (Anthology of Electricity, 1814) to explain the principles of electricity and physics using the *yin-yang* theory. He attributed his ideas to two pioneers of electricity in Japan, Katsuragawa Hoshū (1751–1809) and Takamori Kankō (1750–1830). Kasamine's most significant idea was, perhaps, the use of *yin* and *yang* to illustrate the functions of negative and positive ions. For instance, he explained the occurrence of electricity in nature:

> Electricity is a force of *yang* caused by the physical reaction of two *yang*. Applying this principle to reality, when the force of *yang* in the sky collides with the force of *yang* on the ground, thunder and lighting will occur. This explains why we have thunder in the summer but not in the winter.[44]

These *Rangaku* scholars demonstrated in their thinking the prevalent attitude toward the relationship between Confucianism and Western science. There were, of course, many more late-Tokugawa scientists who used the *I Ching* to illustrate the principles of Western science,[45] and other branches of science besides astronomy and physics underwent the same process of acculturation. In the remaining chapters, we survey two other major fields in Western studies—medicine and weaponry.

Concluding Remarks

The main intellectual and cultural theme of Tokugawa Japan is not the conflict between tradition and modernity, or between East and West, but the accommodation of Western ideas to Japan's traditional cultural system.[46] Historians of Japan tend to emphasize the modernity of popularizers of Western learning in Tokugawa times, overlooking the fact that such Japanese had received a Confucian education and viewed Western ideas through the lens of the Confucian intellectual system.[47] Very few abandoned their belief in Confucianism, although individual scholars questioned this or that doctrine, such as the *wu-hsing* theory of promotion and control. Their use of the *I Ching* illustrates both the subtle relationship between traditional culture and Western learning and the continuity between tradition and modernity as well.

Students of Western learning freely used the *I Ching* to advocate their understanding of Western ideas. As they did so, they developed two important methods of absorbing Western ideas. The first was to contend that Western ideas had existed in ancient China and had been lost or forgotten during later generations, so that the acceptance of Western ideas meant a return to a lost or neglected cultural tradition. The second involved transplanting Western ideas into a Confucian metaphysical framework—namely, a framework primarily based on the *I Ching*.

The pre-modern Confucian mind required a metaphysical base for knowledge. Theory devoid of metaphysics was unacceptable. Western scientific writings did not necessarily come with a metaphysical framework, and when they did, those metaphysics were little understood and were considered incompatible with the Confucian cultural tradition and Tokugawa setting. Neo-Confucian metaphysics, which drew on the interpretation of the *I Ching* by Sung scholars, had become an integral part of Tokugawa thought. As a result, Tokugawa intellectuals tried to provide Western science with a Confucian metaphysical foundation.[48] The *I Ching* was used more often than other Chinese classics because its abstract ideas provided more theoretical flexibility and metaphysical wisdom than other texts did.

As Western science developed within neo-Confucianism in Tokugawa Japan, the traditional cultural system was sustained and left largely unchallenged, at least until the end of the Tokugawa period. In other words, Western science was transplanted into the neo-Confucian tradition without causing bitter metaphysical disputes.[49] Most scholars of Western learning were indeed quite Confucian in their intellectual orientation. The use of the *I Ching* and other Chinese classics to elucidate Western ideas was a product of this cultural naturalization, which was a common phenomenon in nineteenth-century East Asia. Of course, the degree to which this movement was successful and conducive to Japan's cultural development is debatable. It is clear that Western science and traditional learning were not always fully compatible, and that the adaptation or naturalization of Western science was sometimes farfetched and incomplete.[50]

To use a modern metaphor, Tokugawa scholars' efforts to integrate Western knowledge into the neo-Confucian system amounted to installing advanced software in an antiquated computer. Japan had to wait until the Meiji period to have its intellectual hardware upgraded; this occurred only when Western education produced a new, modern generation of thinkers.[51]

9. The *I Ching* and Medicine

Chinese medical philosophy had been strongly influenced by the *yin-yang* tradition and Confucianism. The *I Ching*, a sacred book in both traditions, provided Chinese physicians in different periods with the point of departure from which they developed their medical principles.[1] The influence of the text on medicine increased during the Sung period (960–1279), following the rise of neo-Confucianism, and reached its peak in the Chin (1115–1234) and Yüan (1279–1368) periods. Beginning in the seventeenth century, Western medicine was gradually introduced into China, but it did not challenge the hegemony of Chinese medicine until the last decades of the Ch'ing period.

In Japan, the challenge of Western medicine came earlier and was felt more strongly. Basic assumptions of the Chinese medical system were questioned and gradually replaced in the late eighteenth and early nineteenth centuries, when *Rangaku* (Western learning) became influential.[2] Through a critical reading of the rich Japanese literature on medicine, we here study the role of the *I Ching* in Tokugawa medicine. The influence of the text reached its apex during the first half of the Tokugawa period, when the *goseiha* (school of latter-day medicine) was dominant and spread neo-Confucian medical philosophy throughout Japan. Its influence declined dramatically when the *goseiha* was challenged by two medical schools, the *kohōha* (school of ancient medicine) and *ranpō-igaku* (school of Dutch medicine), in the latter half of the Tokugawa period.

Although the *kohōha* and *ranpō-igaku* were very critical of neo-Confucian medical ideas, they continued to use the *I Ching*. Physicians of *kohōha* and *ranpō-igaku* respected the text, and some even used it to explicate their medical views. This chapter focuses on neo-Confucian medical ideas of *goseiha* and other intellectual forces, thus investigating both the philosophy and divination of the *I Ching* in Tokugawa medicine. The last section surveys the decline of neo-Confucian medical philosophy and the role of the *I Ching* in *kohōha* and Dutch medicine.

The *I Ching* in Neo-Confucian Medical Thought

The history of medicine in traditional Japan consists mainly of the history of Chinese medicine in Japan.[3] Chinese medicine was brought to Japan in the fifth century by Korean doctors, and in Japan as in China and Korea, Chinese medicine and the *I Ching* were inseparable. The Taihō Code of 702 established the Bureau of Medicine (Tenyakuryō), which was staffed with *I Ching* diviners as well as physicians. In ancient Japan, Chinese medicine was studied primarily by the aristocracy, who produced only a handful of medical writings. The oldest and most important text was the *Ishinpō* (Essentials of Medicine, 984), complied by Tamba Yasuyori (912–995). Early Japanese medical texts showed little originality; most quoted heavily from Chinese texts that used *yin-yang wu-hsing* as their major interpretive framework.

Medieval Japan brought two important changes to medical studies. First, Buddhist monks replaced aristocrats as the main authors of medical texts. Second, a sophisticated neo-Confucian medical philosophy was introduced in the late fifteenth century and eventually became the basis of a medical school, the *goseiha*. Neo-Confucian medicine was dominant in the early Tokugawa period, until it was challenged by the *kohōha* and *ranpō-igaku* in the eighteenth century.

The *goseiha* adopted neo-Confucian medical ideas developed during the Chin and Yüan dynasties by physicians like Li Kao (1180–1251) and Chu Chen-heng (1281–1358), who had put medicine into a sophisticated metaphysical system derived primarily from the *I Ching*. Hence the *goseiha* was also called *"ekiironha"* (school of *I Ching* Medicine). Its medical system included a set of *I Ching* related theories, such as *yin-yang wu-hsing, wu-tsang liu-fu* (the five viscera and the six bowels), *wu-yün liu-ch'i* (the five agents and the six climatic factors), *yüan-ch'i* (the inborn life force), and *ching-luo* (main and collateral channels).

According to neo-Confucian ontology, the natural law is subject to the principle of *yin-yang wu-hsing*. Life begins when *yin* and *yang* meet, and ends when they are separated. When they are in a state of dynamic balance, the five agents are in control, and thus health is guaranteed. Sometimes the movements and changes in nature destroy this equilibrium.[4] Thus the ultimate aim of *goseiha* was not merely to fix the sick part of the body but to restore the equilibrium of the whole system.

The theory of the five viscera and the six bowels applies the principle of *yin-yang wu-hsing* to human organs. The five viscera (heart, liver, spleen, lungs, and kidneys) are the five solid organs of storage, which serve as the centers of physiological activity in the human body and which are analogous to the five agents.[5] The six bowels (gall bladder, stomach, small intestine, large intestine, urinary bladder, and triple burner) are the hollow organs of transfer. The relationship between the five viscera and the six bowels is governed by the principle of *yin* (viscera) and *yang* (bowels). They interact with each other in five pairs: heart and small intestine, liver and gall bladder, spleen and stomach, lungs and large intestine, and kidneys and urinary bladder.

Table 11: Correlation between the Five Agents and the Five Viscera

Promotion	*Control*
Water promotes wood—the kidneys (water) store essence and nourish the liver (wood)	Water controls fire—the kidneys control the heart
Wood promotes fire—the liver stores blood and supplies the heart (fire)	Wood controls earth—the liver controls the spleen
Fire promotes earth—the heart produces heat and warms the spleen (earth)	Fire controls metal—the heart controls the lungs
Earth promotes metal—the spleen transforms and conveys the essence of food to replenish the lungs (metal)	Earth controls water—the spleen controls the kidneys
Metal promotes water—the lungs aid in providing the kidneys with water through their descending movement	Metal controls wood—the lungs control the liver

Goseiha medicine regards the spleen and stomach as the most important human organs because they belong to the agent of earth, the origin of the other four agents.[6]

Wu-yün liu-ch'i is a highly speculative theory which suggests that climatic change is a major pathogenic factor. The five agents and the six climatic factors (wind, cold, heat, dampness, dryness, and fire) become unbalanced under extreme seasonal change. The five agents have ten seasonal symbols, whereas the six climatic factors have twelve zodiac signs. The climatic changes of a year in the 240-year cycle can be designated by the sequential use of one of the ten seasonal and one of the twelve zodiac signs.[7]

Yüan-ch'i is an abstract concept that refers to the inborn life force. According to this theory, everyone is endowed with this life force from heaven. Its main functions are to activate growth of the body and to adjust the balance between the *yin* and *yang* of the organs. *Yüan-ch'i* can be strengthened through medical care and moral education. When this force is vigorous, the body is healthy. Diseases occur when *yüan-ch'i* becomes weak or disordered. *Yüan-ch'i* departs the body when life is over. This theory links medicine with the supernatural and with ethics.[8]

The theory of *ching-luo* suggests that the human body has twelve main channels and numerous collateral channels, either *yin* or *yang* in nature, through which *ch'i* and blood can reach the organs of the whole body. This theory has been widely applied in clinical treatments like acupuncture, moxibustion, massage, and herbal prescriptions.

Neo-Confucian Medical Thought in *Goseiha*
(the School of Latter-Day Medicine)

The neo-Confucian medical philosophy was introduced to Japan in the late fifteenth and early sixteenth centuries by two Zen Buddhist monks, Tashiro Sanki (1465–1537) and Manase Dōsan (1507–1594). Both were from the Ashikaga School, the center of *I Ching* studies in the medieval period. Their educational background enabled them to study neo-Confucian interpretations of the *I Ching* and other Confucian classics.

Tashiro spent twelve years studying Chin-Yüan medicine in China before returning to Japan with many Chinese medical books in 1498. He is remembered for spreading neo-Confucian medicine in the Kanto region. Of the Chin-Yüan masters, he admired Li Kao and Chu

Chen-heng, whose medical theories suggested that mild medicine should be used to nourish the *yin (yang yin)* of the five organs and to restore the balance of *yin-yang* in the human body.

Tashiro was succeeded by his best student, Manase Dōsan, who is commonly regarded as the founder of *goseiha*. Manase served the court, the shogun, and prominent warriors. He gained their sponsorship and established a private school in Kyoto, the Keitekiin (Academy for Enlightenment), which attracted hundreds of student who came to study medicine and neo-Confucianism. The branch of *goseiha* he founded, known as Dōsan-ryū (the Dōsan lineage), became influential in the early Tokugawa period.[9] On the main idea of his teaching, Manase said: "Diseases are all caused by either excessive *yin* or excessive *yang*. Therapy simply balances these. This is the secret of our school."[10] He popularized the basic premises of neo-Confucian medicine all over Japan.

The seventeenth century was the heyday of *goseiha*. Manase's medical views were developed by his students, many of whom served the bakufu, court, and daimyō as attendant physicians.[11]

Tomiyama Michi'nao (1585–1634), a disciple of Gensaku (1545–1631), Manase Dōsan's son, was the author of a best-selling *kanazōshi* (story book in the vernacular script) entitled *Chiku-sai* (Bamboo Hut, 1621). He suggested that every doctor should study the *I Ching* thoroughly and familiarize himself with the ideas of *yin-yang wu-hsing* and of the five viscera and six bowels.[12]

Nakayama Sanryū (1613–1684) was famous for having healed ex-emperor Gomizunoo (r. 1611–1629). His major theoretical contribution was to apply the principle of *yin-yang wu-hsing* to prescriptions. He believed that mixtures of dozens of medicine were necessary to restore a patient's own resistance mechanism, because *yin-yang* and *wu-hsing* were delicately balanced in the human body.

Aeba Tōan (1615–1673) was a champion of the theory of *wu-yün liu-ch'i*. He was influenced by Liu Yüan-su (1120–1200) of the Chin dynasty, who established a school of medical thought that explained pathogenesis in terms of the relationship between the agents of fire and water. Liu's idea was inspired by the hexagram *chi chi* (after completion), which reads: "Water over fire: the image of the condition in [the hexagram] 'after completion.' Thus the superior man takes thought of misfortune and arms himself against it in advance."[13] According to Liu, water over fire represents the ideal physical condition. Of the six climatic factors, fire is the most difficult to control and tends to overpower the others. Illnesses occur when fire increases and releases heat, which burns water. Thus the function of medicine is to constrain fire in order to restore water over fire.[14]

Aeba introduced this idea to Japan and attempted to apply the principle of *wu-yün liu-ch'i* to the functions of the five viscera and the six bowels and of the main and collateral channels. He said: "There are six climatic factors in the universe from which everything is created. There are five viscera and six bowels in the human body from which the energy of life is formed. The increase and decrease of everything follow the impact of seasonal change on the five agents and the six climatic factors. Human illnesses begin in the organs and bowels."[15] Despite his efforts, the theory of *wu-yün liu-ch'i* was too abstract and never became widely accepted in Tokugawa medical circles.

Okamoto Ippō (1654–1716), a student of the Aeba Tōan lineage of *goseiha*, attempted to simplify and popularize the ideas of *wu-yün liu-ch'i* and *ching-luo* in his *Unkiron genkai* (A Simple Explanation of the Theory of *Yün-ch'i*) and *Nankei genkai* (A Simple Explanation of the *Book of Difficult Medical Questions*). Okamoto made a contribution to acupuncture and moxibustion; he discussed them in terms of *wu-yün liu-ch'i, wu-tsang liu-fu,* and *ching-luo.* He upheld the traditional views that Fu Hsi had invented acupuncture and moxibustion, and that there was a close relationship between acupuncture and moxibustion and the *I Ching.* Okamoto said: "We have the principle of heaven-earth-man three powers *(san-ts'ai)* in human beings; acupuncture and moxibustion also have the principle of heaven-earth-man three powers."[16]

The map of the medical world changed in the eighteenth and nineteenth centuries. The hegemony of *goseiha* was followed by the coexistence of the three schools of *goseiha, kohōha,* and *ranpō-igaku.* The decline of *goseiha* was obvious in both the material and ideological realms. Patrons were lost to other medical schools; few figures of great stature defended neo-Confucianism medicine; and in the course of defending their own doctrines, ordinary practitioners nevertheless absorbed some influences from *kohōha* and *ranpō-igaku.*

Hata Kōzan (1720–1804), an attendant physician of the emperor and shogun, wrote the *Seki idan* (A Critique of *Idan,* 1762) as a counterattack on *kohōha.* As the title suggests, this work attacks the *Idan,* an influential book written by the champion of *kohōha,* Yoshimasu Tōdō (1702–1773). Hata wrote: "His [Yoshimasu's] book categorically rebukes the medical classics, discards the theory of *yin-yang,* and wants to change what is unchangeable in the universe. It is a heresy."[17] He pointed out that even Pien Chüeh and Chang Chung-ching, the two most respected ancient Chinese physicians in *kohōha*, believed in the *yin-yang* doctrine. Hata's most interesting defense of *goseiha* was the use of the *I Ching* to uphold the idea of *yüan-ch'i*:

> Although the term *"yüan-ch'i"* cannot be found in the Six Classics, its meaning is there. . . . *Yüan* means the beginning of everything. In the teaching of the *I Ching, yüan* is very crucial. The *I Ching* reads: "Great indeed is the sublimity of the *ch'ien* (creation), to which all beings owe their beginning," and "Perfect indeed is the sublimity of the *k'un* (the receptive). All beings owe their birth to it." It is the great virtue of the universe. If the power which supports the everlasting movement of all creatures is not *ch'i*, then what would it be?[18]

Goseiha was further weakened in the last decades of the Tokugawa era. Abe Rōsai, a *goseiha* physician, regretted that the principle of *yin-yang wu-hsing* was no longer the core theory of the Tokugawa medical world. *Goseiha* physicians became more eclectic; they absorbed ideas from other schools of medicine and discarded some of their far-fetched elements. For example, during the Kyōwa years (1801–1803), Kondō Takamasa, in his defense of *goseiha* in the *Tōshi idan* (Medical Discourses of the Kondō Family), did not completely deny the ideological contributions of *kohōha*, and even accepted some of its ideas. He wrote:

> The theories of viscera-bowels and channels-collateral are the essence of medicine, and [spreading them is] the major responsibility of the physician. Today, the so-called students of the school of ancient medicine do not use the principles of *yin-yang* and *yüan-ch'i*, and also discard the use of the major channels and collateral channels to correspond [to *yin* and *yang*], in order to establish their own theory. Some of their arguments are convincing enough to overthrow the useless, corrupted views, and therefore they are not without merit. . . . Using *yüan-ch'i* to correspond to *yin-yang wu-hsing* is too abstract an idea and is no good for therapy. It is not for those physicians who aim to cure diseases. However, things like viscera-bowels and channels-collateral are unquestionable principles, and thus must not be discarded.[19]

Kaneko Keizan, in his *Byōkon seigi ben* (An Analysis of the Origins of Disease), attempted to minimize the differences between *goseiha* and *kohōha* by arguing that the favorite text of *kohōha*, the *Shang han lun* (A Treatise on Fever, c. 200 C.E.), and the *I Ching* agreed on medical issues. He used the hexagrams to discuss the functions of the human organs and also pathology and therapy:

> The *I Ching* and *Shang han lun* are two expressions of one truth. The
> sages, on the bases of the *Ho T'u* (Yellow River Diagram) and *Lo Shu*
> (Writings from the Lo River) and of the principles of *yin-yang,* created
> the teaching that could cure ten thousands diseases. The *Shang han
> lun* was based on the teaching of the sages. . . . One can understand
> the cause of the disease by looking at the change of the sixty-four
> hexagrams, and know the pathology and therapy by reading the text
> and commentary of the 384 hexagrams.[20]

During the nineteenth century, even the prestigious Tamba family,
which had served the court and, later, the shogun as attendant physicians for a thousand years, absorbed some elements from *kohōha* and
Dutch medicine in their defense of *goseiha.* For example, Tamba
Genkan did not believe in *wu-yün liu-ch'i* and suggested that it had
been created by Sung scholars. Although he still used the ideas of
yin-yang wu-hsing, and *wu-tsang liu-fu,* he admitted that they were not
directly related to medicine. He attempted to provide textual proof
that many Western medical ideas could be found in ancient Chinese
texts, and thus that the study of human anatomy was not new to
China.

The same idea was echoed by Imamura Ryō in his *Iji keigen* (The
Origins of the Medical Affair, 1862). Ikeda Zuisen (1733–1816), a
smallpox and measles specialist, was a lecturer in the Medical Academy (Igakukan) of the bakufu. Supplemented by Dutch and Japanese
medical ideas, his medical thought was primarily based on Chin-Yüan
medicine. In the *Tōka benyō* (A Critical Review of Medical Studies of
Smallpox, 1821), Ikeda used the ideas of *yin-yang* and *wu-yün liu-ch'i* to
explain the treatment of smallpox and measles:

> Heaven and earth use *yin-yang* and *wu-yün liu-ch'i* as principles. *Yün*
> [seasonal movement of the five agents] can be either big or small. A
> big movement takes every sixty years for one cycle, while a small move-
> ment takes one year for one cycle. *Yün* can be excessive or inadequate
> in a certain year. The changes in *ch'i* and *yün* are continual. Hence the
> treatment of smallpox and measles, from ancient times to the present,
> varies according to the changes in *ch'i* and *yün.*[21]

In brief, *goseiha* had established itself as the dominant medical
school with distinguishing theories and practices by the seventeenth
century, but declined and lost its distinct characteristics during the
late Tokugawa period. Some farfetched ideas associated with the *yin-
yang wu-hsing* system became the main target of attack from within
and without.

Neo-Confucian Medical Thought outside Medical Circles

Outside medical circles, neo-Confucian medicine was widely accepted by different schools of thought and religion. Its most important and ardent intellectual ally was neo-Confucianism. *Jui-ippon* (the unity of Confucianism and medicine) was a common belief among Tokugawa intellectuals; many early Tokugawa Confucians practiced medicine on the side. Although the majority of Chu Hsi and Wang Yang-ming scholars did not have a systematic medical philosophy, their medical views were similar to those of *goseiha*. Fujiwara Seika (1561–1619) suggested that one could find therapeutic references in the *I Ching*.[22] Hayashi Razan (1583–1657) was famous for his practice of *ken pei*, a kind *ch'i kung* (exercise of the movement of *ch'i*) inspired by the hexagram *ken* (keeping still) that was widely practiced by Taoists and Buddhists as well as Confucians in both China and Japan. Tokugawa Confucians were enthusiastic about this practice. Unlike Zen meditation *(zazen),* which was intended to help one attain spiritual enlightenment, *ken pei* aimed at strengthening the body.

Nakae Tōju (1608–1648) used *yin-yang wu-hsing* as the basic framework in his *Igaku seisho* (A Comprehensive Book on Medicine), in which he emphasized the importance of the stomach and spleen. Yamazaki Ansai (1618–1682), in his *Gogyō jintai seijō zu* (The Diagram of the Relationship Between *Wu Hsing* and the Human Body and Emotions), illustrated that human physical and emotional activities are controlled by *wu-hsing.* Kaibara Ekken (1630–1714) studied medicine under some *goseiha* physicians. In the *Yōjōkun* (Lectures on the Maintenance of Life), he stressed the importance of the stomach and spleen and the exercise of *ch'i.*

Buddhism played a crucial role in transplanting neo-Confucianism and its medical theories to Japan in late medieval times. This historical link between Buddhism and neo-Confucianism partly explains why most Tokugawa Buddhists accepted neo-Confucian medicine. Two famous Zen monks are good examples of this link.

Takuan Sōhō (1573–1645) identified himself as a follower of the *goseiha* tradition of medicine. In his *Isetsu* (Discourse on Medicine), he explained the relationship between the five viscera and *wu-hsing.* His interpretation was faithful to the original Chinese teaching: The five viscera represent the *wu-hsing* of the universe and are related to the processes of promotion and control. For example, he argued that if there is a heart (fire) problem, one should deal with the liver (wood), explaining that "The heart belongs to fire. Fire is derived from wood. Wood is the mother of fire. If the heart is weak, we should nourish the liver because the liver belongs to wood."[23] Influenced by Li Kao, Takuan argued that the stomach is the most important organ because it represents the agent of earth, from which all other agents are derived. He suggested specific ways to protect the stomach. For instance, he used the *wu-hsing* theory to explain why sour things are bad for the stomach: "We should refrain from eating too many sour things. Sour is the taste of wood. The stomach and spleen belong to earth. Since earth is controlled by wood, [sour things] will hurt our stomach and spleen."[24]

Hakuin Ekaku (1685–1768) accepted all the major theories of *goseiha* and believed that the health of a person hinges on the balance of *yin* and *yang*. He analyzed the function of *yin* and *yang* in the body:

> The Great Way is divided into the two fundamental principles, the negative and positive, the *Yin* and the *Yang*. When these two are in harmony, men of character are produced. For then there is an innate vitality silently moving within the body, the five organs are so arranged that the correct rhythmical movements of the pulse are carried on. . . . The heart is then doing its work regularly and easily. It is fire which burns upwards. The lungs do not get tired or become heated with their constant effort to keep in tune with an excited heart. None of the agents which makes up the material of the body are worked to exhaustion. . . . But when these fundamental principles are out of harmony, then the structure of the body goes wrong, each part and all the agents of it become disordered and any or all of the hundred diseases may be produced.[25]

Hakuin used the hexagrams to illustrate his methods of maintenance and nourishment of life:

> Roughly speaking, for maintaining life, the upper parts of the body should be kept pure and cool, and the lower parts warm. Then the twelve pulses and the twelve branches [veins] will be in agreement and in accord with the twelve months and the twelve hours [of the day]. This is just the same as when the six lines of the system of divination [*Eki, I Ching*] complete the circuit and the year is completed. When the five negative lines are on top and one positive line is at the bottom [of the divination sign], this represents the winter solstice. This is what is meant, perhaps, by breathing through the heels. When the three positive lines are on top and the three negative lines at the bottom [of the divination sign], this points to the beginning of spring, when all things are full of the spirit of growth and the hundred herbs receive the abundance of the growth of springtime. . . . When the five

negative lines of divination are underneath [in the divination sign] and one positive line is on top, this means deprivation. It is the season of the ninth month. When the sky receives this, the trees and gardens lose their colors, the hundred herbs wither away. This is the sign that the ordinary man in breathing is breathing through his throat, and his looks become emaciated, and his teeth will fall out.[26]

The ideal state of having the upper body cold and lower body warm could be reached by a physical exercise of *ch'i*. Hakuin healed his diarrhea by practicing this exercise. He guaranteed his students that if this exercise of *ch'i* could not cure any disease, he would cut his head off.[27]

In brief, the philosophy of the *I Ching* exerted its influence on Tokugawa medicine mainly through the neo-Confucian system. *Goseiha* physicians, Chu Hsi scholars, Buddhists, and courtiers were champions of neo-Confucian medicine and made it the most influential medical school of thought in the Tokugawa period.

Divination of the *I Ching* in Tokugawa Medicine

In China, *I Ching* diviners and physicians were closely allied. The Chinese have a saying that goes, "Work as a diviner when young; become a physician when old" *(Shao pu lao i)*. In China and Japan, most *I Ching* diviners practiced medicine, and many physicians employed *I Ching* divination. The use of divination in medicine had a long tradition in Japan. In the sixteeenth century, it was very common for physicians —even those who attended prominent warriors and members of the court—to use *I Ching* oracles to determine the cause and treatment of illness. This shamanistic medical practice survived into the Tokugawa period. Until the mid-Tokugawa period, most medical books in Japan included chapters on divination, cosmology, possession, and similar topics.

There are numerous records in Tokugawa writings of physicians and Confucians from different backgrounds using divination for medical purposes. For example, in 1621 the daimyō of Tsushima, Sō Yoshinari, suddenly began to suffer from a tumor while stopping over in Kyoto on the way to Edo to fulfill his *sankin kōtai* ("alternative attendance") duty. He went to ask the Hino family, a prestigious family in the Kyoto court, for medical advice. The Hino family used the oracles of the *I Ching* to see how serious the problem was. The result was the hexagram *chun* (difficulty at the beginning), which includes the line,

"Bloody tears flow. How could one tarry long in this?"[28] Hence, Hino explained, this was a serious problem and would require a long period of recovery.[29] Shōji Kōki (1787–1857), a merchant-Confucian, also consulted the *I Ching* whenever he was sick. Later he realized that it went against the true intention of the sages and asked his family to stop this practice.[30] And one Tokugawa physician deplored the fact that even the attendant physicians acted like *I Ching* diviners and used the oracles frequently.[31]

In late Tokugawa times, a group of professional *I Ching* diviners, the Arai Hakuga school, attempted to bring elements of mysticism and shamanism into *goseiha*. They had produced considerable literature on *I Ching* medicine. Although many of these texts have not survived, we need only look at their titles for proof of the tenor of this period: Arai Hakuga's (1725–1792) *Koeki heidan* (The Diagnosis of Illness by the Ancient *I Ching*) and *Koeki satsuheiden* (The Observation of Illness by the Ancient *I Ching*); Mase Chūshū's *Ieki kōketsu* (An Oral Transmission of *I Ching* Medicine); and Tanigawa Ryūzan's (1831–1888) *Ieki hongi* (The Original Meaning of *I Ching* Medicine). The Arai school was very influential in the Osaka region, and some courtiers even went there to study in it. However, its impact was regional, and its teachings were not widely accepted by late Tokugawa intellectuals.

The *I Ching* and *Kohōha* (the School of Ancient Medicine)

Kohōha began as early as *goseiha* but did not challenge it until the turn of the eighteenth century. *Kohōha* disapproved of neo-Confucian medicine and advocated a return to the medical classics of the Han period (206 B.C.E.–C.E. 220). In particular, Chang Chung-ching's *Shang han lun* was the bible of the school, and it put more emphasis on treatment than theory.[32] See Table 12 for the main differences between *goseiha* and *kohōha*.

As a school of Chinese medicine, *kohōha* was not free from the influence of the *I Ching*. Although it discarded most Chin-Yüan medical doctrines (such as *wu-hsing, wu-yün liu-ch'i, wu-tsang liu-fu, yüan-ch'i* and *ching-luo*), it still upheld the *yin-yang* theory and respected the medical value of the text.

Early students of *kohōha* were tolerant of *goseiha*. The founding father of *kohōha*, Nagoya Gen'i (1628–1696), still used the theory of *yin-yang* extensively, and particularly stressed the importance of the

Table 12: Differences between the *Goseiha* and *Kohōha*

	Goseiha	*Kohōha*
Nature of Medicine	*it is a nutrition which can nourish *yin* *extensive use of herbal medicine	*it is a poison which can kill the disease *prefer using natural therapies such as a hot-spring bath and massage to medicine
Prescription	from ten to twenty ingredients; each in small quantities, mild in nature	limited to five ingredients; each in substantial quantities, strong in nature
Purpose of Treatment	to restore the balance of the whole body, and eliminate all symptoms	to cure the disease where it appears, and to eliminate the principle symptom
Medical Theories	**yin-yang wu-hsing, wu-yün liu-ch'i* and *wu-tsang liu-fu*	*first-hand observation, actual practice, clinical experience, and *yin-yang*
	*Importation of Chinese medical theories with few changes	*Japanization of Chinese medicine
Principle Texts	*Su Wen* and *Ling Shu*	*Shang han lun*

harmony of *yin-yang*. Applying the *yin-yang* theory to sexual relationships, he remarked: "According to the way of strength and softness, the harmony of *yin* and *yang* in intercourse is very important. Neither a single *yang* nor a single *yin* can survive long. However, one should not fuse them too early. If they are fused too early, illness and fragility are unavoidable."[33] Nagoya did not regard the balance or harmony of *yin* and *yang* as an equality of the two, and preferred *yang* to *yin*. He applied the same principle to acupuncture, calling it *kinyō senin* (respect *yang* and deprecate *yin*) and *fuyō yokuin* (uphold *yang* and suppress *yin*). Following the medieval tradition, Nagoya was skillful in using the oracles of the *I Ching*, which he studied under the *I Ching* master Ushū Shōjun.

Gotō Konzan's (1659–1733) attitude toward *goseiha* was similar to that of his mentor, Nagoya. Gotō respected the *I Ching* but rebuked later generations who created speculative medical theories derived from it. He wrote:

> *Goseiha* physicians say that Fu Hsi drew the trigrams and Shen Nung tasted hundreds of herbal medicines. The eight trigrams show the *yin-yang wu-hsing* doctrine. Because it was the creation of the sages, [this world] cannot do without *yin-yang wu-hsing*. However, *goseiha* physicians apply this idea to identify human organs and bowels, and have developed different theories which have caused many arguments. [These theories] do not help present-day patients at all.[34]

Gotō nevertheless used the *yin-yang* theory extensively. In his explanation of pathology and therapy, he wrote:

> Disease caused by the weakness of *yang* is easy to cure, but disease caused by the weakness of *yin* is difficult to cure. Ordinary people think that the weakness of *yin* only means the weakening of *yin*. However, the fact is that when *yin* becomes weak, *yang* will gradually weaken and become incurable. Tuberculosis is a kind of weakness of *yin*. Therefore, it is the number-one incurable disease. Heart disease is the next.[35]

Gotō did not completely deny the medical philosophy of *goseiha*, and was himself influenced by Ch'en Yen, a Sung physician who had contributed many theories of pathogenesis to Chin-Yüan medicine. He used some abstract neo-Confucian medical ideas, such as *ch'i*, the six climatic factors, and the meridian, to construct his original concept that all diseases occur from the stagnation of *ch'i* (which contains *yin* and *yang*). According to Gotō, the stagnation of *ch'i* could be caused by change in the seven human emotions, the six climactic conditions, or other factors. The principle of his treatment was to remove the stagnation of *ch'i* by moxibustion, hot-spring baths, bear liver, and other natural therapies.[36] However, his notion of *ch'i* was different from the idea of *yüan ch'i* held by *goseiha*, and he did not identify *ch'i* with *yin-yang wu-hsing*.

Gotō trained three brilliant students, Kagawa Shūan (1683–1755), Yoshimasu Tōdō (1702–1773), and Yamawaki Tōyō (1705–1762), who made *kohōha* into a distinct medical school and who were more critical of *goseiha* than their predecessors had been.

Kagawa Shūan had a critical mind and refused to accept any medical knowledge without proof from clinical experience. Unlike Nagoya Gen'i and Gotō Konzan, Kagawa did not accept the idea of *yin-yang,* and even criticized his favorite medical text, the *Shang han lun,* for using this concept.

Yoshimasu Tōdō was perhaps the most important figure in *kohōha.* He was an empiricist and was skeptical of medical theory. He opposed virtually all Chin-Yüan medical theories, including the ideas of *yin-yang* and *ch'i,* two concepts heretofore accepted by most *kohōha* followers. He defended the *Shang han lun* by arguing that its passages about *yin-yang wu-hsing* had been added by later generations. Although he disagreed with others about the use of neo-Confucian medical ideas, Yoshimasu did not deny the value of the *I Ching* itself. In his explanation of a key medical idea of *kohōha*—namely, that medicines are poisons that can kill disease—he quoted the hexagram *wu-wang* (innocence, or the unexpected) to remind people to be cautious in taking medication because it cannot nourish or supplement the human body:

> The nine in the fifth place [of the hexagram *wu-wang*] of the *I Ching* reads: "Use no medicine for an illness incurred through no fault of your own." The *Commentary on the Image* reads: "One should not try an unknown medicine." Tamenori [i.e., Yoshimasu] said: ". . . If you become sick without having done anything wrong, like the situation in the nine in the fifth place, taking no medicine will bring you good fortune." Poisonous medicines are applied to the sick in order to restore the body to a normal state by attacking the virus. If you attack [your body by taking medicine] when you have no diseases, it will hurt your body and upset the normal condition. Therefore, [the *I Ching* said that] "the problem will be solved without taking medicine."[37]

Yamawaki Tōyō attacked the ideas of *yin-yang wu-hsing* and *wu-tsang liu-fu* from an empirical and positive perspective. Observing the dissection of the male body of an executed criminal in 1754, he found that the traditional Chinese knowledge of human organs was erroneous. As a result, many of his students turned to Dutch medicine.

Thanks to the four masters of *kohōha*—Gotō, Yoshimasu, Kagawa, and Yamawaki—*kohōha* became very powerful in late Tokugawa times. Ironically, the expansion of the school led to the dilution of its doctrines. Nineteenth-century *kohōha* was an eclectic doctrine with fewer distinctive features. It became less critical of *goseiha* and even adopted some of the ideas that had been refuted by earlier *kohōha* masters. For example, Nakakawa Shigeaki, a student of Yoshimasu, used *yin-yang* and the five viscera in his *Shōji tekiyō* (The Selected Records of Medical Treatment).

Odai Chō, in his *Iyo* (Records of Medicine, 1863), used the *I Ching* in different places to explicate the medical views of *kohōha*. Like Yoshimasu, Odai quoted the hexagram *wu-wang* to assert that all medicines are poisons and should never be abused. He suggested two ways to acquire health and longevity. First, one needed to be emotionally stable. He quoted from a Han text, the *Ch'un-ch'iu fan-lu* (Luxuriant Gems of the *Ch'un Ch'iu,* by Tung Chung-shu), to illustrate the ideal condition in terms of the hexagram *t'ai* (peace):

> Moving and resting should follow the nature of life. Happiness and anger should stop in the middle level. Sorrow and fear disappear and things return to normal. Having internal harmony inside the body, one reaches the level of "peace of heaven and earth" *(t'ien-ti t'ai)* [from the hexagram *t'ai*]. Those who acquire the peace of heaven and earth will enjoy longevity.[38]

Second, one should be temperate in eating and drinking. Odai used the hexagram *hsü* (nourishment) to explain:

> The *I Ching* says: "Contenting oneself with drinking and eating will bring good fortune" [nine in the fifth place of the hexagram *hsü*]. The *Commentary on the Image* says: "Contenting oneself with drinking and eating will bring good fortune because it is central and correct." If a man can content himself with drinking and eating, it will bring him no loss naturally. Our lives take nourishment from eating and drinking in order to survive, but if we lose our constraint, it may cause more than disorder and even lead to physical harm or death.[39]

In brief, the *I Ching* still played a considerable role in *kohōha*. Most *kohōha* physicians were Confucians themselves, and therefore they respected the *I Ching,* and even cited it to explicate their medical ideas. To maintain the authority of their teachings and of the text, they separated the *I Ching* from neo-Confucian medicine. My investigation also indicates that some *kohōha* physicians were not completely free of the influence of neo-Confucian medical ideas.

The *I Ching* and *Ranpō-igaku* (the School of Dutch Medicine)

Early scholars of Western learning did not necessarily reject neo-Confucian medical ideas; indeed, some even tried to accommodate them to Western learning. Sawano Chūan (1580–1652) trained a number of *nanban-ryū* (Portuguese-style) physicians. His student Kobayashi Kentei (1601–1684) upheld the ideas of *wu-yün liu-ch'i* in his *Nigi ryaku-*

setsu (A Brief Explanation of Heaven and Earth, 1667), writing: "In medicine, if we do not give a prescription after taking *liu-ch'i* of heaven and *wu-yün* of earth into consideration, it will be very difficult to cure a human illness completely."[40] In the early eighteenth century, a maverick popularizer of Western astronomy, Baba Nobutake, emphasized that the *I Ching* and medicine share a natural principle and that no one can understand medicine without the help of the *I Ching*.[41]

Western medicine became very influential in the late Tokugawa period. Historians tend to emphasize the modernity of the school of Dutch medicine while overlooking its interaction with traditional knowledge. Over the years, Western medicine came to supplement rather than replace Chinese medicine. Physicians of Dutch medicine were critical of the speculative mode of medical thought expounded by neo-Confucians, but a closer investigation shows that their attitude toward traditional Chinese medical ideas and practices was actually complicated and ambivalent. Students of Western medicine reached two conclusions: (1) that Western methods were more advanced in surgery and pathology, while Chinese techniques were superior in internal medicine and anesthesia, and (2) that Western and Eastern medicines share many features. Some *ranpō* physicians (such as Nagatomi Dokushōan, 1731–1766, and Ogata Korekatsu) even suggested that Western medical ideas had existed in ancient China.

They were many attempts to fuse Dutch medicine with Chinese medicine using the *I Ching* and other Chinese classics. Hirokawa Kai, a physician attendant to the court, studied Dutch medicine in Nagasaki and in 1803 translated and annotated some Dutch medical sources in a book entitled *Ranryōhō* (The Treatment of Dutch Medicine). Hirokawa still used the concepts of *yin-yang* and *wu-tsang liu-fu* in his analysis, and recommended Chinese herbal medicine for treatment. His translations were influenced by Chinese medical terms, which inevitably carried Chinese meanings with them. For example, he translated the word "distiller" as *inyō-kisei-ro* (literally, "a furnace fusing *yin* and *yang*"); both *inyō* and *kisei* were terms borrowed from the *I Ching*.[42]

Ōtsuki Gentaku (1757–1827), one of the most important *Rangaku* scholars, stressed the similarities between Western and Chinese medicines in his *Ranyaku teikō* (An Introduction to Translations from Dutch Sources). He pointed out that the ideas of *yin-yang wu-hsing* and *ching-luo* do not contradict theories of Western medicine.[43] And Komori Tōu (1782–1843) strove to fuse Western and Chinese medicines, using *yin-yang wu-hsing* theory frequently in his medical writings. His student Ikeda Tōzō used the principles of the *I Ching* to explicate Western medical ideas in his *Igaku engen* (The Origins of Medicine).

Concluding Remarks

These three medical schools represent three stages in the transformation from Chinese to Western medicine in early modern Japan. In a sense, medicine was a battleground for the Chu Hsi school, *kogaku,* and *Rangaku,* which supported *goseiha, kohōha,* and *ranpō-igaku,* respectively. The prevalence of neo-Confucian medicine was a byproduct of the rise of the Chu Hsi school in the Tokugawa period. Neo-Confucian medicine included a set of *I Ching* related theories.

When the Chu Hsi school was challenged by *kogaku* and *Rangaku* in mid-Tokugawa times, the power relations among these three medical schools also changed. The hegemony of *goseiha* was followed by the coexistence of the three schools. The *yin-yang wu-hsing* theory was no longer the core theory in the late-Tokugawa medical world. Although *kohōha* and *ranpō-igaku* physicians were critical of some far-fetched medical ideas of *goseiha,* they did not deny the role of the *I Ching* in medicine. Some of their students used the *I Ching* to explain and justify their medical views.

The influence of the *I Ching* on medicine diminished gradually over the course of the Tokugawa period. The text played a crucial role in *goseiha,* a lesser role in *kohōha,* and an unimportant role in *ranpō-igaku.* Its ideas served as the cornerstone of the Chinese medical system and were less congenial to Western medicine. In the field of medicine, the text played a less significant role in the adaptation of Western science in Tokugawa Japan than it did in astronomy, physics, and weaponry.

10. The *I Ching* and the Military

The *I Ching* is not a military book, but its principles have had a tremendous influence on military literature in China and Japan. Almost all military schools in traditional East Asia employed it in one way or another. Some used it merely for cosmetic purposes, while others adopted its theory of *yin-yang wu-hsing* as their underlying principle.

The *I Ching* played an important role in the history of military thought in Japan. It was significant in three different periods. From the Heian (794–1186) to the *sengoku* (Warring States) period (1467–1600), the text carried a strong *yin-yang* or Taoist tone and was affiliated with *gunbai shisō,* or military oracles. During the first half of the Tokugawa period, it resumed its Confucian role, and its *yin-yang wu-hsing* doctrine was accepted as the central philosophy by many newly founded military schools. Finally, during the latter half of the Tokugawa period, the *I Ching* became a bridge between traditional military thought and Western weaponry, being used to explicate and rationalize the study and use of Western weapons. This chapter examines the role of the *I Ching* both in traditional military thought and the martial arts and in the adaptation of Western weaponry in the Tokugawa period through a textual study of Tokugawa writings.

Yin-Yang Military Thought in the *Sengoku* and Early Tokugawa Periods

The *yin-yang* school in China produced a large body of literature on military affairs; such books were brought to Japan by the Koreans as early as the sixth century.[1] In the Nara period (712–793), *yin-yang* military books were studied by officials of the Bureau of Divination (Onmyōryō) and some courtiers, such as Kibi no Makibi (695–775). *Yin-yang* military thought was institutionalized and popularized during the Heian period. From the ninth century on, the central government dispatched Onmyōryō officials to regional regiments to give military advice using *I Ching* divination and geomancy.[2] In the late Heian period, Ōe no Koretoki translated and edited *yin-yang* military books he brought from T'ang China; his book, the *Kun'etsushū* (A Collection of Military Lessons and Reviews, 120 scrolls), became the bible of *gunbai shisō* in Japan.

In a sense, *gunbai shisō* was a Japanized version of *yin-yang* military thought. It used *I Ching* divination, astrology, and geomancy to make military decisions about issues such as the date of combat, type of tactics, and so forth. *I Ching* divination involved using yarrow stalks to make a hexagram. Other divination methods also used the theory of *yin-yang wu-hsing* as their basic framework. The theory of *wu-hsing* was developed into sophisticated systems of thought—the theory of correspondence and the theory of promotion and control, in particular—that had important implications for military affairs. The correspondence between the five agents and other military factors (such as color, direction, season, star, zodiac sign, and month) is shown in Table 13. The relationships among the five agents are also subject to the principle of promotion and control (see Table 14).

By combining these two theories, diviners could decide the date and time of combat, the color and form of military symbols, which general to choose for a given campaign, and other military matters. For example, knowing that the enemy's general belonged to the agent

**Table 13: Correspondence between the Five Agents
and Other Military Factors**

Five Agents	Wood	Fire	Earth	Metal	Water
Five Colors	Green	Red	Yellow	White	Black
Five Directions	East	South	Center	West	North
Season	Spring	Summer	—	Autumn	Winter
Five Stars	Jupiter	Mars	Saturn	Venus	Mercury
Zodiac Signs	Rabbit	Horse	—	Cock	Rat
Numbers	8	7	5	9	6
Month	1–3	4–6	—	7–9	10–12

Table 14: The Five Agents and the Principle of Promotion and Control

Promotion	*Control*
Water promotes wood	Water controls fire
Wood promotes fire	Wood controls earth
Fire promotes earth	Fire controls metal
Earth promotes metal	Earth controls water
Metal promotes water	Metal controls wood

of fire, diviners would likely offer the following suggestions: Choose a general who belongs to the agent of water; start the military campaign in the winter; attack from the north; and use the color black for the military flag and uniforms.

Medieval Japanese wrote many books advocating *gunbai shisō*. Perhaps the most influential was Yoshida Kanetomo's *Heishō jinkun yōryaku shō* (A Commentary on Military Regulations for Generals and Soldiers, 1450), which gives detailed instructions and regulations for an army. For instance, it stresses the importance of knowing to which of the *wu-hsing* the enemy's general belongs, so as to choose an appropriate general belonging to a stronger agent.[3]

Gunbai shisō reached its peak during the sixteenth century. All *sengoku* daimyō used *I Ching* diviners as their military advisors. Takeda Shingen (1521–1573) is a good example. He employed a group of *I Ching* diviners as his "think tank"; these included Tenkai (1536–1643), Hyōgo, and Sakugen.[4] Takeda consulted the *I Ching* on every important military matter. In 1561 he used the text twice to determine whether he should go to war with his arch-rival, Uesugi Kenshin (1530–1578). Following the oracle, he went to war in Kōzuke and won both battles.[5] On another occasion, he asked Tōshōan, a graduate of the Ashikaga School, to use the text to comment both on his own life and on those of Uesugi Kenshin, Oda Nobunaga (1534–1582), and Tokugawa Ieyasu (1542–1616).[6]

Influenced by the Ashikaga School, Takeda practiced the worship of *I Ching* sages. He constructed statues of the four sages of the *I Ching*—Fu Hsi, Shen Nung, King Wen, and the Duke of Chou—and enshrined them in a temple. Every time he used the *I Ching* for divination, he faced the North, bowed to the statues, and then recited a prayer inviting all the sages of the text to come to help him.[7] He also asked his retainers to copy the text. Takeda's son, Katsuyori (1546–

1582), also used the *I Ching* frequently. In 1576, for example, following the oracles, Katsuyori postponed his campaign to retake Mikawa from Tokugawa Ieyasu and Oda Nobunaga.

There are numerous records of the use of *I Ching* divination by other *sengoku* daimyō as well. Hōjō Ujiyasu (1515–1571) used it to decide the date of going to war in 1564. Date Masamune (1567–1636) asked a monk, Gen'etsu, to consult the text on his military campaign of 1588. The last Ashikaga shogun, Ashikaga Yoshiaki (1537–1597), had Taika, a student of Ippaku Genshin, use it to foretell the political future of his regime.[8]

Although *gunbai shisō* did not play a dominant role in Tokugawa military thought, it remained an important element in most military schools. The most popular military texts in the Tokugawa period were the Seven Chinese Military Classics and Ōe no Koretoki's *Kun'etsushū.* The Seven Chinese Military Classics contain some basic elements of *gunbai shisō*, while the *Kun'etsushū* is a huge collection of *gunbai shisō* literature. The *Kun'etsushū* was reprinted and edited many times in the Tokugawa period. The most popular edition (18 volumes, 85 *kan*) was edited by Okamoto Nobunari. The most influential book within the *Kun'etsushū* seems to have been the *Heihō hijutsu ikkan sho* (Secret Methods in Military Studies), which discusses the military uses of magic, astrology, and geomancy. In the eighth scroll, it uses the hexagrams to explain eight strategic patterns of attack.[9]

Gunbai shisō, which was derived from Chinese *yin-yang* military thought, was expressed in a peculiar form in the Tokugawa period— namely, *taisei heihō* (military methods of the great star). Although contemporary Japanese scholars assert that *taisei heihō* was an indigenous and creative idea, it was really no more than an explanation of *yin-yang* military thought using Shinto rhetoric.[10] Yamamoto Kannosuke, a *sengoku* warrior, is usually credited with founding *taisei heihō*. Most Tokugawa military schools incorporated aspects of this idea in their teachings. For example, Hōjō Ujinaga (1609–1670) and Yamaga Sokō (1622–1685) were famous for their efforts to provide *gunbai shisō* with a neo-Confucian metaphysical basis.

Neo-Confucian Military Thought
in the Early Tokugawa Period

The mid-sixteenth through early seventeenth century was the most creative and vital period in the history of Japanese military studies.[11] Two traditions, *yin-yang* teaching and neo-Confucianism, coexisted and became the dominant forces in military thought. In general, the balance of power shifted from *yin-yang* to neo-Confucian teachings. Military philosophy in this period was characterized by its neo-Confucian overtones. In particular, Confucian interpretations of *yin-yang wu-hsing* served as the cornerstone of most military and martial arts schools.

Schools of Military Thought

There were five major schools of military thought in the Tokugawa period: Kōshū-ryū, Echigo-ryū, Hōjō-ryū, Naga'numa-ryū, and Yamaga-ryū. All were influenced by both Confucian and *yin-yang* aspects of the *I Ching*.

The Kōshū school attributed its ideas to Takeda Shingen. Its founder was Obata Kage'nori (1571–1663), the offspring of one of Takeda's retainers. Obata copied and popularized the *Kōyō gunkan* (Military Records of Shingen), which contains many stories about *gunbai shisō,* a major teaching of the school. He wrote two commentaries on the book that use the *yin-yang wu-hsing* theory to explicate military ideas. These works read more like neo-Confucian commentaries than military treatises. Obata paraphrased the following sentence from the *I Ching* to spread the ideal military spirit and ethics of the school: "Equipped with reason, a clear mind, knowledge and wisdom of the past, a man possesses divine military power *(shen-wu)* but refrains from killing *(pu-sha).*"[12] This sentence was often quoted by Tokugawa intellectuals to suggest the essence of Japan's military spirit. The six-stage training of the school was explained by the six lines of the hexagram *ch'ien* (creation): hidden dragon, appearing dragon, nine in the third place, nine in the fourth place, flying dragon, and arrogant dragon. Various texts and practical combat skills were included in the first five stages. The final stage was a pure mental-training exercise.[13]

The Echigo school attributed its ideas to Uesugi Kenshin. Compared to other military schools, it was strongly Shintoist and made less use of Chinese military books. Takayama Kentei explained the excellence of the Japanese military in terms of *yin-yang:* "The military philosophy of my country respects *yang* and forbids *yin*. It is what the other military schools cannot match."[14] Usami Yoshikata reduced all military tactics to changes of *yin* and *yang*. He wrote: "Although many military tactics have appeared since ancient times, these are merely derived from the *pa-chen* (eight-pattern) pattern. . . . Indeed, they can be reduced to the work of the two forces of *yin* and *yang*. Knowing these changes, one can subdue his enemies without fail."[15]

The Hōjō school was founded by Hōjō Ujinaga, the martial arts tutor to Tokugawa Iemitsu (1604–1651). This was an eclectic school that included Chinese, Japanese, and even Western elements in its system but that adopted *yin-yang wu-hsing* as its central philosophy. Hōjō classified everything according to *yin-yang* (e.g., castle, landscape, navy, and army) and *wu-hsing* (e.g., direction, time, day, and name). Military decisions were made in accordance with his preference for *yang* over *yin,* and with the *wu-hsing* theory of promotion and control. According to Satō Kinji, a historian of Japanese martial arts, Hōjō represents the apex of *gunbai shisō* in Japanese history.[16] Before combat, Hōjō calculated names, date, and time to find the strongest agent of *wu-hsing.* He remarked: "Those who want to lead the army must consider *wu-hsing*—wood, fire, earth, metal, and water —to investigate the principle of control and promotion of names and to choose the auspicious date and hour to go into battle."[17]

Another important figure of the Hōjō school was Matsumiya Kanzan (1685–1780), who used the *yin-yang wu-hsing* doctrine to strengthen the ideological underpinning of the school. He said: "We should know the way of *yin-yang.* The variation in *yin-yang* brings about *wu-hsing.* The *pa-chen* pattern is developed from the change in *wu-hsing.* We should know that there is a [divine] principle behind all these changes and should use it to accommodate change."[18] Matsumiya's analysis focused on the use of geographical settings in battle. He used the hexagrams to explain his ideas: "The deduction of the sixty-four hexagrams shows the unlimited potentials of change. We can also easily understand the landscape of the world thoroughly by this approach."[19] For instance, using the hexagram *k'an* (the abysmal) to stress the importance of building a castle surrounded by moats, he explained that the symbol of the hexagram ䷜ represents a castle surrounded by water, and that the ideal castle has natural fortresses in the North and artificial moats in the East, South, and West.[20]

Matsumiya was also a champion of *gunbai shisō,* and set out military regulations in his *Taiseiden kōketsu ōhi* (The Oral Transmission of the Secrets of *Taiseiden,* 1760). For example, he believed that the best position for daytime battle is south, and for nighttime battle, north: "During the daytime [from 9 a.m. to 3 p.m.], *yang* becomes very active. We should move southward so our backs will face the sun. In the nighttime [from 9 p.m. to 3 a.m.], *yin* becomes very active. When we fight at night, we should move northward."[21]

The Naga'numa school was founded by Naga'numa Sensai (1635–1690). This school adopted Chinese military thought as its major

teaching but also absorbed Japanese and Western elements. Naga'-
numa was also a Chu Hsi scholar and was particularly fond of the *I
Ching* and *Tso Chuan* (Tso's Commentary on the *Ch'un Ch'u*). Influenced by neo-Confucianism, writings of this school sound rational
and scholarly. This was the only major military school that rejected the
ideas of *gunbai shisō*.[22] Stressing the importance of winning the hearts
of the people through virtue, Naga'numa recognized only the ritual
value of divination, denying its military and ethical implications. He
argued that because battles are national events, worshipping the deities and ancestors in a temple is normal etiquette. However, military
decisions do not hinge on the outcome of oracles: "For urgent things,
even though the oracles predict misfortune and the weather is not in
our favor, we raise our army without doubt."[23] He cited the famous
historical precedent in which King Wu overthrew the Shang regime
even while he was at odds with divinational predictions and weather:

> A good rule will lead to the harmony of *yin* and *yang*. When the ad-
> ministration is chaotic, evils and changes arise. . . . *Yin* and *yang* change
> according to human actions. Can natural disasters determine human
> actions? Hence, when famous generals manipulate their troops, they
> do not seek results from magic and numerology but only concern
> themselves with whether or not their causes are righteous.[24]

Despite his reservations about using oracles, Naga'numa held that
the *I Ching* should play a major role in military affairs. As a student of
the text himself, he believed that it was the source of tactics. In his explanation of the two most famous Chinese tactics, the *wo-ch'i* pattern
and the *pa-chen* (eight-pattern) pattern, in his *Akki hachijin shūkai* (Collective Explanations of the *Wo-ch'i* and *Pa-chen* Tactics, 1666), Naga'-
numa pointed out that both were in accordance with the *Ho T'u*
(Yellow River Diagram), the *Lo Shu* (Writings from the Lo River), and
the trigrams:

> In the investigation of tactics, Feng Hou's [a minister of Huang Ti] *wo-
> ch'i* pattern and K'ung Ming's *pa-chen* pattern were the point of depar-
> ture. From heaven we have the images of the *Star Chart;* from the
> earth we have the numbers from the *Ho T'u* and *Lo Shu;* and from man
> we have trigrams drawn by Fu Hsi. I think that when these two masters
> created the tactics, they did not necessarily associate their ideas with
> the universe. They only decided things that facilitated military activi-
> ties, but their ideas turned out to be in accordance with the symbols
> and numbers [of the universe].[25]

The Yamaga school was founded by Yamaga Sokō, who made his
name as a military master. He added neo-Confucian and Chinese mili-

tary ideas to the Kōshū and Hōjō schools' theories to create his own doctrine. The Yamaga school seems to use ideas from the *I Ching* more frequently than the other four schools of military thought. In general, neo-Confucianism served as the framework, while the *yin-yang* tradition was used for applications. Among Yamaga's many writings on military affairs, the *Gengen hakki* (Tracing of Origins, 1678), a treatise on the *I Ching,* constructed a Confucian metaphysics for his military thought, and the *Heihō Jimmu yūbishū* (The Tactics of Emperor Jimmu) explicated the applications of *gunbai shisō.*

Yamaga believed that natural law and the military principle are the same: "The origin of military ideas is *yin-yang.* . . . The way of the universe is the source of military ideas. . . . Although we call it 'the source of military ideas,' it is not different [from the way of *yin-yang*]. The military way is to follow the principle of the universe; killing and fighting happen only when they are unavoidable."[26] Hence Yamaga believed that the primary aim of the military arts is to live or govern, not to kill: "The principles of the military affair came from the first stroke of Fu Hsi, and its applications were established by Huang Ti. People in this world only know the military as a method to fight battles. They do not know that it is indeed the source of daily life."[27] Here Chinese and Shinto military ideals were united in the oft-quoted phrase *shen-wu pu-sha* (literally, "a man with divine power acts without killing") from the *Hsi Tz'u* (Commentary on the Appended Judgments) of the *I Ching.* Because of the phonetic coincidence, Tokugawa Japanese also referred to *shen-wu* as the legendary emperor, Jimmu (660–588 B.C.E?).

Yamaga criticized most Japanese military thinkers for being concerned solely with the way of killing and with forgetting the spirit of Emperor Jimmu. He pointed out that warriors should read the *Jimmu-ki* (Records of Emperor Jimmu) in the *Nihon shoki,* allegedly the earliest Japanese record of military philosophy, to see how Jimmu conquered Eastern Japan without resorting to killing. According to Yamaga's explanation, the phrase *shen-wu pu-sha* (or *jimmu busatsu*) implies the unity of *bun* (governance) and *bu* (the military). Therefore, he stated, "The *I Ching* and *Jimmu-ki* discuss the cultural sages and the military sages together."[28] Yamaga attributed this ideal to Confucius: "Imbued with the spirit of *shen-wu pu-sha,* editing the *I Ching,* Confucius set down the holy rules of teaching both culture (etiquette and music) and the military way."[29]

In the Yamaga school, the *I Ching* was also used to explain concrete military rules. For example, Yamaga used the hexagram *shih* (army) to illustrate two things: the likelihood that waging a war will backfire politically, and the proper way of positioning an army in an open field. He explained:

> The hexagram *shih* in the *I Ching* illustrates the fundamental thing about positioning troops. The Ten Wings point out that the way of the general is based on righteousness. Engaging in an unjustified battle will disturb and harm the people; the people will not follow. It becomes forced business. The image of the hexagram is ䷆. Tactics in the army follow this pattern. The broken lines [of *yin*] represent the location of the troops, while the unbroken line [of *yang*] is the location of the lord or generals. Thousands of tactics are derived from this pattern.[30]

Yamaga was also a champion of *taisei heihō*, which paid special attention to the changes of *ch'i* and *yin-yang*. For example, he explained that the changing distribution of *yin* and *yang* in nature in the different seasons of a year and hours of a day has an impact on military activities, stressing that a successful general can correctly observe the change of *yin-yang* to find out the right time of *yang* for his troops.[31]

In addition to the five largest schools of military thought, there were dozens of smaller schools in the Tokugawa period. To a certain extent they were all influenced by ideas of *yin-yang wu-hsing* and *gunbai shisō*. The Fūzan school, for instance, was influenced by the *I Ching* and was also indebted to the *Sun Tzu* and other Chinese military classics. Its founder, Iga Fūzan (1644–1718), was also a Confucian. The most important teachings of this school were the tactics of *yin-yang wu-hsing* and the *pa-chen* pattern. Iga explained these tactics in his *Inyō gogyō jinzu* (An Illustration of the *Yin-Yang Wu-Hsing* Tactics) and *Hachijin zusetsu* (An Illustrative Explanation of the *Pa-chen* Pattern). He believed that Fu Hsi was the father of tactics because all tactics were derived from the hexagrams and charts of the *I Ching*. For instance, K'ung Ming had supposedly used the *Ho T'u* and *Lo Shu* to create the *pa-chen* pattern. Even the military ideas of the *Sun Tzu* were no exception, Iga wrote:

> Indeed, K'ung Ming created the *pa-chen* tactics and the nine-army tactics from his reading of the *Sun Tzu*. Sun Tzu learned from T'ai Kung. T'ai Kung learned from Huang Ti. Huang Ti learned from Fu Hsi. Fu Hsi based his ideas on the *Star Chart*. From past to present, the principle has always been the same, and served as the unchangeable law for ten thousand generations. Hence the hexagrams of the *I Ching* are the origins [of all tactics].[32]

Iga also applied the *I Ching* to the positioning of different units of the army on a battlefield. His six-line pattern was comparable to the six lines in a hexagram, and was also influenced by the theory of *san-ts'ai* (the three powers of heaven, earth, and man) and the hexagram *shih* (army). He wrote:

> On the battlefield, we have six units in a lineup. We place artillery and archers in the first line, spearmen in the second line, cavalry in the third line, generals and officers in the fourth line, flag bearers in the fifth line, and horses in the sixth line. . . . This idea originates in the *Shuo Kua* (Commentary on the Trigrams) of the *I Ching*. It reads: "Therefore the sages determined the way of heaven and called it the *yin* and *yang*. They determined the way of earth and called it the yielding and the firm. They determined the way of man and called it benevolence and righteousness. They combined these three fundamental powers and doubled them; therefore in the *I Ching* a sign is always formed by six lines." Here, my six-line pattern follows the six lines [in a hexagram], and its principle is based on the hexagram *shih*.[33]

Imbued with neo-Confucian rationalism, Iga disagreed with *gunbai shisō* and even declared that anyone who used *I Ching* divination and *yin-yang* speculation in the army should be executed.[34]

From these six Tokugawa military schools, we know that military thought had been Confucianized in this period. Thanks to neo-Confucianism, Tokugawa military thought became rationalistic, humanistic, and ethical. Shamanistic notions (such as *taisei heihō*) and Shintoist ideas (such as *jimmu busatsu*) also had a certain impact. The *I Ching* played a role in all three traditions.

Schools of Martial Arts

Not only military thought but martial arts reached their zenith in Tokugawa Japan. Many martial arts schools appeared, but their writings were much narrower in focus than those of the six schools of military thought. Ideas of the *I Ching*, and *yin-yang*, in particular, played a major role in their teachings. In this section, we look at several forms of Japanese martial arts.

Fencing was the most popular martial art in the Tokugawa period.[35] Most schools of fencing were influenced tremendously by neo-Confucian metaphysics. We examine five major schools.

Itō Ittōsai (1560–1653), the founder of the Ittō (one-stroke) school, found the highest spirit of swordsmanship in Zen and the *I Ching*. He explained that only with a mind of "transcendental emptiness" could one cope with ever-changing situations:

But when there prevails a state of "purposelessness," the Spirit harbors nothing in it, nor is it tipped in any one direction; it transcends both subject and object; it responds empty-mindedly to environmental vicissitudes and leaves no tracks. We have in the *Book of Changes:* "There is in it no thinking, no doing, absolute quietness, and no motion; but it feels, and when it acts, it flows through any objects and events of the world." When this is understood in connection with the art of swordsmanship, one is nearer to the Way.[36]

Yagyū Mune'nori (1571–1646), the representative of the Shinkage school, also based his teachings on the idea of *yin-yang.* The main purpose of this school was to achieve internal movement in the state of *yang* and external motionlessness in the state of *yin,* following the way of the universe. Swordsmen of this school were famous for standing motionless and then, with one stroke, cutting their opponents in two. Yagyū explained the secret of the school:

Yin and *yang* are two corresponding terms that we should consider together. *Yang* is moving and *yin* is quiet. As regards *yin* and *yang,* in terms of internal and external, *yang* moves inside; *yin* is quiet outside. If the internal is *yin,* then *yang* moves and appears from outside. To apply it to tactics, we should keep *ch'i* moving inside restlessly and make the outside motionless and silent. Moving inside and being quiet outside is [a state] in agreement with the principles of the universe.[37]

The Taisha school was a branch of the Shinkage school. Its founder was Marume Nagayoshi (1539–1629), and its doctrine borrowed heavily from the *yin-yang wu-hsing* theory. Transmission in this school included a peculiar ritual: The patriarch sat in the middle, while disciples presented him with two wooden swords marked with hexagrams. The patriarch then sang and swung the wooden swords to cut the image of the hexagram *k'un* (receptive), a symbol of pure *yin.* Although the religious meanings of this ceremony are not clear, it demonstrates the influence of the *I Ching* and the importance of *yin* to this school.[38]

The Shigen school was founded by Tōgō Shigei (1561–1643), who built his military ideas on Confucian and Buddhist views of nature. This school pursued the unity of *yin* and *yang* through mental training. In Tōgō's metaphor, there is a narrow bridge linking *ch'ien (yang)* in heaven and *k'un (yin)* on earth. One can only cross this bridge by mentally training to be quiet and emptying one's mind.[39] According to Tōgō, swordsmanship is only an expression of the natural principle that can be found everywhere. In his words, "a brick and a grass root can tell the principles of [the hexagrams] *ch'ien* and *k'un*."[40] He also said: "*Ch'ien* is heaven; *k'un* is earth. They are the natural principles of the universe. Fencing also uses the same natural principles to hit."[41]

The Heijō-muteki school was founded by Yamanouchi Naokazu. Yamanouchi wrote the *Heijō muteki sho* (Book of the Heijō-muteki School, 1663), which quoted extensively from the *I Ching*. He used the *yin-yang wu-hsing* principle and the eight trigrams to explicate his military ideas. "The essence of swordsmanship is the unity of *yin* and *yang*" was the central motif of his school.[42] He explained that the natural principle is a never-ending circular movement of *yin* and *yang;* in the state of the unity of *yin* and *yang*, the enemy would fail to make appropriate responses to change.

Archery was the most important traditional shooting technique. The main purpose of the Insai school was the pursuit of the unity of *yin* and *yang*. The founder of the school was Yoshida Shigeuji (1561–1638), the archery tutor to the first three Tokugawa shoguns. This school stressed the importance of having a balance of *yin* and *yang* in bow and arrow, and in the left hand and the right hand. It identified the bow-holding hand as *yang* and the arrow-drawing hand as *yin*, and pointed out that accuracy can only be reached through a subtle balance of the two forces in each hand.[43]

The Yamato school was founded by Morikawa Kōzan in the early Tokugawa period. Although this school had strong Shinto overtones, its ideas borrowed heavily from the *I Ching*. Morikawa used the ideas of *yin-yang, wu-hsing* and the hexagrams to explain archery in his *Nihon-ryū shinmei shagi* (Godly Archery of the Yamato School). He compared *yin-yang* to the bow, *wu-hsing* to the arrow, and the eight trigrams to eight arrows in a set.[44] He said: "*Wu-hsing* are derived from *yin-yang*. *Wu-hsing* are the arrows. This is called the principle of archery."[45] He attributed the origins of Japanese archery to the Sun Goddess and the origins of Chinese archery to Fu Hsi. His explanation of the coordination of bow and arrow is a reminder of the influence of the *I Ching* on the *Nihon shoki:* "Izanagi and Izanami were in the middle, the God of *Yang* to the left, and the God of *Yin* to the right. They formed the image of drawing a bow with an arrow, and it became the origin of [the custom of] using the left hand for holding and the right hand for drawing."[46]

The Ogasawara school was headed by the Ogasawara family, which had a tradition of archery stretching back to the medieval period. This school favored the numbers eight and nine because they represent the numbers of the universe in the *I Ching*. In the *Shareiki* (On the Regulations on Archery, 1699), Ogasawara Tsunetomi explained: "Nine is the number of old *yang*, which originates from the eight trigrams and becomes the origin of the *pa-chen* tactics. The eight trigrams are the origin of everything. The *pa-chen* tactics, the essence of the military, copy the theory of the eight trigrams."[47] Therefore, the school decided that when an archer kneels down to prepare to let an arrow go, the bow pull should be either eight (old *yin*) or nine (old *yang*) inches.

Jūjutsu, the prototype for *jūdō*, was the most important unarmed fighting skill. It was imported to Japan by a Ming refugee, Ch'en Yüan-yün (1587–1671). *Jūjutsu* masters found legitimacy for practicing their techniques in the *Hsi Tz'u* and *Shuo Kua* of the *I Ching*. Katayama Shōsai remarked:

> [The *Hsi Tz'u* reads:] "Movement and quietness have their definite laws; according to these, firmness and softness are differentiated." The *Shuo Kua* reads: "Therefore the sages determined the way of heaven and called it *yin* and *yang*. They determined the way of earth and called it the yielding and the firm. They determined the way of man and called it benevolence and righteousness. They combined these three fundamental powers and doubled them." The three powers of heaven, earth, and man are not beyond the dualism of firmness and softness. . . . Because the heavenly principle is like that, it goes without saying that it is also applicable to the martial arts. Therefore, even things like spear-fighting, fencing, archery, and horsemanship are not excluded from the dualism of firmness and softness.[48]

The Shibukawa school, founded by Shibukawa Yoshikata (1652–1704), admitted that its teachings were based on the *I Ching*. The classic of the school, the *Jūjutsu taisei roku* (The Synthesis of *Jūjutsu*), explains the true meaning of *jūjutsu*:

> The *I Ching* reads: "The sages determined the way of earth and called it the yielding and the firm.". . . . Therefore, from the *I Ching* we come to know that a change in strength hinges on softness and yielding. Following the development of things forward and backward, moving and stopping is called *jūjutsu*. . . . The teachings of our school were established based on the text of the *I Ching*. This is also the reason for the name.[49]

Other *jūjutsu* schools, such as Takeuchi-ryū, Kitō-ryū, Sekiguchi-ryū, and Oguri-ryū, were all indebted to the *I Ching*.

The spear was the second important traditional weapon. The Ōshima school was founded by Ōshima Yoshitsuna (1588–?). The main idea of the school is that spear-fighting is a way of *yang;* the ideal situation is having a *yang* spear and *yang* heart at the same time. This means that the heart is more important than the weapon. A *yin* spear with a *yang* heart will win, while a *yang* spear with a *yin* heart will lose. Ōshima explained: "Even though our spear is *yin,* if we have a *yang* heart, we will not lose. Even though our spear is *yang,* if our heart is *yin,* it will be dangerous. There are *yin* and *yang* in spear and heart."[50]

The Utsumi school was founded by Utsumi Shigetsugu (d. 1648). Like the Ōshima school, it pursued a state of pure *yang.* The main goal of this school was to achieve the transformation from nothing to all *yang* in a stroke. The first hexagram that appears after the formation of the universe is *ch'ien* (creation), a symbol of all *yang.* Utsumi Shigemune, a descendant of Shigetsugu, wrote: "Applying this [principle] to the martial arts [means that] we face our enemy with the spirit of nothingness. We should know that the result happens at the beginning [of the action], like the budding [of a plant]. When we take our first step, it represents the birth of *yang.*"[51]

Ninjutsu, a form of Japanese espionage, was established during the *sengoku* period and institutionalized in the early Tokugawa period. Fujibayashi Yasutake wrote the *Bansen shūkai* (A Hundred Streams Running into the Sea) in 1676; it became the bible of *ninjutsu* for the Iga and Kōga schools. The *Bansen shūkai* uses the ideas of *yin-yang,* *wu-hsing,* and the eight trigrams extensively. For instance, Fujibayashi divided *ninjutsu* into two types, *yang ninjutsu (yō-nin)* and *yin ninjutsu (in-nin).* One of the jobs of a *ninja* is to know the *wu-hsing* of the enemy's generals, an idea left over from *gunbai shisō.* "The *I Ching* says that if important things do not go secretly, misfortunes come," Fujibayashi stated to justify this practice.[52] He also traced the origins of *ninjutsu* to Fu Hsi: "*Ninjutsu* is an important military skill. It was created during the eras of Fu Hsi and Huang Ti, although there are no books left on *ninjutsu.* [Ancient Chinese] already possessed the substance of *ninjutsu* [although they did not name it]."[53]

Thus the philosophy of the *I Ching* was included in the teachings of different Japanese martial arts. Both *yin-yang wu-hsing* and other aspects of the text were used creatively to explicate and justify martial arts teachings.

The Military Views of Tokugawa Confucians

There was great concern with military affairs outside military circles. Most Tokugawa Confucians believed that the *I Ching* played an important role in the military. They studied military ideas and practices and were associated with certain military schools. Like most military scholars, Confucians tended to apply neo-Confucian metaphysics in order to interpret military matters. Many suggested that Fu Hsi was the father of tactics and that all tactics were related to the *I Ching*.

Hayashi Razan was influenced by *gunbai shisō*. For example, he stressed the importance of using proper music during a military campaign. Hayashi thought that "the five types of music" corresponded to *wu-hsing*, and believed that choosing a kind of music with a stronger *wu-hsing* agent than the enemy's was vital to achieving victory. He remarked: "The application of the five types of music to military affairs is written in the *Liu T'ao* (Six Military Classics). The five types of music match the five agents; the five agents match the five points [or directions]. By analyzing the principle of promotion and control, we can determine the result."[54] Hayashi also believed in the use of talismans in the army and held that this tradition had originated in the *Ho T'u*.

Matsunaga Sekigo argued that the *I Ching*, the well-pattern field system, and military methods were all derived from the *Ho T'u* and *Lo Shu*, both of which reflect the numbers and principles of the universe. He said: "The sages established the division of the well-field system and the tactics based on the numerology of the *Ho T'u* and *Lo Shu*. There is nothing in the world excluded from these numbers and principles."[55]

Nakae Tōju maintained that the *I Ching* was the origin of all tactics and criticized the poor quality of many Japanese translations of, and commentaries on, Chinese military classics: "The way of the military and the diagrams of tactics were originally from the *I Ching*. They were completed during the rule of Huang Ti and were transmitted through T'ai Fung, K'ung Ming, and wise men of different eras. In Japan, they were translated into Japanese with many mistakes."[56]

Asami Keisai used the hexagrams to explain tactics. Like Matsunaga Sekigo, he discussed these in terms of the numbers of the universe. In his lecture on the *pa-chen* tactics, he explained: "Military books reached their pinnacle in the *pa-chen* pattern. . . . The eight trigrams in the *I Ching* share the same number eight. . . . The number of the universe is based on the five agents which are four. . . . Therefore the *pa-chen* pattern has four in the middle and four on all sides. . . . If we always prepare the pattern of four in the middle and four on the sides, we will never be penetrated. . . . This is the essence of the *pa-chen* pattern that I have just taught."[57] Although the meaning of

Asami's numerology is far from clear, his attempt to use the *I Ching* to explain tactics is important. He was surprised to realize that although many ancient Japanese warriors did not study the *pa-chen* pattern, their tactics followed it.

Kaibara Ekken stressed that both the way of the *I Ching* and the way of military affairs are the same in nature—namely, the way of benevolence and righteousness. He said: "The *I Ching* is the ultimate teaching of the sages and the mirror for ten thousand generations. We should believe it without doubt. The way of the military is also a way of benevolence and righteousness."[58]

Such attitudes toward the military implications of the *I Ching* were prevalent among Confucians of the time. Although most Tokugawa Confucians did not put forth a complete system of military thought, the scattered quotations given here show the role of the *I Ching* in their military thinking.

The Adaptation of Western Weaponry in the Late Tokugawa Period

If *gunbai shisō* was the dominant school of military thought in the *sengoku* period and neo-Confucian metaphysics became the theoretical mainstream in early Tokugawa times, what was the leading school in the late Tokugawa period? This is not easy to answer. Although neo-Confucian military thought remained very powerful, by the mid-Tokugawa period we see a dramatic increase in the number of students who studied and translated books on Western weaponry. Yet the growing influence of Western military techniques outweighed the influence of Western military thought. Thus some artillerists used the *I Ching* to provide Western weaponry with a neo-Confucian base and hence legitimize its use.

Western artillery had been studied and promoted enthusiastically ever since the Portuguese introduced it to Japan in 1543, and it became one of the six major martial arts during the Tokugawa period. The resulting writings on artillery give a more rational impression than those on the traditional martial arts, for they seldom refer to ideas such as *gunbai shisō* and the deities. From the beginning, however, Japanese writers tried to give Western artillery a neo-Confucian metaphysical framework.

During the early Tokugawa period, there were some efforts to link artillery techniques with Chinese military ideas. For instance, the

Fūzan and Gōden schools were famous for using the *Sun Tzu* to explicate artillery methods. Yamaga Sokō was also interested in cannons and gunpowder, and believed that the principles and manufacturing methods of machines and weapons were concealed in the images and numbers of the *I Ching*.[59]

Among major schools of artillery in the Tokugawa period, the Jikaku, Inoue, Tenzan, Morishige, and Takashima schools frequently used the *I Ching* to interpret Western artillery ideas.

The Jikaku school was founded by Minamoto Tane'naga, who had studied gunnery under the Dutch in Nagasaki. He used *yin-yang wu-hsing* to illustrate the structure of a cannon. Identifying the barrel with *yin* and the gunpowder with *yang*, he pointed out that the unity of *yin* and *yang* was reached in cannoning. He manufactured and tested a variety of cannons and concluded that range and trajectory were subject to the fluctuations of *yin-yang* and to the promotion and control of *wu-hsing*. His grandson, Taneoki, recalled Minamoto Tane'naga's teaching:

> One day, my grandfather suddenly realized the ultimate principle of gunnery. He elaborated it and, surprisingly, found out that it was in accordance with the principle of *yin-yang wu-hsing*, the wonderful application of the theory behind the universe. Hence he treated the barrel as *yin* and the gunpowder as *yang*. Considering the change of *yin-yang* and the promotion and control of *wu-hsing*, the range and trajectory of the cannonball would not err beyond a one-mile range. Developing the numerology [of the *I Ching*], he classified nine kinds of cannon according to their length and size.[60]

The Inoue school served the bakufu as chief artillerists *(teppō yaku)* during the entire Tokugawa period. The school's founder was Inoue Shimotsugu (d. 1646), who believed that the principles of cannons could be found in the *I Ching* and in Buddhist sūtras. His successor, Shimokage, used "the five rings" (a Buddhist version of the five-agent theory) to explain the principles of gunnery, stating that "the cannon was brought to Japan by the Southern barbarians. Although it has been used extensively by our people, very few understand its principles. It is like the five agents of human beings: earth, water, fire, wind, and emptiness. The battery is earth, the gunpowder is water, the fuse is fire, the cannonball is wind, and the muzzle is emptiness."[61]

The Tenzan school was founded by Sakamoto Tenzan (1745–1803), who is remembered for inventing a movable gun carriage known as the *shūhatsudai*. Its principle was similar to today's anti-aircraft gun, in that it could rotate 180 degrees horizontally and 80 degrees vertically; some Japanese scholars regard it as one of the most important innovations of the Tokugawa period, and even of eighteenth-century world military history. Cannons of the Tenzan school proved extremely powerful during the Anglo-Satsuma Conflicts of the 1860s. Using the *I Ching* to interpret artillery techniques was a characteristic of this school. Sakamoto wrote two books to illustrate his movable gun carriage using the symbols and numbers of the *I Ching*: the *Shūhatsu zusetsu* (An Illustrative Explanation of the Movable Carriage) and the *Shūhatsu shuekishō benshaku* (An Explanation of the Movable Carriage Through Images of the *I Ching*).

The Morishige school was developed from the Mishima school in the late Tokugawa period. This school used the *yin-yang* principle to demonstrate the functions of saltpeter and sulfur in explosive devices such as cannons and firearms. For example, Mishima Bokushū explained how these chemicals were mixed: "When *yin* becomes extreme, *yang* arises. When *yang* becomes extreme, *yin* arises. . . . There is *yang* inside *yin* and *yin* inside *yang*. . . . Saltpeter is heaven; it is *yin* caused by *yin* entering *yang* under the sun. Sulfur is the earth; it is *yang* caused by *yang* entering *yin* above the sun."[62]

Sakuma Shōzan (1811–1864) himself serves as the best footnote to his famous motto, "Eastern ethics and Western art"—a common intellectual response during the transitional stage of cultural interchange. Sakuma was a student of the Takashima school, the most active and westernized school of artillery in the late Tokugawa period. He studied the *I Ching* under Satō Issai and Takeuchi Sekimei, and learned gunnery under Egawa Tairō. These two traditions were combined in his *Hōka* (The Hexagram of a Cannon, 1852), a book highly regarded by Satō and Takeuchi.

According to Sakuma, one day when he was teaching his students artillery, a student asked whether Westerners were superior to the sages because they knew artillery, whereas the sages only knew archery. Sakuma replied that the sages had created the wonderful images in the *I Ching*, which could explain everything, including the principles of artillery and archery. As a result of this exchange, he wrote the *Hōka*, in which he reinterpreted the hexagram *k'uei* (opposition) to explain the structure, functions, and political implications of Western artillery and, following the structure of the *I Ching*, wrote a *Judgment of the Trigram, Commentary on the Six Lines*, and *Commentary on the Images* himself.

In this explanation of the whole image, Sakuma associated each of the six lines of the hexagram *k'uei* with a different part of a cannon: "In terms of the whole picture, the rear [the first line from the bottom] represents the tail-end; the next [the second line] is the tail. These two are fairly heavy and are symbols of a solid cannon's tail. The tail has a hole in the middle; it is the fire-hole [the third line]. The thing lying vertically is the barrel [the fourth line]. The empty space at the head is the muzzle [the fifth line]. It solidifies the upper part [the top line]. Who can say that this is not the image of a cannon?"[63] This quotation can be demonstrated by the illustration below.[64]

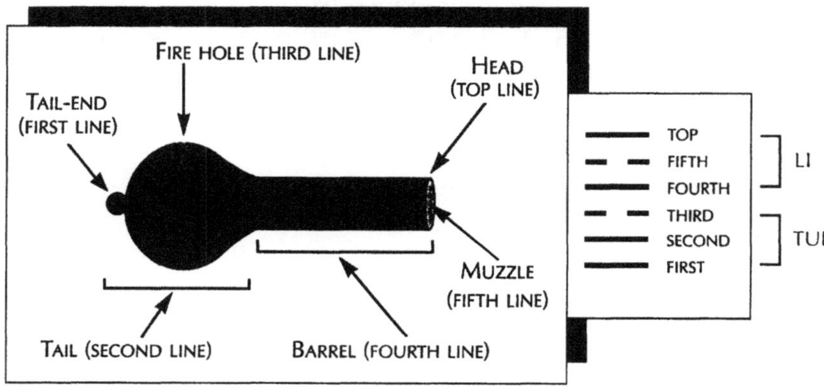

Sakuma also used the *wu-hsing* theory to interpret the image of the hexagram *k'uei*.[65] This hexagram is composed of two parts: the *li* trigram ☲ at the top, and the *tui* trigram ☱ at the bottom. According to the principles of *wu-hsing, li* represents fire and *tui* represents metal. Sakuma claimed that this represents the image of a cannon, showing that the cannonball causes fire when it flies out of the metal barrel and muzzle. He explained: "The meaning [of the image] is that the fire comes out of a golden mouth. Fire also means flying; mouth also means shooting. Hence it is an image of gunnery."[66]

Concluding Remarks

The role of the *I Ching* in Tokugawa military history has been underestimated. The prevalent but unscholarly view is that the *I Ching* was only a book of oracles and was insignificant in Tokugawa history.[67] Yet the *I Ching* played a crucial role in the formation of traditional military thought and the martial arts, and a significant role in the adaptation of Western weaponry.

For centuries, the *I Ching* had been associated with *yin-yang* and Onmyōdō traditions in the form of *gunbai shisō*. Using *I Ching* divination, astrology, and geomancy to make military decisions, *gunbai shisō* reached its peak during the sixteenth century. "The Tokugawa Peace" and the rise of Confucianism changed military ideas and techniques tremendously. Large-scale combat tactics gave way to small-scale martial arts. Military philosophy was baptized by the rationalism of neo-Confucianism. The *I Ching* was flexible enough to be interpreted in different ways that fit these new circumstances. Neo-Confucianism infiltrated different schools of military thought and the martial arts. Its metaphysical framework of *yin-yang wu-hsing* replaced *gunbai shisō* as the central tenet of military thinking.

Far from weakening the role of the *I Ching* in Tokugawa military studies, the importation of Western military technology broadened the possible applications of the text. In late Tokugawa times, some significant attempts were made to use the *I Ching* to integrate Western weaponry into the neo-Confucian system. Scholars from various artillery schools used the text to provide Western weaponry with a neo-Confucian base and to legitimize the use of Western weapons. Although its principal role changed several times, the *I Ching* had a strong impact on military thought throughout the Tokugawa period.

11. The *I Ching* and Popular Culture

The Tokugawa was one of the most important periods in Japanese cultural history.[1] Although it lacked the Heian era's elegance and nobility (794–1186) and the Momoyama's creativity and flamboyance (late sixteenth century, when Japan was under Toyotomi Hideyoshi), Tokugawa culture was unique in many ways. Various artistic and cultural forms reached their maturity and the peak of their popularity during the Tokugawa period. Forms of high culture such as *nō* drama, *gagaku* (an ancient Chinese music), *renga* (linked poetry), the painting of the Kanō and Tosa schools, and porcelain and lacquer ware continued to be patronized by courtiers, the upper samurai, and Buddhist priests.

However, the most striking development was perhaps the emergence of a popular culture among the lower social classes—namely, the *chōnin* (townsmen), the lower samurai, and Confucians. *Chōnin* became the main producers and consumers of forms of Tokugawa popular culture—*kabuki, jōruri* (puppet theater), and *kana zōshi* (writings in Japanese syllabary), among other new genres. Indeed, the boundary between high culture and popular culture became blurred. Popular culture was primarily derived from high culture; it also aroused the interest of the upper classes. High culture became less exclusive, as wealthy commoners also joined the social elite to support it. For these reasons, I do not clearly distinguish between high and popular culture here.

As *I Ching* scholarship reached its apex in the Tokugawa period, its idea of *yin-yang wu-hsing* also penetrated different aspects of Tokugawa culture. This chapter examines the role of the *I Ching* in the theory and practice of various forms of art and culture in the Tokugawa period,[2] highlighting those that seem to have had stronger ties with the *I Ching*. I hope this investigation sheds new light on the nature of Tokugawa culture and helps us understand the role of Chinese traditions in the formation of Japanese culture.

Tea Ceremony *(Chanoyu)*

The Japanese tea ceremony was of interest to all classes in the Tokugawa period. It was influenced by Chinese tea philosophy in its early formation in the medieval period. In China, tea and the *I Ching* were already linked in Lu Yü's (d. 804) *Ch'a Ching* (The Classic of Tea), the bible of Chinese tea philosophy. Lu's philosophy was influenced by his knowledge of the *I Ching*.[3] He not only decorated his brazier with the hexagrams but also emphasized the importance of harmonizing the *wu-hsing*. For example, he pointed out that since wind stirs fire and fire boils water in preparing tea, tea is subject to the *wu-hsing* principle of promotion and control.

Other important Chinese books on tea, such as the *Ta-kuan ch'a-lun* (Treatise on Tea, attributed to the Sung emperor Hui-tsung) and *Ch'a Lüeh* (A Short Discussion on Tea), also mention the *yin-yang wu-hsing* doctrine. Thus when Eisai (1141–1215) introduced tea drinking to Japan in the *Kissa yōshōki* (Drinking Tea for Nourishment, 1214), it is no wonder that he used the *yin-yang wu-hsing* theory to illustrate the medical value of tea. Tea drinking was promoted by Zen Buddhist monks in the medieval period. In the late fifteenth and sixteenth centuries, the Japanese began to formulate their own tea philosophy and rituals. In particular, Sen no Rikyū (1522–1591) is remembered for his role in perfecting *chanoyu*.

The tea ceremony became very popular among urban commoners in the Tokugawa period. However, Tokugawa Japanese made few theoretical contributions. Major tea schools promoted and Confucianized Rikyū's teachings. For instance, Nambō Sōkei, a disciple of Rikyū, compiled Rikyū's teachings in the *Nampō roku* (Records on Tea Drinking in the South, 7 *kan*) in the early Tokugawa period. This classic of *chanoyu* used the *yin-yang wu-hsing* principle extensively. According to the book, Rikyū believed that everything in *chanoyu* is based on the principle of *yin-yang*:

> It is only after years of practice you will grasp in its details the fact that everything—from the hundred thousand ways of displaying utensils to the straw-thatched *wabi* [an aesthetic of *chanoyu* connoting a feeling of loneliness and shabbiness] tearoom—is governed by the measurements, based on *yin* and *yang*, that are applied in using the *daisu* [a rectangular tea stand].[4]

A standard tea ceremony consists of three parts: the first gathering *(shoza* or *shoiri),* the middle break *(nakadachi),* and the second gathering *(goza* or *goiri).* During the first gathering, a light meal with *sake* (Japanese wine) and sweets is served, and the charcoal is prepared. In the middle break, the guest may use the toilet while the host prepares for the second gathering. At the second gathering, flowers are set out, tea utensils are viewed, and, finally, thick and thin tea are served. In his explanation of Rikyū's teachings, Nambō regarded the first gathering as *yin* and the second gathering as *yang*. Because of the change in *yin* and *yang* between the two gatherings, he pointed out that the decorations, utensils, and rituals must be changed:

> In a *wabi* tearoom, we should pay attention to the differences between the first gathering and the second gathering. Sen no Rikyū said: "The first gathering is *yin;* the second gathering is *yang*." This is a fundamental teaching. In the first gathering, we have a *kakemono* [an object hanging in the alcove] hanging in the *tokonoma* [the alcove in a tearoom], a kettle with a small flame, and the rush blinds on the window. These are all in the state of *yin*. The host and his guests also share the same spirit [of *yin*]. In the second gathering, we have flower arrangements, a kettle with a strong flame, and the rush blind removed. These all embody the spirit of *yang*.[5]

Nambō also warned that the misplacement of *yin* and *yang* would cause the tea to taste bitter. It is obvious that he had a preference for *yang* over *yin,* which explains why the second gathering sounds more important than the first. This preference can also be seen from his ideas on the interior design of the *shoin,* a formal Japanese reception room: "In terms of fortune, *yang* is good and *yin* is bad. The *shoin,* alcove, and tea stand should all be decorated according to the spirit of *yang* [most of the time], not to mention during special religious ceremonies."[6] For the same reason, Nambō preferred *yang* numbers, such as three and five, and opposed the use of the *yin* number six in the interior design of a *shoin.*[7]

Another champion of Rikyū's teachings was Fujūzai Chikushin (1678–1745), who wrote the *Genryū chawa* (On the Origins of Tea).

He recorded an interesting conversation between Takuan Sōhō and a friend to demonstrate a common belief that *chanoyu* is subject to *wu-hsing* theory. Takuan's friend said: "If you understand that all teachings are one, you will know immediately that [*chanoyu*] has all the five agents: the ladle is wood, the fire is fire, the fire pit is earth, the kettle is metal, and the water in the kettle is water."[8] This reflects a popular view prevalent among tea masters from Tokugawa times to the present.

With the exception of the *Nampō roku,* Tokugawa writings on tea are less explicit on the role of the *I Ching,* and seldom refer directly to the *yin-yang wu-hsing* doctrine. Textual analysis seems less useful in unlocking the subtle relationship between *chanoyu* and the *I Ching;* hence we look into this issue by reconstructing and analyzing the rituals and settings of *chanoyu* in the Tokugawa period.

The tea ceremony is a microcosm manifesting the principle of *yin-yang wu-hsing.* All its aspects—from the architecture and decoration of the teahouse and tearoom to the tools and utensils used in preparing the tea, the season, date, and time of the gathering, and the gestures, regulations, and food and drink served—reflect the principle of *yin-yang wu-hsing.* In general, Japanese tea philosophy has a preference for *yang,* although its ultimate objective is to achieve the unity of *yin* and *yang.*

Both the external and internal designs have important symbolic meanings. Several stone lanterns are located around the teahouse. They have three basic models—the square (earth), circle (water), and triangle (fire)—representing the balance of *yin* (water) and *yang* (fire) in the tea bowl (earth).[9] A standard tearoom is called a *yojōhan* (four-and-a-half-mat tearoom), which can be divided into nine equal squares representing the universe. The middle segment is identified with *t'ai-chi* (the Supreme Ultimate), whereas the eight peripheral segments are associated with the eight trigrams. The actions of tea practitioners and the setting, design, and decoration of the room are all subject to this idea of geomancy.[10]

During the tea ceremony, both the host and his guests are supposed to use their right *(yang)* and left hands *(yin)* alternately to follow the circulation of *yin* and *yang* in the universe.[11] *Wu-hsing* can also be found in the tea ceremony. Fire (fire, *yang*) is used to make water (water, *yin*) through a kettle (metal). The hot water in the kettle is later carried by a ladle (wood) to a tea bowl (earth). Thus the five agents interact with each other in accord with the principle of promotion and control. Fire and water also represent *yang* and *yin*, which are harmonized in the ceremony.[12]

Water is a crucial element in making tea. As *chanoyu* has a preference for *yang*, it considers the dawn water *(yang)* ideal for making tea. Water drawn at night *(yin)* is believed to be bitter and even sometimes poisonous. Another tradition involves writing the trigram for water *(k'an)* on the ash under the brazier.

Many tea utensils, such as the *chataku* (a lacquer tea tray used to present the tea bowl) and *chaire* (a ceramic tea container), are decorated with hexagrams of the *I Ching*. The color of the tea tray must match *wu-hsing* in different seasons. The arrangements are as follows: spring (wood, blue); summer (fire, red); *toyō*, or the season between summer and fall (earth, yellow); fall (metal, white); and winter (water, black). For example, a tea ceremony in the spring should use a blue tea tray because blue is the color for the agent of wood, to which spring belongs.[13] On the surface of the *chataku* and other lacquered tools and utensils, there are usually two *makie* patterns (a Japanese innovation by which patterns are created on lacquer using gold powder)—the chrysanthemum *(yang)* and the leaf of the firmiana tree *(yin)*—demonstrating the balance of *yin* and *yang*.[14] An unlacquered food tray *(hassun)* is used to make offerings to Shinto spirits. It is sixty-four square *sun* (one *sun* is about one inch) in size, and thus represents the sixty-four hexagrams.

Inside the tearoom, there are several important decorations. *Ikebana* or *chabana* represents *yin-yang* and *wu-hsing* in the universe. An incense container *(kōgō)* is used to harmonize *yin* and *yang*. We will discuss *ikebana* and *kōdō* (the way of incense) in greater detail later. A bronze gong *(dōra)* and a metal bell with a mallet *(kanshō)* are used to call guests back to the tearoom after the middle break of the tea ceremony. The gong is considered to have a *yang* sound and is used in the daytime; the bell has a *yin* sound and is used in the evening. *Kakemono* is usually a calligraphic scroll, and sometimes a painting. Many of these items use terms or ideas from the *I Ching* to show the Zen spirit. The Japanese have developed their own way of framing *kakemono*, called *kanewari*, which is in agreement with the *yin-yang wu-hsing* theory. For instance, the upper section of the frame is divided into five major lines and numerous small lines, which represent *wu-hsing* and *yin-yang*, respectively. In a daytime tea gathering, the *kakemono* is hung along *yang* lines; at an evening tea gathering, it is hung along *yin* lines.[15]

As a modern Japanese scholar of *chanoyu* points out, the relationship between *chanoyu* and the *yin-yang wu-hsing* doctrine is a major topic for future research.[16] The symbolism in the tea ritual provides us with important clues about this little-studied topic.

Flower Arrangement *(Kadō or Ikebana)*

The origin of the way of flowers, or flower arrangement *(kadō),* can be traced to the Kamakura period (1186–1336), when flower arranging developed into a Buddhist art. In the Muromachi period (1392–1573), it was associated with the *nenbutsu* (chanting to Amida Buddha) and *renga* (linked poetry) traditions. It drew closer to *chanoyu* in the sixteenth century. The Tokugawa period was the heyday of flower arrangement. A large number of writings on *kadō* emerged, although their authors and times of completion or publication are mostly uncertain. Compared to *chanoyu, kadō* has a more explicit and closer relationship with the *I Ching.* Most writings on *kadō* in the Tokugawa period use the *yin-yang wu-hsing* principle as their underlying metaphysical and aesthetic framework.

The ideal of flower arrangement is to express and achieve the harmony of the universe in terms of *I Ching* related concepts: *yin-yang, san-ts'ai* (the three powers of heaven, earth, and man), and *wu-hsing.* The most basic and important idea among all *kadō* schools is to divide the flower arrangement into three parts, or branches, to symbolize the harmony of heaven, earth, and man. The *Enshū sōka ikō kōden shō* (Oral Transmission of *Sōka* of the Enshū School, author unknown, 1801) reads: "The three branches are the heavenly branch, earthly branch, and human branch. They represent the *san ts'ai*."[17] These three parts differ in size, weight, direction, strength, and speed of growth. The first part rises up to the top to represent heaven; the second lies down at the bottom to symbolize earth; and the third part grows between heaven *(yang)* and earth *(yin)* to illustrate man's role in harmonizing *yin* and *yang.* The *Senkei-ryū ikebana kōden* (Oral Transmission of *Ikebana* of the Sen School, author unknown, written in the late eighteenth century) explains: "In the flower arrangement, we will find *yin-yang,* heaven-earth-man, father-mother-son, primary-secondary-tertiary, standing-walking-running, and upper-middle-lower. If you do not find these principles, that is not *ikebana.*"[18]

Besides the standard three-branch pattern, there are many other varieties. The *Enshū sōka ikō kōden shō* introduces two other important patterns. The first is the two-branch pattern, in which the upper part is a blossoming flower representing *yang* and heaven and the lower part is a leaf or flower bud representing *yin* and earth. The second is the five-branch pattern. In this pattern, the center and the top are the agent of earth (yellow), in the front is fire (red), in the back is water (black), in the left bottom is metal (white), and in the right bottom is wood (blue).[19] With the exception of the two-branch pattern, which represents *yin-yang,* all the patterns described are odd *(yang)* numbers, such as seven, nine, eleven, thirteen, and fifteen, reflecting the preference for *yang* in *ikebana.* The *Senkei-ryū ikebana kōden* explains: "In *ikebana,* we do not prefer *yin* numbers, such as two, four, six, and eight. However, the number two is used because it has the principle of *yin-yang.* We must not use the rest [of the even numbers], such as four, six, and eight."[20] In particular, the author of this book disagreed with the six-flower, six-leaf pattern adopted by some schools because such a pattern contradicts the principle of *yin-yang.*

The *yin-yang* theory is applied to the position of the leaf and flower and to the number of branches. The front of the leaf and flower are *yang* and the back is *yin.* Branches with odd numbers are *yang* and those with even numbers are *yin. Yang* leaves and flowers are preferable for daytime *ikebana; yin* leaves and flowers are suitable for evening *ikebana.* Tōfuku Ken'i explained this idea in his *Tōfuku kadan* (Tōfuku's Discussions on Flower Arrangement, 1729):

> What is *yin-yang* in flower and leaf? Back is *yin* and front is *yang.* Things with odd numbers are *yang,* and with even numbers are *yin.* . . . I have read the *Taiseishū.* It says: "Daytime *ikebana* uses more *yang* leaves, evening *ikebana* uses more *yin* leaves. . . . Although we have the principle of *sōka* [or *nageire,* a technique of flower arranging, often used in the tea ceremony, that puts the side branch along the top of the vase], the character of a flower, and several teachings from oral transmissions, they are all derived from the principle of *yin-yang* in *ikebana.* Beyond *yin-yang,* there are no more teachings.[21]

The *Kyokugi hihon daikan* (Great Scroll of the Ultimate Secret, author unknown, compiled in the early Tokugawa period) mentions another practice of *ikebana: yin* leaves should face upward and *yang* leaves downward.[22]

Not only the positions and numbers of the plants but the plants themselves were classified as either *yin* or *yang* according to their nature. The *Sanzai-ryū ikebana (Ikebana* of the Hosokawa Sanzai School, author unknown, 1730) points out that flowers from wood are *yang* and flowers from grass are *yin*. It suggests that *yang* flowers, such as the lotus, should be appreciated during the daytime, whereas *yin* flowers, such as the plum and the orchid, should be appreciated in the evening. It also identifies different flowers with *wu-hsing* according to their color: blue (wood), red (fire), yellow (earth), white (metal), and purple/black (water).[23]

The *Ikebana shōdenki* (Legitimate Transmission of *Ikebana*, by Shunjūken Ichiha, compiled in the early nineteenth century) has some interesting discussions of *yin-yang* theory in *ikebana*. Shunjūken emphasized that *yang* flowers grow in the summer and *yin* flowers in the winter. Like other *ikebana* masters, he preferred *yang* to *yin*. For instance, he said: "We only dedicate living *yang* flowers to deities. *Yin* flowers are not wanted because we prefer something that has grown strong."[24] He also applied the *yin-yang* theory when discussing the use of water in a vase and the shapes of flowers and vases, and suggested that the use of water in a vase should be different in each of the four seasons according to the change of *yin-yang* in the universe. In the winter, when *yin* is strong, little water is required (water itself being *yin* in nature), whereas in the spring, when *yang* is strong, more water is needed to achieve the balance of *yin* and *yang*.[25] As for the shape of the vase and flower, square is *yin* and circle is *yang*. If the flower is square, we should put it in a round vase; if round, it is better to use a square vase. By doing this, *yin* and *yang* are harmonized and the flower grows healthily. To this effect, Shunjūken wrote: "Round *ikebana* grows in the *yin* place. Square *ikebana* grows in the *yang* place. Round [*ikebana*] is *yang*. When it discovers a square place, it will grow there. Square is *yin*. Square [*ikebana*] is *yin*. When it discovers a round place, it will grow there."[26]

Despite differences in style, origin, and teaching, many schools of flower arrangement used the *yin-yang wu-hsing* theory as their central philosophy. Few other cultural practices in the Tokugawa period used the *yin-yang wu-hsing* theory as much as *ikebana* did.

Popular Drama *(Kabuki* and *Jōruri)*

It is no exaggeration to say that the flower of Tokugawa popular culture blossomed on the stage of the theater. Two of the most creative and popular cultural forms in the Tokugawa period were *kabuki* and *jōruri*. These two types of popular drama were influenced tremendously by *nō* drama, a theatrical form that declined in the Tokugawa period but continued to enjoy the patronage of courtiers and upper samurai. Thus an examination of the theory of *nō* drama can help us understand *kabuki* and *jōruri*.

The theory of *nō* drama was formulated in the fifteenth century by talented playwrights and actors such as Zeami (1363–1443). From the beginning, *nō* had been a form of high culture intended for the entertainment of the ruling class, the upper samurai in particular. In the Tokugawa period, the Edo bakufu, the Kyoto court, and daimyō were the major sponsors of *nō* drama. Except on special occasions, commoners were not even allowed to watch it. Yet Tokugawa *nō* drama seems to have lost its early spirit and creativity, becoming longwinded and lifeless. It made few new theoretical innovations and basically followed Zeami's artistic theory and aesthetics. We investigate the role of the *I Ching* in the theory of *nō* drama through an examination of Zeami's writings.

The *I Ching* played an important role in the development of *nō* drama theory. The interplay of *yin* and *yang* became the source of *nō*'s artistic imagination. The harmony of *yin* and *yang* was a central philosophy emphasized throughout Zeami's writings. In contrast to the common practice of matching *yang* things with *yang* time and *yin* things with *yin* time, Zeami argued that, to harmonize *yin* and *yang* and thus make the performance interesting and touching, the actor should play with the spirit of *yin* during the daytime *(yang)* and with the spirit of *yang* in the evening *(yin)*. He explained this teaching in his *Fūshikaden* (Teachings on Style and the Flower, 1402 and 1418):

> According to a secret teaching, any endeavor will meet success at the point when the principles of *yin* and *yang* are harmonized. The spirit of the daytime hours can be represented by the positive principle, *yang*. Thus to plan to play the *nō* as gently as possible provides a spirit of the complementary negative principle, *yin*. Giving birth to *yin* during the hours of *yang* produces that sought-for harmony. The creation of this harmony is the first step in producing a successful *nō* performance. Performers and spectators alike will find such a performance moving. On the other hand, the spirit of the night is represented by the negative principle, *yin*. Therefore, the *nō* must be played as buoyantly as possible; what lifts the feelings of the audience is the positive principle, *yang*. Success comes from harmonizing the spirit of *yang* with the spirit of *yin* of night. On the other hand, if the spirit of *yang* is applied to *yang*, or the spirit of *yin* to *yin*, no harmonization can take place, and no success will be forthcoming. And without such a harmony, such a fulfillment, there will be nothing of interest in the performance.[27]

Not only time of day but also season, temperature, location, and even the mood of the audience can change the balance of *yin* and *yang*. A successful actor can feel *yin* and *yang* and does appropriate things to harmonize them. For example, if *yin* is strong when the temperature is cold, bright music *(yang)* should be used to increase *yang*. Likewise, if *yang* is strong when the temperature is warm, sad music *(yin)* should be played to increase *yin*. In the *Shūgyoku tokka* (Finding Gems and Gaining the Flower), Zeami wrote:

> The reason that the same actor who performs with the same highly developed skill will achieve different results from different performances may well be because, depending on the occasion, the balance between *yin* and *yang* may not be in harmony [with the rhythm of his performance]. Conditions vary because of the four seasons, day and night, morning and evening. The nature of the audience itself changes. . . . Cold weather is related to *yin,* and warm weather to *yang;* appropriately, therefore, bright music should be performed to balance cold weather, and melancholy music played to counteract the warm weather.[28]

Zeami also applied the *yin-yang* theory to analyze details in acting, music, setting, and other details of *nō* drama.

If the harmonization of *yin* and *yang* is the highest artistic level in *nō* drama, then what is the ideal state of mind for the actor and audience? The answer is the spirit of nothingness. This is a state in which actor and audience no longer use their minds and consciousness but simply respond to the play instinctively. Zeami explained:

> When relating this matter to the highest levels in our own art, it can be said that this moment of fascination represents an instant sensation that occurs before the rise of any consciousness regarding that sensation, a feeling that transcends cognition. In the *Book of Changes, hsien* 咸 in Chinese is given the meaning of a sensation before consciousness, and so the usual character 感 is written without the bottom part of the character *hsin* 心, which stands for "mind" and "consciousness."[29]

Compared to *nō* drama, *kabuki* was not as well conceptualized or as refined. As a performing art for commoners, it was more successful in performing great plays than in creating theories. This makes its relationship to the *I Ching* less obvious. Tokugawa writings on *kabuki* were mostly on the plays and the ranking of actors. Theoretical discussions were rare. Fortunately, Tame'naga Itchō, a playwright himself, set out some artistic ideas of *kabuki* in the *Kabuki jishi* (Origins of *Kabuki,* 1771), which gives us some clues about the influence of the *yin-yang* theory.

　　　　　　　　　　　　　　　　　　　　　　　　　　

Tame'naga traced the origins of *kabuki* to the Age of the Gods, and used the ideas of *t'ai chi* and *yin-yang* to explain the beginning of the universe. He pointed out that early Shinto deities danced to praise the purity of nature and creation, and held that *kabuki* is a dance to praise the harmony of *yin* and *yang* and of heaven and earth.[30] He also maintained that *kabuki* should only be performed in the daytime because it needs *yang ch'i* to support the actor and the audience, whereas at night, when *yin ch'i* is prevalent, human nature will become impure and the performance strange. Tame'naga believed that the same principle also applied to the puppet theater:

> In a theater, it requires *yang ch'i* to help it move on. Human beings, imbued with *yang ch'i,* will become very energetic. At night, when *yin ch'i* comes, only a very small part of human nature remains. Some people will even become half-human half-animal and take the form of ghosts and evil spirits. The puppet theater also takes on a strange atmosphere at night.[31]

Tame'naga's preference for *yang* can also be seen in his explanation of a special *kabuki* performance held in July in Osaka and Kyoto. According to the theory of the annual circulation of *yin-yang, yin* begins to rise from the earth in July and may cause the destruction to crops and natural disasters. The July *kabuki* performance was a prayer to the gods to keep *yin* and *yang* in harmony. He remarked:

> In July, *yin* and *yang* will once again come together. *Yin ch'i* will rise from the ground and cause the disharmony of *yin* and *yang.* This is a month of changes. Strong wind will destroy the five crops. In order to have *yin ch'i* move gently, we light up the lantern and dance, hoping that *yang ch'i* will not abate, the five crops will ripen, and the people will live in peace.[32]

Jōruri, a serious dramatic form combining puppetry, storytelling, and music, seems to have developed a stronger theoretical base than *kabuki.* These two popular dramatic forms, which were both interdependent and in competition with each other, had many things in common, including plays, acting techniques, music and narrative, audience, and so forth. Most playwrights wrote plays for both forms, and it was not unusual for the same play to be performed by troupes from both traditions. Through the writings on *jōruri,* we can therefore gain some understanding of the role of the *I Ching* in Tokugawa popular drama.

In his *Danbutsushū* (1687), a short treatise on the principles of *jōruri,* Takemoto Gidayū (1651–1714), the father of *jōruri,* mentions that one can find *yin* and *yang* in music and *wu-hsing* in *jōruri*. As these teachings were supposed to be orally transmitted, he does not elaborate on them in his book.[33] Fortunately, playwrights after Takemoto disclosed more about the role of *yin-yang wu-hsing* in *jōruri*. They usually attributed their ideas to Takemoto and his disciple, Toyotake Echizen no Shōjō (1681–1764), although some seem to have created their own ideas.

The *Gidayū shisshinroku* (Records of Gidayū, 1760s, author unknown) states that the spirit of Japanese drama is to harmonize *yin* and *yang*. It traces the beginning of *jōruri* to 808 C.E. and the reign of Emperor Heizei (r. 806–809). It was in 808, in Kyoto, that a gigantic hole suddenly appeared, emitting black smoke, terrifying people, and spreading disease. The *hakase* family (specially designated scholarly family) of the time believed that *yin ch'i* arose from the earth, and thus suggested that someone dance, sing, and act in front of the Buddhist temple Kyōfukuji to expel *yin ch'i* and restore the balance of *yin* and *yang*. This was said to be the origin of *nō, sarugaku* (a form of entertainment involving dance, acting, and singing that was meant to provoke laughter), *sumō* (Japanese wrestling), *kabuki,* and *jōruri*.[34]

The *Chikuhō koji* (Story of Masters Takemoto and Toyotake, 1756, by Ichiraku) seems to have preserved some teachings of the early *jōruri* masters. Ichiraku, a Tokugawa *jōrur* master, cited the *Chou-i lüeh-chu* (A Brief Commentary on the *I Ching,* author unknown) to praise Takemoto and Toyotake for their efforts to bring benefit to the world through *jōruri*. This commentary reads: "It is very appropriate to make efforts according to the way of the sages, to facilitate everything in the world."[35] Ichiraku's discussion of music is very interesting. Following the Chinese tradition, *jōruri* classified sound into two systems: five *t'iao* (five notes) and twelve *lu* (twelve tubes, which are comprised of six *lu* and six *lu*).

In its analysis of the characteristics of these sounds, the *Chikuhō koji* identifies the five *t'iao* with the *wu-hsing*. On the twelve *lu,* it does not follow the Chinese mainstream view, which regards *lu* 律 as *yang* tubes and *lu* 呂 as *yin* tubes. As Ichiraku wrote: "*Lu* 呂 is the tone of happiness, and thus belongs to *yang.* . . . *Lu* 律 is the tone of sadness, . . . it is *yin*."[36] Although critics might think that the brittle sound of the *samisen* (a three-stringed musical instrument used in both *kabuki* and *jōruri*) is vulgar and corrupt, Ichiraku praised its sound as the embodiment of the principles of *yin-yang* and *san-ts'ai,* and believed that it had the power to purify the human mind. He described the structure of the *samisen* as follows: "Its length is three *shaku*, which represents heaven-man-earth, *san ts'ai*. Its handle is more than one *shaku* long, which represents the two forces of *yin* and *yang*."[37]

Toyotake Konodayū (1726–1796), the second-generation head of the Toyotake troupe in Osaka, wrote the *Jōruri setsushōshū* (On *Jōruri* Musical Notes, 1777). He said: "Musical notes [of *jōruri*] represent *yin-yang wu-hsing* in the universe; they symbolize the four seasons of a year and seventy-two climatic changes."[38] He argued that the four seasons correspond to different agents of *wu-hsing*, and that the performance of *jōruri* should change in accordance with the four seasons to express their different characters: spring (wood) is a time for celebrations and entertainment, summer (fire) a time for strong emotions, fall (metal) a time of sadness, and winter (water) is a time of quietude and waiting.[39]

Another early *jōruri* master, Gidayūbuji Nemotodayū, used the *yin-yang* doctrine extensively to discuss music in his *Jōruri hidenshō* (Secret Teachings of *Jōruri*, 1757). He classified sounds into three levels according to their tone: *yin* sound (level one) is heavy and low; *yang* sound (level three) is light and high; and the sound of *yin-yang* (level two)—the ideal sound for *jōruri*—is mild and balanced. He gave his idea the following cosmological base:

> In antiquity, when heaven and earth had not yet separated, there was no *yin* or *yang*. The universe was in a formless state like an egg. [Later,] the light and clear stuff rose and became heaven, and the heavy and impure stuff descended and became earth. One is *yin* and three is *yang*. The sound of one is heavy and impure; it is *yin*. The three is light and clear; it is *yang*. The reason that three is above and one is below is that *yin* descends and *yang* ascends. . . . The place where *yin* and *yang* meet is two. The more it is filled with *yin* and *yang*, the more it produces sounds and songs.[40]

He also used the *yin-yang* principle to explain rhythm. According to Gidayūbuji, rhythm, like *yin* and *yang*, must be harmonic and consistent. He used this metaphor: "Rhythm is like a man's walking. . . . If the right foot moves a foot, the left foot should also move a foot. There must be no differences in pace. This regulation matches the principle of *yin-yang*."[41]

All these ideas were cited, paraphrased, or commented on in a large number of writings on *jōruri* published in the nineteenth century. The *yin-yang wu-hsing* theory seems to have infiltrated the innermost aspects of *jōruri*.

Other Artistic and Cultural Forms

We have discussed the role of *I Ching* related concepts in *chanoyu, ikebana,* and the theater, for all have substantial materials that have allowed us to provide a brief picture of them. This section examines other cultural areas in which we have gathered only piecemeal material at this stage of research.

The way of incense, or *kōdō,* was a popular art among warriors, monks, courtiers, and merchants in the Tokugawa period. It started as a Buddhist art during the Muromachi period and developed into a mature art form associated with *chanoyu* in the sixteenth century. Incense gathering was a competition in which different types of incense were identified and ranked. Tokugawa writings suggest a close relationship between *kōdō* and the *I Ching.*

An important work on *kōdō,* the *Kōdō kihan* (Guidelines on the Way of Incense), was compiled in the early Tokugawa period. It is attributed to Mineya Shūgo (d. 1554), a tea master who studied under Takeno Jōō (1504–1555). The book contains some interesting and somewhat bizarre ideas. For instance, it points out that the proper way to smell incense is to use half of the left nostril *(yang)* and all of the right nostril *(yin),* believing that this ratio of one to two matches the *yin-yang* principle of the universe:

> When we smell incense, remember the "right-full, left-half" theory. This is a secret teaching about the use of the nose. This is an oral transmission. My explanation is that the *yang* numbers are half [or odd], such as one, three, five, seven, nine, and the like. . . . On the other hand, the *yin* numbers are double [or even], such as two, four, six, eight, ten, and so forth. . . . In terms of our human body, the left hand side is *yang,* whereas the right hand side is *yin.* . . . Hence our left nostril smells half and our right nostril [smells fully] to balance the *yang* number [of the left]. The other method is to use the left nostril to smell once, then the right nostril to smell twice. By doing this, we will not go against the principle of *yin-yang.*[42]

More mysteriously, the book even suggests that we can tell the *yin-yang* of the hour by using our nostrils: "If you want to know the *yin-yang* of an hour, you can always use your nostrils to distinguish it. When the left nostril smells, it is *yang;* when the right nostril smells, it is *yin.*"[43]

The book contains sophisticated discussions on the incense container. For instance, it suggests that different shapes of containers represent different theories of the *I Ching;* round represents the four cardinal virtues; the pentagon represents *wu-hsing;* the hexagon stands for the *yin* number; and the octagon symbolizes the eight trigrams.[44] Applying geomancy to discuss the proper place for locating the incense container, the book points out that in a standard square Japanese room, the incense container can be put in all corners except the southeast one, which is a *yin* position.[45]

Incense itself was divided into either *yin* or *yang.* The *Kokin kōkan* (Appreciation of Incense from Past to Present, 1815, author unknown) mentions that the wood from Southeast nations produces the *yang* odor, whereas the wood from Northeast nations produces the *yin* odor.[46] The *Gokeryū kōdō hyakukajō kōjuden* (A Hundred Items of the Way of Incense of the Goke School by Oral Transmission, 1820s, by Iyoda Muneshige) even specifically distinguishes the *yin* and *yang* of incense imported from different nations.[47]

Cooking *(ryōri)* also became a specific field of knowledge in the Tokugawa period. The Chinese usually attribute the beginning of cooking to Fu Hsi, and believe that both cooking and the *I Ching* belong to the same natural principle. This idea was echoed by Hayashi Razan in his *Hōtei shoroku* (A Bibliographical Guide to Cooking, 1652).[48] Yaoya Zenshirō used the *yin-yang* theory to explain his philosophy of cooking in the *Ryōritsū taizen* (Anthology of Cooking, 1822). For example, he suggested that the ideal dining table should have a triangular or square top and round feet. This design is in accord with the Chinese cosmological idea of *t'ien-yüan ti-fang* ("heaven is circular and the earth is square"). The top represents *yin,* or earth, and the foot stands for *yan,* or heaven. Thus the dinner table forms the image of the hexagram *t'ai,* one of the best hexagrams in the *I Ching.* Yaoya noted:

> The top has angles on three or four sides; it is the form of *yin.* The feet are round and *yang.* This combination forms the hexagram earth-heaven *t'ai,* representing *yang* inside *yin.* In the *I Ching,* it is the hexagram for the first month of the year. We should know that nothing in this world can survive without *yin* and *yang.*[49]

Even the position of utensils on a table is something to be learned, according to Yaoya: "Round plates [*yang*] are placed in front of guests. Square wooden plates [*yin*] are placed on the other side of guests. This is the principle of *yin-yang.*"[50]

Phonetics, poetry, and music are an inseparable trinity. Phonetics is a basic form of training for poets, songwriters, and playwrights. Its ideas are associated with the *I Ching*. The Chinese trace the beginning of phonetics to a Han scholar, Li Shen, who based his theory on the sixty-four hexagrams. In Korea, Emperor Sejŏng (1418–1450) used the *I Ching* to explain the Korean writing system, *hangul*. In Tokugawa Japan, many Confucians accepted this Chinese tradition. For example, Chu Shun-sui (1600–1682), a refugee from Ming China, stressed the role of the *I Ching* in Chinese phonetics. His view influenced a Mito scholar, Ugai Sekisai (1615–1664). Minakawa Kien even attempted to reconstruct the lost learning of Li Shen by applying the sixty-four hexagrams to phonetics and philology.

In poetry, Tamiya Nakanobu, an Osaka Confucian, pointed out in his *Tōyūshi* (1803) that Japanese poetry is subject to the principle of the *I Ching*. For example, he used the numerology of the *I Ching* to explain the relationship between the *I Ching* and *tanka* (short poems that consist of five lines with a 5–7–5–7–7 syllable pattern) using the following obscure phrases: "Seven is the constant number of small *yang*. When it is divided [by three], it becomes one. It represents the number of the hexagram earth-thunder *fu* of the *I Ching*. Likewise, a *tanka* has thirty-one words and becomes one if it is divided [by three]."[51] He also pointed out that the *go* game (enclosing black and white stones on a lined board) and *shōgi* (Japanese chess) share the same numerology.

Music was an essential part of Tokugawa life. Many Tokugawa Confucians believed that music was based on the *yin-yang wu-hsing* principle. As Kaibara Ekken said in his *Gojōkun* (Lectures on the Five Constant Virtues):

> In regard to the origins of music, it is like *yin-yang* and *wu-hsing* in the universe. They [*yin-yang* and *wu-hsing*] circulate from past to present, from season to season, and never stop for a moment. The harmony of these forces gives birth to everything. They are the music of the universe. The sages created music in accordance with these principles.[52]

Kumazawa Banzan viewed Fu Hsi as the founder of music and suggested that it was Fu Hsi who had created the *shitsu* (a musical instrument with fifty strings symbolizing the number of the universe).[53] Minakawa Kien wrote the *Ekigen kyūchū no setsu awasete jūniritsu no setsu no shōkai* (Comprehensive Explanation of the Unity of the Nine-Category Theory in the *Ekigen* and the Theory of Twelve Tubes) to discuss the relationship between the *I Ching* and the twelve tubes. Even

Andō Shōeki (1703–1762), a critic of the *I Ching*, admitted that Chinese music was based on the *yin-yang wu-hsing* theory. In his *Shizen shineidō* (The Way of Nature and the True Vocation), he explained how the Chinese had applied the principles of the *I Ching* to divide the tubes into twelve—six *yang* and six *yin*—and match them with different musical instruments. Andō condemned this method of association as "mistakes of fabrication."[54]

Tamiya Nakanobu emphasized that *gagaku* (an ancient Chinese music) is in agreement with the numerology of the *I Ching*. *Gagaku* had been brought to Japan in the early Nara period and had exerted tremendous influence on *renga*, *nō*, and other Japanese music and poetry. Tamiya said: "In my country, during the time of Prince Shōtoku, Hata Kawakatsu taught us the original rhythm of *gagaku*. By adjusting the high *yang* number of 9–9 to the low *yang* number of 5–7, it became twelve tubes."[55] Although now we might not understand the numerology, his attempt to link *gagaku* to the *I Ching* remains obvious.

The role of the *I Ching* in many other forms of Tokugawa culture, such as architecture, painting, *bonsai* (the Japanese mini-landscape), *karesansui* (dry-rock landscape), literature, games, dance, sports, and folklore, was significant and provides fertile ground for new research by those who are interested in Japanese cultural history and Sino-Japanese cultural interchange.

Concluding Remarks

This chapter demonstrates that the *I Ching* played a considerable role in Tokugawa art and culture. The text influenced Japanese culture mainly through its *yin-yang wu-hsing* doctrine, which penetrated every cultural arena in the Tokugawa period, becoming an integral part in some (such as *ikebana*, *jōruri*, and *kōdō*) but occupying only a peripheral position in others (such as *kana zōshi*).[56] *Yin-yang wu-hsing* was influential in both high and popular culture. Art and cultural historians like to emphasis the "Japaneseness" of Tokugawa culture, but my research suggests that the formation of Japanese art and culture was indebted in part to the Chinese *yin-yang wu-hsing* theory.

Generally speaking, the influence of the *yin-yang wu-hsing* theory on Tokugawa culture was consistent and strong. It played an important role in both the importation of Chinese culture and the formation of Japanese culture. Hence the simultaneous rise in Tokugawa

Japan of both Chinese learning and popular culture was by no means coincidental. Even though the *yin-yang wu-hsing* doctrine was questioned in some areas, such as medicine and physics, from the late eighteenth century onward, it was basically unchallenged in the realm of art and culture. The change of worldview and the rise of Western learning had a minimal impact on the relationship between the *I Ching* and Tokugawa culture. These theoretical ties have survived into modern and contemporary Japan.

12. Epilogue

There is a Chinese saying that runs, "Not knowing the real face of Mount Lu, I merely wander along its paths." During these years of preparation and writing, I have gotten lost, every now and then, in a mountain of primary sources and have struggled to find my way out. This work records my first impressions of that academic journey.

This study uses the *I Ching* to investigate the role of Chinese learning in the development of thought and culture in Japan during the Tokugawa period. The philosophy and divination of the *I Ching* were an integral part of Chinese civilization. In particular, its ideas of *yin-yang* and *wu-hsing* were extremely powerful in the Chinese cultural system. Because traditional Japan was within the orbit of Chinese culture, the *I Ching* has been a book of particular significance and interest in Japanese history. Thanks to the solid foundation laid down by medieval scholars and to the rise of neo-Confucianism, *I Ching* scholarship reached its apex in Japan during the Tokugawa period. As a result, the *I Ching* became one of the most popular and influential Chinese texts read by Tokugawa intellectuals, penetrating many different areas of Tokugawa life: politics, the economy, religion, science, medicine, the military, and popular culture.

In Tokugawa thought, the *I Ching* played an important role in formulating political, economic, and religious ideas. In their interpretations of the political implications of the text, Tokugawa Japanese altered Chinese political ideals to fit the Tokugawa political system. The abstraction and ambiguity of the text's ideas left them open to interpretation; these ideas were thus used in different ways in different political contexts. Early Tokugawa scholars used the *I Ching* to legitimize the Tokugawa shogunate, whereas late Tokugawa reformers and loyalists used it to express anti-bakufu ideas. The doctrine of *yin-yang wu-hsing* provided a basic interpretative framework in Tokugawa agriculture. This doctrine was also used by economists to develop their "free-market" economic ideas, and provided early entrepreneurs with the wisdom and confidence to engage in modern industry and business.

Tokugawa Shinto and Buddhism recognized the significance of the *I Ching*, although Shinto interacted more closely with the text than did Buddhism. Early Tokugawa Confucians and Shintoists used the book to uphold the doctrine of the unity of Confucianism and Shinto, and Shinto was Confucianized by borrowing many ideas from it. In late Tokugawa times, in contrast, the school of national learning *(koku-gaku)*, Unden Shinto, and the Mito school all Shintoized the text by suggesting that it had Shinto origins and by emptying it of Chinese content. The relationship between the *I Ching* and Tokugawa Buddhism was subtle. The text served as an ideological battleground for Buddhists and Confucians. Buddhists quoted it to illustrate that both teachings share the ideas of karmic retribution, transmigration of three lives, gods and ghosts, and universal flux, whereas Confucians interpreted it in their own way to deny any affinity with Buddhism.

The *I Ching* had three major functions in Tokugawa culture. First, it popularized Chinese culture. Neo-Confucian medicine was the dominant medical school in early Tokugawa times. It included a set of *I Ching* related theories, such as *yin-yang wu-hsing*, the five viscera and the six bowels, and the five agents and the six climatic factors. Hence it was also called "the school of *I Ching*-medicine." The *I Ching* played a crucial role in formulating theories in Chinese astronomy, calendrical studies, mathematics, geography, architecture, and botany. It had a tremendous impact on the scientific thought of Tokugawa scholars, who studied science mainly through Chinese texts.

Second, the *I Ching* provided a set of basic ideas that were employed in many facets of native Japanese culture. Thus the text influenced the theory and practice of different forms of Tokugawa art and culture, such as the tea ceremony, flower arrangement, and popular theater. In general, Tokugawa culture had a preference for *yang* over *yin*, although its ultimate goal was to achieve the unity or harmony of the two. The tea ceremony and flower arrangement were seen as microcosms that manifest the principles of *yin-yang wu-hsing* in the universe. In popular theaters such as *kabuki* and *jōruri*, the interplay of *yin* and *yang* inspired the Japanese artistic imagination. The *yin-yang wu-hsing* doctrine also served as the underlying principle for schools of military thought and martial arts in the Tokugawa period.

Third, the *I Ching* was used to promote the adaptation of Western science. It was utilized extensively by scholars of Western learning to explicate and rationalize Western science. Some cited it to claim that Western ideas had existed in ancient China, and even maintained that they had originated in China; others attempted to transplant Western science and technology into a Confucian metaphysical framework. In astronomy and physics, the *I Ching* was used to accommodate the Aristotelian theory of the four elements, the Ptolemaic global theory, Copernican astronomy, Newtonian physics, and other Western scientific ideas into the Chinese-Japanese cultural system. Some students of Dutch medicine tried to use the text to fuse Western medicine with Chinese medicine, and it was common practice to use it to explain Western weaponry in different Tokugawa artillery schools. This suggests that the major intellectual and cultural theme of Tokugawa Japan was neither the conflict between tradition and modernity nor that between East and West, but the accommodation of Western ideas to Japan's traditional cultural system.

To plumb this body of research was an ambitious task. Although I stretched myself to the limit, many areas lay beyond my grasp. For instance, metaphysics, ethics, literature, historical thought, and divination have not been specially treated in the present volume.

I have asked myself two basic questions since the beginning of this project. The first is how to define the nature of the *I Ching*, and how to place it within the context of Chinese culture and the East Asian tradition. Some "contemporary Confucians" and "*I Ching* authorities" insist that the text has nothing to do with divination, *yin-yang wu-hsing*, and other "non-Confucian" ideas and practices. I find this view ahistorical and unscholarly. The *I Ching* is a rich text that has influenced different aspects of the East Asian tradition. Regarded as the top Confucian classic, its nature became a focus of controversy among East Asian Confucians for more than two thousand years. Some view it as a book of wisdom while others use it as a book of magic. Here I have examined different facets of the *I Ching* and their historical significance in Tokugawa Japan.

Broadly speaking, the *I Ching* not only played a crucial role in Confucianism but also influenced the development of many other East Asian traditions, such as Taoism, Buddhism, and the *yin-yang* tradition. Some schools of thought and religion do not necessarily view it as a Confucian classic per se, and even try to claim it as their own. In historical terms, the *I Ching* began as an oracle book; it was then "moralized" and became a Confucian classic during the Chou period. In Ch'in and Han times, Taoists and *yin-yang* scholars added the doctrine of *yin-yang wu-hsing* to it and formulated an *I Ching* system. Sung scholars borrowed from Taoism and Buddhism, transforming the text into a book of metaphysical wisdom.

In which of these versions of the text do we see the "real" *I Ching*? My answer is "In all of them." In my research, I avoid narrowly defining the text as a purely Confucian classic, but see it, rather, as a textual tradition and metaphysical system representing different aspects of Chinese culture. In the context of Tokugawa Japan, the *I Ching* was an "intellectual crossover" that represented not only Confucianism but the entire Chinese cultural tradition. Tokugawa Japanese, including Confucians, never confined themselves to one aspect of its tradition. The *I Ching* became an integral part of basic cultural training; all literate groups studied and used it, although they had different attitudes toward its philosophy and divination. As already mentioned, some Tokugawa Japanese saw it as a non-Confucian or even non-Chinese text. Hence the *I Ching* demonstrates the complicity and dynamism in Sino-Japanese intellectual and cultural interchange.

The second question I asked myself was how to locate my research within current (particularly Western) scholarship on Japanese history. In other words, what kinds of contributions would this research make to Tokugawa intellectual and cultural studies? Locating this research proved no easy task. For example, Peter Nosco's taxonomy divides Western scholarship of Tokugawa intellectual history into five genres: biography, source book and general history, monograph, local history, and theoretical analysis.[1] My work does not fit comfortably into any of these categories. So far, the vast majority of intellectual and cultural studies about Tokugawa Japan have been presented as individual biographies, textual analyses of certain works, or discussions of particular issues. My research examines the scholarship surrounding a text and its influence on different areas of thought and culture over a long period of time. This approach is parallel to biblical and Koranic studies in Western historiography, but is relatively new in Japanese studies.[2]

In addition, Samuel Yamashita points out four "distinct interpretive communities" in Tokugawa intellectual history: the modernization school, the de Bary group, the "new" intellectual history, and the post-modern theorists.[3] Obviously, my research has little to do with theories. Its textual approach is closer to that of the first two schools, but its ideas rectify and even challenge the modernization and de Bary accounts of Tokugawa thought and culture. Methodologically, I have been influenced by Ch'ing *k'ao cheng* ("evidential research") scholarship; the narrative and analysis in this study are based on my reading of primary sources without any theoretical premises.

Thus this is a pioneering work that aims at opening new investigative areas in Japanese history and Sino-Japanese cultural interchange. Although the *I Ching* in China is a well-researched topic, very few historians have studied the history of the text in Japan.[4] My research argues that the *I Ching* was one of the most popular and influential Chinese classics among Tokugawa intellectuals and that it saturated Tokugawa thought and culture. This study covers much ground that heretofore has been "sacred land" accessible only to a small circle of specialists. Each chapter represents a scholarly attempt to expose new research territory, offering new analysis and new materials. Because direct secondary references are extremely limited, my work relies heavily on textual studies of primary sources, many of which have never been used in research or rendered into English. The secondary materials I have used provide only some background information, and my investigations at this stage are only preliminary. I am fully aware of how much more remains to be done on—and of the potential for developing independent research projects from—each topic.

This research also attempts to fill a gap in Tokugawa intellectual and cultural history. Historians of Japan usually focus on a particular aspect of Tokugawa thought and culture, and many works have been written on the impact of the West and on Japanese tradition in Tokugawa Japan. Although it is generally agreed that the influence of Chinese culture reached its apex in the Tokugawa period, very few academic works have examined this important aspect of Japanese history.[5] My study aims to correct that imbalance and deepen our understanding of the impact of Chinese learning in Tokugawa Japan.

However, my larger ambition is to provide a balanced picture of the interplay of Chinese, Japanese, and Western elements in the formation of Tokugawa thought and culture using the *I Ching* as an example. My research demonstrates that the text played important roles in the cultural interchanges among these three cultural systems by spreading Chinese culture, formulating Japanese culture, and accommodating Western culture. My hope is that it will also enrich our scholarship on the naturalization of Confucianism and on the cultural identity of Tokugawa Japanese in response to the importation of foreign ideas.[6]

Notes

Chapter 1: The Adaptation of the *I Ching* in the Pre-Tokugawa Period

1. According to the *Nihon shoki*, the doctor of the Five Classics *(gokyō hakase)*, Dan Yangmi, and the doctor of the *I Ching (eki hakase)*, Wang Dolyang, came to Japan from Paeche in 516 and 554, respectively. Yoshino Hiroko's works indicate that the principle of *yin-yang wu-hsing* had an impact on Japanese culture well before the sixth century. See note 11 below.

2. According to Miyamoto Shōson, articles 1, 10, and 15 of the *Code of Seventeen Articles* were influenced by the *yin-yang* principle. See Miyamoto, "The Relation of Philosophical Theory to Practical Affairs in Japan," in Charles A. Moore, ed., *The Japanese Mind* (Honolulu: East-West Center Press, 1967), pp. 6–7.

3. Yen Shao-yang, *Han-chi tsai Jih-pen ti liu-pu yen-chiu* (Nanking: Chiang-su ku-chi ch'u-pan-she, 1992), pp. 96–107. The *I Ching* was outnumbered by the *Li Chi* (Book of Rites), *Lun Yü* (Analects), and *Ch'un Ch'iu* (Spring and Autumn Annals); ibid., p. 103. However, another record raises the number to thirty-five books (177 *kan*). See "Kaidai," in Imai Usaburō, trans., *Ekikyō* (Tokyo: Meiji tosho shuppansha, 1987), p. 61. Classified under the category of "*I Ching* literature" *(ekika)*, these books were commentaries written between the Eastern Han and T'ang eras. Some *I Ching* related works were classified under the categories of the school of *wu-hsing (gogyōka)*, the school of medicine *(ihōka)*, and the school of calendrical studies and mathematics *(rekisūka)*.

4. See "Kaidai," in Imai, trans., *Ekikyō*, p. 71.

5. According to Chinese tradition, the reign name should be changed and reforms implemented in the year of *kinoene*. Although this idea did not originate in the *I Ching*, its arguments were based on its symbolism and numerology.

6. The taboo against the *I Ching* being studied by anyone younger than fifty was a peculiar feature in *I Ching* studies in Japan. Its origins seem to stem from a misinterpretation of the following statement from the *Lun Yü:* "If [heaven] gives me a few more years so that I can study the *I Ching* at the age of fifty, I will probably not make a major mistake." The Chinese saw this as a declaration of the

text's difficulty and moral value, whereas ancient Japanese narrowly interpreted it as an age restriction.

7. Fujiwara no Yorinaga, in *Daiki*, quoted in Kohi ruien kankōkai, ed., *Koji ruien, hōgibu* 7 (Tokyo: Koji ruien kankōkai, 1909), p. 474.

8. See Yamamoto Yūichi, *Ekisen to Nihonbungaku* (Tokyo: Shimizu kōbundō, 1976), pp. 22–150.

9. See Ivan Morris, *The World of the Shining Prince: Court Life in Ancient Japan* (New York: Penguin Books, 1964), pp. 44, 137–144, 169–178, 225.

10. For instance, according to the principle of *yin-yang,* the Taihō and Yōrō Codes made the minister of the left *(sadaijin)* and the minister of the right *(udaijin)* in charge of the affairs of the central court government. In contrast, the grand minister *(dajōdaijin)* was merely an honorary position with the duty to "harmonize the *yin* and *yang."* See Robert Borgen, *Sugawara no Michizane and the Early Heian Court* (Cambridge, Mass.: Harvard University Press, 1986), pp. 154–155.

11. Yoshino Hiroko is the author of a number of books on the *I Ching* in ancient Japanese culture. They include the *Daijōsai* (Tokyo: Kōbundō, 1987), *Inyō gogyō shisō to Nihon no minzoku* (Kyoto: Jimbun shoin, 1983), *Yama no kami* (Kyoto: Jimbun shoin, 1989), *Kakusareta kamigami* (Kyoto: Jimbun shoin, 1992), and *Gogyō junkan* (Kyoto: Jimbun shoin, 1992).

12. For a general review, see Ōta Masao, ed., *Onmyōdō no hon* (Tokyo: Gakushū kenkyūsha, 1993). See also Shigeru Nakayama, *A History of Japanese Astronomy* (Cambridge, Mass.: Harvard University Press, 1969), pp. 7–73.

13. Unfortunately, the *Keishisan* has not survived. Having examined the use and description of it in other Japanese writings, Joseph Needham was surprised to have found some elements of modern mathematics in it. See Needham, *Science and Civilization in China,* vol. 3, part 1, "Mathematics," in Yamanaka Shigeru, trans., *Chūgoku no kagaku to bunmei* (Tokyo: Shisakusha, 1975), pp. 71, 153.

14. The character *I* literally means "change," and the *I Ching* elucidates the philosophy of change. According to the text, a wise man should follow the changes of the times, not because this is a moral law that one is constrained to obey, but because by following the new developments, he will survive and flourish. See Hellmut Wilhelm, *Change: Eight Lectures on the I Ching* (Princeton, N.J.: Princeton University Press, 1973), p. 19. See also Richard Smith, *China's Cultural Heritage: The Ch'ing Dynasty, 1644–1912* (Boulder, Colo.: Westview Press, 1983), p. 248.

15. For a historical overview of the growth of Confucian studies within the Zen Buddhist framework, see chapter 3, "Zen and the Study of Confucianism," in Daisetsu Suzuki, *Zen and Japanese Culture* (Princeton, N.J.: Princeton University Press, 1973), pp. 39–57.

16. Shunjō (1166–1227) and Enni Ben'en (1202–1280) were typical of those who contributed to the growth of non-government collections of Chinese books. Shunjō brought back 256 volumes of Confucian texts from Sung China in 1212 and lectured on the *I Ching.* Unfortunately, we do not know how many and what kind of *I Ching* commentaries he brought. See Linda Walton, "Sino-Japanese Relations in the Early Thirteenth Century: The Buddhist Monk Shunjō (1166–1227) in China, 1199–1212," in Ryū Shiken hakase shōju kinen Sōshi kenkyū ronshū kankōkai, ed., *Ryū Shiken hakase shōju kinen Sōshi kenkyū ronshū* (Kyoto: Dōhōsha,

1989), pp. 567–576. Among the Chinese books that Enni brought from Sung China in 1241 there were several pre-Sung commentaries on the *I Ching*, including the *Chou-i yin-i* (The Sound and Meaning of the *I Ching*), *I tsung-shuo* (A General Discussion of the *I Ching*), *I chi-chieh* (A Collective Explanation of the *I Ching*), and *Tsuan-t'u hu-chu Chou-i* (A Graphic Commentary of the *I Ching*). However, we have no evidence that Enni had studied the *I Ching*.

17. Quoted in Haga Kōshirō, *Chūsei Zenrin no kakumon oyobi bungaku ni kansuru kenkyū* (Tokyo: Maruzen shoten, 1956), p. 72.

18. For Kokan's views on Buddhist-Confucian relations, see Marian Ury, trans., "*Genko Shakusho:* Japan's First Comprehensive History of Buddhism" (Ph.D. dissertation, University of California, Berkeley, 1971), pp. 116–128.

19. In *Kaizō oshō kinenroku*, quoted in Haga, *Chūsei Zenrin no kakumon oyobi bungaku ni kansuru kenkyū*, p. 89.

20. Ibid., p. 72.

21. Ashikaga Enjutsu rates Chūgan Engetsu as the best *I Ching* scholar in medieval Japan. See Ashikaga, *Kamakura Muromachi jidai no Jukyō* (Tokyo: Nihon koten zensho, 1932), p. 268.

22. Having read the *Kakukaihen*, Fujiwara Seika (1561–1616) praised Chūgan for understanding the idea of change in the *I Ching*.

23. In *Kūka nikkōshū* (entry December 3, 1381), quoted in Haga, *Chūsei Zenrin no kakumon oyobi bungaku ni kansuru kenkyū*, p. 74.

24. Ibid., p. 76.

25. Another of Kiyō's top students was Kōshi Ehō (1362–1465), who rated the *I Ching* higher in importance than the Four Books. He was critical of all pre-Sung commentaries on the *I Ching* for their association with divination and numerology, and praised Sung Confucians—Chou Tun-i in particular—for restoring the tradition of Confucius.

26. For a long time, people believed that Unshō was the first person in Japan who read and introduced the *Chou-i chuan-i*. Haga Hōshirō has doubts about this because there is lack of documentary support; see Haga, *Chūsei Zenrin no kakumon oyobi bungaku ni kansuru kenkyū*, p. 77. Ōe Fumiki alleges that Gidō punctuated the *Chou-i chuan-i;* see his *Honpō Jugakushi ronkō* (Tokyo: Zenkoku shobō, 1944), p. 20.

27. Shōchū Shōzui was a master of divination who gave the *Chou-i ming-ch'i ching* (Book of Fate Calculation Using the *I Ching*) to Tōgen. Jikuun Tōren and Zuikei Shūhō seem to have influenced Tōgen on philosophy.

28. In particular, Tōgen focused on the following commentaries: (Wei) Wang Pi's *Chou-i chu*, (T'ang) Kung An-kuo's *Chou-i shu*, (T'ang) Li Chun-feng's *Chou-i meng-ch'i ching*, (Sung) Shao Yung's *I-chien meng t'uan*, (Sung) Ch'eng I's *I Chuan*, (Sung) Chu Hsi's *I-hsüeh ch'i-meng*, (Sung) Hu Fang-p'ing's *I-hsüeh ch'i-meng t'ung-shih*, (Yüan) Tung Kai's *Chou-i chuan-i*, (Yüan) Hu I-kuei's *I-hsüeh ch'i-meng i-chuan*, and (Ming) Hu Kuang's *Chou-i ta-ch'üan*.

29. Influenced by the *gunbai shisō* (theory of military oracles) of the Ashikaga School, Tōgen used the *I Ching* to predict the fate of warriors and the result of battles. He also lectured on the *Chou-i meng-ch'i ching*, and taught people how to use the *I Ching* to foretell the whole life of a person. See Ashikaga, *Kamakura Muromachi jidai no Jukyō*, p. 403.

30. In the fifth *kan* of the *Hyakunōbusuma*, quoted in Haga, *Chūsei Zenrin no kakumon oyobi bungaku ni kansuru kenkyū*, p. 82. For more examples of Tōgen's originality in the explanation of the *I Ching*, see Ashikaga, *Kamakura Muromachi jidai no Jukyō*, pp. 404–407.

31. Since he did not have access to Chu Hsi's *Chou-i pen-i*, Tōgen sometimes had to use Wang Pi and Kung An-kuo's commentaries to explain the text. See Haga, *Chūsei Zenrin no kakumon oyobi bungaku ni kansuru kenkyū*, p. 90.

32. The only famous student of Tōgen was a Tokudaiji monk, Sanjōnishi Sanetaka (1455–1537), who was particularly interested in divination.

33. This ancient taboo did not disappear completely in the medieval period. For details, see Imaizumi Toshio, "*Eki* no batsu ga atarukoto," in Imaizumi, *Chūsei Nihon no shosō*, vol. 2 (Tokyo: Yoshikawa kōbunkan, 1989), pp. 571–587.

34. In *Hanazonoin tennō shinki* (The Diary of the Cloistered Reigning Hanazono), quoted in Koji ruien kankōkai, ed., *Koji ruien, hōgibu* 7, p. 476.

35. Quoted in Yamanaka Hiroyuki, "Nihonjin to *Eki*," in Kaji Nobuyuki, ed., *Eki no sekai* (Tokyo: Shin jimbutsu ōraisha, 1987), p. 52.

36. Ibid., pp. 47–49.

37. The changing reign name serves as a barometer of the growing influence of the *I Ching* at court. According to Uda Naoshi, there were 94 reign names used from the Heian to Kamakura periods. They were quoted from the following six Confucian classics: *Shu Ching* (37), *I Ching* (27), *Shih Ching* (15), *Li Chi* (8), *Tso Chuan* (4), and *Hsiao Ching* (3). The *I Ching* was second in terms of frequency. It was used more often during the Kamakura period. See Uda Naoshi, *Nihon bunka ni oyoboseru Jukyō teki eikyō* (Tokyo: Tōyō shisō kenkyūjo, 1935), p. 120.

38. In *Jōkō kokushi goroku*, quoted in Ashikaga, *Kamakura Muromachi jidai no Jukyō*, p. 175.

39. Wajima Yoshio, *Chūsei no Jugaku* (Tokyo: Yoshikawa kōbunkan, 1962), p. 249.

40. See Yasui Kōzan, *Chūgoku shimpi shisō no Nihon he no tenkai* (Tokyo: Taishō daigaku shuppanbu, 1983), p. 129.

41. See Murayama Shūichi, *Nihon Onmyōdōshi sōsetsu* (Tokyo: Hanawa shobō, 1981), pp. 293–294.

42. For details on the impact of the *I Ching* on the *Jinnō shōtoki*, see Nakamura Shōhachi, trans., *Gogyō taigi zenshaku* (Tokyo: Meiji shoin, 1986), pp. 22–25.

43. Ashikaga, *Kamakura Muromachi jidai no Jukyō*, p. 677.

44. Imaizumi, "*Eki* no batsu ga atarukoto," in Imaizumi, *Chūsei Nihon no shosō*, vol. 2, pp. 572–573.

45. *Gunbai shisō*, or military oracles, had a long tradition in Japan. It is said that ever since the Heian period the government had sent officials of the Bureau of Divination to regional regiments. This idea became more prevalent in the medieval period. Minamoto no Yoritomo (1147–1199), Hōjō Yoshitoki, Hōjō Masako, Nitta Yoshisada, and Ashikaga Yoshimitsu had used the *I Ching* oracles for military and political purposes. *Gunbai shisō* reached its apex during the *sengoku* period. Almost all *sengoku* daimyō (warrior-leaders of the *sengoku* period) employed *I Ching* diviners in their armies. For an overview of *gunbai shisō* at the Ashikaga School, see Lee A. Butler, "The Way of Yin and Yang: A Tradition Revived, Sold, Adopted," *Monumenta Nipponica* 51, 2 (1996):197–201.

46. In *Hyakunōbusuma*, quoted in Yūki Rikurō, *Kanazawa bunko to Ashikaga gakkō* (Tokyo: Shibundō, 1959), p. 231.

47. The new commentaries in the library of the Ashikaga School included some books that Tōgen did not see, such as Chu Hsi's *Chou-i pen-i*, (Sung) Li Chung-cheng's *Ch'in-hsien Chou-i-chuan*, and (Yüan) Tung Chen-ching's *Chou-i hui-t'ung*. See Cheng Liang-sheng, *Yüan-Ming shih-tai tung-chuan Jih-pen ti wen-hsien* (Taipei: Wen-shih-che ch'u-pan-she, 1984), p. 112.

48. Quoted in Ashikaga, *Kamakura Muromachi jidai no Jukyō*, p. 616. In this ritual, we see the fusion of Shinto, Confucianism, and *yin-yang* (or Onmyōdō) thought. *I Ching* scholarship became eclectic and naturalized in this process.

49. Quoted in Haga, *Chūsei Zenrin no kakumon oyobi bungaku ni kansuru kenkyū*, p. 85.

50. See Suzuki Hiroshi, *Shūekishō no kokugogaku teki kenkyū* (Tokyo: Seibundō, 1972), pp. 1–3.

51. There is an interesting story in the *Kōyō gunkan* (Military Records of the Takeda House). One day, Nagasaka Chōkan, a senior retainer, recommended his own shaman, Tokugan, to Takeda. Takeda refused, on the grounds that Tokugan had not graduated from the Ashikaga School. See Yamanaka, "Nihonjin to Eki," in Kaji, ed., *Eki no sekai*, pp. 54–55.

52. For a basic understanding of the influence of the *I Ching* on medieval culture, see Murayama, *Nihon Onmyōdōshi sōsetsu*, pp. 393–410.

Chapter 2: The Popularization of the *I Ching* in the Tokugawa Period

1. The *Hsiao Ching* (Book of Filial Piety) and *Lun Yü* seem to have exerted a stronger impact on ancient and medieval Japan than the *I Ching*. When *I Ching* scholarship reached its apex in the Tokugawa period, its popularity and influence matched and even surpassed those of these two classics.

2. Miyazaki Michio, *Kumazawa Banzan no kenkyū* (Tokyo: Shibunkaku, 1990), p. 256.

3. Imai Usaburō, trans., *Ekikyō* (Tokyo: Meiji tosho shuppansha, 1987), p. 76.

4. The *Nihon keikai* (also called *Dai-Nihon keikai mokuroku*) was compiled by Terada Hiroshi and collated by Shigeno Yasutsugu (1826–1910) in the Meiji period. The book closely followed the format of Ch'ing scholar Juan Yüan's (1764–1849) *Huang-ch'ing ching-chieh* (An Explanation of Confucian Books in the Ch'ing Period) and Wang Hsien-ch'ien's (1842–1918) *Huang-ch'ing ching-chien hsu-pien* (*Huang-ch'ing ching-chieh*, supplement, 1886–1888). See Uchino Dairei, "*Nihon keikai* ni tsuite," in Fukushima Kinoezō, ed., *Kindai Nihon no Jugaku* (Tokyo: Iwanami shoten, 1939), pp. 1132–1135.

5. Ibid., pp. 1141–1143.

6. The school of textual interpretation understands the *I Ching* by studying its main text and commentaries. It has three branches: the school of explanation focuses on the general understanding of the text, the school of commentary annotates the text, and the school of textual criticism studies the text by sophisticated methods of textual criticism. The school of symbols and numbers speculates on the symbolism and numerology of the text. The school of divination treats it as a divination manual. The school of application applies the text's ideas to different aspects of political and cultural activities.

7. A terrifying example of such devotion to *I Ching* studies is that of Asami Keisai, who finished one of his works on the text with his own blood because he could not find any ink in jail.

8. Yi T'oegye's idea of separating Chu Hsi's *Chou-i pen-i* from Ch'eng I's *I Chuan* influenced Yamazaki Ansai and other early Tokugawa Confucians to restore Chu Hsi's original commentary. Muro Kyūsō (1658–1734) praised Yi's book as a faithful transmission of Chu Hsi's scholarship on the *I Ching*. See Abe Yoshio, *Nihon no Shushigaku to Chōsen* (Tokyo: Tōkyō daigaku shuppankai, 1965), pp. 311, 439.

9. See Ōba Osamu, *Edo jidai ni okeru Tōsen mochiwatarisho no kenkyū* (Kyoto: Kansai daigaku gakujutsu kenkyūjo, 1967).

10. On the relationship between the two books punctuated by Bunshi, see Murakami Masataka, "Bunshi Genshō to *Shūeki dengi taizen*," *Nihon bunka kenkyūjo kenkyū hōkoku* 25 (Sendai: Daitō bunka daigaku Nihon bunka kenkyūjo, 1989), pp. 19–60.

11. Since the early Tokugawa period, some people have alleged that Fujiwara pilfered Bunshi's punctuation. The first to make this accusation was Jochiku in the *Kikigaki* (A Book of Hearings). This issue has yet to be settled by modern scholars. Nishimura Tenshū (1865–1924), Ijichi Ieyasu, and Inoue Tetsujirō (1885–1944) have maintained that the text was pilfered, while Ōe Fumiki and Abe Yoshio believe Fujiwara to be innocent. See Abe, *Nihon no Shushigaku to Chōsen*, p. 69.

12. On the differences between Hayashi Razan and Gahō's punctuation, see Murakami Masataka, "Kinsei ekigaku juyōshi ni okeru Gahōten *Ekikyō hongi* no igi," *Bungei kenkyū*, no. 100 (Sendai: Nihon bungei kenkyūkai, 1982), pp. 79–88.

13. Besides working on punctuation, a number of people worked on collation and editing. Unlike commentators or punctuators, most of them were little known. They came from various backgrounds and included Chu Hsi scholars, Wang Yang-ming scholars, and scholars of national learning.

Chapter 3: Study and Uses of the *I Ching* in the Tokugawa Period

1. See Herman Ooms, *Tokugawa Ideology: Early Constructs, 1570–1680* (Princeton, N.J.: Princeton University Press, 1985), and Watanabe Hiroshi, *Kinsei Nihon shakai to Sōgaku* (Tokyo: Tōkyō daigaku shuppankai, 1985). I think this view is sound in terms of its analysis of Confucian-bakufu relations, but less so in its assessment of the intellectual influence of neo-Confucianism. Ironically, neo-Confucianism had lost its early vitality when it was adopted as the official ideology by the bakufu during the Kansei era (1789–1800).

2. Fujiwara Seika, "Baison saihitsu," in Nihon zuihitsu taisei henshūbu, ed., *Nihon zuihitsu taisei*, vol. 1 (Tokyo: Yoshikawa kōbunkan, 1975), p. 57.

3. This account is questionable. Hayashi Razan read the *Chou-i chuan-i ta-ch'üan* before he met Fujiwara Seika. The Hayashi family liked to contrast Fujiwara and Hayashi with Kiyohara Hidekata, and misleadingly portrayed Kiyohara and his family as stubborn supporters of the old commentaries. Actually the Kiyohara family began to adopt the new commentaries as early as the early fifteenth century. Indeed, almost all traditions of *I Ching* scholarship in the late medieval period used both the new as well as the old commentaries. Fujiwara and Hayashi represented a continuation of, rather than a departure from, this trend.

4. I think this story may have been fabricated by the Hayashi family to legiti-mize their orthodoxy. The real successor to Fujiwara's *I Ching* scholarship seems to have been Matsunaga Sekigo (1592–1657), who lectured Toyotomi Hideyori (1593–1615) on the text.

5. In the "preface" of Hayashi Gahō (punctuator), *Ekikyō hongi* (1674, 5 *kan*). Quoted in Murakami Masataka, "Kinsei ekigaku juyōshi ni okeru Gahōten *Ekikyō hongi* no igi," *Bungei kenkyū*, no. 100 (Sendai: Nihon bungei kenkyūkai, 1982): 81–82.

6. Ooms is right to point out that Yamazaki Ansai's scholarship of the *I Ching* has often been overlooked. See his *Tokugawa Ideology*, p. 203.

7. Although Ansai criticized Yi T'oegye's (1501–1570) *Chǔyok gyemong chŏnǔi*, many of his ideas seem to have been inspired by Yi. See Abe Yoshio, *Nihon no Shu-shigaku to Chōsen* (Tokyo: Tōkyō daigaku shuppankai, 1965), p. 311.

8. The four stages were calligraphy, Chu Hsi's *Chin-ssu lu* (Reflections on Things at Hand), the Four Books, and the Chu and Ch'eng commentaries on the *I Ching*. The *I Ching* represented the most advanced and difficult part of Yama-zaki Ansai's Confucian curriculum. See Ooms, *Tokugawa Ideology*, p. 255.

9. Asami and Miyake were prolific writers of the *I Ching*, writing thirty-six and twenty-six books, respectively, to elucidate Yamazaki's teachings. Unlike Yamazaki and his classmates, Satō was more interested in symbols and numbers than in the text.

10. The dispute was over the meaning of *ching i chih nei, i i fang wai* ("by devo-tion we strengthen ourselves within; by righteousness we square the world with-out"), a phrase from the *Wen Yen* (Commentary on the Words of the Text) of the *I Ching*. "Inside" and "outside," according to the standard interpretation pre-sented by Chu Hsi, referred to the heart and the self. Influenced by Shinto thought, Yamazaki Ansai argued that the two represented oneself and the out-side world. Satō and Asami disagreed over this unorthodox view, and this caused their expulsion from the Ansai school.

11. Kaibara Ekken, *Yamato zokkun* (Moral Teachings in Japan). The translation is from Mary Tucker, *Moral and Spiritual Cultivation in Japanese Neo-Confucianism: The Life and Thought of Kaibara Ekken* (Albany: State University of New York, 1989), pp. 147–148.

12. For details of the story, see Yamanaka Hiroyuki, "Nihonjin to *Eki*," in Kaji Nobuyuki, ed., *Eki no sekai* (Tokyo: Shin jimbutsu ōraisha, 1987), pp. 61–62.

13. Having read Chu Hsi's *I-hsüeh ch'i-meng* at the age of twenty-eight, Nakae believed that he had grasped the essence of the book. However, he did not under-stand its divination methods. He went to Kyoto to look for a teacher but gave up when he found the tuition outrageous. He came to understand the divination methods later, through self-study.

14. Nakae Tōju, *Okina mondō*, in Yamashita Yū and Bitō Masahide, eds., *Nakae Tōju, Nihon shisō taikei*, vol. 29 (Tokyo: Iwanami shoten, 1974), p. 96.

15. Nakae Tōju, "Taijō tenson Taiitsushinkyō jo" (1640), in Koide Tetsuo, ed., *Nakae Tōju, Kumazawa Banzan shū* (Tokyo: Tamagawa daigaku shuppanbu, 1976), p. 195.

16. A general review of Banzan's thought can be found in James McMullen, "Kumazawa Banzan: The Life and Thought of a Seventeenth-Century Japanese Confucian" (Ph.D. dissertation, University of Cambridge, 1969).

17. Kumazawa Banzan, *Eki keijiden shōkai* (A Brief Explanation of the *Hsi Tz'u Commentary* of the *I Ching*), in Masamune Atsuo, ed., *Kumazawa Banzan zenshū*, vol. 4 (Tokyo: Meicho shuppan, 1978), p. 402.

18. Although Itō Jinsai (1627–1705) was called "Kogaku sensei" (master of ancient learning) shortly after his death, the use of the term *"kogaku"* to refer to the intellectual school that included Yamaga Sokō (1622–1685), Itō Jinsai, Ogyū Sorai (1666–1728), and their students only gained currency after the publication of the *Nihon kogakuha no tetsugaku* by Inoue Tetsujirō in 1902.

19. *Kogaku* scholars' disapproval of the use of divination did not mean that they did not research this aspect of the book. Indeed, *kogaku* scholars produced two important works on divination: Itō Tōgai's *Kahensetsu* (The Theory of Changing Lines in a Hexagram) and Dazai Shundai's *Ekisen yōryaku* (An Outline of *I Ching* Divination, 1753). However, they seldom used the text for divination.

20. Unlike Ch'ing scholars, Itō Jinsai and his son Tōgai were critical of Han scholarship for adding the *wu-hsing* doctrine to Confucianism. See Ryusaku Tsunoda, Wm. Theodore de Bary, and Donald Keene, eds., *Sources of the Japanese Tradition* (New York: Columbia University Press, 1958), pp. 413–414.

21. The Hirata school of *kokugaku* (national learning) later borrowed this idea, but inverted it.

22. This commentary was also the favorite book of Fukuzawa Yukichi's father. When the Fukuzawa family was in financial difficulty, they sold everything except this book. Fukuzawa Yukichi's father said: "These thirteen volumes of ethics [the *I Ching*] with Tōgai sensei's notes are a rare treasure. My descendants shall preserve them generation after generation in the Fukuzawa family." Eiichi Kiyooka, trans., *The Autobiography of Yukichi Fukuzawa* (New York: Schocken Books, 1972), pp. 45–46.

23. For a textual analysis of the *Tokueki shiki*, see Hama Hisao, "Itō Tōgai no ekigaku," *Tōyō kenkyū* (Tokyo: Daitō-bunka daigaku tōyō kenkyūjo, 1989), no. 90, pp. 8–15.

24. The similarity between *kogaku* and *k'ao-cheng* scholarship has drawn a lot of attention, particularly in the case of the studies of the *Meng Tzu* by Itō Jinsai and Tai Chen (1724–1777). Here we find a similar case in *I Ching* scholarship, with Dazai Shundai and Hui Tung. In both cases the *kogaku* scholars published their works prior to their Chinese counterparts. Some may speculate that *kogaku* had a certain influence on Ch'ing scholars, and it is true that some works by Tokugawa intellectuals were brought to China: Itō Tōgai and Ogyū Sorai's books, for example, were known among Ch'ing intellectuals. However, there is no documentary evidence to suggest that *kogaku* scholars influenced Ch'ing *k'ao-cheng* scholarship. Rather, similar developments in the intellectual history of the two countries probably contributed to this coincidence.

25. The term *"setchūgakuka"* (eclectic school) was first used by Inoue Tetsujirō in his *Nihon rinri ihen, Setchūgakuha no bu*, vol. 9 (Tokyo: Ikuseikai, 1903). It was a loose concept designed to include a group of late-Tokugawa Confucian scholars who belonged neither to the Chu Hsi school nor to the school of ancient learning *(kogaku)*.

26. For the intellectual development and activities of the academy, see Najita Tetsuo, *Visions of Virtue in Tokugawa Japan: The Kaitokudō Merchant Academy of Osaka* (Chicago: University of Chicago Press, 1987).

27. Nakai Riken, *Shūeki hōgen*, scroll 3. I have read the unpublished original manuscript kept in the Kaitokudō Collection (Kaitokudō bunko) at Osaka University. Nakai Riken also pointed out that most scholars made mistakes in punctuating the sentences of the Ten Wings. See Tao De-min, *Kaitokudō Shushigaku no kenkyū* (Osaka: Ōsaka daigaku shuppankai, 1993), pp. 327–328.

28. These *I Ching* scholars include Hara Kyōsai (1734–1790), Hachida Kayō (1743–1815), Shimoda Hōtaku (1749–1820), and Yamamoto Hokuzan (1751–1812).

29. Others students of Ōta include Tsutsumi Tazan (1782–1849), Ōta Seiken (1794–1873), Tōjō Kindai (1794–1878), and Nakai Kansai.

30. Minakawa Kien's linguistic method of studying the *I Ching* was passed on to his students Kaneko Kakuson (1767–1840), Tōjō Ichidō (1776–1857), and Miyanaga Gushin (1797–1855).

31. For details on Hirata's views on *I Ching* divination, see Kitō Gennosuke, "Hirata Atsutane no zeihōkan," *Ekikyō kenkyū* (Tokyo: Waseda University), 21 (October 1968):7–12, and 21 (December 1968):5–10.

32. The *Chou-i che-chung* was the representative work of Ch'ing scholarship. Shao Yung was famous for his divination skill. It is inappropriate to portray Arai Hakuga and his students as profit-seeking diviners; rather, they were Confucian specialists on the *I Ching*, and their works show evidence of fine scholarship and originality. Suzuki Yoshijirō has given a balanced account of Arai's scholarship in his "Arai Hakuga no ichimen," in *Ekikyō kenkyū* 16 (May 1963):2–6.

33. For details of Mase's divination, see Katō Taigaku, "Mase Chūshū no zeihō ni tsuite," *Ekikyō kenkyū* 34 (April 1981):52–60.

34. For an analysis of political thought of the Mito school, see Victor Koschmann, *The Mito Ideology: Discourse, Reform and Insurrection in Late Tokugawa Japan, 1790–1864* (Berkeley and Los Angeles: University of California Press, 1987). See also Bob Wakabayashi, *Anti-Foreignism and Western Learning in Early Modern Japan: The New Thesis of 1825* (Cambridge, Mass.: Harvard University Press, 1986).

35. In Ch'ing China, the government adopted Sung commentaries, whereas scholars favored Han commentaries.

36. Ch'ing scholarship on the text also underwent three stages but showed a clear direction toward reconstructing a "Confucian *I Ching*."

Chapter 4: The *I Ching* and Political Thought

1. In addition to its role in political thought, the *I Ching* had a number of functions in Tokugawa politics. First, the shoguns, daimyō, and ministers left many records of using its oracles to make political and judicial decisions. As a Tosa retainer argued in 1787, using the oracles of the *I Ching* in decision making was a tradition in Japan and helped to win the trust of the people. See *Toyochika-kōki*, entry of the seventh year of Tenmei (1787), in *Yamauchike shiryō* (photocopy of unpublished Tokugawa sources kept in Yamauchi jinja hōbutsu shiryōkan, Kochi Prefecture, Japan), pp. 78–79. Second, the Onmyōdō developed into a strong, nationwide organization whose functions included performing ceremonies and divinational rituals, supervising blind monks, spying on regions through its branches and inspection tours, pursuing calendrical, astronomical, and scientific studies, etc. See Kōno Yoshihiko, *Kinsei onmyōdō no hensei to soshiki* (Tokyo: Yoshikawa kō bunkan, 1984), pp. 253–294. Third, the *I Ching* was used for polit-

ical symbols, such as reign names *(nengō)* and crests *(kamon)*. Of thirty-five *nengō* used in the Tokugawa period, four were from the *I Ching:* Keian (1648–1651), Jōkyō (1684–1688), Bunka (1804–1818), and Genji (1864–1865). See Morimoto Kakuzō, *Kinsei Nihon no Jugaku* (Tokyo: Iwanami shoten, 1935), pp. 17–18. The pattern of the eight trigrams *(hakkamon)* was one of the major patterns of family crests. See Niwa Motoji, *Seishi, chimei, kamon sōgō jiten* (Tokyo: Shinjimbutsu ōrai-sha, 1988), p. 498.

2. Hellmut Wilhelm emphasizes the importance of the Son of Heaven ideology and the idea of change in the making of the East Asian political mentality. See "Preface," in Wilhelm, *Changes: Eight Lectures on the I Ching* (Princeton,N.J.: Princeton University Press, 1973), pp. viii–ix.

3. The pioneering and now classic work is Maruyama Masao's *Studies in the Intellectual History of Tokugawa Japan,* trans. Mikiso Hane (Princeton, N.J.: Princeton University Press, 1974), which traces the rise of a "modern consciousness" by highlighting the Sorai school. Herman Ooms, in his *Tokugawa Ideology: Early Constructs, 1570–1680* (Princeton, N.J.: Princeton University Press, 1985), attempts to "reconstruct" early Tokugawa ideology by examining the thought of Yamazaki Ansai. Herschel Webb's *The Japanese Imperial Institution in the Tokugawa Period* (New York: Columbia University Press, 1968) and David M. Earl's *Emperor and Nation in Japan* (Seattle: University of Washington Press, 1964) outline the development of imperial loyalism. Harry Harootunian studies the growth of political consciousness before the Meiji Restoration in his *Toward Restoration* (Berkeley and Los Angeles: University of California Press, 1970). Marius B. Jansen's *Sakamoto Ryōma and the Meiji Restoration* (Princeton, N.J.: Princeton University Press, 1961), E. H. Norman's articles on Andō Shōeki, and Tetsuo Najita's articles on Dazai Shundai and Yamagata Daini are also noteworthy.

4. The main text reads: "When one's own day comes, one may create revolution. Starting brings good fortune. No blame"; "Changing the form of government brings good fortune." The *T'uan Chuan* justifies revolution as a principle of heaven and earth: "Heaven and earth bring about revolution, and the four seasons complete themselves thereby. T'ang and Wu brought about political revolutions because they were submissive toward heaven and in accord with men." In Richard Wilhelm, trans., *The I Ching or Book of Changes* (Princeton, N.J.: Princeton University Press, 1977), pp. 636, 638–639.

5. Joyce Ackroyd, trans., *Told Round a Brushwood Fire: The Autobiography of Arai Hakusei* (Princeton, N.J.: Princeton University Press, 1976), pp. 102–103. Arai also cited the hexagram *ko* on other occasions (ibid., p. 271).

6. Ryusaku Tsunoda, Wm. Theodore de Bary, and Donald Keene, eds., *Sources of the Japanese Tradition* (New York: Columbia University Press, 1958), p. 431. This quotation shows that Ogyū Sorai's view of the relationship between the way of heaven and the way of man was more complicated than Maruyama Masao's analysis suggests.

7. Yamazaki and Yamaga blamed the founder of the Chou dynasty for breaking the ultimate moral principle of loyalty to the sovereign.

8. Itō Jinsai, *Dōjimon* (Questions from the Children), in Kaizuka Shigeki, ed., *Itō Jinsai, Nihon no meicho,* vol. 13 (Tokyo: Chūō kōronsha, 1972), p. 452.

9. Kate Nakai suggests that the Hayashi, Mito school, and Arai Hakuseki used

the concept of *kakumei* (revolution) to justify the bakufu. See her "Tokugawa Confucian Historiography: The Hayashi, Early Mito School and Arai Hakuseki," in Peter Nosco, ed., *Confucianism and Tokugawa Culture* (Princeton, N.J.: Princeton University Press, 1984), p. 79. John Tucker points out that the Confucian notion of rebellion against tyranny was distorted so that it could be used to legitimize the bakufu. See Tucker, "Two Mencian Political Notions in Tokugawa Japan," *Philosophy East and West* 47, 2 (April 1997):233–253. This discussion continued into the modern period. For example, Netomo Michiaki (1821–1906) tried to give the *I Ching* a "modern" character and linked it to *tennōsei* (emperor-state) ideology. Criticizing the traditional interpretation of the hexagram *ko*, which suggested the ideas of change and revolution, Netomo held that the *I Ching* was in fact a book stressing the idea of "non-change" and the unbroken lineage of the Japanese imperial family; the hexagram *ko* was intended to forbid revolution by describing the horror of it.

10. Wilhelm, trans., *The I Ching or Book of Changes*, pp. 286–287, 298, 302.

11. Takuan Sōhō, *Tōkai yawa* (Evening Talks on the Eastern Sea), in Takuan oshō zenshū kankōkai, ed., *Takuan oshō zenshū*, vol. 5 (Tokyo: Kogisha, 1929), pp. 11–12.

12. Izumi Makuni, *Meidōshō* (Book to Explicate the Truth), in Haga Noboru and Matsumoto Sannosuke, eds., *Kokugaku undō no shisō, Nihon shisō taikei*, vol. 51 (Tokyo: Iwanami shoten, 1971), p. 198.

13. Quoted in Maruyama Masao's *Studies in the Intellectual History of Tokugawa Japan*, p. 196.

14. Matsunaga Sekigo, *Irinshō* (Notes on Morality, 1640), in Ishida Ichirō and Kanaya Osamu, eds., *Fujiwara Seika, Hayashi Razan, Nihon shisō taikei*, vol. 28 (Tokyo: Iwanami shoten, 1975), pp. 310–311.

15. Ibid., p. 317.

16. Satō Issai, *Genshiroku* (Records of My Aspirations), in Inoue Tetsujirō, ed., *Nihon rinri ihen, Yōmeigakuha no bu*, vol. 3, part 2 (Tokyo: Ikuseikai, 1903), p. 15.

17. Yamaga Sokō, *Yamaga gorui* (The Analects of Yamaga Sokō), in Hirose Yutaka, ed., *Yamaga Sokō zenshū*, vol. 4 (Tokyo: Iwanami shoten, 1941), p. 65.

18. Kumazawa Banzan, *Shūgi gaisho* (Book of Moral Teaching), in Inoue Tetsujirō, ed., *Nihon rinri ihen, Yōmeigakuha no bu*, vol. 2, part 2 (Tokyo: Ikuseikai, 1903), p. 144.

19. Kumazawa Banzan, *Daigaku wakumon* (Questions about the *Ta Hsüeh*), in Gotō Yōichi and Tomoeda Ryūtarō, eds., *Kumazawa Banzan, Nihon shisō taikei*, vol. 30 (Tokyo: Iwanami shoten, 1971), pp. 413–414.

20. Yamagata reiterated this idea to criticize the bakufu throughout his life. See Bob T. Wakabayashi, *Japanese Loyalism Reconstructed: Yamagata Dai'ni's Ryūshi Shinron of 1759* (Honolulu: University of Hawai'i Press, 1995), pp. 45, 78–79, 168.

21. Kumazawa Banzan, *Ekikyō shōkai*, quoted in Miyazaki Michio, *Kumazawa Banzan no kenkyū* (Tokyo: Shibunkaku, 1990), p. 192.

22. Kumazawa Banzan, *Shūgiwashō* (Books on Morality in Japanese), in Gotō and Tomoeda, eds., *Kumazawa Banzan, Nihon shisō taikei*, vol. 30, p. 209.

23. Yamaga, *Yamaga gorui*, in Hirose, ed., *Yamaga Sokō zenshū*, vol. 4, p. 77.

24. Yamagata Shūnan, *Igaku shomon* (Basic Questions Concerning Study), in

Saigusa Hiroto, ed., *Jukyō hen, Nihon tetsugaku zensho*, vol. 3 (Tokyo: Daiichi shobō, 1936), p. 330.

25. Ibid., p. 321.

26. In the preface of the *Shūeki hansei*, quoted in Chu Ch'ien-chih, *Jih-pen ti ku-hsüeh yü Yang-ming hsüeh* (Shanghai: Jen-min ch'u-pen-she, 1962), p. 192.

27. See Dazai, *Keizairoku*, in Rai Tsutomu, ed., *Sorai gakuha, Nihon shisō taikei*, vol. 37 (Tokyo: Iwanami shoten, 1972), pp. 37, 39, 41, 44.

28. The prototype of the *tendō* theory already existed in medieval writings, including the *Gempei seisuiki* (Account of the Gempei Wars), *Taiheiki*, *Heike monogatari* (Tale of the Taira House), and *Shinchōkōki* (Record of Oda Nobunaga). See Ozawa Eiichi, *Kinsei shigaku shisōshi kenkyū* (Tokyo: Yoshikawa kōbunkan, 1974), pp. 15–17.

29. Quoted in Tsunoda, de Bary, and Keene, eds., *Sources of the Japanese Tradition*, p. 337.

30. See Ronald P. Toby, "Reopening the Question of *Sakoku:* Diplomacy in the Legitimation of the Tokugawa Bakufu," *Journal of Japanese Studies* 3 (Summer 1977):347–355. The term *"taikun"* was at first only applied in Japan-Korean relations but later gained wider currency. It became an honorific title for the shogun in general usage and was employed until the mid-nineteenth century. Arai Hakuseki disapproved of the use of the title *taikun* for two reasons: First, there was the post known as *taikun* in the Korean government. Second, the shogun was the legitimate ruler of Japan and should not use an ambiguous title. He preferred to use "king of Japan" as the diplomatic title for the shogun. See Tsuji Zennosuke, *Nihon bunka shi*, vol. 5, *Edo jidai*, part 1 (Tokyo: Shunjūsha, 1960), p. 240. Yoshida Shōin opposed its use on the grounds that *taikun* should only refer to the emperor. See Earl, *Emperor and Nation in Japan*, p. 196.

31. Yamanaka Hiroyuki, "Nihonjin to *Eki*," in Kaji Nobuyuki, ed., *Eki no sekai* (Tokyo: Shinjimbutsu ōraisha, 1987), pp. 55–58. See also R. P. Dore, *Education in Tokugawa Japan* (London: The Athlone Press, 1965), p. 21.

32. *Jōkenin zō daishōkokukō jikki*, vol. 14, entry of April 21, 1693. Quoted in Fukui Tamotsu, *Edo bakufu kankōbutsu* (Tokyo: Yūshōdō, 1985), p. 65.

33. Besides special editions under the auspices of Ieyasu and Tsunayoshi, the official publication bureau, Shōheizaka gakumonjo, reprinted at least seven books on the *I Ching*. These were written either by Chu Hsi himself or by post-Sung Chu Hsi scholars. In addition, some domains had their own publication facility to promote *I Ching* scholarship. For example, Kaga domain reprinted the *Chou-i che-chung*. See Fukui, *Edo bakufu kankōbutsu*, pp. 144, 330.

34. Yamanaka, "Nihonjin to *Eki*," in Kaji, ed., *Eki no sekai*, pp. 58–60.

35. The Onmyōdō, together with the Jingidō (Bureau of Shinto), became the two largest religious and ceremonial institutions at court. The Tsuchimikado (originally Abe) defeated the Kamo house to become the head of the Onmyōdō. However, it did not bring back the glory of *I Ching* scholarship that the court had enjoyed in the past. For example, Abe Yasuhide, the head of the Onmyōdō, asked the famous diviner Matsui Rashū for guidance on the *I Ching*. See Kō Shōga, *Chung-kuo i-chan hsüeh* (Hong Kong: Kwan Tun Press, 1972), p. 104.

36. For example, in the *bakumatsu* period, the bakufu used this system to survey the situation in regions through its nationwide branches and inspection tours. See Harootunian, *Toward Restoration*, pp. 255–256.

37. See Ackroyd, trans., *Told Round a Brushwood Fire,* pp. 74–76.

38. On the dilemma of Confucians in early Tokugawa times, see Najita Tetsuo, *Visions of Virtue in Tokugawa Japan: Kaitokudō* (Chicago: University of Chicago Press, 1987), p. 61.

39. The *I Ching* provided textual support for a political and social hierarchy. For example, the hexagram *lü* (treading) reads: "Heaven above, the lake below: The image of Treading. Thus the superior man discriminates between high and low, and thereby fortifies the thinking of the people." In Wilhelm, trans., *The I Ching or Book of Changes,* p. 437.

40. Quoted in Ooms, *Tokugawa Ideology,* p. 159.

41. Asayama, like most Tokugawa intellectuals, still respected the court. In 1653, he was invited to lecture on the *I Ching* to Emperor Gokōmyō (r. 1643–1654) and courtiers in Kyoto. See Tsuji, *Nihon bunka shi,* vol. 5, *Edo jidai,* part 1, p. 228.

42. Although Kumazawa helped to legitimize the Tokugawa social hierarchy, he was very critical of the bakufu's policies, including the alternate attendance system.

43. Kumazawa Banzan, *Keijijōden,* in Masamune Atsuo, ed., *Kumazawa Banzan zenshū,* vol. 4 (Tokyo: Meicho shuppan, 1978), p. 408.

44. The term *"taikun"* was used here to represent the shogun without referring to Japanese-Korean relations. This is evidence that it became a general term for the shogun no later than the Genroku era (1688–1704), when this work was written.

45. Shinto was also employed by early Tokugawa Confucians, like Asayama Soshin, Kumazawa Banzan, and Arai Hakuseki, to rationalize the depoliticization of the court. Kumazawa argued that since the emperor was the descendant of the gods, it was better for him not to get involved in worldly affairs. He used the downfall of imperial authority during the Ashikaga period as a precedent to hold that the restoration of imperial power would be disastrous. Likewise, Arai, in his philological analysis of the word *"tennō,"* concluded that the emperor should limit his activities to heavenly matters such as ceremonies.

46. Quotation modified from Nakai, "Tokugawa Confucian Historiography," in Nosco, ed., *Confucianism and Tokugawa Culture,* p. 79. Also see Matsumura Akira, ed., *Arai Hakusei, Nihon shisō taikei,* vol. 35 (Tokyo: Iwanami shoten, 1975), p. 534.

47. "Introduction," Joyce Ackroyd, trans., *Lessons from History: The Tokushi Yoron by Arai Hakuseki* (St. Lucia: University of Queensland Press, 1982), pp. xxxix–xi.

48. David M. Earl believes that Arai's theory of the bakufu-court relationship became the official bakufu ideology; see his *Emperor and Nation in Japan,* p. 16. I think the situation was more subtle and complicated; see Lee Butler, "Court and Bakufu in Early Seventeenth-Century Japan" (Ph.D. dissertation, Princeton University, 1991). I have doubts about two issues. First, did Arai really deny the legitimacy of the imperial family? Second, did the bakufu accept Arai's idea as the official ideology? I think that both Arai and the bakufu let the issue of legitimacy remain ambiguous. The bakufu never tried to clearly define bakufu-court relations. Ambiguity was welcome as long as the bakufu's hegemony was not challenged. If the bakufu ever had an intellectual policy, it was a negative one—namely, suppressing unwelcome ideas rather than establishing an official political ideology.

49. Dazai Shundai, *Sekihi* (The Rebuke of Wrong Ideas), in Rai Tsutomu, ed., *Sorai gakuha, Nihon shisō taikei,* vol. 37 (Tokyo: Iwanami shoten, 1972), p. 164. For a study of Dazai Shundai's political thought, see Najita Tetsuo, "Political Economism in the Thought of Dazai Shundai (1680–1740)," *Journal of Asian Studies* 31 (1972):821–839.

50. However, the degree to which the *I Ching* actually penetrated Tokugawa politics is not easy to measure. Watanabe Hiroshi emphasizes the incompatibility of Confucianism with Tokugawa politics and society. In general, Confucianism was flexible enough to be adapted to Tokugawa politics, although some parts of it might have been rejected or altered.

51. Maruyama Masao is insightful in suggesting that Itō Jinsai and Ogyū Sorai's distinction between natural law and human activities, and their logic of invention, shook the very foundation of the *bakuhan* system. He also asserts that these ideas were succeeded by those of Andō Shōeki and Motoori Norinaga, and were incorporated into an anti-bakufu ideology in the *bakumatsu* period. See Maruyama Masao, *Studies in the Intellectual History of Tokugawa Japan.*

52. Ibid., pp. 257–258.

53. Kaihō Seiryō, *Keikodan* (Discourse on Ancient Matters), in Kuranami Seiji, ed., *Kaihō Seiryō zenshū* (Tokyo: Yashiyo shuppansha, 1976), p. 102.

54. Ibid., p. 100.

55. In Naramoto Tatsuya, ed., *Nihon shisō taikei,* vol. 38, *Kinsei seidōron* (Tokyo: Iwanami shoten, 1976), p. 284.

56. Date Chihiro, *Taisei santenkō* (Three Changes in the Historical Trend), in Maruyama Masao, ed., *Rekishi shisō shū, Nihon no shisō,* vol. 6 (Tokyo: Chikuma shobō, 1972), p. 396.

57. Translation is altered from Victor Koschmann, *Mito Ideology: Discourse, Reform and Insurrection in Late Tokugawa Japan, 1790–1864* (Berkeley and Los Angeles: University of California Press, 1987), p. 74.

58. In Kano Masanao, ed., *Bakumatsu shisō shū, Nihon no shisō* (Tokyo: Chikuma shobō, 1969), p. 50.

59. See Imai Usaburō, ed., *Mitogaku, Nihon shisō taikei,* vol. 53 (Tokyo: Iwanami shoten, 1973), pp. 76, 108, 131.

60. Quoted in Bob T. Wakabayashi, *Anti-Foreignism and Western Learning in Early-Modern Japan* (Cambridge, Mass.: Harvard University Press, 1986), p. 277.

61. Aizawa Seishisai, *Tokueki nissatsu,* see Imai Usaburō, "Mitogaku ni okeru Jukyō no juyō," in Imai, ed., *Mitogaku, Nihon shisō taikei,* vol. 53, pp. 552–55.

62. Wakabayashi, *Anti-Foreignism and Western Learning in Early-Modern Japan,* p. 184.

63. Aizawa Seishisai, *Kagaku igen* (A Lesson for Junior Students), in Saigusa Hiroto, ed., *Kokugaku hen, Nihon tetsugaku zensho,* vol. 5 (Tokyo: Daiichi shobō, 1935), p. 395. The loyalist Ōhashi Totsuan (1816–1862), probably influenced by the Mito school, suggested similar ideas. Ōhashi asserted that Westerners lived in the land of *yin,* whereas "our country is located in East Asia, and because it is a realm rich and prosperous in the spirit of *yang,* we have been confirmed with the benevolence of the human heart." See Harootunian, *Toward Restoration,* p. 266. This argument seems to have been derived from an older Chinese theory that China was *yang* and the nations of barbarians were *yin,* a theme echoed by

Kaibara Ekken in his *Shinshiroku* (A Record of Deep Thoughts). See Inoue Tetsu-jirō, ed., *Nihon rinri ihen, Shushigakuha no bu,* part 3, vol. 8 (Tokyo: Ikuseikai, 1902), p. 88.

64. Fujita Tōko, *Hitachi obi* (1844), in Fukuda Kōjiro, ed., *Mitogaku, Shintō taikei, ronsetsuhen,* vol. 15 (Tokyo: Shintō taikei hensankai, 1986), pp. 151–152. Sugai Masahide, a martial arts master, expressed an idea similar to that of Fujita's in 1853. Sugai urged the bakufu to consult "others" when faced with new international and domestic situations.

65. Quoted in Harootunian, *Toward Restoration,* p. 165.

66. Ibid., pp. 165–66. See also Harry D. Harootunian, "The Functions of China in Tokugawa Thought," in Akira Iriye, ed., *The Chinese and the Japanese* (Princeton, N.J.: Princeton University Press, 1980), p. 30.

67. Wilhelm, trans., *The I Ching or Book of Changes,* pp. 504–509.

68. In Okada Takehiko, ed., *Bakumatsu ishin Shushigakusha shokanshū, Shushigaku taikei,* vol. 14 (Tokyo: Meitoku shuppansha, 1975), p. 37.

69. Ibid., pp. 77–78.

70. See Shimohodo Yūkichi, *Yoshida Shōin no ningengaku teki kenkyū* (Kashiwa City: Kōchigakuen shuppanbu, 1988), pp. 770–916. For a larger picture on the role of Confucianism in Yoshida's loyalist thought, see Thomas Huber, *The Revolutionary Origins of Modern Japan* (Stanford, Calif.: Stanford University Press, 1981), chapter 3, pp. 42–68.

71. Wilhelm, trans., *The I Ching or Book of Changes,* p. 115.

72. Ibid., p. 152.

73. Quoted in Shimohodo, *Yoshida Shōin no ningengaku teki kenkyū,* p. 785.

74. Isobe Eiichi, ed., *Nihon Yōmeigakusha goroku* (Tokyo: Tōa kenkyūkai, 1935), p. 184.

75. Ibid., p. 784.

76. See Harootunian, *Toward Restoration,* p. 221.

77. Takasuga Shinsaku, *Gokuchū shuki* (A Diary from the Prison), in Yoshida Tsunekichi and Satō Seizaburō, eds., *Bakumatsu seiji ronshū, Nihon shisō taikei,* vol. 56 (Tokyo: Iwanami shoten, 1976), p. 355.

Chapter 5: The *I Ching* and Economic Thought

1. The term *"keizai"* is a Confucian ideal meaning "management to benefit the world." Rulers are to use their knowledge to improve the livelihood of the people. Meiji Japanese translated "economy" as *keizai* and "economics" as *keizaigaku.* Indeed, in the Confucian context *keizai* is a broader concept that includes politics, economics, sociology, and ethics. This chapter is a study of economic thought rather than of the broader meaning of *keizai.* On its meaning in the Tokugawa Confucian context, see Sakai Naoki, *Voices of the Past: The Status of Language in Eighteenth-Century Japanese Discourse* (Ithaca, N.Y.: Cornell University Press, 1991), pp. 295–296. See also Eijirō Honjō, *Economic Theory and History of Japan in the Tokugawa Period* (New York: Russell & Russell, Inc., 1965), pp. 1–3.

2. Although economic history is one of the richest areas of Tokugawa studies in the United States, very few works focus on economic thought. Najita Tetsuo's works on Kaitōkudō and Dazai Shundai provide some insightful discussions but cover a much larger ground. Robert Bellah discusses the intellectual origins of

Japan's modernization in *Tokugawa Religion* (New York: The Free Press, 1957). Luke Robert has conducted a study of economic ideology in Tosa domain in "The Merchant Origins of National Prosperity Thought in Eighteenth-Century Tosa" (Ph.D. dissertation, Princeton University, 1991).

3. For instance, some Tokugawa intellectuals believed that Toyotomi Hideyoshi's land survey *(Taikō kenchi)* was conducted in accordance with the *yin-yang wu-hsing* doctrine. Ōishi Kyūkei (1781–1794) questioned this belief in his *Jikata hanreiroku* (Records of General Development in the Regions, 1794), in Takimoto Seiichi, ed., *Nihon keizai sōsho*, vol. 31 (Tokyo: Nihon keizai sōsho kankōkai, 1916), pp. 22–23.

4. See Furushima Toshio, ed., *Nōsho no jidai* (Tokyo: Nōzan gyōson bunka kyōkai, 1980), p. 201.

5. See Tsukuba Hisaharu, *Nihon no nōsho* (Tokyo: Chūō kōronsha, 1987), p. 53.

6. In Furushima Toshio and Aki Kōichi, eds., *Kinsei kagaku shisō*, part 1, *Nihon shisō taikei*, vol. 62 (Tokyo: Iwanami shoten, 1972), p. 18.

7. Ibid.

8. Ibid., pp. 18–20.

9. Ibid., pp. 22–35.

10. This modification of the annual cycle of *yin-yang* seems to have originated in the Heian period, although its exact origins are unknown. In Tokugawa times, this Japanized version gained more popularity. For example, Baba Nobutake used it to explain monthly climatic changes in the *Shosetsu bendan* (Discourses on Miscellaneous Theories, 1715), and Hayakawa Hachirō applied it to explain the growth of wheat in the *Kyūsei jōkyō* (1799).

11. See Furushima and Aki, eds., *Kinsei kagaku shisō*, part 1, *Nihon shisō taikei*, vol. 62, pp. 10–16.

12. Ibid., p. 71.

13. Ibid., p. 115.

14. Ibid., pp. 109–112. Miyazaki's discussions on the nature and use of night soil are perhaps the most sophisticated and interesting part of the *Nōgyō zensho*. Yamada Tatsuo also praises the book for skillfully applying the *yin-yang* theory to fertilizer. See Furushima, ed., *Nōsho no jidai*, p. 160.

15. Furushima and Aki, eds., *Kinsei kagaku shisō*, part 1, *Nihon shisō taikei*, vol. 62, p. 115.

16. Tsuchiya Matasaburō, *Kōka shunjū*, in Takimoto Seiichi, ed., *Nihon keizai sōsho*, vol. 14 (Tokyo: Nihon keizai sōsho kankōkai, 1915), p. 337.

17. However, it seems that after the mid-Tokugawa period, a growing number of agricultural writings used empirical investigation and talked less about abstract principles. Two of the most important late-Tokugawa agricultural scholars, Ōkura Nagatsune (1768–?) and Satō Nobuhiro (1769–1850), seldom mentioned the *yin-yang wu-hsing* theory. Indeed, Satō was critical of the *wu-hsing* theory. See Saigusa Hiroto, ed., *Sangyō gijutsu hen: Jikin, nōgyō, seizōgyō, Nihon kagaku koten zensho*, vol. 13 (Tokyo: Asahi shimbunsha, 1978), p. 172.

18. Issued by the Ming founding emperors in 1398 and later expanded by a late Ming scholar, the *Liu yüan yen-i* became a standard text for moral education in Ch'ing Ching and Tokugawa Japan. For the circulation of the *Liu yü yen-i* in Tokugawa Japan, see De-min Tao, "Traditional Chinese Ethics in Japan, 1721–1943," *Gest Library Journal* 4:2 (Princeton, 1991).

19. In Nagayama Usaburō, ed., *Hayakawa daikan* (Okayama City: Okayama-ken kyōikukai, 1929), p. 290.

20. Ibid., pp. 289–290.

21. See Sugimoto Isao, *Kinsei jitsugakushi no kenkyū* (Tokyo: Yoshikawa kōbunkan, 1962), p. 324.

22. See Ono Takeo, ed., *Kinsei chihō keizai shiryō*, vol. 4 (Tokyo: Yoshikawa kōbunkan, 1958), pp. 391–393. Like Hayakawa, Tokuyama was from Central Japan. The rest of Tokuyama's book consists mainly of lengthy quotations from the *Nōgyō zensho* and other texts. While not very creative, the book did popularize *yin-yang* agricultural ideas in the Chūgoku area.

23. See Iyota Enshi, *Nihon nōgakusha hyōden* (Tokyo: Nihon tōsho senta, 1991), p. 158.

24. Ibid., pp. 158–160.

25. See "Preface" of the *Nōgyō jitoku*, in Furushima and Aki, eds., *Kinsei kagaku shisō*, part 1, *Nihon shisō taikei*, vol. 62, p. 221.

26. Two famous examples include Sugawara Dōmo's *Nōgyō yowa shō* (A Commentary on the *Nōgyō Yowa*) and Santō Kyōden's *Hōnen hyakushō kagami mansaku odori* (*Kagami Mansaku* Dance for the Bumper Year, 1837).

27. Ko'nishi Atsuyoshi, *Nōgyō yowa*, in Tanaka Kōji, ed., *Nōka gyōji, Nōgyō yowa, Nihon nōsho zenshū*, vol. 7 (Tokyo: Nōzan gyōson bunka kyōkai, 1979), p. 227.

28. Ibid., p. 295.

29. Ibid., p. 314.

30. Furushima and Aki, eds., *Kinsei kagaku shisō*, part 1, *Nihon shisō taikei*, vol. 62, p. 224.

31. Tamura Yoshishige, *Nōgyō jitoku furoku* (Appendix to the *Nōgyō jitoku*, 1871), in Kumashiro Yukio, ed., *Nōgyō jitoku, Nōgyō jitoku furoku, Nihon nōsho zenshū*, vol. 21 (Tokyo: Nōzan gyōson bunka kyōkai, 1981), p. 232–233.

32. Furushima and Aki, eds., *Kinsei kagaku shisō*, part 1, *Nihon shisō taikei*, vol. 62, p. 225.

33. Ibid., pp. 229–230.

34. Ibid., p. 229.

35. Tamura, *Nōgyō jitoku furoku*, in Kumashiro, ed., *Nōgyō jitoku, Nōgyō jitoku furoku, Nihon nōsho zenshū*, vol. 21, p. 87.

36. Ibid., p. 110.

37. See Martin Collcutt, "The Legacy of Confucianism in Japan," in Gilbert Rozman, ed., *The East Asian Region: Confucian Heritage and Its Modern Adaptation* (Princeton, N.J.: Princeton University Press, 1991), p. 143.

38. The translation of Western agricultural books and the introduction of the Western calendar did not destroy traditional agriculture in modern Japan. Since Western methods of agriculture were not always appropriate to Japan, Meiji agricultural writers seem to have drawn more from their past than from the West. The Meiji government also promoted Tokugawa agricultural literature. However, the *yin-yang wu-hsing* theory was no longer generally accepted by modern writers.

39. See Buyō Inshi, *Seji kenmonroku* (Hearing and Witnessing Current Affairs), in Naramoto Tatsuya and Kimugasa Yasuki, eds., *Edo jidai no shisō* (Tokyo: Tokuma shoten, 1966), p. 168.

40. See Nakamura Yukihiko, ed., *Kinsei chōnin shisō, Nihon shiō taikei*, vol. 59 (Tokyo: Iwanami shoten, 1975), p. 141.

41. Shōji Kōki, *Kashoku yōdō*, in Takimoto Seiichi, ed., *Nihon keizai sōsho*, vol. 24 (Tokyo: Nihon keizai sōsho kankōkai, 1916), p. 127.

42. See Nihon keizai sōsho kankōkai, ed., *Tsūzoku keizai bunko* (Tokyo: Nihon keizai sōsho kankōkai, 1917), pp. 281–312.

43. See Kurosawa Motoshige, *Kōsan shihō yōroku*, in Saigusa Hiroto, ed., *Saihō, jikin*, part 2, *Nihon kagaku koten zensho*, vol. 10 (Tokyo: Asahi shimbunsha, 1978), p. 12.

44. Kanazawa Kenkō, *Wakan senyōshū*, in Saigusa Hiroto, ed., *Kaijō kōtsū, Nihon kagaku koten zensho*, vol. 12 (Tokyo: Asahi shimbunsha, 1978), p. 167.

45. Ibid., pp. 173–174.

46. Tessa Morris-Suzuki believes that the Confucian notion of nature influenced the development of Western economic thought through French physiocrats and Adam Smith, and that the similarities between Japanese and European economic thought in the eighteenth century were not coincidental. She has also compared the agricultural philosophy of Kumazawa Banzan and the French physiocrats. See Morris-Suzuki, *A History of Japanese Economic Thought* (London: Routledge, 1989), pp. 7–117. See also John Hall, *Tanuma Okitsugu, 1719–1788: Forerunner of Modern Japan* (Westport, Conn.: Greenwood Press, 1982), p. 60.

47. Kaibara Ekken, *Jigoshū* (A Collection for Self-Entertainment), quoted in Nomura Kanetarō, *Tokugawa jidai no keizai shisō* (Tokyo: Nihon hyōronsha, 1935), p. 109. Yamaga Sokō aired a similar idea.

48. Nishikawa Joken, *Chōnin bukuro*, in Nakamura Yukihiko, ed., *Kinsei chōnin shisō, Nihon shiō taikei*, vol. 59, p. 101.

49. Hatanaka Tachū, *Kashokuron*, in Takimoto Seiichi, ed., *Nihon keizai sōsho*, vol. 11 (Tokyo: Nihon keizai sōsho kankōkai, 1915), p. 531.

50. Ibid., pp. 552–553.

51. Ninomiya Sontoku, *Ninomiya sensei goroku* (The Sayings of Master Ninomiya), in Nakamura Yukihiko, ed., *Andō Shōeki, Tominaga Nakamoto, Miura Baien, Ishida Baigan, Ninomiya Sontoku, Kaihō Seiryō, Nihon no shisō*, vol. 18 (Tokyo: Chikuma shobō, 1971), pp. 47–48.

52. Tsutsumi Masatoshi, *Shōdō kyūhen kokujikai*, in Takimoto Seiichi, ed., *Nihon keizai sōsho*, vol. 20 (Tokyo: Nihon keizai sōsho kankōkai, 1916), p. 417.

53. Kusama Naokata, *Sanka zui*, in Takimoto Seiichi, ed., *Nihon keizai sōsho*, vol. 28 (Tokyo: Nihon keizai sōsho kankōkai, 1916), p. 156. Ironically, the *yin-yang* theory can also be used to support a planned economy. For instance, Matsudaira Sadanobu (1758–1829) used it to justify his regulative economic policies during the Kansei Reform (1787–1800). He explained the income-expenditure relationship in terms of the natural principle of *yin-yang*: "Just as the Way of Heaven is *yin-yang*, when *yin* is income and *yang* outgo, and just as the Way of Man is inhalation and exhalation, so income in economy means storing in storehouses, and outgo means use of the stored goods." He thus believed that the bakufu should play a role in regulating income and expenditure. Quoted in Herman Ooms, *Charismatic Bureaucrat: A Political Biography of Matsudaira Sadanobu, 1758–1829* (Chicago: University of Chicago Press, 1975), p. 34.

54. For discussions of the influence of religious ethics on economic modernization, see Max Weber, *The Protestant Ethics and the Spirit of Capitalism* (London: Unwin Hyman, Ltd., 1930) and Robert Bellah, *Tokugawa Religion* (New York: Free Press, 1985).

Chapter 6: The *I Ching* and Shinto

1. The relationship between the *I Ching* and Shinto can be traced to the ancient and medieval periods. Shinto classics like the *Kojiki, Nihon shoki,* and *Gobusho* (Five Shinto Classics) contain *yin-yang wu-hsing* and other *I Ching* related ideas. Medieval scholars like Kitabatake Chikafusa (1243–1354), Ichijō Kanera (1402–1481), and Yoshida Kanemoto (1435–1511) used the ideas of the *I Ching* extensively to develop their Shinto thought.

2. On the myth formation of Shinto, see Helen Hardacre, "Creating State-Shinto: The Great Promulgation Campaign and the New Religions," *Journal of Japanese Studies* 12, 1 (Winter 1986):29–63. An overview of Western scholarship on Shinto studies can be found in Susan Tyler, "Is There a Religion Called Shinto?" in Adriana Boscaro et al., eds., *Rethinking Japanese,* vol. 2 (Sandgate, England: Japan Library Limited, 1990), pp. 261–720.

3. For its semantic change, see Kuroda Toshio, "Shinto in the History of Japanese Religion," *Journal of Japanese Studies* 7, 1 (Winter 1981):1–21. See also Murooka Tsunetsugu, *Studies in Shinto Thought* (New York: Greenwood Press, 1988), pp. 1–11.

4. Discussions of Confucian-Shinto relations in the early Tokugawa period can be found in Peter Nosco, "Masaho Zankō (1655–1742): A Shinto Popularizer between Nativism and National Learning," in Nosco, ed., *Confucianism and Tokugawa Culture* (Princeton, N.J.: Princeton University Press, 1984), pp. 166–178. See also Abe Akio, "Juka Shintō to kokugaku," and Taira Shigemichi, "Kinsei no Shintō shisō," both in Abe and Taira, eds., *Kinsei Shintōron, zenki kokugaku, Nihon shisō taikei,* vol. 39 (Tokyo: Iwanami shoten, 1972), pp. 497–558.

5. Hayashi Razan, *Shintō denju,* in Saigusa Hiroto, ed., *Shintō hen, Jukyō hen, Nihon tetsugaku zensho,* vol. 4 (Tokyo: Daiichi shobō, 1936), pp. 80, 94. Hayashi used neo-Confucian ideas of the heavenly way, mind, heart, human nature, and principle to construct his Shinto views. See Nosco, "Masaho Zankō," in Nosco, ed., *Confucianism and Tokugawa Culture,* pp. 171–172, and Taira, "Kinsei no Shintō shisō," in Abe and Taira, eds., *Kinsei Shintōron, zenki kokugaku, Nihon shisō taikei,* vol. 39, pp. 514–519.

6. Hayashi, *Shintō denju,* in Saigusa, ed., *Shintō hen, Jukyō hen, Nihon tetsugaku zensho,* vol. 4, pp. 43, 50.

7. Ibid., p. 79. This idea was influenced by Watarai Nobuyoshi, a Shinto priest who was associated with Yamazaki Ansai and Hayashi Razan, and it had a tremendous impact on their Shinto views.

8. Ibid., p. 53. Hayashi also believed that Emperor Jimmu was the Chinese Prince Wu T'ai-po, and that the Three Regalia were of continental rather than divine origin. See Ryusaku Tsunoda, Wm. Theodore de Bary, and Donald Keene, eds., *Sources of the Japanese Tradition* (New York: Columbia University Press), p. 358. Kumazawa Banzan held similar views.

9. Hayashi, *Shintō denju,* in Saigusa, ed., *Shintō hen, Jukyō hen, Nihon tetsugaku zensho,* vol. 4, p. 94.

10. Hayashi Razan, *Shintō hiden setchū zokukai,* in Shintō taikei hensankai, ed., *Fujiwara Seika, Hayashi Razan, Shintō taikei, ronsetsu hen,* vol. 20 (Tokyo: Shintō taikei hensankai, 1988), p. 449. The original sentence is longer. There are two reliable English translations. James Legge translates this as: "When we contem-

plate the spirit-like way of heaven, we see how the four seasons proceed without error. The sages, in accordance with this spirit-like way, laid down their instructions, and all under heaven yield submission to them." In Legge, trans., *The Yi King: Book of Changes* (Cambridge: Oxford University Press, 1882), p. 230. Richard Wilhelm translates: "He affords them a view of the divine way of heaven, and the four seasons do not deviate from their rule. Thus the holy man uses the divine way to give instruction, and the whole world submits to him." In Wilhelm, trans., *The I Ching or Book of Changes* (Princeton, N.J.: Princeton University Press, 1977), p. 486. This was the most-quoted passage when Tokugawa intellectuals discussed the relationship between Confucianism and Shinto.

11. Atobe Yoshiaki, *Suikaō shinsetsu* (Shinto Ideas of Master Suika, 1707, 3 *kan*), in Ishida Ichirō, ed., *Shintō shisō shū, Nihon no shisō*, vol. 14 (Tokyo: Chikuma shobō, 1970), p. 264. Atobe Yoshiaki (1658–1729) succeeded his teacher Yamazaki as the champion of Suika Shinto.

12. Kondō Keigo, ed., *Suika Shintō*, part 1, in Shintō taikei hensankai, ed., *Shintō taikei, ronsetsu hen*, vol. 12 (Tokyo: Shintō taikei hensankai, 1984), p. 410.

13. The essence of Suika Shinto was *keigi-naigai gaii-hōgai* ("by devotion we strengthen ourselves within; by righteousness we square the world without"), a phrase from the *Wen Yen* of the *I Ching*. Yamazaki's interpretation was that people should purify their bodies with reverence, and could then execute their duty to family and country. This was different from the Chu Hsi commentary that took the "within" and "without" in this phrase as referring to the heart and self. Yamazaki also used the *wu-hsing* theory to establish his metaphysics and ethics. He stressed the importance of the interaction of the agents of earth and metal in regulating fire, the most fundamental agent, identifying the agents of earth and metal with the virtues of devotion and righteousness.

14. Yamazaki Anzai, *Kōhan zensho* (An Anthology of the *Hung Fan*), quoted in Herman Ooms, *Tokugawa Ideology: Early Constructs, 1570–1680* (Princeton, N.J.: Princeton University Press, 1985), p. 234.

15. Taira Shigemichi, "Suika Shintō," in Ishida Ichirō, ed., *Kinsei no shisō*, part 1, *Nihon shisōshi kōza*, vol. 4, (Tokyo: Yūzankaku, 1977), p. 176.

16. Kumazawa Banzan, *Miwa monogatari* (Stories of the Three-Wheel Doctrine), in Saigusa Hiroto, ed., *Nihon tetsugaku zensho*, vol. 4 (Tokyo: Daiichi shobo, 1936), p. 220.

17. Kumazawa Banzan, *Keijijōden* (A Commentary on the First Half of the *Hsi Tz'u*), in Masamune Atsuo, ed., *Kumazawa Banzan zenshū*, vol. 4 (Tokyo: Meicho shuppan, 1978), p. 421.

18. Kumazawa, *Miwa monogatari*, in Saigusa, ed., *Nihon tetsugaku zensho*, vol. 4, p. 155.

19. Ibid., p. 221

20. Ibid., p. 176.

21. Kumazawa, *Keijijōden*, in Masamune, ed., *Kumazawa Banzan zenshū*, vol. 4, p. 421.

22. In Hirose Yutaka, ed., *Yamaga Sokō zenshū, shisō hen*, vol. 9 (Tokyo: Iwanami shoten, 1941), p. 579.

23. Ogyū Sorai, "Sorai shū," in Yoshikawa Kōjirō, ed., *Ogyū Sorai, Nihon shisō taikei*, vol. 36 (Tokyo: Iwanami shoten, 1973), p. 543.

24. Ogyū Sorai, *Rongochō* (An Investigation of the *Lun Yü*), in Ogawa Tamaki, ed., *Ogyū Sorai zenshū*, vol. 3 (Tokyo: Misuzu shobō, 1974), p. 291.

25. Ibid.

26. See Togawa Yoshio and Konda Nobuo, eds., *Ogyū Sorai zenshū*, vol. 2 (Tokyo: Misuzu shobō, 1974), p. 683, and Nishida Taichirō and Hino Tatsuo, eds., *Ogyū Sorai zenshū*, vol. 18 (Tokyo: Misuzu shobō, 1976), p. 599. This issue spilt Ogyū Sorai's disciples into two factions. One group, represented by Yamagata Shūnan (1687–1752), remained faithful to Ogyū, and believed that Shinto and the way of the sages were basically the same. The other group, led by Dazai Shundai, was more critical of Shinto.

27. Shimonaka Yasaburō, ed., *Shintō daijiten* (Kyoto: Rinsen shoten, 1986), p. 110.

28. Watarai Nobuyoshi, *Yōfukki*, in Ishida Ichirō, ed., *Shintō shisō shū, Nihon no shisō*, vol. 14 (Tokyo: Chikuma shobō, 1970), pp. 188–189.

29. Ibid.

30. Watarai Nobuyoshi, *Jingū hiden mondō* (The Secret Transmission of the Ise Shrine: Questions and Answers), in Nishikawa Junshi, ed., *Ise Shintō*, part 2, *Shintō taikei, ronsetsu hen*, vol. 7 (Tokyo: Shintō taikei hensankai, 1982), p. 74.

31. Kikkawa matched the first sentence of the prayer to the five agents as follows: *to—shui* (water), *o—huo* (fire), *kami—mu* (wood), *emi—chin* (gold), *tame —t'u* (earth). He matched the second sentence to the eight hexagrams: *kan— k'an* (abysmal), *ken—ken* (keeping still), *shin—chen* (arousing), *son—sun* (gentle), *ri—li* (clinging), *kon—k'un* (receptive), *sui—tui* (joyous), *ken—ch'ien* (creative). See Taira Shigemichi, *Kikkawa Shintō no kiso teki kenkyū* (Tokyo: Yoshikawa kōbunkan, 1966), pp. 284–285. This was a secret teaching of Ise Shinto that originated in late medieval times. It became very prevalent among different schools of early Tokugawa Shinto. Some Confucian Shintoists, such as Hayashi Razan, Yamazaki Ansai, and Tamaki Masahide, put forth similar ideas. See Shimonaka, ed., *Shintō daijiten*, p. 1026.

32. See Taira Shigemichi, ed., *Kikkawa Shintō, Shintō taikei, ronsetsu hen*, vol. 10 (Tokyo: Shintō taikei hensankai, 1983), pp. 18–21.

33. Peter Nosco has pinpointed two tendencies that emerged in mid-Tokugawa Shinto—simplification of metaphysical speculations, and the separation from the neo-Confucian synthesis, using Masuho Zankō as an example. See Nosco, "Masuho Zankō," in Nosco, ed., *Confucianism and Tokugawa Culture*, pp. 178–187. However, Masuho was a transitional figure and used the *yin-yang wu-hsing* theory frequently in his explanations of Shinto. See "Jinji no maki," in Masuho Zankō, *Endō tsūkan* (1715), in Noma Kōshin, ed., *Kinsei shokudōron, Nihon shisō taikei*, vol. 60 (Tokyo: Iwanami shoten, 1976), pp. 206–235.

34. Muro Kyūsō, *Shundai zatsuwa*, in Inoue Tetsujirō, ed., *Nihon rinri ihen*, vol. 3, *Shushigakuha no bu*, part 1 (Tokyo: Ikuseikai, 1902), p. 104. A century later, Yamagata Bantō expressed the same idea in his *Yume no shiro*. See Yamagata, *Yume no shiro*, in Saigusa Hiroto, ed., *Shūkyō ron, heihō bujutsu ron, Nihon tetsugaku zensho*, vol. 12 (Tokyo: Daiichi shobō, 1935), p. 118.

35. Muro Kyūsō, "Shokan," in Araki Kengo, ed., *Kaibara Ekken, Muro Kyūsō, Nihon shisō taikei*, vol. 34 (Tokyo: Iwanami shoten, 1970), p. 249.

36. Ibid., p. 245.

37. Ibid., p. 371.

38. Muro recognized the historical value of the Three Regalia as relics but rejected their religious and ethical implications. Thus, to him, the Three Regalia were no longer sacred treasures and did not represent the Three Confucian Values of wisdom, benevolence, and courage (ibid., p. 289).

39. Dazai Shundai, *Bendōsho* (Book Differentiating the Way), in Inoue Tetsujirō, ed., *Nihon rinri ihen*, vol. 6, *Kogakuha no bu*, part 2 (Tokyo: Ikuseikai, 1902), pp. 205–206.

40. Dazai stated that ancient Japanese behaved like animals. For example, he discovered that marriage between brother and sister was not unusual in the *Kojiki* and *Nihon shoki*, and argued that Japan became civilized only after the importation of the way of the sages from China.

41. Dazai, *Bendōsho*, in Inoue, ed., *Nihon rinri ihen*, vol. 6, *Kogakuha no bu*, part 2, p. 208.

42. The rise of nativist thought was one of the most striking developments in eighteenth-century Japan. It can be observed in the growing influence of *kokugaku*, the increasing independence of Shinto from Confucianism and Busshism, the formation of a vernacular language, and the naturalization of Chinese learning. For details on the formation of a vernacular language, see Sakai, *Voices of the Past: The Status of Language in Eighteenth-Century Japanese Discourse* (Ithaca, N.Y.: Cornell University Press, 1991).

43. Many "new religions" affiliated with Shinto founded in late Tokugawa times used the oracles of the *I Ching* frequently. They included the Kurozumikyō and Misogikyō.

44. Influenced by *kogaku*, Jiun strove to return to original Buddhism by studying Buddhist sūtras in Sanskrit. For his Buddhist views, see Paul B. Watt, "Jiun Sonja (1718–1804): A Response to Confucianism within the Context of Buddhist Reform," in Nosco, ed., *Confucianism and Tokugawa Culture*, pp. 188–214.

45. Jiun Sonja, *Shinju gūdan* (Discursive Talks on Shinto-Confucian Relations), in Imai Atsushi and Yamamoto Masao, eds., *Unden Shintō, Shintō taikei, ronsetsu hen*, vol. 14 (Tokyo: Shintō taikei hensankai, 1990), p. 31.

46. Ibid., p. 50.

47. Some early *kokugaku* scholars recognized the divinational and metaphysical value of the *I Ching*. Amano Sadakage (1661–1733) and Yoshimi Kōwa (Yukikazu, 1672–1761) wrote several books on it. Peter Nosco also points out that Kada no Azumamaro (1669–1736) was influenced by the *yin-yang* theory in constructing his cosmology and ontology. See Nosco, *Remembering Paradise: Nativism and Nostalgia in Eighteenth-Century Japan* (Cambridge, Mass.: Harvard University Press, 1990), pp. 87, 94.

48. Motoori Norinaga, *Kuzubara* (Arrowroot, 1780), in Kamada Jun'ichi, ed., *Fukko Shintō*, part 3, *Motoori Norinaga, Shintō taikei, ronsetsu hen*, vol. 25 (Tokyo: Shintō taikei hensankai, 1982), pp. 227, 253.

49. Modified from Harry Harootunian, *Things Seen and Unseen: Discourse and Ideology in Tokugawa Nativism* (Chicago: University of Chicago Press, 1988), p. 99.

50. For Motoori's criticisms of Hayashi Razan and Watarai Nobuyoshi's Shinto views, see Motoori Norinaga, *Kojikiden* (Commentary on the *Kojiki*), vol. 3 (1767), in Kamada ed., *Fukko Shintō*, part 3, *Motoori Norinaga, Shintō taikei, ronsetsu hen*, vol. 25, pp. 331, 386. In addition, he criticized the *Nihon shoki* for describing Izanagi

as *"yang kami"* and Izanami as *"yin kami."* See ibid., pp. 176–177. See also Matsumoto Shigeru, *Motoori Norinaga* (Cambridge: Harvard University Press, 1970), p. 89.

51. Motoori Norinaga, *Naobi no mitama* (The Rectifying Spirit, 1771), in Kamada ed., *Fukko Shintō*, part 3, *Motoori Norinaga, Shintō taikei, ronsetsu hen*, vol. 25, pp. 17–18.

52. Izumi Maku'ni, *Meidōsho*, in Haga Noboru and Matsumoto Sannosuke, eds., *Kokugaku undō no shisō, Nihon shisō taikei*, vol. 51 (Tokyo: Iwanami shoten, 1971), pp. 51, 184.

53. Ibid., p.186.

54. See Kiyohara Sadao, *Kokugaku hattatsushi* (Tokyo: Unebi shobō, 1940), pp. 315–316.

55. Although scholars of later generations paid little attention to Hirata's scholarship on the *I Ching*, his student, Ōkuni Takamasa, rated the *Taikō koekiden* with three others as Hirata's greatest works. See Fujii Sadafumi, *Edo kokugaku tensei shi no kenkyū* (Tokyo: Yoshikawa kōbunkan, 1987), p. 37.

56. Indeed, Ueda Akinari (1734–1809), an arch-rival of Motoori in *kokugaku* circles, had already alleged that Fu Hsi was a Shinto deity. This idea was denied by Motoori. Hirata used the *wu-hsing* theory to rationalize this idea. According to Hirata, since some ancient Chinese books suggested that Fu Hsi belonged to the agent of wood, Fu Hsi was a Japanese deity who had come to China from Japan because wood implied the direction of the East.

57. Hirata Atsutane, *Taiko koekiden*, in Hirata Atsutane zenshu kankōkai, ed., *Hirata Atsutane zenshū*, vol. 6 (Tokyo: Hōbunkan, 1935), p. 2.

58. Ibid., p. 6.

59. The first person I can trace in Japan who advocated the Shinto origins of Chinese classics was a Suika Shintoist, Suzuki Teisai, a student of Asami Keisai (1652–1711), in his *Shingaku kokinben* (Discourse on the Differences between Ancient and Today's Shinto). See Denki gakkai, ed., *Yamazaki Ansai to sono monryū* (Tokyo: Meiji shobō, 1933), p. 268.

60. See Muraoka Tsunetsugu, *Norinaga to Atsutane* (Tokyo: Sōbunsha, 1957), pp. 170–175. Hirata used Confucian texts and apocrypha to reconstruct the ancient *I Ching*. However, his contributions were minor because he did not break new ground in either textual reconstruction or intellectual discussion. As early as the Southern Sung, Wang Ying-lin (1223–1296) had already pointed out that the *Kui Ts'ang* had only forty-five yarrow stalks in his *Yü Hai*. *K'ao-cheng* scholarship in Ch'ing China also discussed this issue.

61. Furukawa Tetsushi, ed., *Kinsei no shisō, Nihon shisōshi kōza*, vol. 4 (Tokyo: Yūzankaku, 1977), p. 235.

62. Ikuta Yorozu, *Tan'eki seigi* (The Essence of the *T'uan Chuan* of the *I Ching*), in Haga Noboru, ed., *Ikuta Yorozu zenshū*, vol. 3 (Tokyo: Kyōiku shuppan senta, 1986), p. 469.

63. Ikuta Yorozu, *Koeki taishōkyō den*, in Haga Noboru, ed., *Ikuta Yorozu zenshū*, vol. 2 (Tokyo: Kyōiku shuppan senta, 1986), pp. 412–413.

64. Ōkuni Takamasa, *Gakutō benron* (Discussions on Intellectual Lineage), in Tahara Tsuguo, ed., *Hirata Atsutane, Ban Nobutomo, Ōkuni Takamasa, Nihon shisō taikei*, vol. 50 (Tokyo: Iwanami shoten, 1973), p. 487.

65. Ibid., p. 489. Motoori did not believe in the existence of *jindai moji*,

whereas Hirata accepted it in his last years. Ōkuni's student, Ōhata Harukuni (1818–1875) elaborated on this idea in the *Kanjigen* (The Origins of the Chinese Characters). He believed that Chinese characters came from Japanese, and that Sanskrit letters were derived from Chinese.

66. Ōkuni Takamasa, *Koden tsūkai* (An Explicit Explanation of the Classics), in Nomura Denshirō, ed., *Ōkuni Takamasa zenshū*, vol. 7 (Tokyo: Yūkōsha, 1939), pp. 1–12.

67. Thus Ōkuni felt comfortable using the ideas from the *I Ching* to interpret the Age of the Gods in his *Naobi no mitama hochū* (*Naobi no Mitama:* Supplement and Annotation). He also used the *I Ching* for divination, and some of his students applied it to agriculture. In addition to Ikuta and Ōkuni, other late *kokugaku* scholars who studied the *I Ching* along the lines suggested by Hirata Atsutane included Hirata Kanetane (1798–1880), Arai Shuson (1808–?), and Izumi Ietane (1819–1886).

68. See Aizawka Seishisai, *Toku Naobi no mitama* (Reading *Naobi no mitama*), in Takasu Yoshijirō, ed., *Aizawa Seishisai shū, Mitogaku taikei,* vol. 2 (Tokyo: Ida shoten, 1941), pp. 453–454.

69. Aizawa did not create this argument. Its origins can be traced to an early Mito scholar, Mori Shōken (1653–1746), who openly replaced China with Japan in the discussion of the relationship between Confucianism and Shinto. Mori said: "The *I Ching* reads: 'The sages, in accordance with Shinto, laid down their instructions, and all under heaven yield submission to them.' Here, it refers to one country." See Mori, *Nijūyonron* (Twenty-Four Arguments), in Takasu Yoshijirō, ed., *Mito Gikō, Rekkō shū, Mitogaku taikei,* vol. 5 (Tokyo: Ida shoten, 1941), p. 323. Yamaga Sokō also expressed a similar idea. In his explanation of the hexagram *kuan,* he praised the Japanese political tradition from the Sun Goddess. See Yamaga, *Takkyō dōmon* (Questions from Children During My Exile), in Hirose Yutaka, ed., *Yamaga Sokō zenshū,* vol. 12 (Tokyo: Iwanami shoten, 1941), pp. 284–285.

70. Aizawa Seishisai, *Shinron,* in Saigusa Hiroto, ed., *Kokugaku hen, Nihon tetsugaku zensho,* vol. 5 (Tokyo: Daiichi shobō, 1936), p. 155.

71. Aizawa, *Toku Naobi no mitama,* in Takasu, ed., *Aizawa Seishisai shū, Mitogaku taikei,* vol. 2, p. 454.

72. For details on Shinto-Buddhist relations in Tokugawa Japan, see Helen Hardacre, *Shintō and the State, 1868–1988* (Princeton, N.J.: Princeton University Press, 1989), pp. 3–19.

Chapter 7: The *I Ching* and Buddhism

1. For instance, Iulian K. Shchutskii remarks that the *I Ching* had a tremendous impact on Confucianism, less on Taoism, and very little on Buddhism. He points out that only Ch'en-yen (Shingon) Buddhists sometimes used *I Ching* terms, and that only one Chinese monk, Chih-hsü Ou-i, wrote an important commentary on it in late Ming times. See Shchutskii, *Researches on the I Ching* (Princeton, N.J.: Princeton University Press, 1979), pp. 222–223.

2. On the metaphysical exchange between the *I Ching* and Buddhism, Chang Hsüeh-ch'eng, in his *Wen-shih t'ung-i* (General Meaning of Literature and History), suggests that Buddhism basically "proceeds from the teaching of the *Book*

of Changes," that "it does not differ from the words of the sages," and that both use fantastic imagery and symbolic images (see Shchutskii, *Researches on the I Ching,* p. 86). Andō Shōeki expresses a similar idea: "The sages have made the *Book of Changes* the basis of all other writings. When those such as Xuan Zhuang (Hsüan Chuang) translated the Buddhist scriptures, they did it based on the *Book of Changes.* All Buddhist writings are thus in accord with the *Book of Changes.*" (Andō, *Shizen shineidō,* quoted in Toshinobu Yasunaga, trans., *Andō Shōeki: Social and Ecological Philosopher in Eighteenth-Century Japan* [New York: Weatherhill, 1992], pp. 223–224). Kenneth K. Inada also believes that the metaphysics of the *I Ching* equipped the Chinese mind with "the form of understanding" to adapt Buddhism in its early stages in China (see Inada, "*I Ching* Metaphysics and the Buddhist Introduction to China," in Committee Appointed to Commemorate Professor Yūki's Retirement and Sixtieth Birthday, ed., *Bukkyō shisōshi ronshū* [Tokyo: Daizo shuppansha, 1964], pp. 19–32). For a study of T'ang Buddhist uses of the *I Ching,* see Tanaka Toshiaki, "Tōzan *Hōkyō zammai* no eki to gen *Taikyokuzu* teki hassō," *Tōhō shūkyō* (Tokyo: Nihon dōkyō gakuin, 1985), 66:87–102, and (1986) 67:38–58. William R. LaFleur maintains that the Buddhist doctrines of karma, *rokudō* (six paths), and *jikkai* (relativity of good and evil) in medieval Japan were in accord with the *yin-yang* principle. See LaFleur, *The Karma of Words: Buddhism and the Literary Arts in Medieval Japan* (Berkeley and Los Angeles: University of California Press, 1983), pp. 27–31, 53.

3. Modified from Richard Wilhelm, trans., *The I Ching or Book of Changes* (Princeton, N.J.: Princeton University Press, 1977), p. 393.

4. In China, people used this passage to discuss Buddhism shortly after its importation from India. See Furuta Kazuhiro, "Shoki Chūgoku Bukkyō ni okeru gōron," in Kumoi Shōzen, ed., *Gō shisō kenkyū* (Kyoto: Heirakuji shoten, 1979), pp. 628–634. It also laid the foundation for the Chinese mind to accept the idea of karmic retribution. See Tōdō Kyōshun, "Chūgoku Jōdōkyō ni okeru inga ni kansuru shomondai," in Nakamura Hajime, ed., *Inga, Bukkyō shisō,* vol. 3 (Kyoto: Heirakuji shoten, 1978), p. 294. In Japan, Zen monks started to cite this most-quoted passage during the Kamakura period, and for the Tokugawa era I have found many intellectuals of various backgrounds who used it to explain the relationship between Confucianism and Buddhism, including Takuan Sōhō, Nishikawa Joken, Mori Shōken, Arai Hakuseki, Ishida Baigan (1685–1748), Okada Hakuku (1692–1767), and Tsurumine Kaisei (1750–1826).

5. Modified from Wilhelm, trans., *The I Ching or Book of Changes,* p. 294.

6. Ibid., pp. 340–341. One Buddhist treatise that makes this argument is the *Myō kōjin den* (Biography of Wonderful Good People, 1842) by a Jōdo Shin (New Pure Land) monk, Jun (1791–1872). See Jun, *Myō kōjin den,* in Kashiwabara Yūsen and Fujii Manabu, eds., *Kinsei Bukkyō no shisō, Nihon shisō taikei,* vol. 57 (Tokyo: Iwanami shoten, 1973), p. 175.

7. See Sasaki Genjun, *Gō to unmei* (Tokyo: Shimizu kōbundō, 1976), pp. 283–284.

8. In Yōmeigaku taikei hensankai, ed., *Nihon no Yōmeigaku, Yōmeigaku taikei,* vol. 8 (Tokyo: Meitoku shuppansha, 1972), p. 41. Two years later, in another poem he composed after a visit to the Ise Shrine, Nakae compared Fu Hsi to Amaterasu because they both did a wonderful creative work (ibid., p. 46).

His belief in the God of the Hexagrams was uncommon in the Tokugawa period.

9. For additional details, see Muraoka Tsunetsugu, *Shintōshi* (Tokyo: Sōbunsha, 1964), pp. 45–46.

10. Arai Hakuseki, *Kishinron*, in Saigusa Hiroto, ed., *Shūkyō ron, heihō bujutsu ron, Nihon tetsugaku zensho,* vol. 12 (Tokyo: Daiichi shobō, 1936), pp. 32–33.

11. For instance, Arai refuted the Buddhist idea of gods and ghosts but did not deny their existence. He even admitted that worshipping them could bring power.

12. Okada Hakuku, *Jikoku shūshinroku* (Records of Ruling the Nation and Self-Cultivation, 1794), in Takimoto Seiichi, ed., *Nihon keizai sōsho*, vol. 6 (Tokyo: Nihon keizai sōsho kankōkai, 1914), p. 505.

13. Yamagata Bantō, *Yume no shiro*, in Saigusa Hiroto, ed., *Shūkyō ron, heihō bujutsu ron, Nihon tetsugaku zensho,* vol. 12 (Tokyo: Daiichi shobō, 1935), p. 114.

14. Itō Jinsai, *Gomōjigi* (The Meanings of Words in the *Lun Yü* and *Meng Tzu*), in Yoshikawa Kōjirō and Shimizu Shigeru, eds., *Itō Jinsai, Itō Tōgai, Nihon shisō taikei,* vol. 33 (Tokyo: Iwanami shoten, 1971), pp. 125–126.

15. Hara Sōkei, *Katei kidan*, in Nihon zuihitsu taisei henshūbu, ed., *Nihon zuihitsu taisei,* series 1, vol. 9 (Tokyo: Yoshikawa kōbunkan, 1975), pp. 39–40.

16. Ōta Kinjō, *Gimonroku*, in Nagasawa Kikuta, ed., *Nihon zuihitsu shūsei*, vol. 8 (Tokyo: Kyūko shoin, 1978), p. 182.

17. Ibid., pp. 182–184.

18. Hirose Yokusō, *Kyūkeisōdō zuihitsu*, in Mori Senzō and Kitagawa Hirokuni, eds., *Zoku Nihon zuihitsu taisei*, vol. 2 (Tokyo: Yoshikawa kōbunkan, 1979), p. 140.

19. Okada Kōtei, *Shichikyō tatsuki* (Notes on the Seven Classics), in Seki Giichirō, ed., *Kaisetsubu, Zokuzoku Nihon Jurin sōsho,* vol. 1 (Tokyo: Tōyō tōsho kankōkai, 1935), pp. 4–5.

20. Isobe Tadakata, *Shōcha wakumon* (Questions about Tea Appreciation), in Geinōshi kenkyūkai, ed., *Sūki, Nihon shomin bunka shiryō shūsei,* vol. 10 (Tokyo: San'ichi shobō, 1976), p. 64.

21. See Kumakura Isao, *Kan'ei bunka no kenkyū* (Tokyo: Yoshikawa kōbunkan, 1988), p. 108. See also Ogino Dokuen, *Kinsei Zenrin sōhōden* (Kyoto: Shibunkaku, 1980), pp. 91–92.

22. The tenth rector, Ryūha Kanshō (1548–1636), was the author of two books, the *Taieki danrei bokuzei genki* (*I Ching* Laws for Divination Using Yarrow Stalks and Tortoise Shell) and *Dan'eki etoki* (Elucidation of Divining [According to the] *I Ching*), in which he advocated the unity of Buddhism and Confucianism. The eleventh rector, Myōtetsu, and the thirteenth rector, Den'ei (d. 1687), annotated the *I Ching*. The fourteenth rector, Kyūshitsu Genchō (d. 1713), wrote the *Ekigaku hisho* (Secret Book on *I Ching* Studies). The sixteenth rector, Gekkō Genchō, wrote the *Kizō sho* (Book on Returning to the *Kuei Ts'ang*) and *Bokuzei genkisho* (Book on the Origin of Divination with Yarrow Stalks).

23. See Yūki Rikuo, *Ashikaga gakkō no kyōikushi teki kenkyū* (Tokyo: Daiichi hōkei, 1985), pp. 339–575.

24. Quoted in Tsuji Zennosuke, *Nihon Bukkyō shi, kinsei hen,* vol. 4 (Tokyo: Iwanami shoten, 1955), p. 439.

25. Quoted in Fukui Tamotsu, *Edo bakufu kankōbutsu* (Tokyo: Yūshōdō, 1985), pp. 23–24.

26. Takuan laid down his argument in the *Ketsujōshū*, which is included in Takuan oshō zenshū kankōkai, ed., *Takuan oshō zenshū*, vol. 5 (Tokyo: Kogisha, 1929), pp. 11–12.

27. In Royall Tyler, trans., *Selected Writings of Suzuki Shōsan* (Ithaca, N.Y.: China-Japan Program of Cornell University, 1977), p. 228.

28. Unshō, *Sankyō shiki chū* (A Collection of Ideas of the Three Teachings, 1657), in Takaoka Ryūshin, ed., *Shingonshū zensho* (Tokyo: Shingonshū zensho kankōkai, 1935), pp. 160–161. The idea that Fu Hsi was actually a bodhisattva was not very popular in the Tokugawa period but seems to have exerted some impact on *kokugaku* scholars.

29. See Paul Peachey, *A History of Zen Buddhism* (New York: Pantheon Books, 1963), pp. 113–118.

30. Although the doctrine of the five ranks *(goisetsu)* originated in Chinese Buddhism, it was discussed more by Japanese monks. It was no longer a major teaching in Ming-Ch'ing Ch'an (Zen) Buddhism. In contrast, the doctrine became a central issue in the Sōtō school of Zen Buddhism during medieval times, and eventually reached its peak in the Tokugawa period. Famous advocates in Japan were Gazan Shōseki (1274–1365, Sōtō), Nan'ei Kenshū (1387–1459, Sōtō), Renzan Kōeki (1635–1694, Sōtō), Shōju Etan (1642–1672, Sōtō), Shōkai Kensetsu (Sōtō), Muzin Seitō (Rinzai), Taihaku Kokusui (Sōtō), Hakuin Ekaku (Rinzai), Shigetsu Ein (1689–1764, Sōtō), Katsudō Honkō (1710–1773, Sōtō), Genrō Ōryū (1720–1813, Sōtō), Kinbyō Ketsukan (1728–1803, Sōtō), Kōzan Kakuryū (Sōtō), Koun Ikushū (Sōtō), and Teishū (Rinzai). Unlike the situation in medieval Japan, the Sōtō sect studied the *I Ching* more seriously than the Rinzai sect in the Tokugawa period.

31. Taihaku Kokusui, *Sōtō gokokuben*, in Sōtōshū zensho kankōkai, ed., *Sōtōshū zensho*, vol. 5, *Chūkai* (Tokyo: Sōtō zensho kankōkai, 1930), p. 418.

32. Ibid., p. 413.

33. Ibid., pp. 377, 379.

34. Quoted in R. Shaw, trans., *The Embossed Tea Kettle and Other Works of Hakuin Zenji* (London: George Allen & Unwin, 1963), p. 150.

35. Quoted in Philip B. Yampolsky, trans., *The Zen Master Hakuin: Selected Writings* (New York: Columbia University Press, 1971), p. 214.

36. Ichihara Toyota, ed., *Munan, Shōju, Nihon no Zen goroku*, vol. 15 (Tokyo: Kōdansha, 1979), pp. 36–38.

37. In Kamada Shigeo, ed., *Hakuin, Nihon no Zen goroku*, vol. 19 (Tokyo: Kōdansha, 1977), pp. 81, 391.

38. Quoted in Ōsaki Ryūen, *Hakuin Zenshi den* (Tokyo: Morikawa shoten, 1922), p. 161.

39. Historians of Japanese Buddhism have viewed this situation with interest. Charles Eliot says: "During more than two centuries of anti-Buddhist attacks, no Buddhist champion came forward to defend the faith." See Eliot, *Japanese Buddhism* (London: Edward Arnold & Co., 1935), p. 315. O. Kressler, in his paper on Confucian-Buddhist philosophical relations, remarks that all attacks by Tokugawa Confucians were superficial because they did not touch on the inner metaphysical value and logic of Buddhism. Ironically, he points out that the charges made against the Buddhists were well deserved, since no outstanding figures emerged among them to take up the challenge. See Kressler, "Die mitteljapan-

ischen konfuzianischen philosphen und ihr Verhäitnis zum Buddhismus ihres Landes," *Zeitschrift der deutschen morgenländischen Gesellschaft*, vol. 88 (1934), pp. 65–82. This article is introduced in Joseph Spae, *Itō Jinsai* (New York: Paragon Book, 1967), p. 62. In fact, many Buddhist monks—particularly those from the Jōdo Shin, Pure Land, and Nichiren sects—stood up to defend their beliefs, but with limited success.

40. The best overview of the anti-Buddhist movement in the Tokugawa period was presented by a Jōdo Shin monk, Ryūon (1800–1885), who witnessed the movement himself. See Ryūon, *Sōseki haibutsu ben* (A Comprehensive Critique of Anti-Buddhist Ideas, 1865), in Kashiwabara Yūsen and Fujii Manabu, eds., *Kinsei Bukkyō no shisō, Nihon shisō taikei*, vol. 57 (Tokyo: Iwanami shoten, 1973), pp. 105–146.

41. From the seventeenth rector, Senkei (1722–1795), to the twenty-third and the last rector, Kendō (1822–1875), the masters of the Ashikaga School lectured less on the *I Ching*, and more on Buddhist sūtras. None of them wrote comments on the text anymore. In addition, enrollment declined and finances were strained. See Yūki Rikuo, *Ashikaga gakkō no kyōikushi teki kenkyū* (Tokyo: Daiichi hōkei, 1985), pp. 339–575.

42. Sakurai Hideo, ed., *Zengaku daijiten* (Tokyo: Taishūkan shoten, 1985), p. 480. Chih-hsü's other work, the *Ju-shih tsung-chuan ch'ieh-i* (A Private Discussion on the Transmission of Confucianism and Buddhism), was also reprinted in Japan; it suggests the unity of the two teachings.

43. Modified from Shchutskii, *Researches on the I Ching*, pp. 205–206.

44. For instance, Amano Sadakage (1661–1733), a Shintoist and early *kokugaku* scholar, attacked the book in his *Shioshiri;* see Amano, *Shioshiri*, in Nihon zuihitsu taisei henshūbu, ed., *Nihon zuihitsu taisei*, series 3, vol. 13 (Tokyo: Yoshikawa kōbunkan, 1976), p. 81. Namikawa Tenmin (1678–1718), also a *kokugaku* scholar, condemned it as a work which distorted the *I Ching;* see Namikawa, *Tenmin igon* (Testament of Tenmin, 1722), in Seki Giichirō, ed., *Nihon Jurin sōsho*, vol. 5, *Kaisetsubu*, part 1 (Tokyo: Tōyō tōsho kankōkai, 1929), p. 1.

45. Chūmoku Gikai, *Shōsō manhitsu*, in Nagasawa Kikuya, ed., *Nihon zuihitsu shūsei*, vol. 3 (Tokyo: Kyūko shoin, 1978), p. 11.

46. See Imai Atsushi and Ozawa Tomio, eds., *Nihon shisō ronsōshi* (Tokyo: Perikansha, 1979), pp. 150–154.

47. Wilhelm, trans., *The I Ching or Book of Changes*, p. 294.

48. Inkei Chidatsu, *Jubutsu gōron* (A Combined Discussion of Confucianism and Buddhism, 1668), in Shūo Junkei, ed., *Nihon shisō tōsō shiryō*, vol. 1 (Tokyo: Tōhō shoin, 1931), p. 51.

49. Ibid., p. 18.

50. Jiun Sonja, *Shintō kokka* (National Songs of Shinto), in Imai Atsushi and Yamamoto Masao, eds., *Unden Shintō, Shintō taikei, ronsetsu hen*, vol. 14 (Tokyo: Shintō taikei hensankai, 1990), p. 115.

51. Jiun Sonja, *Jūzen hōgō* (Lectures on Ten Goodnesses), in Nihon kyōiku shisō taikei, ed., *Bukkyō kyōiku shisō*, part 3, *Nihon kyōiku shisō taikei*, vol. 17 (Tokyo: Nihon tōsho senta, 1980), pp. 322–323.

52. Jiun Sonja, *Mudaishō* (Book Without a Title, 1788), in Imai and Yamamoto, eds., *Unden Shintō, Shintō taikei, ronsetsu hen*, vol. 14, p. 348.

53. See Takizawa Bakin, *Enseki zasshi* (1809), in Nihon zuihitsu taisei hensubu, ed., *Nihon zuihitsu taisei,* series 2, vol. 19 (Tokyo: Yoshikawa kōbunkan, 1975), pp. 340–342.

Chapter 8: The *I Ching* and Natural Science

1. Joseph Needham separates the *yin-yang wu-hsing* doctrine from the *I Ching*: "While the five-element and two-force theories were favorable rather than inimical to the development of scientific thought in China, the elaborated symbolic system of the *Book of Changes* was almost from the start a mischievous handicap. It tempted those who were interested in Nature to rest in explanations which were no explanations at all." See Needham et al., *Science and Civilization in China,* vol. 2 (Cambridge: Cambridge University Press, 1956), p. 336. This dismissal is ahistorical, since *yin-yang wu-hsing* theory had been incorporated into the *I Ching* system by the Ch'in and Han periods.

2. On the role of the *I Ching* in Chinese scientific thought, see Wallace A. Sherrill and Wen-kuan Chu, *An Anthology of I Ching* (London: Arkana, 1977), chapters 3, 6, 7, and 8. See also Peng-yoke Ho, "The System of the Book of Changes and Chinese Science," *Japanese Studies in the History of Science* (Tokyo, 1972), no. 11, 23–39.

3. The Bureau of Divination (Onmyōryō) was the official center of *I Ching* studies. It consisted of three divisions: the Onmyōdō (Office of *Yin-Yang*), Tenmondō (Office of Astronomy and Astrology), and Rekidō (Office of Calendrical Studies). The first two offices specialized in *I Ching* divination; the third applied *I Ching* metaphysics and ideas to calendrical studies and other applied sciences. On the impact of the *yin-yang* doctrine on pre-Tokugawa science, see Nakayama Shigeru, *A History of Japanese Astronomy* (Cambridge, Mass.: Harvard University Press, 1969), chapters 2 through 5.

4. "Western science" is a very loose concept. I use it here only to refer to European scientific knowledge and technology brought to Tokugawa Japan and its perceptions by the Tokugawa Japanese. Western science after the scientific revolution is experimental, empirical, mechanical, and utilitarian, whereas traditional or Chinese science is not an independent discipline but is affiliated with metaphysics (e.g., *yin-yang wu-hsing*), theology (e.g., the theory of correspondence between heaven and man), ethics, and superstitions (e.g., astrology, numerology, and geomancy). For a historical overview of Western science in Tokugawa Japan, see James Bartholomew, *The Foundation of Science in Japan* (New Haven, Conn.: Yale University Press, 1989), pp. 9–48. See also Tuge Hideomi, ed., *Historical Development of Science and Technology in Japan* (Tokyo: Japan Cultural Society, 1968), pp. 23–88.

5. Other scholars have already questioned this view. See Albert Craig, "Science and Confucianism in Tokugawa Japan," in Marius Jansen, ed., *Changing Japanese Attitudes Toward Modernization* (Princeton, N.J.: Princeton University Press, 1965), pp. 133–160.

6. On the early European impact on Japan, see Charles Boxer, "Some Aspects of Portuguese Influence in Japan, 1542–1640," in Michael Moscato, ed., *Papers on Portuguese, Dutch and Jesuit Influences in Sixteenth- and Seventeenth-Century Japan* (Washington, D.C.: University Publications of America, Inc., 1979), pp. 95–146.

See also C. R. Boxer, *The Christian Century in Japan, 1549–1650* (Berkeley and Los Angeles: University of California Press, 1951).

7. The bakufu limited its contacts with the West to the Dutch and adopted a rigid cultural policy by the 1640s. Hence very few Chinese books on Western science were imported. Although Dutch books were not censored, Dutch merchants seldom carried them because they were not viewed as profitable. As a result, seventeenth-century Japanese could only read outdated Western texts. Even the knowledge of sixteenth-century Western science was incomplete because the Jesuits had their own censorship. The situation improved only after the loosening of book censorship by the eighth shogun Yoshimune (1684–1751) in the 1720s.

8. The Ptolemaic system, suggested by the Hellenistic astronomer Ptolemy (c. 90–168), dominated scientific thinking in the West until the sixteenth century.

9. Quoted in Sugimoto Isao, *Kinsei jitsugakushi no kenkyū* (Tokyo: Yoshikawa kōbunkan, 1962), p. 207.

10. Quoted in Nakayama, *A History of Japanese Astronomy*, p. 91.

11. In scroll 2, entry 19 of *Kenkon bensetsu*, quoted in Tamura Sensosuke, *Nihon kishōgakushi kenkyū*, vol. 1 (Mishima: Mishima kagakushi kenkyūjo, 1979), pp. 227–228.

12. Ibid., scroll 2, entry 14, p. 226.

13. There were some discussions on the shape of heaven and earth in the early Tokugawa period. See Tōkyō kagaku hakubutsukan, ed., *Edo jidai no kagaku* (Tokyo: Hakubunkan, 1934), p. 4.

14. The six climatic factors *(liu-ch'i)* are cold, heat, dampness, dryness, wind, and fire. If the balance of the six climatic factors is disturbed by the variation in *yin-yang wu-hsing* in the universe, dramatic climate changes will occur. Kobayashi used this theory to explain the four qualities (hot, cold, wet, and dry) of the four elements.

15. Quoted in Nakayama, *A History of Japanese Astronomy*, p. 112.

16. Quoted in Sugimoto, *Kinsei jitsugakushi no kenkyū*, p. 190.

17. According to Takahashi, Nishikawa separated natural science from the influence of the *I Ching* by introducing the global theory. See Takahashi Shin'ichi, *Yōgaku shisōshi ron* (Tokyo: Shin Nihon shuppansha, 1972), p. 79. Takahashi tends to overemphasize the modernity of Western learning and has overlooked the fact that Nishikawa used *I Ching* related concepts to explain global theory.

18. Saigusa Hiroto, ed., *Tenmon, butsurigakuka no shizenkan, Nihon tetsugaku zensho*, vol. 8 (Tokyo: Daiichi shobō, 1936), p. 91.

19. However, Nishikawa became very "rational" when he used his knowledge of geography to debase China, stressing that China is only a tiny part of the world.

20. Baba Nobutake, *Shosetsu bendan* (A Critique of Miscellaneous Ideas, 1715), in Nagasawa Kikuya, ed., *Nihon zuihitsu shūsei*, vol. 2 (Tokyo: Kyūko shoin, 1978), p. 42.

21. In Saigusa, ed., *Tenmon, butsurigakuka no shizenkan, Nihon tetsugaku zensho*, vol. 8, p. 29.

22. Quoted in Rai Kiichi, ed., *Jugaku, kokugaku, yōgaku, Nihon no kinsei*, vol. 13 (Tokyo: Chūō kōronsha, 1993), p. 201.

23. The change of worldview in the late eighteenth century has been noted

by several scholars. For instance, Marius Jansen regards the 1770s as the beginning of a decisive change in the way the Japanese perceived their world. He attributes this change to the beginning of the "age of translation of Western books in Japanese." See Jansen, *Japan and Its World* (Princeton, N.J.: Princeton University Press, 1980). On the Western impact on Japanese perception, see also Donald Keene, *The Japanese Discovery of Europe* (Stanford, Calif.: Stanford University Press, 1969) and Grant Goodman, *Japan: The Dutch Experience* (London: Athlone Press, 1986). Maruyama Masao traces the intellectual origins of the change after Ogyū Sorai in *Studies in the Intellectual History of Tokugawa Japan*, trans. Mikiso Hane (Princeton, N.J.: Princeton University Press, 1974).

24. Nakayama Shigeru suggests that after the mid-Tokugawa period, "practical learning" no longer needed the *yin-yang wu-hsing* theory as a source of authority. See Nakayama, "Kindai kagaku to yōgaku," in Hirose Hideo, ed., *Yōgaku*, part 2, *Nihon shisō taikei*, vol. 65 (Tokyo: Iwanami shoten, 1972), p. 458. This evaluation is most applicable to the circle of those who practiced Dutch medicine.

25. Maeno Ryōtaku, *Kanrei higen* (Secret Words from a Narrow Perspective, 1777), in Numata Jirō and Matsumura Akira, eds., *Yōgaku*, part 1, *Nihon shisō taikei*, vol. 64 (Tokyo: Iwanami shoten, 1976), p. 155.

26. The Copernican system is a sun-centered concept of the solar system, advanced by the Polish astronomer Copernicus (1473–1543), in which the planets are considered to move in circular orbits around the sun. Modern astronomy was built on the foundation of the Copernican system, which was introduced to China in 1767.

27. Motoki Yoshi'naga, *Seijutsu hongen taiyō kyūri ryōkai shinsei tenchi nikyū yōhōki*, in Numata and Matsumura, eds., *Yōgaku*, part 1, *Nihon shisō taikei*, vol. 64, p. 343.

28. The importance of Western science was generally recognized by late Tokugawa scholars. Unlike earlier scholars, who identified Western science with *ch'i* (material, physical knowledge), late Tokugawa scholars equated Western science with Chu Hsi's philosophy of *ch'iu-li* (*kyūri*, investigation of principle), and thus made it a central part of the neo-Confucian system. See Craig, "Science and Confucianism in Tokugawa Japan," in Jansen, ed., *Changing Japanese Attitudes Toward Modernization*, pp. 133–160. See also Sugimoto Masayoshi and David L. Swain, *Science and Culture in Traditional Japan* (Cambridge, Mass.: MIT Press, 1978), pp. 303–306.

29. Newtonian physics, introduced to China in 1852, refers to the law of gravitation formulated by Isaac Newton (1642–1727). It explains how every particle of matter in the universe attracts every other particle, and why the planets move in orbits and do not fly off into space.

30. "The theory of native origin" was indeed a very common means of cultural adaptation. Not only Tokugawa Confucians but also *kokugaku* and Buddhist scholars sought to integrate Western science into their own systems. Hirata Atsutane argued for the Japanese origins of Western science using Shinto mythology. For instance, he asserted that the notions of heliocentricity and gravitation had already appeared in the *Kojiki* (Records of Ancient Matters, 712), and that these ideas had been transmitted to the West from Japan in ancient times. Monno (1700–1763), a Pure Land monk, accommodated Western astronomy to tradi-

tional Indian and Buddhist cosmology, or the Sumeru theory, believing that many Western ideas could be found in Buddhist sūtras. In the Sumeru system, the universe consists of eight levels, with Mt. Sumeru at the center and the sun, moon, and stars revolving around it. All heavenly bodies are spheres and move in concentric orbits. Some Tokugawa and Meiji Buddhists also found the ideas of the four-element theory and the seven-day week in Buddhist sūtras. In addition, Buddhist ideas of *gokumi* (extremely small) and *fukaken-ryoku* (force unseen) functioned as background for the introduction of Western chemistry in late Tokugawa Japan. See Togo Tsukahara, *Affinity and Shinwa Ryoku: Introduction of Western Chemical Concepts in Early Nineteenth-Century Japan* (Amsterdam: J. C. Gieben, 1993), pp. 50–55, 90–97. We find parallel developments in China and Korea. In late Ming and Ch'ing China, many scholars espoused the theory of the Chinese origins of Western science. Famous advocates included the Confucian scholars Juan Yüan (1764–1849), Huang Tsun-hsien (1848–1905), the emperor K'ang-hsi (r. 1661–1772), and even the Jesuit Matteo Ricci (1552–1610). In eighteenth-century Korea, some *sirhak* (practical learning) scholars used the *I Ching* to illustrate Western ideas. Kim Sŏkmun (1658–1735), Yi Sŏngho (1681–1763), and Chŏng Yagyong (1762–1836) employed the *I Ching* to explain Western astronomy and physics, such as the Ptolemaic system and the rotation of the earth.

31. Shizuki Tadao, *Konton bunhan zusetsu*, in Saigusa Hiroto, ed., *Jukyōka no shizenkan, tenmon, butsurigakuka no shizenkan, Nihon tetsugaku zensho*, vol. 9 (Tokyo: Daiichi shobō, 1936), p. 200.

32. Shizuki Tadao, *Rekishō shinsho*, in Saigusa Hiroto, ed., *Shizenhen, Nihon tetsugaku shisō zensho*, vol. 6 (Tokyo: Heibonsha, 1956), pp. 145–146.

33. Quoted in Nakayama, *A History of Japanese Astronomy*, p. 183. By using *ch'i* to explain the force of particles, Shizuki was close to Miura Baien (1723–1785), a student of Western learning who mixed the *I Ching* with Western philosophy and physics. Both these scholars discussed this important aspect of the Newtonian theory within the context of the *I Ching*. See Nihon gakushiin, ed., *Meijizen Nihon butsurikagakushi* (Tokyo: Nihon gakujutsu shinkyōkai, 1964), p. 45. On Shizuki's application of *ch'i* to explain the concept of particles and the law of gravitation, see Yoshida Tadashi, "The *Rangaku* of Shizuki Tadao: The Introduction of Western Science in Tokugawa Japan" (Ph.D. dissertation, Princeton University, 1974), pp. 234–243.

34. Saigusa, *Shizenhen, Nihon tetsugaku shisō zensho*, vol. 6, p. 136.

35. Ibid., p. 139.

36. See Hirose Hideo, "Yōgaku toshite no tenmongaku," in Hirose, ed., *Yōgaku*, part 2, *Nihon shisō taikei*, vol. 65, p. 155.

37. Ibid., p. 232.

38. Ibid., pp. 33–35, 38–39. Nakayama Shigeru explains that since there were no words in the Sino-Japanese vocabulary that could adequately express Newtonian physics, Shizuki had to use Chinese terminology in his translation of Keill's work. See Nakayama, *Academic and Scientific Traditions in China, Japan and the West* (Tokyo: University of Tokyo Press, 1984), p. 194.

39. See Craig, "Science and Confucianism in Tokugawa Japan," in Jansen, ed., *Changing Japanese Attitudes Toward Modernization*, p. 142.

40. See Mizuta Norihisa, ed., *Tominaga Nakamoto, Yamagata Bantō, Nihon shisō taikei*, vol. 43 (Tokyo: Iwanami shoten, 1973), pp. 429–430.

41. Yoshio Nankō, *Chidō wakumon,* in Hirose, ed., *Yōgaku,* part 2, *Nihon shisō taikei,* vol. 65, pp. 161–162.

42. Ibid., p. 162.

43. Hashimoto Sōkichi, *Oranda shisei erekiteru kyūrigen,* in Saigusa Hiroto, ed., *Rigaku, Nihon kagaku koten zensho,* vol. 6 (Tokyo: Asahi shimbunsha, 1978), p. 584.

44. Kasamine Tachū, *Erikiteru zensho,* in Saigusa Hiroto, ed., *Edo kagaku koden sōsho,* vol. 11 (Tokyo: Kanwa shuppan, 1978), p. 14.

45. These included Nishimura Tōsato (d. 1787, astronomer and mathematician), Shiba Kōkan (1738–1818, astronomer), Takahashi Yoshitoki (1764–1804, astronomer), Suzuki Bokushi (1770–1842, physicist), Hoashi Banri (1778–1852, physicist), Hirata Atsutane (calendrical scholar), Itō Keisuke (1803–1901, botanist), Satō Setsuzan (1813–1859, astronomer and mathematician), and Takeuchi Sekimei (d. 1871, astronomer and mathematician).

46. Current scholarship on the cultural relations between East Asia and the West has been influenced by the so-called modernization theory, which regards modernization as a lineal and universal development based on Western models. See Marion J. Levy, Jr., *Modernization: Latecomers and Survivors* (New York: Basic Books, Inc., 1972) and John Hall, "Changing Conceptions of the Modernization of Japan," in Jansen, ed., *Changing Japanese Attitudes Toward Modernization.* Fairly speaking, the discussion of Japan's modernization has enhanced Western scholars' academic interest in Japan and can be understood as an attempt to put Japan in a larger context of world history. Despite its contributions, some of its ideas are too mechanical and Western-centered. John Dower has provided a critical but somewhat emotional overview in his "Japan and the Uses of History," in Dower, ed., *Origins of the Modern Japanese State* (New York: Pantheon Books, 1975), pp. 3–101. For a balanced account of the Western scholarship on Japan's modernization, see Ng Wai-ming, "Nihon kindaikaron," *Jiyū,* vol. 36, no. 10 (Tokyo, October 1994), pp. 10–20.

47. The dramatic change in Grant Goodman's view of the nature of Western learning is extremely interesting. In his earlier work, *The Dutch Impact on Japan* (Leiden: Brill, 1967), Goodman emphasizes the modernity of Dutch studies and treats it as a force that weakened Confucianism. In his recent work, *Japan: The Dutch Experience* (1986), he views Dutch studies as a "technology without ideology" (p. 228) and points out that most *Rangaku* scholars were still very Confucian in their intellectual orientation. Likewise, Nakayama Shigeru has modified his perception of the relationship between Western science and Japan's tradition. In his *A History of Japanese Astronomy* (1969), Nakayama views Western astronomy and traditional cosmology as two basically incompatible systems, whereas in his *The Academic and Scientific Traditions in China, Japan and the West* (1984), he concludes that Western astronomy was "simply incorporated into the old framework" (p. 195) and was used "to strengthen the fabric of their [East Asian] tradition" (p. 197).

48. Tokugawa intellectuals were perhaps unfair in accusing Western science of lacking a metaphysical base. Indeed, the West had developed different versions of natural law, theological and atheist beliefs, and cosmological and ontological speculations. However, none of these seemed compatible with the East Asian cultural tradition, or tolerable in the Tokugawa political and cultural setting. Grant Goodman also points out that the theoretical basis of Western astron-

omy was little understood during the Tokugawa period; see his *Japan: The Dutch Experience*, p. 8. Nakayama Shigeru documents how Tokugawa translators left out the theological argumentation in the Western texts; see his "Abhorrence of God in the Introduction of Copernicanism into Japan," *Japanese Studies in the History of Science* (Tokyo, 1964), no. 3, 60–67.

49. Nakayama Shigeru is surprised that Western astronomy had such a smooth reception in late Tokugawa Japan, and that the Copernican and Newtonian theories did not evoke bitter ideological opposition; see his *A History of Japanese Astronomy*, p. 187. He explains the role of Confucianism in the adaptation of Western science as follows: "The Confucian framework of ideas became flexible enough to include Western science with no serious ideological difficulty. The acceptance of Western learning was facilitated by two assumptions: that it was historically of Chinese origin, and that as a mere technique it supplemented eastern values without threatening them" (ibid., p. 214). I think the *I Ching* demonstrates the flexibility of Confucianism.

50. The incomplete importation of Western science arose from the following conditions: First, Tokugawa scholars seldom translated original Western works and only translated secondary materials from the Dutch. For instance, Shizuki did not translate Newton's *Principia* itself but secondary works by John Keill. Second, Tokugawa translations were partial and rough because most translators did not have a strong scientific background—or even an advanced Dutch reading ability. Many did not translate the whole work and left out the mathematical, theoretical, and otherwise difficult parts. Third, Tokugawa scholars were mainly interested in Western technology and applied science, so they paid little attention to scientific methods, the philosophy of science, and pure science and mathematics. This partly explains why Western science did not inspire the equivalent of the Enlightenment in Tokugawa Japan.

51. The role of traditional learning in the adaptation of Western science diminished but did not disappear in the modern period. Some Meiji and Taishō scholars used Buddhism and Shinto to accommodate the theory of evolution, pointing out that Buddhist ideas of transmigration and Shinto views of nature were compatible with the theory of evolution. See Masao Watanabe, *The Japanese and Western Science* (Philadelphia: University of Pennsylvania Press, 1990), chapters 4, 5, and 6. Likewise, in late Ch'ing and early Republican China, many scholars used the three-world theory in the *Kung Yang Commentary* on the *Ch'un Ch'iu* to explain Darwinism and Social Darwinism.

Chapter 9: The *I Ching* and Medicine

1. The relationship between the *I Ching* and Chinese medicine has been a subject of interest to the general reader but has provoked few scholarly discussions. A historical account is provided by Li Chün-ch'uan in his *I-i hui-t'ung ching-i* (Peking: Jen-min wei-sheng ch'u-pan-she, 1991). For a basic analysis of the theoretical relationship between the *I Ching* and Chinese medicine, see Huang Tun-han, *I-hsüeh yü i-hsüeh chih tsung-ho yen-chiu* (Taipei: Palace Publishing Co., 1979) and T'an Wei-ch'ung, [*The*] *Five Element System of Traditional Chinese Medicine in* [*the*] *West* (Peking: Hsüeh Yüan Press, 1990).

2. Marius Jansen points out that the Confucian order was challenged by West-

ern approaches to natural science in the 1770s, and regards the decision of the doctor Sugita Gempaku (1733–1817) to be present at a dissection as the epoch-making event. See Jansen, *Japan and Its World* (Princeton, N.J.: Princeton University Press, 1980), pp. 7–8.

3. Some Buddhist and indigenous medical ideas and practices were incorporated into the Chinese medical system in traditional Japan.

4. For details on the medical implications of the theory of *yin-yang wu-hsing*, see Chang En-ch'in, ed., *Basic Theory of Traditional Chinese Medicine*, vol. 1 (Shanghai: Publishing House of Shanghai College of Traditional Chinese Medicine, 1989), pp. 22–165.

5. See Liu Yen-ch'ih, *The Essential Book of Traditional Chinese Medicine*, vol. 1, *Theory* (New York: Columbia University Press, 1988), pp. 58–59, 63–93.

6. See Ōtsuka Yoshinori, "Kinsei zenki no igaku," in Hirose Hideo, Nakayama Shigeru, and Ōtsuka Yoshinori, eds., *Kinsei kagaku shisō*, part 2, *Nihon shisō taikei*, vol. 63 (Tokyo: Iwanami shoten, 1971), p. 512.

7. For details, see Huang, *I-hsüeh yü i-hsüeh chih tsung-ho yen-chiu*, pp. 345–374. See also Earl Miner, Hiroko Odagiri, and Robert E. Morrell, eds., *The Princeton Companion to Classical Japanese Literature* (Princeton: Princeton University Press, 1985), pp. 399–408.

8. T'an, [*The*] *Five Element System of Traditional Chinese Medicine in [the] West*, pp. 104–107.

9. There were several reasons for the Dōsan lineage's popularity in the early Tokugawa period: (1) it was a byproduct of the rise of neo-Confucianism, (2) the Chin-Yüan medical approach was more appropriate to people who suffered from malnutrition, (3) it was patronized by political leaders, and (4) Manase and his students used simple language to explain difficult medical ideas and practices. See Sōda Hajime, *Nihon iryō bunka shi* (Kyoto: Shibunsha, 1989), pp. 106–108.

10. Manase Dōsan, *Kirigami* (Cutting Paper), quoted in Ōtsuka, "Kinsei zenki no igaku," in Hideo et al., eds., *Kinsei kagaku shisō*, part 2, *Nihon shisō taikei*, vol. 63, p. 514.

11. *Goseiha* received political patronage from the shogunate and the court; both employed *goseiha* physicians from the Dōsan lineage as their attendant physicians in the early Tokugawa period. For instance, Hata Sōha (1550–1607), Hori Kyōan (1584–1642), Misono Isai (d. 1616), Okamoto Genya (1584–1645), Noma Gentaku (1587–1645), Inoue Gentetsu (1601–1686), and Iseki Gensetsu (1618–1699) served the shogun; Manase Gensaku, Manase Shōrin (1565–1611), Yamawaki Genshin (1598–1678), and Nakayama Sanryū (1613–1684) served the court.

12. See Hattori Toshirō, *Edo jidai igakushi no kenkyū* (Tokyo: Yoshikawa kōbunkan, 1978), p. 553.

13. Wilhelm, trans., *The I Ching or Book of Changes*, pp. 710–711.

14. Li Chün-ch'uan, *I-i hui-t'ung ching-i*, pp. 162–174.

15. Quoted in Hattori Toshirō, *Nihonshi shōhyakka*, vol. 20, *Igaku* (Tokyo: Kondō shuppansha, 1985), p. 76.

16. Okamoto Ippō, *Shinkyū hasshu taisei* (Tokugawa edition, Rare Book Collection of Gest Oriental Library, Princeton University), p. 92. Another of Okamoto's important work on acupuncture and moxibustion was the *Jūyonkei keiryaku shōkai* (A Comprehensive Explanation of the Systems of Main and Collateral Channels

in the Fourteen Medical Classics). Terajima Ryōan, an Osaka physician of *goseiha*, expressed similar opinions in his famous *Wakan sansai zue* (An Illustrated Encyclopedia of the Three Powers in Japan, 1713).

17. In Saigusa Hiroto, ed., *Bukkyōka no shizenkan, igakuka no shizenkan, Nihon tetsugaku zensho*, vol. 7 (Tokyo: Daiichi shobō, 1936), p. 324.

18. Huang han i-hsüeh ts'ung-shu hui, ed., *I-an, i-hua, Huang han i-hsüeh ts'ung-shu*, vol. 13 (Peking: Ping-fang ch'u-pan-she, 1935), p. 18.

19. Ibid., p. 10.

20. Quoted in Fujikawa Yū, *Nihon igakushi kōyō*, vol. 2 (Tokyo: Heibonsha, 1974), p. 59.

21. In Huang han i-hsüeh ts'ung-shu hui, ed., *Nuk'o-hsüeh, erhk'o-hsüeh, Huang han i-hsüeh ts'ung-shu*, vol. 9 (Peking: Ping-fang ch'u-pan-she, 1935), p. 24.

22. Fujiwara Seika gave the example of Huang Tzu-hou, who found in the *I Ching* the source of a method to cure diarrhea. See Shushigaku taikei kankōkai, ed., *Nihon no Shushigaku*, part 2, *Shushigaku taikei*, vol. 13 (Tokyo: Meitoku shuppansha, 1975), p. 74.

23. Saigusa, ed., *Bukkyōka no shizenkan, igakuka no shizenkan, Nihon tetsugaku zensho*, vol. 7, p. 159.

24. Takuan Sōhō, *Kottō roku* (Records of Antiquity, 1644), in ibid., p. 174.

25. R. Shaw, trans., *The Embossed Tea Kettle and Other Works of Hakuin Zenji* (London: George Allen & Unwin, 1963), pp. 36–37.

26. Ibid., pp. 38–39.

27. See Hattori, *Edo jidai igakushi no kenkyū*, pp. 85–87. This idea was also adopted by some Tokugawa Confucians and *kokugaku* scholar (e.g., Hirata Atsutane).

28. Wilhelm, trans., *The I Ching or Book of Changes*, p. 403.

29. See Kumakura Isao, *Kan'ei bunka no kenkyū* (Tokyo: Yoshikawa kōbunkan, 1988), p. 102.

30. Shōji Kōki, *Kashoku yōdō* (Major Ways of Managing the Family), in Takimoto Seiichi, ed., *Nihon keizai sōsho*, vol. 24 (Tokyo: Nihon keizai sōsho kankōkai, 1916), p. 113.

31. Ogata Korekatsu, *Kyōrin naisei roku* (Records of Self-Examination of Medical Matters, 1836), in Mori Senzō and Kiyagawa Hirokuni, eds., *Zōku zuihitsu taisei*, vol. 10 (Tokyo: Yoshikawa kōbunkan, 1979), p. 109. In the same text, it is recorded that Takeda Shingen (1521–1573) asked his attendant physician to use *I Ching* divination to trace the whereabouts of a lost boy. It seems that the role of physician and *I Ching* diviner sometimes overlapped in pre-Tokugawa Japan; ibid., pp. 109–110.

32. The medical theory of the *Shang han lun* is rather simple. The main idea is based on the change of balance of *yin-yang* in the human body. The book suggests that diseases progress through six stages—great *yang*, middle *yang*, small *yang*, great *yin*, middle *yin*, and small *yin*—and that each stage has its own symptoms that require different treatments. In general, the natural resistance of a patient in the *yang* state is still strong, and the disease is not serious; thus a *yin* medicine should be used. When the patient reaches the *yin* state, then a stronger *yang* medicine is necessary.

33. Nagoya Gen'i, *Tansuishi*, in Saigusa, ed., *Bukkyōka no shizenkan, igakuka no shizenkan, Nihon tetsugaku zensho*, vol. 7, p. 247.

34. Gotō Konzan, *Shisetsu hikki* (Notes from My Teacher's Lectures, 1780), in Hideo et al., eds., *Kinsei kagaku shisō,* part 2, *Nihon shisō taikei,* vol. 63, p. 390.

35. Ibid., p. 386.

36. See Otsuka Yasuo, "Chinese Traditional Medicine in Japan," in Charles Leslie, ed., *Asian Medical Systems: A Comparative Study* (Berkeley and Los Angeles: University of California Press, 1976), pp. 328–329.

37. Yoshimasu Tōdō, *Kosho igen* (Medical Discussions about Ancient Books, published 1813), in Huang han i-hsüeh ts'ung-shu hui, ed., *I-an, i-hua, Huang han i-hsüeh ts'ung-shu,* vol. 13, p. 1.

38. Ibid., p. 9.

39. Ibid., p. 6.

40. Hideo et al., eds., *Kinsei kagaku shisō,* part 2, *Nihon shisō taikei,* vol. 63, p. 96.

41. Baba Nobutake, *Shosetsu bendan* (1715), in Nagasawa Kikyua, ed., *Nihon zui-hitsu shūsei,* vol. 2 (Tokyo: Kyūko shoin, 1978), pp. 47–48.

42. Hirokawa Kai, *Ranryōhō,* in Sōda Hajime, ed., *Ranryōhō, Ranryō yakukai, Edo kagaku koten sōsho,* vol. 27 (Tokyo: Kanwa shoten, 1980), p. 5.

43. See Yamazaki Akira, "Wakon yōsai teki shii kōzō no keisei to kokka ishiki," in Arisaka Takamichi, ed., *Nihon yōgakushi no kenkyū,* vol. 3 (Tokyo: Sōgensha, 1974), p. 141.

Chapter 10: The *I Ching* and the Military

1. According to an official record, a number of *yin-yang* books on military strategy were imported from Paekche in 602. See Yasui Kōzan, *Chūgoku shimpi shisō no Nihon eno tenkai* (Tokyo: Taishō daigaku shuppanbu, 1983), pp. 111–112.

2. For example, according to the *Ruijū sandai kaku* (A Comprehensive Record of the Institutions in the Three Eras), in 882 officials of the Onmyōryō were sent to Chinjufu in Mutsu no kuni. See Ono Yasuhiro, ed., *Nihon shūkyō jiten* (Tokyo: Kōbunkan, 1985), p. 429.

3. For details, see Shirai Takamasa, "Gunshi," *Rekishi dokuhon* 32, 13 (Tokyo, 1987), p. 99.

4. Tenkai studied under Kyūka at the Ashikaga School for four years. He was famous for his knowledge on the *I Ching,* and was influential in early Tokugawa politics.

5. See Ashikaga Enjutsu, *Kamakura Muromachi jidai no Jukyō* (Tokyo: Nihon koten zensho, 1932), pp. 808–812.

6. See Takasaka Masanobu, *Ryū, tora, hyō sanpon* (Three Chapters on the Dragon, Tiger, and Leopard), in Ishioka Hisao, ed., *Kōshūryū heihō, Nihon heihō zenshū,* vol. 1 (Tokyo: Jimbutsu ōraisha, 1967), pp. 150–156. The result was that Takeda Shingen was represented by the hexagram *feng* (abundance); Tōshōan compared Takeda's military talent to K'ung Ming (Chu-ko Liang, 181–234) but implied that he would not live a long life. For the others, according to the oracles, Uesugi had the talent of an emperor (hexagram *lü,* treading); Oda was immoral but could govern the nation (hexagram *ku,* decay); and Tokugawa was a man of virtue and good fortune (hexagram *chin,* progress).

7. For details on the ritual and the text of the prayer, see ibid., pp. 108–109.

8. Owada Tetsuo, *Gunshi, sanbō* (Tokyo: Chūō kōronsha, 1990), pp. 73–76.

9. Ishioka Hisao, *Nihon heihō shi,* vol. 1 (Tokyo: Yūzankaku, 1972), pp. 91–101.

10. For example, two scholars of Japanese military studies, Ishioka Hisao and

Satō Kinji, praise the Japaneseness of *taisei heihō;* see Ishioka, *Nihon heihō shi,* vol. 1, p. 111, and Satō, *Nihon bugakushi* (Tokyo: Taitō shokan, 1942), pp. 37–39.

11. Ōmori Nobumasa, *Bujutsu densho no kenkyū* (Tokyo: Seiunsha, 1991), p. 11.

12. This is quoted from chapter 11 of part one of the *Hsi Tz'u.* See Obata Kage'nori, *Kōyō gunkan nukigaki kōshū* (The Afterword to the *Kōyō Gunkan,* 1647), in Ishioka, ed., *Kōshūryū heihō, Nihon heihō zenshū,* vol. 1, p. 186.

13. Many writings of the Kōshū school mention this six-stage training. Two examples are Hattori Naokage's *Kangu no maki* (1658?) and Nagano Naoteru's *Heihō hiden bimyō zenshūsetsu* (A Comprehensive Explanation of the Mystery of the *Heihō Hiden,* 1763). See Ishioka, ed., *Kōshūryū heihō, Nihon heihō zenshū,* vol. 1, pp. 340–348.

14. Takayama Kentei, *Nihonden chiran yōketsu* (The Essence of Politics in the *Nihon Shoki,* 1753), in Ishioka Hisao, ed., *Echigo-ryū heihō, Nihon heihō zenshū,* vol. 2 (Tokyo: Jimbutsu ōraisha, 1967), p. 199.

15. Usami Yoshikata, *Bukei yōryaku* (The Essence of Military Classics, 1740), in ibid., p. 350.

16. Satō Kinji, *Nihon bugakushi* (Tokyo: Taitō shokan, 1942), p. 39.

17. Hōjō Ujinaga, *Shikanshō* (A Commentary on My Teacher's Lectures, 1635), in Ishioka Hisao, ed., *Hōjō-ryū heihō, Nihon heihō zenshū,* vol. 3 (Tokyo: Jimbutsu ōraisha, 1967), p. 41.

18. Matsumiya Kanzan, *Dokanyōhō chokushi shō* (A Commentary on the *Dokanyōhō*), in Kokumin seishin bunka kenkyūjo, ed., *Matsumiya Kanzan shū,* vol. 3 (Tokyo: Kokumin seishin bunka kenkyūjo, 1937), p. 239.

19. Ibid., p. 136.

20. Ibid., pp. 125–127.

21. Matsumiya Kanzan, *Taiseiden kōketsu ōhi,* in Hisao, ed., *Hōjō-ryū heihō, Nihon heihō zenshū,* vol. 3, p. 261.

22. However, the teachings of the Naga'numa school were not free from the influence of *gunbai shisō.* For example, the army regulations set out by Naga'-numa included the clauses "Those that send troops during the day of misfortune will be punished later"and "Military masters prefer *yin* to *yang* [in movement]. Therefore, right is first and left is after." See Ishioka Hisao, ed., *Naga'numa-ryū heihō, Nihon heihō zenshū,* vol. 4 (Tokyo: Jimbutsu ōraisha, 1967), pp. 135, 219.

23. Naga'numa Sensai, *Heiyōroku* (Records of Essential Military Matters, 1666), in ibid., p. 55.

24. Ibid., p. 54.

25. Ibid., p. 311.

26. Yamaga Sokō, *Heihō ōgi kōroku* (Lectures on the Mystery of Tactics, 1651), in Saigusa Hiroto, ed., *Shūkyōron, heihōbujutsuron, Nihon tetsugaku zensho,* vol. 12 (Tokyo: Daiichi shobō, 1935), pp. 239–241.

27. Yamaga Sokō, *Bukyō zensho* (An Anthology of Military Education, 1656), in Ishioka Hisao, ed., *Yamaga-ryū heihō, Nihon heihō zenshū,* vol. 5 (Tokyo: Jimbutsu ōraisha, 1967), p. 253.

28. Yamaga Sokō, *Bukyō honron* (The Essential Lecture on Military Education, 1656), quoted in Satō Kinji, *Nihon bugakushi* (Tokyo: Taitō shokan, 1942), p. 580.

29. Yamaga Sokō, *Chūchō jijitsu* (The True Facts Concerning the Central Kingdom, 1681), quoted in Satō, *Nihon bugakushi,* p. 582.

30. Yamaga, *Heihō ōgi kōroku*, in Saigusa, ed., *Shūkyōron, heihōbujutsuron, Nihon tetsugaku zensho*, vol. 12, p. 316. Bitō Jishū (1745–1813) also stressed the military implications of this hexagram. See Rai Tsutomu, ed., *Sorai gakuha, Nihon shisō taikei*, vol. 37 (Tokyo: Iwanami shoten, 1972), p. 273.

31. Yamaga Sokō, *Heihō jinmu yūbishū* (A Collection of the Jimmu Tactics), in Hirose Yutaka, ed., *Yamaga Sokō zenshū*, vol. 1 (Tokyo: Iwanami shoten, 1942), p. 579.

32. Iga Fūzan, *Keiken teiyō* (The Essential of the Power of the Military Classics, 1670), in Ishioka Isao, ed., *Shoryū heihō*, part 2, *Nihon heihō zenshū*, vol. 7 (Tokyo: Jimbutsu ōraisha, 1967), p. 215.

33. Ibid., p. 162.

34. Ibid., p. 150.

35. The six major forms of martial arts in the Tokugawa period were fencing, archery, *jūjutsu*, spear-fighting, horsemanship, and gunnery.

36. Quoted in Suzuki Daisetsu, *Zen and Japanese Culture* (Princeton, N.J.: Princeton University Press, 1973), pp. 433–434.

37. Yagyū Mune'nori, *Heihō kadensho* (Book of Family Tradition in Military Arts, 1632), in Imamura Yoshio, ed., *Kenjutsu*, part 1, *Nihon budō zenshū*, vol. 1 (Tokyo: Jimbutsu ōraisha, 1966), pp. 63–64.

38. For details of this ritual, see Marume Nagayoshi, *Kenjutsu taiisha-ryū kaden yōkyoku* (The Essence of Family Transmission of Fencing of the Taisha School), in Imamura, ed., *Kenjutsu*, part 1, *Nihon budō zenshū*, vol. 1, pp. 218–219.

39. See Tōgō Shigei, *Shigen-ryū heihōsho* (Martial Arts of the Shigen School), in Imamura Yoshio, ed., *Ken, Nihon budō taikei*, vol. 3 (Kyoto: Tōhōsha, 1982), pp. 87–88.

40. Ibid., p. 120.

41. Imamura Yoshio, ed., *Kenjutsu*, part 2, *Nihon budō zenshū*, vol. 2 (Tokyo: Jimbutsu ōraisha, 1966), p. 403.

42. Yamanouchi Naokazu, *Heijō muteki sho*, in Imamaura, ed., *Ken, Nihon budō taikei*, vol. 3, p. 401.

43. Ishioka Hisao, ed., *Kyūjutsu, Nihon budō taikei*, vol. 4 (Kyoto: Tōhōsha, 1982), p. 280.

44. Imamura Yoshio, ed., *Kyūjutsu, bajutsu, Nihon budō zenshū*, vol. 3 (Tokyo: Jimbutsu ōraisha, 1966), pp. 379–387.

45. Ishioka, ed., *Kyūjutsu, Nihon budō taikei*, vol. 4, p. 349.

46. Ibid., p. 350.

47. Imamura, ed., *Kyūjutsu, bajutsu, Nihon budō zenshū*, vol. 3, p. 63.

48. Imamura Yoshio, ed., *Jūjutsu, karate, kempō, aikijutsu, Nihon budō zenshū*, vol. 5 (Tokyo: Jimbutsu ōraisha, 1966), p. 18.

49. Tashiro Tokihide, *Jūjutsu taisei roku*, in Oimatsu Shin'ichi, ed., *Jūjutsu, aikijutsu, Nihon budō taikei*, vol. 6 (Kyoto: Tōhōsha, 1982), pp. 336–337.

50. Ōshima Yoshitsuna, *Unheiryūchūdō* (The Central Philosophy of the Unhei School), in Shimada Teiichi, ed., *Sōjutsu, naginatajutsu, bōjutsu, kusarigamajutsu, shurikenjutsu, Nihon budō taikei*, vol. 7 (Kyoto: Tōhōsha, 1982), p. 128.

51. Utsumi Shigemune, *Rōsōron* (Discourse on Spear-Fighting, 1841), in ibid., p. 298.

52. Fujibayashi Yasutake, *Bansen shūkai*, in Imamura Yoshio, ed., *Hōjutsu, suijutsu, ninjutsu, Nihon budō zenshū*, vol. 4 (Tokyo: Jimbutsu ōraisha, 1966), p. 444.

53. Ibid., p. 423.

54. Hayashi Ranzan, *Gunji daisetsu* (A Brief Discussion of Military Matters, 1619), in Ueki Naoichirō, ed., *Bushidō zensho*, vol. 2 (Tokyo: Jidaisha, 1942), p. 34.

55. Matsunaga Sekigo, *Irinshō*, in Ishida Ichirō and Kanaya Osamu, eds., *Fujiwara Seika, Hayashi Razan, Nihon shisō taikei*, vol. 28 (Tokyo: Iwanami shoten, 1975), p. 325.

56. Nakae Tōju, *Okina mondō*, in Yamashita Yū and Bitō Masahide, eds., *Nakae Tōju, Nihon shisō taikei*, vol. 29 (Tokyo: Iwanami shoten, 1974), p. 63.

57. Asami Keisai, *Satsuroku*, in Nishi Junzō and Maruyama Masao, eds., *Yamazaki Ansai gakuha, Nihon shisō taikei*, vol. 31 (Tokyo: Iwanami shoten, 1980), pp. 356–358.

58. Kaibara Ekken, *Bunbukun* (Lectures on Literary and Military Matters), in Imamura Yoshio, ed., *Bugei zuihitsu, Nihon budō taikei*, vol. 9 (Kyoto: Tōhōsha, 1982), p. 25.

59. See Yamaga Sokō, *Yamaga gorui*, in Hirose Yutaka, ed., *Yamaga Sokō zenshū*, vol. 10 (Tokyo: Iwanami shoten, 1941), p. 381.

60. Minamoto Taneoki, *Jikaku meigikai* (An Explanations of Terms Used in the Jikaku School), in Imamura Yoshio, ed., *Hōjutsu, suijutsu, ninjutsu, Nihon budō zenshū*, vol. 4 (Tokyo: Jimbutsu ōraisha, 1966), p. 105.

61. Inoue Shimokage, *Chōsekishū*, in Tokoro Sōkichi, ed., *Hōjutsu, suijutsu, ninjutsu, bajutsu, Nihon budō taikei*, vol. 5 (Kyoto: Tōhōsha, 1982), p. 65.

62. Mishima Bokushū, *Morishige-ryū hōjutsu sanshukan* (On the Three Kinds of Artillery Technique of the Morishige School), quoted in Nishizawa Yūshichi, *Nihon kajutsu yakuhō no maki* (Tokyo: Tōgakusha, 1935), pp. 15–16.

63. In Shinano kyōikukai, ed., *Shōzan zenshū*, vol. 1 (Nagano: Shinano kyōikukai shuppanbu, 1975), p. 4.

64. This illustration is modified from Maeno Kiyoji, *Sakuma Shōzan saikō* (Naganoshi: Ginka shobō, 1977), p. 114.

65. In a letter to a friend in 1837, Sakuma declared that *wu-hsing* theory was "clearly compatible" with Western learning.

66. Shinano kyōikukai, ed., *Shōzan zenshū*, vol. 1, p. 4.

67. For example, Nakayama Shigeru remarks: "Japanese military strategists in warlike ages frequently used the *I Ching* in making crucial decisions. In peacetime under the Tokugawa regime, the book gradually lost its importance and became a handbook for unemployed samurai, who told individual fortunes." In Nakayama, *A History of Japanese Astronomy* (Cambridge, Mass.: Harvard University Press, 1969), pp. 58–59.

Chapter 11: The *I Ching* and Popular Culture

1. Western works on Tokugawa culture can be classified into two major categories—general histories and literary studies. Two useful textbooks in the first category are G. Sansom, *Japan: A Short Cultural History* (Stanford, Calif.: Stanford University Press, 1977), chapter 7, and Paul Varley, *Japanese Culture: A Short History* (Honolulu: University of Hawai'i Press, 1984), chapter 7. See also Donald Shively, "Popular Culture," in John Hall, ed., *Cambridge History of Japan* (Cam-

bridge: Cambridge University Press, 1991), vol. 4. Within literary studies, introductory narratives can be found in Donald Keene, *World Within Walls* (New York: Holt, Rinehart & Winston, 1977) and Howard Hibbett, *The Floating World in Japanese Fiction* (Cambridge: Oxford University Press, 1959). Many important *ukiyo-zōshi* have been translated into English. *Kabuki, jōruri,* and *ukiyoe* (woodblock prints of the daily life of the people) have also drawn some academic attention. Chinese influence on Tokugawa art and culture is little studied. Two useful references are Peter Nosco, ed., *Confucianism and Tokugawa Culture* (Princeton, N.J.: Princeton University Press, 1984) and Marius B. Jansen, *China in the Tokugawa World* (Cambridge, Mass.: Harvard University Press, 1992). See also David Pollack, "The Intellectual Contexts of Tokugawa Aesthetics," in Pollack, *The Fracture of Meaning* (Princeton, N.J.: Princeton University Press, 1986), pp. 185–226, and Stephen Addis, ed., *Japanese Quest for a New Vision: The Impact of Visiting Chinese Painters, 1600–1900* (Kansas City: University of Kansas Press, 1986).

2. For a comparative reference on the impact of the *I Ching* on Ch'ing culture, see Richard Smith, *China's Cultural Heritage: The Ch'ing Dynasty, 1644–1912* (Boulder, Colo.: Westview Press, 1983), chapters 5 to 8, pp. 80–189.

3. It is well known that Lu was an orphan who did not know his own name. When he grew up, he became familiar with the *I Ching,* and used it to find his name.

4. Modified from Jennifer L. Anderson, *An Introduction to Japanese Tea Ritual* (Albany: State University of New York Press, 1991), p. 55.

5. Nambō Sōkei, *Nampō roku,* in Sen no Sōshitsu, ed., *Chadō koten zenshū,* vol. 4 (Kyoto: Tankō shinsha, 1964), p. 212.

6. Ibid., p. 216.

7. Ibid., pp. 198–210.

8. In Sen no Sōshitsu, ed., *Chadō koten zenshū,* vol. 3 (Kyoto: Tankō shinsha, 1957), p. 471.

9. Rand Castile, *The Way of Tea* (New York: Weatherhill, 1971), p. 123.

10. For details on the relationship between the *I Ching* and the geomancy of the tearoom, see Anderson, *An Introduction to Japanese Tea Ritual,* pp. 161–162, 257.

11. Yasui Kōzan, *Seiza no bunka* (Tokyo: Satsuki shobō, 1987), p. 79.

12. Herbert E. Plutchow, *Historical chanoyu* (Tokyo: Japan Times, 1986), p. 30.

13. Yasui, *Seiza no bunka,* pp. 82–83.

14. Sue Munehiro, *Chajin no kenkyū* (Tokyo: Shibunkaku, 1981), p. 92.

15. For details on the relationship between the *yin-yang wu-hsing* doctrine and *kakemono,* see Tanaka Senō, *Cha no bi* (Tokyo: Asahi sononama, 1976), pp. 50–57. *Kanewari* framing, created during the Momoyama period, became prevalent in the Tokugawa period.

16. Ibid., p. 57.

17. Zoku kadō kosho shūsei kankōkai, ed., *Zoku kadō kosho shūsei,* vol. 2 (Kyoto: Shibunkaku, 1972), p. 421.

18. Ibid., vol. 4 , p. 321.

19. Ibid., vol. 4, pp. 424–425.

20. Ibid., vol. 4, p. 322.

21. Ibid., vol. 3, p. 105.

22. Ibid., vol. 1, pp. 66–67.

23. Ibid., vol. 1, pp. 210, 213, 215.

24. Ibid., vol. 3, p. 407.

25. Ibid., vol. 3, p. 412.

26. Ibid., vol. 3, p. 384.

27. Thomas Rimer and Yamazaki Masakazu, trans., *On the Art of the Nō Drama: The Major Treatise of Zeami* (Princeton, N.J.: Princeton University Press, 1984), pp. 19–20. The original text can be found in Nogami Toyoichirō, ed., *Fūshikaden* (Tokyo: Iwanami shoten, 1991), pp. 41–42.

28. Rimer and Yamazaki, trans., *On the Art of the Nō Drama*, pp. 126–127.

29. Ibid., p. 133.

30. See Geinōshi kenkyūkai, ed., *Kabuki, Nihon shomin bunka shiryō shūsei*, vol. 6 (Tokyo: San'ichi shobō, 1973), p. 113.

31. Ibid., p. 107.

32. Ibid., p. 115.

33. See Nishiyama Matsunosuke et al., eds., *Kinsei geidōron, Nihon shisō taikei*, vol. 61 (Tokyo: Iwanami shoten, 1972), pp. 409, 414.

34. See Geinōshi kenkyūkai, ed., *Ningyō jōruri, Nihon shomin bunka shiryō shūsei*, vol. 7 (Tokyo: San'ichi shobō, 1974), p. 57.

35. Ibid., p. 29.

36. Ibid.

37. Ibid., p. 30.

38. Ibid., p. 213.

39. Ibid.

40. Ibid., p. 228.

41. Ibid., p. 227.

42. See Geinōshi kenkyūkai, ed., *Sūki, Nihon shomin bunka shiryō shūsei*, vol. 10 (Tokyo: San'ichi shobō, 1976), p. 406.

43. Ibid.

44. Ibid., pp. 390–391.

45. Ibid., p. 403.

46. Ibid., p. 443.

47. Ibid., p. 506.

48. In Hayashi Razan, *Hōtei shoroku*, in Nihon zuihitsu taisei henshūbu, ed., *Nihon zuihitsu taisei*, series 1, vol. 23 (Tokyo: Yoshikawa kōbunkan, 1976), p. 337.

49. Geinōshi kenkyūkai, ed., *Sūki, Nihon shomin bunka shiryō shūsei*, vol. 10, p. 557.

50. Ibid.

51. Tamiya Nakanobu, *Tōyūshi*, in Nihon zuihitsu taisei henshūbu, ed., *Nihon zuihitsu taisei*, series 1, vol. 19 (Tokyo: Yoshikawa kōbunkan, 1976), p. 191.

52. Kaibara Ekken, *Gojōkun*, in Inoue Tetsujirō, ed., *Nihon rinri ihen, Shushigaku no bu*, part 2, vol. 8 (Tokyo: Ikuseikai, 1902), p. 309.

53. See Kumazawa Banzan, *Shūgi gaisho* (1709), in Shintō taikei hensankai, ed., *Shintō taikei, ronsetsuhen*, vol. 21, *Kumazawa Banzan* (Tokyo: Shintō taikei hensankai, 1992), p. 402. Regarding fifty as the number of the universe, the *I Ching* also suggests using fifty yarrow stalks for divination.

54. See Andō Shōeki, *Shizen shineidō,* in Bitō Masahide, ed., *Nihon shisō taikei,* vol. 45, *Andō Shōeki, Satō Nobuhiro* (Tokyo: Iwanami shoten, 1977), p. 138.

55. Tamiya Nakanobu, *Tōyūshi,* in Nihon zuihitsu taisei henshūbu, ed., *Nihon zuihitsu taisei,* series 1, vol. 19, p. 136.

56. *Ukiyo zōshi* (prose about the life of townsmen) was a new genre of fiction. Its relationship with the *I Ching* was not close. However, we can use this genre as a source to understand the impact of the *I Ching* on the daily life of commoners. It is interesting to note that the *wu-hsing* theory was applied in many *ukiyo zōshi* to describe erotic human relationships. Human characters were classified according to *wu-hsing.* For example, Ihara Saikaku (1642–1693), in his famous *Kōshoku ichidai otoko* (The Erotic Life of a Man, 1682), described playboys as follows: "Their love is like a fortune-telling book. At the beginning it is good and later it is bad. These men have the attribute of the agent of metal." There are many superstitions recorded in *ukiyo zōshi.* For examples, the *Joyō chie kanhōshiki* (Records of Woman's Wisdom, 1769, author unknown) emphasizes the importance of matching the *wu-hsing* of a couple before marriage, a common practice in East Asia: "If the man is wood and the female is fire, they will have five children. At the beginning, they will have a hard time, but later [their situation] will improve. They will enjoy longevity. . . . If the man is water and the female is earth, this matching is very bad. They will have four children. They will be very poor and have a hard time. Nothing can be achieved." The *Nagesen seirō sen* (The Divination of the Pleasure Quarter by Throwing Money, 1774, by Kinhi Razanjin) describes how people used the money-throwing method to acquire a hexagram to predict the relationship between courtesans and their patrons. All these examples indicate that *I Ching* divination was omnipresent in Tokugawa life. See Takao Kazuhiko, *Kinsei no shomin bunka* (Tokyo: Iwanami shoten, 1968), pp. 296–304.

Chapter 12: Epilogue

1. Nosco, Peter, "Rethinking Tokugawa Thought," in Adriana Boscaro et al., eds., *Rethinking Japan,* vol. 2 (Sandgate, England: Japan Library Limited, 1987), pp. 304–312.

2. There are very few studies on the history of the commentary and influence of Confucian, Buddhist, and Shinto texts in Tokugawa Japan. They include Peter Nosco, "*Manyōshū* Studies in Tokugawa Japan," *Transactions of the Asiatic Society of Japan,* fourth series (1986), no. 1, pp. 109–146; Minamoto Ryōen, *Edo no Jugaku: Daigaku juyō no rekishi* (Tokyo: Shibunkaku, 1988); and Ōe Fumiki, *Honpō Shisho kunten narabi ni chūshakushi teki kenkyū* (Tokyo: Seki shoin, 1935).

3. See Samuel Yamashita, "Reading the New Tokugawa Intellectual Histories," *Journal of Japanese Studies* 22, 1 (1996):1–48.

4. There are several Japanese articles on the history of the *I Ching* in Japan. For a historical overview, see Wajima Yoshio, "Chūsei ni okeru *Shūeki* no kenkyū ni tsuite," *Kōbe jogakuin daigaku ronshū* 5, 1 (Kobe, 1958):1–26. Imai Usaburōo provides a fine account in the "preface" of Imai, trans., *Ekikyō* (Tokyo: Meiji tosho shuppansha, 1987). Murakami Masataka studies the punctuation of some early Tokugawa commentaries in "Kinsei ekigaku juyōshi ni okeru Gahōten *Ekikyō hongi* no igi," *Bungei kenkyū* (Sendai, 1982), no. 100:79–88, and in "Bunshi Genshō to *Shūeki dengi taizen,*" *Nihon bunka kenkyūjo kenkyū hōkoku* (Sendai, 1989),

no. 25:19–60. See also Hama Hisao, "Itō Tōgai no ekigaku" (Tokyo, 1989), no. 90:1–31. A number of articles on divination can be found in *Ekikyō kenkyū* (Tokyo, 1958–1983).

5. For representative English and Japanese works on Sino-Japanese cultural and intellectual relations during the Tokugawa period, see "Bibliographical Note," in Marius B. Jansen, *China in the Tokugawa World* (Cambridge, Mass.: Harvard University Press, 1992), pp. 128–129.

6. The best scholarship is presented in Kate Nakai, "The Nationalization of Confucianism in Tokugawa Japan: The Problem of Sinocentrism," *Harvard Journal of Asiatic Studies* 40, 1 (June 1980):157–199, and Harry Harootunian, "The Functions of China in Tokugawa Thought," in Akira Iriye, ed., *The Chinese and the Japanese* (Princeton, N.J.: Princeton University Press, 1980), pp. 9–36.

Bibliography

This bibliography only lists the works cited in the main text.

Abe Akio, "Juka Shintō to kokugaku," in Abe Akio and Taira Shigemichi, eds., *Kinsei Shintōron, zenki kokugaku, Nihon shisō taikei,* vol. 39 (Tokyo: Iwanami shoten, 1972).

Abe Yoshio, *Nihon no Shushigaku to Chōsen* (Tokyo: Tōkyō daigaku shuppankai, 1965).

Ackroyd, Joyce, trans., *Lessons from History: The Tokushi Yoron by Arai Hakuseki* (St. Lucia: University of Queensland Press, 1982).

———, *Told Round a Brushwood Fire: The Autobiography of Arai Hakuseki* (Princeton, N.J.: Princeton University Press, 1976).

Addis, Stephen, ed., *Japanese Quest for a New Vision* (Kansas City: University of Kansas Press, 1986).

Aizawa Seishisai, *Kagaku igen,* in Saigusa Hiroto, ed., *Kokugaku hen, Nihon tetsugaku zensho,* vol. 5 (Tokyo: Daiichi shobō, 1935).

———, *Shinron,* in Saigusa Hiroto, ed., *Kokugaku hen, Nihon tetsugaku zensho,* vol. 5 (Tokyo: Daiichi shobō, 1935).

———, *Toku Naobi no mitama,* in Takasu Yoshijirō, ed., *Aizawa Seishisai shū, Mitogaku taikei,* vol. 2 (Tokyo: Ida shoten, 1941).

Amano Sadakage, *Shioshiri,* in Nihon zuihitsu taisei henshūbu, ed., *Nihon zuihitsu taisei,* series 3, vol. 13 (Tokyo: Yoshikawa kōbunkan, 1976).

Anderson, Jennifer L., *An Introduction to Japanese Tea Ritual* (Albany: State University of New York Press, 1991).

Andō Shōeki, *Shizen shineidō,* in Bitō Masahide, ed., *Andō Shōeki, Satō Nobuhiro, Nihon shisō taikei,* vol. 45 (Tokyo: Iwanami shoten, 1977).

Arai Hakuseki, *Kishinron,* in Saigusa Hiroto, ed., *Shūkyō ron, heihō bujutsu ron, Nihon tetsugaku zensho,* vol. 12 (Tokyo: Daiichi shobō, 1936).

Araki Kengo, ed., *Kaibara Ekken, Muro Kyūsō, Nihon shisō taikei,* vol. 34 (Tokyo: Iwanami shoten, 1970).

Asami Keisai, *Satsuroku*, in Nishi Junzō and Maruyama Masao, eds., *Yamazaki Ansai gakuha, Nihon shisō taikei*, vol. 31 (Tokyo: Iwanami shoten, 1980).

Ashikaga Enjutsu, *Kamakura Muromachi jidai no Jukyō* (Tokyo: Nihon koten zensho, 1932).

Atobe Yoshiaki, *Suikaō shinsetsu*, in Ishida Ichirō, ed., *Shintō shisō shū, Nihon no shisō*, vol. 14 (Tokyo: Chikuma shobō, 1970).

Baba Nobutake, *Shosetsu bendan*, in Nagasawa Kikuya, ed., *Nihon zuihitsu shūsei*, vol. 2 (Tokyo: Kyūko shoin, 1978).

Bellah, Robert, *Tokugawa Religion* (New York: The Free Press, 1957).

Borgen, Robert, *Sugawara no Michizane and the Early Heian Court* (Cambridge, Mass.: Harvard University Press, 1986).

Boxer, Charles, *The Christian Century in Japan, 1549–1650* (Berkeley and Los Angeles: University of California Press, 1951).

———, "Some Aspects of Portuguese Influence in Japan, 1542–1640," in Michael Moscato, ed., *Papers on Portuguese, Dutch and Jesuit Influences in Sixteenth- and Seventeenth-Century Japan* (Washington, D.C.: University Publications of America, Inc., 1979).

Butler, Lee, "Court and Bakufu in Early Seventeenth-Century Japan" (Ph.D. dissertation, Princeton University, 1991).

———, "The Way of Yin and Yang: A Tradition Revived, Sold, Adopted," *Monumenta Nipponica* 51, 2 (1996):189–217.

Buyō Inshi, *Seiji kenbunroku*, in Naramoto Tatsuya and Kimugasa Yasuki, eds., *Edo jidai no shisō* (Tokyo: Tokuma shoten, 1966).

Castile, Rand, *The Way of Tea* (New York: Weatherhill, 1971).

Chang En-ch'in, ed., *Basic Theory of Traditional Chinese Medicine*, vol. 1 (Shanghai: Publishing House of Shanghai College of Traditional Chinese Medicine, 1989).

Cheng Liang-sheng, *Yüan-Ming shih-tai tung-chuan Jih-pen ti wen-hsien* (Taipei: Wen-shih-che ch'u-pan-she, 1984).

Chu Ch'ien-chih, *Jih-pen ti ku-hsüeh yü Yang-ming hsüeh* (Shanghai: Jen-min sh'u-pen-she, 1962).

Chūmoku Gikai, *Shōsō manhitsu*, in Nagasawa Kikuya, ed., *Nihon zuihitsu shūsei*, vol. 3 (Tokyo: Kyūko shoin, 1978).

Chu Wen-kuan and Wallace Sherill, *An Anthology of I Ching* (London: Arkana, 1977).

Collcutt, Martin, "The Legacy of Confucianism in Japan," in Gilbert Rozman, ed., *The East Asian Region: Confucian Heritage and Its Modern Adaptation* (Princeton, N.J.: Princeton University Press, 1991).

Craig, Albert, "Science and Confucianism in Tokugawa Japan," in Marius Jansen, ed., *Changing Japanese Attitudes Toward Modernization* (Princeton, N.J.: Princeton University Press, 1965).

Date Chihiro, *Taisei santenkō*, in Maruyama Masao, ed., *Rekishi shisō shū, Nihon no shisō*, vol. 6 (Tokyo: Chikuma shobō, 1972).

Dazai Shundai, *Bendōsho*, in Inoue Tetsujirō, ed., *Nihon rinri ihen*, vol. 6, *Kogakuha no bu*, part 2 (Tokyo: Ikuseikai, 1902).

———, *Sekihi*, in Rai Tsutomu, ed., *Sorai gakuha, Nihon shisō taikei*, vol. 37 (Tokyo: Iwanami shoten, 1972).

Denki gakkai, ed., *Yamazaki Ansai to sono monryū* (Tokyo: Meiji shobō, 1933).

Dore, R. P., *Education in Tokugawa Japan* (London: The Athlone Press, 1965).

Dower, John, "Japan and the Uses of History," in Dower, ed., *Origins of the Modern Japanese State* (New York: Pantheon Books, 1975).

Earl, David M., *Emperor and Nation in Japan* (Seattle: University of Washington Press, 1964).

Eliot, Charles, *Japanese Buddhism* (London: Edward Arnold & Co., 1935).

Fujibayashi Yasutake, *Bansen shūkai*, in Imamura Yoshio, ed., *Hōjutsu, suijutsu, ninjutsu, Nihon budō zenshū*, vol. 4 (Tokyo: Jimbutsu ōraisha, 1966).

Fujii Sadafumi, *Edo kokugaku tensei shi no kenkyū* (Tokyo: Yoshikawa kōbunkan, 1987).

Fujikawa Yū, *Nihon igakushi kōyō* (Tokyo: Heibonsha, 1974).

Fujita Tōko, *Hitachi obi*, in Fukuda Kōjirō, ed., *Mitogaku, Shintō taikei, ronsetsu hen*, vol. 15 (Tokyo: Shintō taikei hensankai, 1986).

Fujiwara Seika, "Baison saihitsu," in Nihon zuihitsu taisei henshūbu, ed., *Nihon zuihitsu taisei*, vol. 1 (Tokyo: Yoshikawa kōbunkan, 1975).

Fujūzai Chikushin, *Genryū chawa*, in Sen no Sōshitsu, ed., *Chadō koten zenshū*, vol. 4 (Kyoto: Tankō shinsha, 1964).

Fukui Tamotsu, *Edo bakufu kankōbutsu* (Tokyo: Yūshōdō, 1985).

Furukawa Tetsushi, ed., *Kinsei no shisō, Nihon shisōshi kōza*, vol. 4 (Tokyo: Yūzankaku, 1977).

Furushima Toshio, ed., *Nōsho no jidai* (Tokyo: Nōzan gyōson bunka kyōkai, 1980).

Furushima Toshio and Aki Kōichi, eds., *Kinsei kagaku shisō*, part 1, *Nihon shisō taikei*, vol. 62 (Tokyo: Iwanami shoten, 1972).

Furuta Kazuhiro, "Shoki Chūgoku Bukkyō ni okeru gōron," in Kumoi Shōzen, ed., *Gō shisō kenkyū* (Kyoto: Heirakuji shoten, 1979).

Geinōshi kenkyūkai, ed., *Ningyō jōruri, Nihon shomin bunka shiryō shūsei*, vol. 7 (Tokyo: San'ichi shobō, 1974).

———, *Suki, Nihon shomin bunka shiryō shūsei*, vol. 10 (Tokyo: San'ichi shobō, 1976).

Gidayūbuji Nemotodayū, *Jōruri hidenshō*, in Geinōshi kenkyūkai, ed., *Ningyō jōruri, Nihon shomin bunka shiryō shūsei*, vol. 7 (Tokyo: San'ichi shobō, 1974).

Goodman, Grant, *The Dutch Experience* (London: Athlone Press, 1986).

———, *The Dutch Impact on Japan* (Leiden: Brill, 1967).

Gotō Konzan, *Shisetsu hikki*, in Hirose Hideo, Nakayama Shigeru, and Ōtsuka Yoshinori, eds., *Kinsei kagaku shisō*, part 2, *Nihon shisō taikei*, vol. 63 (Tokyo: Iwanami shoten, 1971).

Haga Kōshirō, *Chūsei Zenrin no kakumon oyobi bungaku ni kansuru kenkyū* (Tokyo: Maruzen shoten, 1956).

Hall, John, "Changing Conceptions of the Modernization of Japan," in Marius Jansen, ed., *Changing Japanese Attitudes Toward Modernization* (Princeton, N.J.: Princeton University Press, 1965).

———, *Tanuma Okitsugu, 1719–1788: Forerunner of Modern Japan* (Westport, Conn.: Greenwood Press, 1982).

Hama Hisao, "Itō Tōgai no ekigaku," *Tōyō kenkyū* (Tokyo: Daitō bunka daigaku tōyō kenkyūjo, 1989), no. 90.

Hara Sōkei, *Katei kidan*, in Nihon zuihitsu taisei henshūbu, ed., *Nihon zuihitsu taisei*, series 1, vol. 9 (Tokyo: Yoshikawa kōbunkan, 1975).

Hardacre, Helen, "Creating State Shintō: The Great Promulgation Campaign and the New Religions," *Journal of Japanese Studies* 12, 1 (Winter 1986).

———, *Shintō and the State, 1868–1988* (Princeton, N.J.: Princeton University Press, 1989).

Harootunian, Harry, "The Functions of China in Tokugawa Thought," in Akira Iriye, ed., *The Chinese and the Japanese* (Princeton, N.J.: Princeton University Press, 1980).

———, *Things Seen and Unseen: Discourse and Ideology in Tokugawa Nativism* (Chicago: University of Chicago Press, 1988).

———, *Toward Restoration* (Berkeley and Los Angeles: University of California Press, 1970).

Hashimoto Sōkichi, *Oranda shisei erekiteru kyūrigen*, in Saigusa Hiroto, ed., *Rigaku, Nihon kagaku koten zensho*, vol. 6 (Tokyo: Asahi shimbunsha, 1978).

Hatanaka Tachū, *Kashokuron*, in Takimoto Seiichi, ed., *Nihon keizai sōsho*, vol. 11 (Tokyo: Nihon keizai sōsho kankōkai, 1915).

Hattori Naokage, *Kangu no maki*, in Ishioka Hisao, ed., *Kōshū-ryū heihō, Nihon heihō zenshū*, vol. 1 (Tokyo: Jimbutsu ōraisha, 1967).

Hattori Toshirō, *Edo jidai igakushi no kenkyū* (Tokyo: Yoshikawa kōbunkan, 1978).

———, *Nihonshi shōhyakka*, vol. 20, *Igaku* (Tokyo: Kondō shuppansha, 1985).

Hayakawa Hachirō, *Kyūsei jōkyō*, in Nagayama Usaburō, ed., *Hayakawa daikan* (Okayama City: Okayamaken kyōikukai, 1929).

Hayashi Razan, *Gunji daisetsu*, in Ueki Naoichirō, ed., *Bushidō zensho*, vol. 2 (Tokyo: Jidaisha, 1942).

———, *Hōtei shoroku*, in Nihon zuihitsu taisei henshūbu, ed., *Nihon zuihitsu taisei*, series 1, vol. 23 (Tokyo: Yoshikawa kōbunkan, 1976).

———, *Shintō denju*, in Saigusa Hiroto, ed., *Shintō hen, Jukyō hen, Nihon tetsugaku zensho*, vol. 4 (Tokyo: Daiichi shobō, 1936).

———, *Shintō hiden setchū zokukai*, in Shintō taikei hensankai, ed., *Fujiwara Seika, Hayashi Razan, Shintō taikei, ronsetsu hen*, vol. 20 (Tokyo: Shintō taikei hensankai, 1988).

Hibbett, Howard, *The Floating World in Japanese Fiction* (New York: Oxford University Press, 1959).

Hirata Atsutane, *Taiko koekiden*, in Hirata Atsutane zenshū kankōkai, ed., *Hirata Atsutane zenshū*, vol. 6 (Tokyo: Hōbunkan, 1935).

Hirose Hideo, "Yōgaku toshite no tenmongaku," in Hirose, ed., *Yōgaku*, part 2, *Nihon shisō taikei*, vol. 65 (Tokyo: Iwanami shoten, 1972).

Hirose Tansō, *Ugen*, in Naramoto Tatsuya, ed., *Kinsei seidōron, Nihon shisō taikei*, vol. 38 (Tokyo: Iwanami shoten, 1976).

Hirose Yokusō, *Kyūkeisōdō zuihitsu*, in Mori Senzō and Kitagawa Hirokuni, eds., *Zoku Nihon zuihitsu taisei*, vol. 2 (Tokyo: Yoshikawa kōbunkan, 1979).

Hirose Yutaka, ed., *Yamaga Sokō zenshū, shisō hen*, vol. 9 (Tokyo: Iwanami shoten, 1941).

Ho Peng-yoke, "The System of the Book of Changes and Chinese Science," *Japanese Studies in the History of Science*, no. 11 (Tokyo, 1972):23–39.

Hōjō Ujinaga, *Shikanshō*, in Ishioka Hisao, ed., *Hōjō-ryū heihō, Nihon heihō zenshū*, vol. 3 (Tokyo: Jimbutsu ōraisha, 1967).

Honjō Eijirō, *Economic Theory and History of Japan in the Tokugawa Period* (New York: Russell & Russell, Inc., 1965).

Huang han i-hsüeh ts'ung-shu hui, ed., *I-an, i-hua, Huang-han i-hsüeh ts'ung-shu,* vol. 3 (Peking: P'ing-fang ch'u-pan-she, 1935).

———, *Nuko-hsüeh, erhko-hsüeh, Huang han i-hsüeh ts'ung-shu,* vol. 9 (Peking: P'ing-fang ch'u-pan-she, 1935).

Huang Tun-han, *I-hsüeh yü i-hsüeh chih tsung-ho yen-chiu* (Taipei: Palace Publishing, Co., 1979).

Huber, Thomas, *The Revolutionary Origins of Modern Japan* (Stanford, Calif.: Stanford University Press, 1981).

Ichihara Toyota, ed., *Munan, Shōju, Nihon no Zen goroku,* vol. 15 (Tokyo: Kōdansha, 1979).

Ichiraku, *Chikuhō koji,* in Geinōshi kenkyūkai, ed., *Ningyō jōruri, Nihon shomin bunka shiryō shūsei,* vol. 7 (Tokyo: San'ichi shobō, 1975).

Iga Fūzan, *Keiken teiyō,* in Ishioka Isao ed., Nihon heihō zenshū, vol. 7, shoryū heihō, part 2 (Tokyo: Jimbutsu ōraisha, 1967).

Ikuta Yorozu, *Koeki taishōkyō den,* in Haga Noberu, ed., *Ikuta Yorozu zenshū,* vol. 2 (Tokyo: Kyōiku shuppan senta, 1986).

———, *Taneki seigi,* in Haga Noberu, ed., *Ikuta Yorozu zenshū,* vol. 3 (Tokyo: Kyōiku shuppan senta, 1986).

Imai Atsushi and Ozawa Tomio, eds., *Nihon shisō ronsōshi* (Tokyo: Perikansha, 1979).

Imai Usaburō, ed., *Mitogaku, Nihon shisō taikei,* vol. 53 (Tokyo: Iwanami shoten, 1973).

———, trans., *Ekikyō* (Tokyo: Meiji tosho shuppansha, 1987).

Imaizumi Toshio, "*Eki* no batsu ga atarukoto," in Imaizumi, *Chūsei Nihon no shosō,* vol. 2 (Tokyo: Yoshikawa kōbunkan, 1989).

Imamura Yoshio, ed., *Jūjutsu, karate, kempō, aikijutsu, Nihon budō zenshū,* vol. 5 (Tokyo: Jimbutsu ōraisha, 1966).

———, *Kenjutsu,* part 2, *Nihon budō zenshū,* vol. 2 (Tokyo: Jimbutsu ōraisha, 1966).

———, *Kyūjutsu, bajutsu, Nihon budō zenshū,* vol. 3 (Tokyo: Jimbutsu ōraisha, 1966).

Inada, Kenneth K., "*I Ching* Metaphysics and Buddhist Introduction to China," Committee Appointed to Commemorate Professor Yūki's Retirement and Sixtieth Birthday, ed., *Bukkyō shisōshi ronshū* (Tokyo: Daizo shuppan, 1964).

Inkei Chidatsu, *Jubutsu gōron,* in Shūo Junkei, ed., *Nihon shisō tōsō shiryō,* vol. 1 (Tokyo: Tōhō shoin, 1931).

Inoue Kakushū, *Bokuzei kashoku kō,* in Nihon keizai sōsho kankōkai, ed., *Tsūzoku keizai bunko* (Tokyo: Nihon keizai sōsho kankōkai, 1917).

Inoue Shimokage, *Chōsekishū,* in Tokoro Sōkichi, ed., *Hōjutsu, suijutsu, ninjutsu, bajutsu, Nihon budō taikei,* vol. 5 (Kyoto: Tōhōsha, 1982).

Inoue Tetsujirō, ed., *Nihon kogakuha no tetsugaku* (Tokyo: Toyamabō, 1902).

———, *Nihon rinri ihen,* vol. 9, *Secchūgaka no bu* (Tokyo: Ikuseikai, 1903).

Ishioka Hisao, *Nihon heihō shi,* vol. 1 (Tokyo: Yūzankaku, 1972).

———, ed., *Kyūjutsu, Nihon budō taikei,* vol. 4 (Kyoto: Tōhōsha, 1982).

Isobe Ei'ichi, ed., *Nihon Yōmeigakusha goroku* (Tokyo: Tōa kenkyūkai, 1935).

Isobe Tadakata, *Shōcha wakumon,* in Geinōshi kenkyūkai, ed., *Sūki, Nihon shomin bunka shiryō shūsei,* vol. 10 (Tokyo: San'ichi shobō, 1976).

Itō Jinsai, *Dōjimon,* in Kaizuka Shigeki, ed., *Itō Jinsai, Nihon no meicho,* vol. 13 (Tokyo: Chūō kōronsha, 1972).

————, *Gomōjigi*, in Yoshikawa Kōjirō and Shimizu Shigeru, eds., *Itō Jinsai, Itō Tōgai, Nihon shisō taikei*, vol. 33 (Tokyo: Iwanami shoten, 1971).

Iyota Enshi, *Nihon nōgakusha hyōden* (Tokyo: Nihon tōsho senta, 1991).

Izumi Maku'ni, *Meidōsho*, in Haga Noboru and Matsumoto Sannosuke, eds., *Kokugaku undō no shisō, Nihon shisō taikei*, vol. 51 (Tokyo: Iwanami shoten, 1971).

Jansen, Marius B., *China in the Tokugawa World* (Cambridge, Mass.: Harvard University Press, 1992).

————, *Japan and Its World* (Princeton, N.J.: Princeton University Press, 1980).

————, *Sakamoto Ryōma and the Meiji Restoration* (Princeton, N.J.: Princeton University Press, 1961).

Jiun Sonja, *Jūzen hōgo*, in Nihon kyōkiu shisō taikei, ed., *Bukkyō kyōiku shisō*, part 3, *Nihon kyōiku shisō taikei*, vol. 17 (Tokyo: Nihon tōsho senta, 1980).

————, *Mudaishō*, in Imai Atsushi and Yamamoto Masao, eds., *Unden Shintō, Shintō taikei, ronsetsu hen*, vol. 14 (Tokyo: Shintō taikei hensankai, 1990).

————, *Shinju gūdan*, in Imai Atsushi and Yamamoto Masao, eds., *Unden Shintō, Shintō taikei, ronsetsu hen*, vol. 14 (Tokyo: Shintō taikei hensankai, 1990).

————, *Shintō kokka*, in Imai Atsushi and Yamamoto Masao, eds., *Unden Shintō, Shintō taikei, ronsetsu hen*, vol. 14 (Tokyo: Shintō taikei hensankai, 1990).

Jun, *Myō kōjin den*, in Kashiwabara Yūsen and Fujii Manabu, eds., *Kinsei Bukkyō no shisō, Nihon shisō taikei*, vol. 57 (Tokyo: Iwanami shoten, 1973).

Kaibara Ekken, *Bunbukun*, in Imamura Yoshio, ed., *Bugei zuihitsu, Nihon budō taikei*, vol. 9 (Kyoto: Tōhōsha, 1982).

————, *Gojōkun*, in Inoue Tetsujirō, ed., *Nihon rinri ihen, Shushigaku no bu*, part 2, vol 8 (Tokyo: Ikuseikai, 1902).

————, *Shinshiroku*, in Inoue Tetsujirō, ed., *Nihon rinri ihen, Shushigakuha no bu*, part 3, vol. 8 (Tokyo: Ikuseikai, 1902).

Kaihō Seiryō, *Keikodan*, in Kuranami Seiji, ed., *Kaihō Seiryō zenshū* (Tokyo: Yashiyo shuppansha, 1976).

Kamada Shigeo, *Hakuin, Nihon no Zen goroku*, vol. 19 (Tokyo: Kōdansha, 1977).

Kanazawa Kenkō, *Wakan senyōshū*, in Saigusa Hiroto, ed., *Kaijō kōtsū, Nihon kagaku koten zensho*, vol. 12 (Tokyo: Asahi shimbunsha, 1978).

Kano Masanao, ed., *Bakumatsu shisō shū, Nihon no shisō* (Tokyo: Chikuma shobō, 1969).

Kasamine Tachū, *Erikiteru zensho*, in Saigusa Hiroto, ed., *Edo kagaku koten sōsho*, vol. 11 (Tokyo: Kanwa shuppan, 1978).

Katō Taigaku, "Mase Chūshū no zeihō ni tsuite," *Ekikyō kenkyū* (Tokyo: Waseda University), 34 (April 1981):52–60.

Keene, Donald, *The Japanese Discovery of Europe* (Stanford, Calif.: Stanford University Press, 1969).

————, *World Within Walls* (New York: Holt, Rinehart & Winston, 1977).

Kitō Gennosuke, "Hirata Atsutane no zeihōkan," *Ekikyō kenkyū* (Tokyo: Waseda University), 21 (October 1968):7–12, and 21 (December 1968):5–10.

Kiyohara Sadao, *Kokugaku hattatsushi* (Tokyo: Unebi shobō, 1940).

Kiyooka Eiichi, trans., *The Antobiography of Yukichi Fukuzawa* (New York: Schocken Books, 1972).

Kō Shōga, *Chung-kuo i-chien hsüeh* (Hong Kong: Kwan tun Press, 1992).

Koji ruien kankōkai, ed., *Kojiruien, hōgibu*, vol. 7 (Tokyo: Kojiruien kankōkai, 1909).

Kondō Keigo, ed., *Suika Shintō*, part 1, *Shintō taikei, ronsetsu hen*, vol. 12 (Tokyo: Shintō taikei hensankai, 1984).

Ko'nishi Atsuyoshi, *Nōgyō yowa*, in Tanaka Kōji, ed., *Nōka gyōji, Nōgyō yowa, Nihon nōsho zenshū*, vol. 7 (Tokyo: Nōzan gyūson bunka kyōkai, 1979).

Kōno Yoshihiko, *Kinsei Onmyōdō no hensei to soshiki* (Tokyo: Yoshikawa kōbunkan, 1984).

Koschmann, Victor, *Mito Ideology: Discourse, Reform and Insurrection in Late Tokugawa Japan, 1790–1864* (Berkeley and Los Angeles: University of California Press, 1987).

Kumakura Isao, *Kan'ei bunka no kenkyū* (Tokyo: Yoshikawa kōbunkan, 1988).

Kumazawa Banzan, *Daigaku wakumon*, in Gotō Yōichi and Tomoeda Ryūtarō, eds., *Kumazawa Banzan, Nihon shisō taikei*, vol. 30 (Tokyo: Iwanami shoten, 1971).

————, *Eki keijiden shōkai*, in Masamune Atsuo, ed., *Kumazawa Banzan zenshū*, vol. 4 (Tokyo: Meicho shuppan, 1978).

————, *Keijijōden*, in Masamune Atsuo, ed., *Kumazawa Banzan zenshū*, vol. 4 (Tokyo: Meicho shuppan, 1978).

————, *Miwa mongatari*, in Saigusa Hiroto, ed., *Nihon tetsugaku zensho*, vol. 4 (Tokyo: Daiichi shobō, 1936).

————, *Shūgi gaisho*, in Inoue Tetsujirō, ed., *Nihon rinri ihen, Yōmeigaku no bu*, vol. 2, part 2 (Tokyo: Ikuseikai, 1903).

————, *Shūgi gaisho*, in Shintō taikei hensankai, ed., *Shintō taikei, ronshetsuhen*, vol. 21, *Kumazawa Banzan* (Tokyo: Shintō taikei hensankai, 1992).

————, *Shūgi washo*, in Gotō Yōichi and Tomoeda Ryūtarō, eds., *Kumazawa Banzan, Nihon shisō taikei*, vol. 30 (Tokyo: Iwanami shoten, 1971).

Kuroda Toshio, "Shinto in the History of Japanese Religion," *Journal of Japanese Studies* 7 (Winter 1981).

Kurosawa Motoshige, *Kōsan shihō yōroku*, in Saigusa Hiroto, ed., *Saihō, jikin*, part 2, *Nihon kagaku koten zensho*, vol. 10 (Tokyo: Asahi shimbunsha, 1978).

Kusama Naokata, *Sanka zui*, in Takimoto Seiichi, ed., *Nihon keizai sōsho*, vol. 28 (Tokyo: Nihon keizai sōsho kankōkai, 1916).

LaFleur, William R., *The Karma of Words: Buddhism and the Literary Arts in Medieval Japan* (Berkeley and Los Angeles: University of California Press, 1983).

Legge, James, trans., *The Yi King: Book of Changes* (Cambridge: Oxford University Press, 1882).

Levy, Marion, Jr., *Modernization: Latecomers and Survivors* (New York: Basic Books, Inc., 1972).

Li Chün-ch'uan, *I-i hui-t'ung ching-i* (Peking: Jen-min wei-sheng ch'u-pan-she, 1991).

Liu Yen-ch'ih, *The Essential Book of Traditional Chinese Medicine*, vol. 1. *Theory* (New York: Columbia University Press, 1988).

Maeno Kiyoji, *Sakuma Shōzan saikō* (Nagano City: Ginka shobō, 1977), p. 114.

Maeno Ryōtaku, *Kanrei higen*, in Numata Jirō and Matsumura Akira, eds., *Yōgaku*, part 1, *Nihon shisō taikei*, vol. 64 (Tokyo: Iwanami shoten, 1976).

Marume Nagayoshi, *Kenjutsu taiisha-ryū kaden yōkyoku*, in Imamura Yoshio, ed., *Kenjutsu*, part 1, *Nihon budō zenshū*, vol. 1 (Tokyo: Jimbutsu ōraisha, 1966).

Maruyama Masao, *Studies in the Intellectual History of Tokugawa Japan,* trans. Mikiso Hane (Princeton, N.J.: Princeton University Press, 1974).

Masuho Zankō, *Endō tsūkan,* in Noma Kōshin, ed., *Kinsei shokudōron, Nihon shisō taikei,* vol. 60 (Tokyo: Iwanami shoten, 1976).

Matsumiya Kanzan, *Dokanyōhō chokushi shō,* in Kokumin seishin bunka kenkyūjo, ed., *Matsumiya Kanzan shū,* vol. 3 (Tokyo: Kokumin seishin bunka kenkyūjo, 1937).

————, *Taiseiden kōketsu ōhi,* in Ishioka Hisao, ed., *Hōjō-ryū heihō, Nihon heihō zenshū,* vol. 3 (Tokyo: Jimbutsu ōraisha, 1967).

Matsumoto Shigeru, *Motoori Norinaga* (Cambridge, Mass.: Harvard University Press, 1970).

Matsumura Akira, ed., *Arai Hakuseki, Nihon shisō taikei,* vol. 35 (Tokyo: Iwanami shoten, 1975).

Matsunaga Sekigo, *Irinshō,* in Ishida Ichirō and Kanaya Osamu, eds., *Fujiwara Seika, Hayashi Razan, Nihon shisō taikei,* vol. 28 (Tokyo: Iwanami shoten, 1975).

McMullen, James, "Kumazawa Banzan: The Life and Thought of a Seventeenth-Century Japanese Confucian" (Ph.D. dissertation, University of Cambridge, 1969).

Minamoto Ta'neoki, *Jikaku meigikai,* in Imamura Yoshio, ed., *Hōjutsu, suijutsu, ninjutsu, Nihon budō zenshū,* vol. 4 (Tokyo: Jimbutsu ōraisha, 1966).

Miner, Earl, Hiroko Odagiri, and Robert E. Morrell, eds., *The Princeton Companion to Classical Japanese Literature* (Princeton, N.J.: Princeton University Press, 1985).

Miyamoto Shōson, "The Relations of Philosophical Theory to Practical Affairs in Japan," in Charles A. Moore, ed., *The Japanese Mind* (Honolulu: East-West Center Press, 1967).

Miyazaki Michio, *Kumazawa Banzan no kenkyū* (Tokyo: Shibunkaku, 1990).

Mizuta Norihisa, ed., *Tominaga Nakamoto, Yamagata Bantō, Nihon shisō taikei,* vol. 43 (Tokyo: Iwanami shoten, 1973).

Mori Shōken, *Nijūyonron,* in Takasu Yoshijirō, ed., *Mito Gikō, Rekkō shū, Mitogaku taikei,* vol. 5 (Tokyo: Ida shoten, 1941).

Morikawa Kōzan, *Nihon-ryū shinmei shagi,* in Ishioka Hisao, ed., *Kyūjutsu, Nihon budō taikei,* vol. 4 (Kyoto: Tōhōsha, 1982).

Morimoto Kakuzō, *Kinsei Nihon no Jugaku* (Tokyo: Iwanami shoten, 1935).

Morris, Ivan, *The World of the Shining Prince: Court Life in Ancient Japan* (New York: Penguin Books, 1964).

Morris-Suzuki, Tessa, *A History of Japanese Economic Thought* (London: Routledge, 1989).

Motoori Norinaga, *Kojikiden,* in Kamada Jun'ichi, ed., *Fukko Shintō,* part 3, *Motoori Norinaga, Shintō taikei, ronsetsu hen,* vol. 25 (Tokyo: Shintō taikei hensankai, 1982).

————, *Kuzuhara,* in Kamada Jun'ichi, ed., *Fukko Shintō,* part 3, *Motoori Norinaga, Shintō taikei, ronsetsu hen,* vol. 25 (Tokyo: Shintō taikei hensankai, 1982).

————, *Naobi no mitama,* in Kamada Jun'ichi, ed., *Fukko Shintō,* part 3, *Motoori Norinaga, Shintō taikei, ronsetsu hen,* vol. 25 (Tokyo: Shintō taikei hensankai, 1982).

Murakami Masataka, "Bunshi Genshō to *Shūeki dengi taizen*," *Nihon bunka ken-kyūjo kenkyū hōkoku*, no. 25 (Sendai: Tōhoku daigaku Nihon bunka kenkyūjo, 1989).

———, "Kinsei ekigaku juyōshi ni okeru Gahōten *Ekikyō hongi* no igi," in *Bungei kenkyū*, no. 100 (Sendai: Nihon bungei kenkyūkai, 1982).

Muraoka Tsunetsugu, *Norinaga to Atsutane* (Tokyo: Sōbunsha, 1957).

———, *Shintōshi* (Tokyo: Sōbunsha, 1964).

———, *Studies in Shinto Thought*, trans. Delmer Brown and James Araki (New York: Greenwood Press, 1988).

Murayama Shūichi, *Nihon Onmyōdoshi sōsetsu* (Tokyo: Hanawa shobō, 1981).

Muro Kyūsō, *Shundai zatsuwa*, in Inoue Tetsujirō, ed., *Nihon rinri ihen*, vol. 3, *Shushigakuha no bu*, part 1 (Tokyo: Ikuseikai, 1902).

Nagano Naoteru, *Heihō hiden bimyō zenshū setsu*, in Ishioka Hisao, ed., *Kōshū-ryū heihō, Nihon heihō zenshū*, vol. 1 (Tokyo: Jimbutsu ōraisha, 1967).

Naganuma Sensai, *Akki hachijin shūkai*, in Ishioka Hisao, ed., *Naganuma-ryū heihō, Nihon heihō zenshū*, vol. 4 (Tokyo: Jimbutsu ōraisha, 1967).

———, *Heiyōroku*, in Ishioka Hisao, ed., *Naganuma-ryū heihō, Nihon heihō zenshū*, vol. 4 (Tokyo: Jimbutsu ōraisha, 1967).

Nagoya Gen'i, *Tansuishi*, in Saigusa Hiroto, ed., *Bukkyōka no shizenkan, igakuka no shizenkan, Nihon tetsugaku zensho*, vol. 7 (Tokyo: Dai'ichi shobō, 1936).

Najita Tetsuo, "Political Economicism in the Thought of Dazai Shundai (1680–1740)," *Journal of Asian Studies* 31 (1972):821–839.

———, *Visions of Virtue in Tokugawa Japan: Kaitokudō* (Chicago: University of Chicago Press, 1987).

Nakae Tōju, *Okina mondō*, in Yamashita Yū and Bitō Masahide, eds., *Nakae Tōju, Nihon shisō taikei*, vol. 29 (Tokyo: Iwanami shoten, 1974).

———, "Taijō tenson Taiitsushinkyō jō" (1640), in Koide Tetsuo, ed., *Nakae Tōju, Kumazawa Banzan shū* (Tokyo: Tamagawa daigaku shuppanbu, 1976).

Nakai, Kate W., "Tokugawa Confucian Historiography: The Hayashi, Early Mito School and Arai Hakuseki," in Peter Nosco, ed., *Confucianism and Tokugawa Culture* (Princeton, N.J.: Princeton University Press, 1984).

Nakai Riken, *Shūeki hōgen*, unpublished manuscript, Kaitokudō bunko, Osaka University.

Nakamura Shōhachi, trans., *Gogyō taigi zenshaku* (Tokyo: Meiji shoin, 1986).

Nakamura Yukihiko, ed., *Kinsei chōnin shisō, Nihon shiō taikei*, vol. 59 (Tokyo: Iwanami shoten, 1975).

Nakayama Shigeru, "Abhorrence of God in the Introduction of Copernicanism into Japan," *Japanese Studies in the History of Science*, no. 3 (Tokyo, 1964): 60–67.

———, *Academic and Scientific Traditions in China, Japan and the West* (Tokyo: University of Tokyo Press, 1984).

———, *A History of Japanese Astronomy* (Cambridge, Mass.: Harvard University Press, 1969).

———, "Kindai kagaku to yōgaku," in Hirose Hideo, ed., *Yōgaku*, part 2, *Nihon shisō taikei*, vol. 65 (Tokyo: Iwanami shoten, 1972).

Namikawa Tenmin, *Tenmin igon*, in Seki Giichirō, ed., *Nihon Jurin sōsho*, vol. 5, *Kaisetsubu*, part 1 (Tokyo: Tōyō tōsho kankōkai, 1929).

Nambō Sōkei, *Nampō roku,* in Sen no Sōshitsu, ed., *Chadō koten zenshū,* vol. 4 (Kyoto: Tankō shinsha, 1964).

Naramoto Tatsuya, ed., *Nihon shisō taikei,* vol. 38, *Kinsei seidōron* (Tokyo: Iwanami shoten, 1976).

Needham, Joseph, et al., *Science and Civilization in China,* vols. 2–3 (Cambridge: Cambridge University Press, 1956).

Ng Wai-ming, "Nihon kindaikaron," *Jiyū,* vol. 36, no. 10 (Tokyo, October 1994): 10–20.

Nihon gakushiin, ed., *Meijizen Nihon butsurigakushi* (Tokyo: Nihon gakujutsu shinkyōkai, 1964).

Ninomiya Sontoku, *Ninomiya sensei goroku,* in Nakamura Yukihiro, ed., *Andō Shōeki, Tominaga Nakamoto, Miura Baien, Ishida Baigan, Ninomiya Sontoku, Kaihō Seiryō, Nihon no shisō,* vol. 18 (Tokyo: Chikuma shobō, 1971).

Nishizawa Yūshichi, *Nihon kajutsu yakuhō no maki* (Tokyo: Tōgakusha, 1935).

Niwa Motoji, *Seishi, chimei, kamon sōgō jiten* (Tokyo: Shinjimbutsu ōraisha, 1988).

Nomura Kanetarō, *Tokugawa jidai no keizai shisō* (Tokyo: Nihon hyōronsha, 1935).

Nosco, Peter, "*Manyōshū* Studies in Tokugawa Japan," *Transactions of the Asiatic Society of Japan,* fourth series (1986), no. 1.

———, "Masaho Zankō (1655–1742): A Shinto Popularizer Between Nativism and National Learning," in Peter Nosco, ed., *Confucianism and Tokugawa Culture* (Princeton, N.J.: Princeton University Press, 1984).

———, *Remembering Paradise: Nativism and Nostalgia in Eighteenth-Century Japan* (Cambridge, Mass.: Harvard University Press, 1990).

———, "Rethinking Tokugawa Thought," in Adriana Boscaro et al., eds., *Rethinking Japan,* vol. 2 (Sandgate, England: Japan Library Limited, 1987).

Ōba Osamu, *Edo jidai ni okeru Tōsen mochiwatarisho no kenkyū* (Kyoto: Kansai daigaku gakujitsu kenkyūjo, 1967).

Obata Kagenori, *Kōyō gunkan nukigaki zenshū,* in Ishioka Hisao, ed., *Kōshūryū heihō, Nihon heihō zenshū,* vol. 1 (Tokyo: Jimbutsu ōraisha, 1967).

Ōe Fumiki, *Honpō Jugakushi ronkō* (Tokyo: Zenkoku shobō, 1944).

———, *Honpō Shisho kunten narabi ni chūshakushi teki kenkyū* (Tokyo: Seki shoin, 1935).

Ogasawara Tsunetomi, *Shareiki,* in Imamura Yoshio, ed., *Kyūjutsu, bajutsu, Nihon budō zenshū,* vol. 3 (Tokyo: Jimbutsu ōraisha, 1966).

Ogata Korekatsu, *Kyōrin naisei roku,* in Mori Senzō and Kitagawa Hirokuni, eds., *Zoku zuihitsu taisei,* vol. 10 (Tokyo: Yoshikawa kōbunkan, 1979).

Ogino Dokuen, *Kinsei Zenrin sōhōden* (Kyoto: Shibunkaku, 1980).

Ogyū Sorai, *Rongochō,* in Ogawa Tamaki, ed., *Ogyū Sorai zenshū,* vol. 3 (Tokyo: Misuzu shobō, 1974).

Ōishi Kyūkei, *Jikata hanreiroku,* in Takimoto Seiichi, ed., *Nihon keizai sōsho,* vol. 31 (Tokyo: Nihon keizai kankōkai, 1916).

Okada Hakuku, *Jikoku shūshin roku,* in Takimoto Seiichi, ed., *Nihon keizai sōsho,* vol. 6 (Tokyo: Nihon keizai sōsho kankōkai, 1914).

Okada Kōtei, *Shichikyō tatsuki,* in Seki Giichirō, ed., *Zokuzoku Nihon Jurin sōsho,* vol. 1, *Kaisetsubu* (Tokyo: Tōyō tōsho kankōkai, 1935).

Okada Takehiko, ed., *Bakumatsu ishin Shushigakusha shokanshū, Shushigaku taikei,* vol. 14 (Tokyo: Meitoku shuppansha, 1975).

Okamoto Ippō, *Shinkyū hasshu taisei* (Tokugawa edition, Rare Book Collection of Gest Oriental Library, Princeton University).

Ōkuni Takamasa, *Gakutō benron*, in Tahara Tsuguo, ed., *Hirata Atsutane, Ban Nobutomo, Ōkuni Takamasa, Nihon shisō taikei*, vol. 50 (Tokyo: Iwanami shoten, 1973).

———, *Kodentsū-kai*, in Nomura Denshirō, ed., *Ōkuni Takamasa zenshū*, vol. 7 (Tokyo: Yūkōsha, 1939).

Ōmori Nobumasa, *Bujutsu densho no kenkyū* (Tokyo: Seiunsha, 1991).

Ono Takeo, ed., *Kinsei chihō keizai shiryō*, vol. 4 (Tokyo: Yoshikawa kōbunkan, 1958).

Ono Yasuhiro, ed., *Nihon shūkyō jiten* (Tokyo: Kōbunkan, 1985).

Ooms, Herman, *Charismatic Bureaucrat: A Political Biography of Matsudaira Sadanobu, 1758–1829* (Chicago: University of Chicago Press, 1975).

———, *Tokugawa Ideology: Early Constructs, 1570–1680* (Princeton, N.J.: Princeton University Press, 1985).

Ōsaki Ryūen, *Hakuin Zenshi den* (Tokyo: Morikawa shoten, 1922).

Ōshima Yoshitsuna, *Unheiryūchūdō*, in Shimada Teiichi, ed., *Sōjutsu, naginatajutsu, bōjutsu, kusarigamajutsu, shurikenjutsu, Nihon budō taikei*, vol. 7 (Kyoto: Tōhōsha, 1982).

Ōta Kinjō, *Gimonroku*, in Nagasawa Kikuta, ed., *Nihon zuihitsu shūsei*, vol. 8 (Tokyo: Kyūko shoin, 1978).

Ōta Masao, ed., *Onmyōdō no hon* (Tokyo: Gakushū kenkyūsha, 1993).

Otsuka Yasuo, "Chinese Traditional Medicine in Japan," in Charlies Leslie, ed., *Asian Medical Systems: A Comparative Study* (Berkeley and Los Angeles: University of California Press, 1976).

Ōtsuka Yoshinori, "Kinsei zenki no igaku," in Hirose Hideo, Nakayama Shigeru, and Ōtsuka Yoshinori, eds., *Kinsei kagaku shisō*, part 2, *Nihon shisō taikei*, vol. 63 (Tokyo: Iwanami shoten, 1971).

Owada Tetsuo, *Gunshi, sanbō* (Tokyo: Chūō kōronsha, 1990).

Ozawa Eiichi, *Kinsei shigaku shisōshi kenkyū* (Tokyo: Yoshikawa kōbunkan, 1974).

Peachery, Paul, *A History of Zen Buddhism* (New York: Pantheon Books, 1963).

Plutchow, Herbert E., *Historical chanoyu* (Tokyo: Japan Times, 1986).

Pollack, David, "The Intellectual Contexts of Tokugawa Aesthetics," in Pollack, *The Fracture of Meaning* (Princeton, N.J.: Princeton University Press, 1986).

Rai Kiichi, ed., *Jugaku, kokugaku, yōgaku, Nihon no kinsei*, vol. 13 (Tokyo: Chūō kōronsha, 1993).

Rimer, Thomas, and Yamazaki Masakazu, trans., *On the Art of the Nō Drama: The Major Treatise of Zeami* (Princeton, N.J.: Princeton University Press, 1984).

Robert, Luke, "The Merchant Origins of National Prosperity Thought in Eighteenth-Century Tosa" (Ph.D. dissertation, Princeton University, 1991).

Ryūon, *Sōseki haibutsu ben*, in Kashiwabara Yūsen and Fujii Manabu, eds., *Kinsei Bukkyō no shisō, Nihon shisō taikei*, vol. 57 (Tokyo: Iwanami shoten, 1973).

Saigusa Hiroto, ed., *Bukkyōka no shizenkan, igakuka no shizenkan, Nihon tetsugaku zensho*, vol. 7 (Tokyo: Daiichi shobō, 1936).

———, *Sangyō gijutsu hen: jikin, nōgyō, seizōgyō, Nihon kagaku koten zensho*, vol. 13 (Tokyo: Asahi shimbunsha, 1978).

————, *Tenmon, butsurigakuha no shizenkan, Nihon tetsugaku zensho,* vol. 8 (Tokyo: Daiichi shobō, 1936).

Sakai Naoki, *Voices of the Past: The Status of Language in Eighteenth-Century Japanese Discourse* (Ithaca, N.Y.: Cornell University Press, 1991).

Sakuma Shōzan, *Hōka,* in Shinano Kyōikukai, ed., *Shōzan zenshū,* vol. 1 (Nagano: Shinano kyōikukai shuppanbu, 1975).

Sakurai Hideo, *Zengaku daijiten* (Tokyo: Taishūkan shoten, 1985).

Sansom, George, *Japan: A Short Cultural History* (Stanford, Calif.: Stanford University Press, 1977).

Sasaki Genjun, *Gō to unmei* (Tokyo: Shimizu kōbundō, 1976).

Satō Issai, *Genshiroku,* in Inoue Tetsujirō, ed., *Nihon rinri ihen, Yōmeigakuha no bu,* vol. 3, part 2 (Tokyo: Ikuseikai, 1903).

Satō Kinji, *Nihon bugakushi* (Tokyo: Taitō shokan, 1942).

Shaw, R., trans., *The Embossed Tea Kettle and Other Works of Hakuin Zenji* (London: George Allen & Unwin, 1963).

Shchutskii, Iulian K., *Researches on the I Ching* (Princeton, N.J.: Princeton University Press, 1979).

Shimonaka Yasuburō, ed., *Shintō daijiten* (Kyoto: Rinsen shoten, 1986).

Shimotohodō Yūkichi, *Yoshida Shōin no ningenguku teki kenkyū* (Kanshiwa City: Kōchigakuen shuppanbu, 1988).

Shirai Takamasa, "Gunshi," *Rekishi dokuhon* 32, 13 (Tokyo, 1987).

Shively, Donald, "Popular Culture," in John Hall, ed., *The Cambridge History of Japan,* vol. 4 (Cambridge: Cambridge University Press, 1991).

Shizuki Tadao, *Konton bunhan zusetsu,* in Saigusa Hiroto, ed., *Jukyōka no shizenkan, tenmon, butsurigakuka no shizenkan, Nihon tetsugaku zensho,* vol. 9 (Tokyo: Daiichi shobō, 1936).

————, *Rekishō shinsho,* in Saigusa Hiroto, ed., *Shizenhen, Nihon tetsugaku shisō zensho,* vol. 6 (Tokyo: Heibonsha, 1956).

Shōji Kōki, *Kashoku yōdō,* in Takimoto Seiichi, ed., *Nihon keizai sōsho,* vol. 24 (Tokyo: Nihon keizai sōsho kankōkai, 1916).

Shunjūken Ichiha, *Ikebana shōdenki,* in Zoku kadō kosho shūsei kankōkai, ed., *Zoku kadō kosho shūsei,* vol. 3 (Kyoto: Shibunkaku, 1972).

Shushigaku taikei kankōkai, ed., *Nihon no Shushigaku,* part 2, *Shushigaku taikei,* vol. 13 (Tokyo: Meitoku shuppansha, 1975).

Smith, Richard, *China's Cultural Heritage: The Ch'ing Dynasty, 1644–1912* (Boulder, Colo.: Westview Press, 1983).

Sōda Hajime, *Nihon iryō bunka shi* (Kyoto: Shibunsha, 1989).

————, ed., *Ranryōhō, Ranryō yakukai, Edo kagaku koten sōsho,* vol. 27 (Tokyo: Kanwa shoten, 1980).

Spae, Joseph, *Itō Jinsai* (New York: Paragon Book, 1967).

Sue Munehiro, *Chajin no kenkyū* (Tokyo: Shibunkaku, 1981).

Sugimoto Isao, *Kinsei jitsugakushi no kenkyū* (Tokyo: Yoshikawa kōbunkan, 1962).

Sugimoto Masayoshi and David L. Swain, *Science and Culture in Traditional Japan* (Cambridge, Mass.: MIT Press, 1978).

Suzuki Daisetsu, *Zen and Japanese Culture* (Princeton, N.J.: Princeton University Press, 1973).

Suzuki Hiroshi, *Shūekishō no kokugogaku teki kenkyū* (Tokyo: Seibundō, 1972).

Suzuki Yoshijirō, "Arai Hakuga no ichimen," *Ekikyō kenkyū* (Tokyo: Waseda University), 16 (May 1963):2–6.

Taihaku Kokusui, *Sōtō gokokuben*, in Sōtōshū zensho kankōkai, ed., *Sōtōshū zensho*, vol. 5, *Chūkai* (Tokyo: Sōtō zensho kankōkai, 1930).

Taira Shigemichi, *Kikkawa Shintō no kiso teki kenkyū* (Tokyo: Yoshikawa kōbunkan, 1966).

———, "Kinsei no Shintō shisō," in Abe Akio and Taira Shigemichi, eds., *Kinsei Shintōron, zenki kokugaku. Nihon shisō taikei,* vol. 39 (Tokyo: Iwanami shoten, 1972).

———, "Suika Shintō," in Ishida Ichirō, ed., *Kinsei no shisō,* part 1, *Nihon shisōshi kōza,* vol. 4 (Tokyo: Yūzankaku, 1977).

———, ed., *Kikkawa Shintō, Shintō taikei, ronsetsu hen,* vol. 10 (Tokyo: Shintō taikei hensankai, 1983).

Takahashi Shin'ichi, *Yōgaku shisōshi ron* (Tokyo: Shin Nihon shuppansha, 1972).

Takao Kazuhiko, *Kinsei no shomin bunka* (Tokyo: Iwanami shoten, 1968).

Takasaka Masanobu, *Ryū, tora, hyō sanpon,* in Ishioka Hisao, ed., *Kōshū-ryū heihō, Nihon heihō zenshū,* vol. 1 (Tokyo: Jimbutsu ōraisha, 1967).

Takasugi Shinsaku, *Gokuchū shuki,* in Yoshida Tsunekichi and Satō Seizaburō, eds., *Bakumatsu seiji ronshū, Nihon shisō taikei,* vol. 56 (Tokyo: Iwanami shoten, 1976).

Takayama Kentei, *Nihonden chiran yōketsu,* in Ishioka Hisao, ed., *Echigo-ryū heihō, Nihon heihō zenshū,* vol. 2 (Tokyo: Jimbutsu ōraisha, 1967).

Takemoto Gidayū, *Danbutsushū,* in Nishiyama Matsunosuke et al., eds., *Kinsei Geidōron, Nihon shisō taikei,* vol. 61 (Tokyo: Iwanami shoten, 1972).

Takizawa Bakin, *Enseki zasshi,* in Nihon zuihitsu taisei henshūbu, ed., *Nihon zuihitsu taisei,* series 2, vol. 19 (Tokyo: Yoshikawa kōbunkan, 1975).

Takuan Sōhō, *Isetsu,* in Saigusa Hiroto, ed., *Bukkyōka no shizenkan, igakuka no shizenkan, Nihon tetsugaku zensho,* vol. 7 (Tokyo: Daiichi shobō, 1936).

———, *Ketsujōshū,* in Takuan oshō zenshū kaikōkai, ed., *Takuan oshō zenshū,* vol. 5 (Tokyo: Kogisha, 1929).

———, *Kottō roku,* in Saigusa Hiroto, ed., *Bukkyōka no shizenkan, igakuka no shizenkan, Nihon tetsugaku zensho,* vol. 7 (Tokyo: Dai'ichi shobō, 1936).

———, *Tōkai yawa,* in Takuan oshō zenshū kaikōkai, ed., *Takuan oshō zenshū,* vol. 5 (Tokyo: Kogisha, 1929).

Tamenaga Icchō, *Kabuki jishi,* in Geinōshi kenkyūkai, ed., *Kabuki, Nihon shomin bunka shiryō shūsei,* vol. 6 (Tokyo: San'ichi shobō, 1973).

Tamiya Nakanobu, *Tōyūshi,* in Nihon zuihitsu taisei henshūbu, ed., *Nihon zuihitsu taisei,* series 1, vol. 19 (Tokyo: Yoshikawa kōbunkan, 1976).

Tamura Sensosuke, *Nihon kishōgakushi kenkyū,* vol. 1 (Mishima: Mishima kagakushi kenkyūjo, 1979).

Tamura Yoshishige, *Nōgyō jitoku,* in Furushima Toshio and Aki Kōichi, eds., *Kinsei kagaku shisō,* part 1, *Nihon shiso taikei,* vol. 62 (Tokyo: Iwanami shoten, 1972).

———, *Nōgyō jitoku furoku,* in Kumashiro Yukio, ed., *Nōgyō jitoku, Nōgyō jitoku furoku, Nihon nōsho zenshū,* vol. 21 (Tokyo: Nōzan gyōson bunka kyōkai, 1981).

T'an Wei-ch'ung, [*The*] *Five Element System of Traditional Chinese Medicine in* [*the*] *West* (Peking: Hsüeh Yüan Press, 1990).

Tanaka Senō, *Cha no bi* (Tokyo: Asahi sononama, 1976).

Tanaka Toshiaki, "Tōzan *Hōkyō zammai* no *eki* to gen *Taikyokuzu* teki hassō," *Tōhō shūkyō* (Tokyo: Nihon dōkyō gakuin, 1985), 66:87–102, and (1986) 67:38–58.

Tao De-min, *Kaitokudō Shushigaku no kenkyū* (Osaka: Ōsaka daigaku shuppankai, 1993).

Tashiro Tokihide, *Jūjutsu taisei roku,* in Oimatsu Shinichi, ed., *Jūjutsu, aikijutsu, Nihon budō taikei,* vol. 6 (Kyoto: Tōhōsha, 1982).

Toby, Ronald P., "Reopening the Question of *Sakoku:* Diplomacy in the Legitimation of the Tokugawa Bakufu," *Journal of Japanese Studies,* vol. 3 (Summer 1977):347–355.

Tōdō Kyōshun, "Chūgoku Jōdokyō ni okeru inga ni kansuru shomondai," in Nakamura Hajime, ed., *Inga, Bukkyō shisō,* vol. 3 (Kyoto: Heirakuji shoten, 1978).

Tōfuku Ken'i, *Tōfuku kadan,* in Zoku kadō kosho shūsei kankōkai, ed., *Zoku kadō kosho shūsei,* vol. 3 (Kyoto: Shibunkaku, 1972).

Tōgō Shigei, *Shigen-ryū heihō-sho,* in Imamura Yoshio, ed., *Ken, Nihon budō taikei,* vol. 3 (Kyoto: Tōhōsha, 1982).

Tōkyō kagaku hakubutsukan, ed., *Edo jidai no kagaku* (Tokyo: Hakubunkan, 1934).

Toyotake Konodayū, *Jōruri setsushōshū,* in Geinōshi kenkyūkai, ed., *Ningyō jōruri, Nihon shomin bunka shiryō shūsei,* vol. 7 (Tokyo: San'ichi shobō, 1974).

Tsuchiya Matasaburō, *Kōka shunjū,* in Takimoto Seiichi, ed., *Nihon keizai sōsho,* vol. 14 (Tokyo: Nihon keizai sōsho kankōkai, 1915).

Tsuji Zennosuke, *Nihon Bukkyō shi, Kinsei hen,* vol. 4 (Tokyo: Iwanami shoten, 1955).

———, *Nihon bunka shi,* vol. 5, *Edo jidai,* part 1 (Tokyo: Shunjūsha, 1960).

Tsukahara Togo, *Affinity and Shinwa Ryoku: Introduction of Western Chemical Concepts in Early Nineteenth-Century Japan* (Amsterdam: J. C. Gieber, 1993).

Tsukuba Hisaharu, *Nihon no nōsho* (Tokyo: Chūō kōronsha, 1987).

Tsunoda Ryusaku, Wm. Theodore de Bary, and Donald Keene, eds., *Sources of the Japanese Tradition* (New York: Columbia University Press, 1958).

Tsutsumi Masatoshi, *Shōdō kyūhen kokujikai,* in Takimoto Seiichi, ed., *Nihon keizai sōsho,* vol. 20 (Tokyo: Nihon keizai sōsho kankōkai, 1916).

Tucker, John, "Two Mencian Political Notions in Tokugawa Japan," *Philosophy East and West* 47, 2 (April 1997):233–253.

Tucker, Mary, *Moral and Spiritual Cultivation in Japanese Neo-Confucianism: The Life and Thought of Kaibara Ekken* (Albany: State University of New York Press, 1989).

Tyler, Royall, trans., *Selected Writings of Suzuki Shōsan* (Ithaca, N.Y.: China-Japan Program of Cornell University, 1977).

Tyler, Susan, "Is There a Religion Called Shinto?" in Adriana Boscaro et al., eds., *Rethinking Japan,* vol. 2 (Sandgate, England: Japan Library Limited, 1990).

Uchino Dairei, "*Nihon keikai* ni tsuite," in Fukushima Kanoezō, ed., *Kindai Nihon no Jugaku* (Tokyo: Iwanami shoten, 1939).

Uda Naoshi, *Nihon bunka ni oyoboseru Jukyō teki eikyō* (Tokyo: Tōyō shisō kenkyūjo, 1935).

Unshō, *Sankyō shikichū,* in Takaoka Ryūshin, ed., *Shingonshū zensho* (Tokyo: Shingonshū zensho kankōkai, 1935).

Ury, Marian, trans., "*Genkō Sakusho:* Japan's First Comprehensive History of Buddhism" (Ph.D. dissertation, University of California, Berkeley, 1971).

Usami Yoshikata, *Bukei yōryaku,* in Ishioka Hisao, ed., *Echigo-ryū heihō, Nihon heihō zenshū,* vol. 2 (Tokyo: Jimbutsu ōraisha, 1967).

Utsumi Shigemune, *Rōsōron, Sōjutsu, naginatajutsu, bōjutsu, kusarigamajutsu, shurikenjutsu, Nihon budō taikei,* vol. 7 (Kyoto: Tōhōsha, 1982).

Varley, Paul, *Japanese Culture: A Short History* (New York: Praeger, 1977).

Wajima Yoshio, "Chūsei ni okeru *Shūeki* no kenkyū ni tsuite," *Kōbe jogakuin daigaku ronshū* (Kobe, 1958), 5:1.

————, *Chūsei no Jugaku* (Tokyo: Yoshikawa kōbunkan, 1965).

Wakabayashi, Bob T., *Anti-Foreignism and Western Learning in Early-Modern Japan* (Cambridge, Mass.: Harvard University Press, 1986).

————, *Japanese Loyalism Reconstructed: Yamagata Daiin's Ryūshi Shiron of 1759* (Honolulu: University of Hawai'i Press, 1995).

Walton, Linda, "Sino-Japanese Cultural Relations in the Early Thirteenth Century: The Buddhist Monk Shunjō (1166–1227) in China, 1199–1212," in Ryū Shiken hakasei shōju kinen Sōshi kenkyū ronshū kankōkai, ed., *Ryū Shiken hakasei shōju kinen Sōshi kenkyū ronshū* (Kyoto: Dōhōsha, 1989).

Watanabe Hiroshi, *Kinsei Nihon shakai to Sōgaku* (Tokyo: Tōkyō daigaku shuppankai, 1985).

Watanabe Masao, *The Japanese and Western Science* (Philadelphia: University of Pennsylvania Press, 1990).

Watarai Nobuyoshi, *Jingū hiden mondō,* in Nishikawa Junshi, ed., *Ise Shintō,* part 2, *Shintō taikei, ronsetsu hen,* vol. 7 (Tokyo: Shintō taikei hensankai, 1982).

Watarai Nobuyoshi, *Yōfukki,* in Ishida Ichirō, ed., *Shintō shisō shū, Nihon no shisō,* vol. 14 (Tokyo: Chikuma shobō, 1970).

Watt, Paul B., "Jiun Sonja (1718–1804): A Response to Confucianism within the Context of Buddhist Reform," in Peter Nosco, ed., *Confucianism and Tokugawa Culture* (Princeton, N.J.: Princeton University Press, 1984).

Webb, Herschel, *The Japanese Imperial Institution in the Tokugawa Period* (New York: Columbia University Press, 1968).

Weber, Max, *The Protestant Ethic and the Spirit of Capitalism* (London: Unwin Hyman, Ltd., 1930).

Wilhelm, Hellmut, *Change: Eight Lectures on the I Ching* (Princeton, N.J.: Princeton University Press, 1973).

Wilhelm, Richard, trans., *The I Ching or Book of Changes* (Princeton, N.J.: Princeton University Press, 1977).

Yagyū Munenori, *Heihō kadensho,* in Imamura Yoshio, ed., *Kenjutsu,* part 1, *Nihon budō zenshū,* vol. 1 (Tokyo: Jimbutsu ōraisha, 1966).

Yamaga Sokō, *Bukyō zensho,* in Ishioka Hisao, ed., *Yamaga-ryū heihō, Nihon heihō zenshū,* vol. 5 (Tokyo: Jimbutsu ōraisha, 1967).

————, *Heihō jinmu yūbishū,* in Hirose Yutaka, ed., *Yamaga Sokō zenshū,* vol. 1 (Tokyo: Iwanami shoten, 1942).

————, *Heihō ōgi kōroku,* in Saigusa Hiroto, ed., *Shūkyōron, heihōbujutsuron, Nihon tetsugaku zensho,* vol. 12 (Tokyo: Daiichi shobō, 1935).

————, *Takkyō dōmon,* in Hirose Yutaka, ed., *Yamaga Sokō zenshū,* vol. 12 (Tokyo: Iwanami shoten, 1941).

————, *Yamaga gorui*, in Hirose Yutaka, ed., *Yamaga Sokō zenshū*, vols. 4–10 (Tokyo: Iwanami shoten, 1941).

Yamagata Bantō, *Yume no shiro*, in Saigusa Hiroto, ed., *Shūkyō ron, heihō bujutsu ron, Nihon tetsugaku zensho*, vol. 12 (Tokyo: Daiichi shobō, 1935).

Yamagata Shūnan, *Igaku wakumon*, in Saigusa Hiroto, ed., *Jukyōhen, Nihon tetsugaku zensho*, vol. 3 (Tokyo: Daiichi shobō, 1936).

Yamamoto Yūichi, *Ekisen to Nihonbungaku* (Tokyo: Shimizu kōbundō, 1976).

Yamanaka Hiroyuki, "Nihonjin to *Eki*," in Kaji Nobuyuki, ed., *Eki no sekai* (Tokyo: Shinjimbutsu ōraisha, 1987).

Yamanaka Shigeru, trans., *Chūgoku no kagaku to bunmei* (Tokyo: Shisakusha, 1975).

Yamanouchi Naokazu, *Heijō muteki sho*, in Imamura Yoshio, ed., *Ken, Nihon budō taikei*, vol. 3 (Kyoto: Tōhōsha, 1982).

Yamauchi-ke shiryō, unpublished source kept in Yamauchi jinga hōbutsu shiryō-kan, Kōchi Prefecture, Japan.

Yamazaki Akira, "Wakon yōsai teki shii kōzō no keisei to kokka ishiki," in Arisaka Takamichi, ed., *Nihon yōgakushi no kenkyū*, vol. 3 (Tokyo: Sōgensha, 1974).

Yampolsky, Philip B., trans., *The Zen Master Hakuin: Selected Writings* (New York: Columbia University Press, 1971).

Yaoya Zenshirō, *Ryōritsū taizen*, in Geinōshi kenkyūkai, ed., *Sūki, Nihon shomin bunka shiryō shūsei*, vol. 10 (Tokyo: San'ichi shobō, 1976).

Yasui Kōzan, *Chūgoku shinpi shisō no Nihon eno tenkai* (Tokyo: Taishō daigaku shuppanbu, 1983).

————, *Seiza no bunka* (Tokyo: Satsuki shobō, 1987).

Yasunaga Toshinobu, trans., *Andō Shōeki: Social and Ecological Philosopher in Eighteenth-Century Japan* (New York: Weatherhill, 1992).

Yen Shao-yang, *Han-chi tsai Jih-pen ti kiu-pu yen-chiu* (Nanking: Chiang-su ku-chi ch'i-pan-she, 1992).

Yōmeigaku taikei hensankai, ed., *Nihon no Yōmeigaku, Yōmeigaku taikei*, vol. 8 (Tokyo: Meitoku shuppansha, 1972).

Yoshida Tadashi, "The *Rangaku* of Shizuki Tadao: The Introduction of Western Science in Tokugawa Japan" (Ph.D. dissertation, Princeton University, 1974).

Yoshikawa Kōjirō, ed., *Ogyū Sorai, Nihon shisō taikei*, vol. 36 (Tokyo: Iwanami shoten, 1973).

Yoshimasu Tōdō, *Kosho igen*, in Huang han i-hsüeh ts'ung-shu hui, ed., *I-an, i-hua, Huang han i-hsüeh ts'ung-shu*, vol. 13 (Peking: P'ing-fang ch'u-pan-she, 1935).

Yoshino Hiroko, *Daijōsai* (Tokyo: Kōbundō, 1987).

————, *Inyō gogyō shisō to Nihon no minzoku* (Kyoto: Jimbun shoin, 1983).

————, *Kakusareta kamigami* (Kyoto: Jimbun shoin, 1992).

————, *Yama no kami* (Kyoto: Jimbun shoin, 1989).

Yoshio Nankō, *Chidō wakumon*, in Hirose Hideo, ed., *Yōgaku*, part 2, *Nihon shisō taikei*, vol. 65 (Tokyo: Iwanami shoten, 1972).

Yūki Rikuo, *Ashikaga gakkō no kyōikushi teki kenkyū* (Tokyo: Daiichi hōkei, 1985).

————, *Kanazawa bunko to Ashikaga gakkō* (Tokyo: Shibundō, 1959).

Zeami, *Fūshikaden*, in Nogami Toyoichirō, ed., *Fūshikaden* (Tokyo: Iwanami shoten, 1991).

Zoku kadō kosho shūsei kankōkai, ed., *Zoku kadō kosho shūsei*, vols. 1–5 (Kyoto: Shibunkaku, 1972).

INDEX

About the Author

WAI-MING NG, who received his doctorate in East Asian studies from Princeton University in 1996, is assistant professor of Japanese studies at the National University of Singapore. His articles have appeared in a number of journals, including *Sino-Japanese Studies, Philosophy East and West, Asian Philosophy,* and *Journal of Asian History. The* I Ching *in Tokugawa Thought and Culture* is his first book.

www.ingramcontent.com/pod-product-compliance
Ingram Content Group UK Ltd.
Pitfield, Milton Keynes, MK11 3LW, UK
UKHW011439151125
465054UK00001B/65

9 780824 822422